THE NATURE OF HUMAN ACTION

THE NATURE OF HUMAN ACTION

EDITED BY MYLES BRAND, UNIVERSITY OF PITTSBURGH

WILLIAM K. FRANKENA, ACADEMIC EDITOR

SCOTT, FORESMAN AND COMPANY

To Wendy and Joshua

PREFACE

A genuine philosophical problem is essentially related to other philosophical problems; or what amounts to the same thing, a genuine philosophical problem is not bound by the traditional categories of metaphysics, epistemology, ethics, logic, and so on. On this criterion, problems about human action are genuinely philosophical. Until approximately two decades ago, almost everything written about human action was written for the purpose of solving the metaphysical puzzle about free will. However, it became apparent to philosophers other than metaphysicians, for example, to philosophers of science, particularly those concerned with psychology and the social sciences, that it is essential to know the nature of human action. One reason for concern is that behavioristic psychology assumes that the conceptual scheme of neurophysiology, and hence, of physics, is adequate to account for all human behavior, including "actions." Critics of behaviorism claim that human action involves an element of purposefulness, of goal-directedness. The behaviorist's conceptual scheme, however, has no room for the concept of purposefulness, for the Aristotelian notion of final cause. In order to evaluate this objection to behaviorism, we must determine whether in fact the behaviorist has misconstrued the nature of action. In another philosophical category, the philosophy of mind, determining the nature of human action is again relevant. What is the connection between desiring and acting, wanting and acting, preferring and acting? What is it to act rationally, to act irrationally? Some philosophers have thought that the issues in the philosophy of mind exhaust the problems connected with human action. Clearly, however, problems about human action have a wider scope.

It is not an exaggeration to say that we are now in the midst of an action theory revolution. In published work and in private and classroom discussion, many philosophers are turning their attention to action theory. One aim of this volume is to make readily available to the student, to the philosopher whose primary interests are in other areas, to the nonphilosopher, the sociologist, the psychologist, the jurist, as well as to the philosopher working in the area, a volume of the most influential and philosophically important work in the basic problems in action theory. Another aim of this volume, and probably a more important one, is to give coherence to a seemingly divergent body of literature, to supply Theseus with the thread to find his way.

To Richard Taylor, my former teacher, I owe thanks for contributing an essay, and more importantly, for introducing me to the problems of action theory and to the methods for examining them. To my colleagues Kurt Baier and Nicholas Rescher, I owe thanks for contributing essays and providing encouragement for this project. I should also like to thank Storrs McCall, who in addition to contributing an essay, spent many noisy lunch hours discussing the problems of "cans" with me. To William Frankena, the publisher's academic editor, I am grateful for helpful comments on the introductions. I wish also to thank Roderick Chisholm for permitting the publication of his revised version of " 'He Could Have Done Otherwise.' " To my other colleagues and students who considered these issues with me, to the secretarial staff of the Pittsburgh philosophy department, especially Rita Pappas, I extend a blanket thanks. I should like, finally, to express my gratitude to a superb teacher and scholar, Robert E. Whallen.

MYLES BRAND
UNIVERSITY OF PITTSBURGH

TABLE OF CONTENTS

section **I**

ACTION AND BEHAVIOR:

ON DEFINING "A PERSON PERFORMS AN ACTION"

INTRODUCTION

ACTION AND BEHAVIOR *

1. THE PROBLEMS

Persons perform actions. They move their muscles, raise their arms, buy loaves of bread, build bridges, and insult other persons. Mental activities, such as solving a mathematical problem or keeping a secret, are also actions. Perhaps some actions are not performed by persons. It may be that apes, dolphins, and bees perform actions; and perhaps God performs (or performed) actions. In any case, it is a fact about the world that persons perform actions.

To claim that it is evident that persons perform actions, however, is not to claim that there are no perplexing problems concerning human action. Indeed problems about action have occupied reflective men since at least the time of Plato. Basically, there are five kinds of philosophical questions that can be raised about human action. First, there are what might be called conceptual questions. These include "What is a human action?" and "What can persons do?" Or stating them more precisely, "What does it mean to say that a person performed an action?" and "What does it mean to say that a person *can* perform an action?" Closely related to the conceptual questions are questions about the explanation of human action. Is the conceptual scheme and methodology of physics and biology adequate to account for human action? Or more exactly, are the concepts or purposiveness and goal-directedness, which presumably are excluded from the conceptual scheme of physics and biology, needed for adequate ex-

---

* Since this and subsequent introductions are, in part, commentaries on the selections, it may be helpful to reread the introductions after reading the selections.

planations of human actions? Third, there are metaphysical questions. These include "Are all human actions caused?" and, more fundamentally, "Can a human action be caused?" Many of these questions have a bearing on the complex of issues known as the Free Will Problem. Fourth, there are epistemological questions. Is it by observation or some other means that we know that we are performing an action? How do we know, if at all, that others perform actions? And fifth, there is the conglomerate group of ethical and metaethical questions. This group includes "Are actions or their consequences good or bad?" and "What does it mean to say that a person is responsible for his actions (or their consequences)?"

Clearly the conceptual questions are the most fundamental. In order to answer adequately questions concerning explanation of actions, causes of actions, knowledge of actions, and evaluation of actions or their consequences, it is necessary first to know just what an action is. Or again, a theory about the nature of action is logically prior to explanatory, metaphysical, epistemological, ethical, and metaethical theories about action. The purpose of this volume, quite simply, is to gather together the most thoughtful answers philosophers have given to the conceptual questions about human action.

There are basically two ways of analyzing, or determining the meaning of, the key action-locutions "A person performed an action" and "A person can perform an action." The first attempts to "reduce" human action to certain kinds of changes or events; or, put linguistically, it attempts to analyze action talk into nonaction talk. This approach to the analysis of action-locutions can be called *extra-systemic*. Behaviorism, which involves the identification of human actions with behavioral events, is characteristic of this approach. (Though it is difficult to explicate "behavior" without begging the question at this stage of the discussion, "behavior" refers, roughly, to any physiological change or process—for example, heartbeats, nerve impulses, and arm risings due to muscular twitches or external forces.) Section I, "Action and Behavior," contains essays that examine reductionistic analyses of "A person performs an action"; and section II, "Ability and Possibility," deals with reductionistic analyses of "A person can perform an action." The second approach explains human action *systemically*. That is, it explicates action-locutions within a constructive system, or calculus. This approach is characteristic of the work of Carnap, Goodman, and others in system construction. Section III, "Action and Logical Systems," contains essays that deal with systemic answers to both conceptual questions about human action.

In the first selection Professor Melden makes an apt analogy between the Naturalistic Fallacy, that is, the attempt to derive "ought" from "is," and the analysis of action in terms of behavior. The group of concepts that concern human action is, if Melden is right, independent of the group that concerns behavior just as the group of moral concepts is, if the Naturalistic Fallacy is a fallacy, independent of the group that concerns matters of fact. Metaphorically speaking, the systemic approach to action or morals, or any area of philosophy, is that there are closed circles of concepts and that the way to explicate one element in the circle is by means of the other elements. On this view, conceptual analysis consists in finding out which concepts belong to which groups, what are the internal relationships between members of a group, and what relationships, if any, exist between groups. Sections I and II can be thought of as a justification for taking a systemic approach to action theory by showing that extra-systemic attempts fail. It is an investigation of the question whether there is a naturalistic fallacy for human action. Section III consists of systemic analyses and preliminaries for systemic analyses.

The remainder of this introduction to section I is concerned with an examination of the more plausible attempts to define "A person performs an action" in nonaction talk.

2. NAÏVE BEHAVIORISM

A first attempt to define "A person performs an action" is to equate an action with bodily behavior. Hence, a person raises his arm if, and only if, his arm rises. But this view is clearly too narrow: persons perform actions that involve more than their bodies. They perform mental actions, which presumably would be identical with mental events; and they perform actions that include the effects of their bodily movements. In picking up a pencil, for example, the pencil's rising is an effect of the movement of my arm. The view that bodily and mental actions are just bodily and mental behavioral events, which might be called with some misgivings "naïve behaviorism," can be formulated in the following way:

(D1) For every person S and every action a, S performed a if and only if: (i) there is a b such that b is the appropriate bit of bodily or mental behavior of S or there is a b such that b is the appropriate bit of bodily or mental behavior of S and the appropriate effects of this bodily or mental behavior; and (ii) b occurred.

In the first selection, "Physiological Happenings and Bodily Actions," Melden examines and rejects naïve behaviorism.[1] As Melden correctly suggests, bodily movements can occur without the person to whom they are happening intentionally bringing them about. Persons undergo twitches and nervous spasms; they have their limbs moved by machines and by other persons. In the mental sphere, thoughts can occur to a person, as in cases of daydreaming and posthypnotic suggestion, without that person performing any action at all. To take a specific case, suppose that my arm rose because of a nervous spasm. The definiens of (D1) is satisfied; the behavior of my arm's rising occurred. However, the definiendum is not satisfied; I did not perform the action of raising my arm. I was a victim of my arm's rising, a mere spectator with a good vantage point: my arm's rising was nothing I *did*, but rather something that happened to me. Definition (D1), further, does not appear to account for refrainings and acts of omission. The patrolman who keeps his arm at his side and refrains from shooting the fleeing youth performed a bodily action but no behavior occurred. This last objection can be met, perhaps, by construing "behavior" in a sufficiently wide sense to include "negative behavior." The patrolman's arm remaining at his side was a bit of behavior in which no overt change occurred.[2]

---

[1] Cf. Richard Taylor, "Simple Action and Volition," pp. 54–55 below.

[2] This reply, however, involves one in the difficult problem of explicating "negative behavior." It cannot refer to the mere nonoccurrence of a bodily event; for if "negative behavior" were explicated in this way, it would have the absurd consequence that everyone is behaving in an infinity of ways at every moment.

In addition to the obvious counterexamples, Melden argues that naïve behaviorism is fundamentally mistaken. According to Melden, the naïve behaviorist is led to claim that what a person does in raising his arm is move certain muscles that cause his arm to rise. But this account cannot be correct. If a person raises his arm by contracting muscles that cause his arm to rise, he must know, or at least be aware of, which muscles he contracts; but the ordinary man who raises his arm has no such knowledge or awareness. The correct explanation, Melden claims, proceeds the other way around. One ordinarily moves his muscles by raising his arm. In raising my arm, I *simply* raise it.

In order to better understand Melden's account of what happens when a person raises his arm, let us consider the following often-made objection. If one contracts his arm muscles by raising his arm, then the arm-raising occurred temporally prior to the muscle contractions. The muscle contractions, however, cause the arm-raising. Here, then, is a case of "backward" causation, a case of the effect occurring prior to the cause. But it is commonly agreed that effects cannot occur before their causes. Thus, the objection concludes, Melden's claim that we ordinarily move our muscles by raising our arms is false.

Melden, however, can answer this objection without altering his view about the way we perform actions. Melden is not claiming that the muscle contractions cause the arm-raising. As he elaborates at the beginning of the second selection, the muscle contractions cause the bit of behavior of the arm's *rising;* they do not cause the *action* of *raising* the arm. The arm-raising temporally includes both the muscle contractions and the arm's rising. Melden must be taken seriously when he says that in raising one's arm, one simply raises it. A person does not perform the action of raising his arm by *first* contracting his muscles. This is not a case of backward causation, in short: the effect of the arm's rising occurs after (or simultaneously with) its cause, the muscle contractions. To make the point in a slightly different way, the expression "I raise my arm by contracting my muscles" is misleading. It suggests that the "by" is causal. But my *raising* my arm and my muscles contracting are causally independent (in the ordinary sense of "cause"), though they temporally overlap.

3. BEHAVIOR PLUS A CONCURRENT MENTAL EVENT

A behaviorist might attempt to "patch up" definition (D1) by suggesting that action is behavior accompanied by a special kind of mental event, perhaps a motive or desire or want. For example, my signaling for the chairman's attention *is* my arm's rising and my wanting to attract his attention. This proposal can be formulated as follows:

(D2) For every person S and every action a, S performed a if and only if: (i) there is a b such that b is the appropriate bit of bodily or mental behavior of S or there is a b such that b is the appropriate bit of bodily or mental behavior of S and the appropriate effects of this bodily or mental behavior; (ii) b occurred; (iii) there is a c such that c is a mental event concurrent with b; and (iv) c occurred.

In considering this revision of naïve behaviorism, we make two assumptions: first, that although it is controversial, motives, wants, desires, and so on, are mental events; second, that the relation between the behavior and the concurrent or accompanying event is not causal. The case in which the relation is causal will be investigated separately.

In the second selection Melden can be interpreted as arguing against definition (D2). His most forceful argument,[3] which is designed to reduce definitions like (D2) to absurdity, is unfortunately both truncated and needlessly complicated. Without elaborating all the details, the argument is fundamentally this. It follows from (D2) that the bit of behavior and the concurrent mental event happened to a person only if that person performed the action in question. However, it is not the case that the occurrence of the behavior and the mental event are (logically) sufficient for the performance of the action. This last claim contradicts what follows from definition (D2); hence, (D2) is untenable.

This argument is sound. The crucial claim, that the occurrence of the behavior and mental event are not sufficient for performing the action, is justified. Suppose that Jones swallowed a strange drug. Whenever he takes this drug, which might be called "the hand-raising-motive-event drug," something happens to him, namely, he acquires a motive for raising his hand. Now at the very moment the drug affects Jones, Smith lifts Jones' hand. In this case Jones' hand rose—Smith lifted it—and Jones had the appropriate motive. However, Jones did not raise his hand: something *happened to* Jones; he was a victim of the drug and his hand's rising. Since this situation is logically possible, the appropriate bit of behavior and motive can, logically, occur to a person without his performing the action in question. The importance of this example lies in the fact that counterinstances of this type can be generated even if intendings, desires, willings, wantings, or so on, are taken as the concurrent mental events. The crucial premise in Melden's *reductio* argument, further, is justifiable by less fanciful examples. Again taking motives as concurrent mental events, suppose that Brown is jealous of Robinson's piano playing. Brown might express his jealousy by suddenly waving his hand near Robinson while he is playing. Brown, however, is aware of his own jealousy and what it can lead him to do, so he *refrains* from moving his hand. But at that very moment Brown's hand moves because of a nervous spasm. In this case Brown exhibited the bodily behavior of his hand's moving and he had a motive for moving it; but he did not perform the action of moving his hand. Brown, as well as Robinson, was a victim of his hand's moving.[4] In short, then, the strange-drug and jealous-piano-player examples show that it is logically possible that the relevant behavior and mental events happen to a person and that the person does not perform the action in question. Since it follows from (D2) that this is not possible, definition (D2), the accompanying event revision of naïve behaviorism, is inadequate.

4. VOLUNTARY BEHAVIOR

The behaviorist remains undaunted. Granted that human action is not mere behavior, nor behavior plus an accompanying mental event, it is nonetheless behavior, *a special kind of behavior*, in particular, *voluntary* bodily or mental be-

---

[3] See Melden, " 'Action Equals Bodily Movement Plus Motive,' " pp. 29–30 below.

[4] This example has an interesting sidelight: namely, the "logic" of refraining is different from performing. If a person performs an overt action, it follows that the behavior in question occurs. However, from the fact that a person refrains from performing an action it does not follow that the behavior in question did not occur. If I raise my hand, then my hand must rise; if I refrain from raising my hand, it is not the case that my hand must not rise—someone or something else could lift it.

havior. What distinguishes my raising my arm from my arm's rising is that in the former case the rising was voluntary. Hence, the definition of "(person) S performed (action) *a*"—call it (D3)—can be formulated by adding "(iii) (behavior) *b* was voluntary" to the two naïve behavioristic conditions.[5]

Obviously the difficulty with this definition is determining the meaning of "voluntary behavior." In the fourth selection, Professor Gilbert Ryle indicates two meanings that this expression can have. The first is the ordinary man's, in which the word "voluntary," and its correlative "involuntary," are used in connection with actions that ought or ought not to be done. A bit of behavior is voluntary, provided that the agent could have helped doing it, or more generally, that he could have done otherwise. But under what conditions could he have done otherwise? One answer often given is that the agent could have done otherwise if he had chosen to do otherwise. For this sense of "voluntary," then, condition (iii) would read "(behavior) *b* would not have occurred if (person) S had chosen otherwise." It is best, however, to return to this interpretation of definition (D3) after we have considered the second meaning of "voluntary."

Ryle claims that a sense of "voluntary" has been introduced by philosophers in which the word applies to all and only those things a person does as opposed to the things that happen to him. The danger in adopting this sense of "voluntary" is that it may lead to circularity when used to explicate "performs an action." Aristotle, on one interpretation, has fallen victim to this peril. A person's behavior is voluntary, according to him, only if "the principle that moves the instrumental parts of the body in such actions is in him."[6] But what is this moving principle? It is that which gives a person power to act and forbear. That is, "voluntary behavior" is to be understood in terms of an internal moving principle, which in turn is to be understood in terms of acting. On this reading of Aristotle, then, definition (D3) is viciously circular.

5. THE VOLITIONAL THEORY

At this point it might be objected that although Aristotle's explication of "voluntary" is no help for our purposes, there is a "philosopher's sense" that does not commit us to circularity. A bit of behavior is voluntary if, and only if, it is *caused by* the occurrence of a special sort of event, namely, a *volition*. I signal for the waiter by raising my hand when, and only when, my hand's rising was caused by a voluntary event, a volition. This theory can be formulated by adding to the naïve behavioristic conditions (i) and (ii):

(iii) there is a v such that v is a volition of (person) S and v caused (behavior) b.

Proponents of the volitional theory—call it (D4)—can argue that the reason we were able to generate counterexamples to definition (D2) is that we failed to specify correctly the relationship between the accompanying event and the be-

---

[5] This view is sometimes adopted by legal theorists. According to Mr. Justice Oliver Wendell Holmes, for example, "An act is always a voluntary muscular contraction, and nothing else." [Quoted by Walter W. Cook in "Act, Intention and Motive," *Yale Law Journal*, XXVI (1917); partially reprinted in *Freedom and Responsibility*, ed. Herbert Morris (Stanford: Stanford University Press, 1961), pp. 123–125.]

[6] *Ethica Nicomachea*, 1110a15–17; cf. 1110b1–3 and 1111a21–22. (See pp. 32–34 below.)

havior. It is not merely that a mental event occurs and the behavior also occurs, but rather that the accompanying event, the volition (which need not be mental), *causes* the behavior to occur. The strange-drug and jealous-piano-player examples do not count against the volitional theory because in both cases the accompanying event, the motive, was causally independent of the behavior, the arm's rising.

The volitional theory had the status of dogma for eighteenth- and nineteenth-century philosophers. John Stuart Mill, for example, says:

> Now what is an action? Not one thing, but a series of two things; the state of mind called a volition, followed by an effect. The volition or intention to produce the effect, is one thing; the effect produced in consequence of the intention, is another thing; the two together constitute the action. I form the purpose of instantly moving my arm; that is a state of my mind: my arm (not being tied or paralytic) moves in obedience to my purpose; that is a physical fact, consequent on a state of mind. The intention followed by the fact, or (if we prefer the expression) the fact when preceded and caused by the intention, is called the action of moving my arm.[7]

Psychologists and legal theorists also accepted this theory. John Austin, the nineteenth-century jurist, for example, says "a voluntary movement of my body, or a movement which follows a volition, is an *act*." [8] Professor H. L. A. Hart points out, moreover, that the volitional theory is currently the orthodox view in Anglo-Saxon law.[9]

From about 1920 to about 1960, most analytic philosophers rejected the volitional theory. One notable exception is Professor H. A. Prichard who, in his paper "Acting, Willing, Desiring," develops and defends a volitional theory. Prichard's terminology differs from the eighteenth- and nineteenth-century theorists, but that may be all. ". . . to act," he says, "is really to will something." [10] What is this something we will? And further, what is the relationship between this something and the willing? What we will, Prichard claims, is a bodily change. We do not will actions: for if acting is willing something and if what is willed were an action, then in acting we would have to will the willing of the willing of . . . and so on *ad infinitum*. His answer to the second question is not as clear. He appears to side with the volitional theorists in claiming that the willing *causes* the bodily change, but he hedges. He says, for example, "Where we have willed some movement of our body and think we have caused it, we cannot have directly caused it. For what we directly caused, if anything, must have been some change in our brain." [11] What is the force of "if anything," and similar remarks in the text? Perhaps Prichard thinks that willing may be a mere accompanying event, or perhaps he suspects that the relation between the willing and the behavior is logical, which would place him among the philosophers to be considered in section III. However, the overall impression is that Prichard agrees with the volitional theorists, who take the relation to be causal.

[7] *A System of Logic*, 8th ed. (London: Longmans, Green and Co. Ltd., 1961), p. 35.
[8] *Lectures on Jurisprudence*, 4th ed., vol. I, Lecture XVIII (London: John Murray Ltd., 1873), 427.
[9] H. L. A. Hart, *Punishment and Responsibility* (Oxford: Oxford University Press, 1968), pp. 90 ff.
[10] P. 43 below.
[11] P. 46 below.

Prichard's version of the volitional theory has several noteworthy features. What the willing actually causes is not the bodily movement, such as an arm rising, but rather the first link in the causal chain, presumably a brain event, that culminates in the bodily movement. Also, the willing is accompanied by a desire, in particular, a desire to will the bodily movement. This version of the theory motivates several questions. Can I not act even though I have no desires concerning this bodily movement at the time? If in acting I am somehow aware of what I am doing, how can acting be causing a certain, specific brain event about which I know nothing? We will not here investigate the details of Prichard's proposal. Rather, let us examine several recurrent general criticisms of the volitional theory.

It is urged that there is no reason to believe that persons experience volitions. Professor Richard Taylor, for example, says ". . . I am quite certain that no such thing [namely, a volition] ever occurred within me. I do not believe that I have merely *failed to find* things that are in fact occurring within me daily, nor that, finding them, I have failed to *recognize* them." [12] Basically, the argument that Taylor and others are appealing to is this.[13] If I experience something, then arguments are not needed to convince me that I experience it. Since I do not recognize something as a volition, arguments by philosophers are needed to convince me that I experience volitions. Hence, I do not experience volitions. But the volitional theory is not so easily defeated. The main premise, "If I experience something, then arguments are not needed to convince me that I experience it," is false. A person can experience something without being immediately aware, or aware at all, that he is experiencing it. In this respect volitions would be like unrecognized desires or motives or like the effects of an undetected brain tumor.

Rather than pursue this argument from introspective evidence—or better, from lack of introspective evidence—let us consider an argument often thought to be conclusive, namely, that the volitional theory leads to a vicious infinite regress.[14] Suppose that there are volitions that cause bodily and mental behavior. Two cases then arise. In case I, a volition is itself something that is caused. In case II, a volition is not caused. Consider case I. If a volition is caused, then either something causes that volition—call it a second-order volition—or it is not the case that something causes that volition. If there is not something that causes that volition, then the situation reduces to case II. If, on the other hand, there is something that causes the second-order volition, then either there is something that causes it—a third-order volition—or there is not, and so on *ad infinitum*. In case I, then, persons would have to do an infinite number of things in order to perform any action, which is impossible. Consider case II. Here a volition, whether first-order or higher, is something that is not caused, at least in the ordinary sense of "cause" that obtains between events. Rather, it is something that a person just *makes happen*. But volitions were introduced in order to avoid saying that in acting we just make something happen. The problem has merely been pushed back one step;

12 "Simple Action and Volition," p. 58 below.
13 For example, cf. A. I. Melden, *Free Action* (New York: Humanities Press, Inc., 1961), pp. 47 ff.
14 Cf. Ryle, "The Will," pp. 64–65 below; there is also a hint of this argument in Taylor, "Simple Action and Volition," p. 60 below. Also cf. Jonathan Edwards, *Freedom of the Will*, first published 1754, and reprinted in the *Works of Jonathan Edwards*, vol. 1, ed. Paul Ramsey (New Haven: Yale University Press, 1957). See especially Part II (pp. 169 ff. in the Yale reprint). Part II is also reprinted (in part) in *The Problem of Free Will*, ed. W. Enteman (New York: Charles Scribner's Sons, 1967), pp. 111 ff.

and hence, the analysis is inadequate. Thus, the objection concludes, if there are volitions that cause bits of behavior, then either a vicious infinite regress results or the volitional theory is an inadequate analysis of human action.

The first horn of this dilemma, however, can be broken. A *nonvicious* regress results from supposing that every volition is caused. There is no reason to think that higher order volitions are voluntary; they may be nerve impulses or muscle contractions. Indeed, calling the causes of volitions "higher order volitions" is misleading; for a volition might be caused by an event external to the agent. What distinguishes action from mere behavior, on this view, is that the causal chain associated with acting includes a volition, whereas the causal chain associated with mere behavior does not. In short, even if every event, including volitions, is caused, there is no reason to claim that a person voluntarily does an infinite number of things in performing an action. Only the event immediately preceding the behavior in question need be voluntary.

6. REASONS AS CAUSES

Philosophers have recently discussed the question whether reasons are causes for actions.[15] This question is essentially no different from the question whether the volitional theory is tenable. "Volitions" can be construed as referring not to mere bodily events, but rather to motives or desires or wants or, to use an all-encompassing term, reasons. There is, however, a superficial difference between the reasons-as-causes debate and the discussion of volitions. The volitional theory conceives the effects of volitions as behavior, whereas the effects of reasons are said to be actions. Though it is contrary to the way we ordinarily talk (we say "My reason for raising my hand was to attract the chairman's attention," rather than "My reason for having my hand rise was to attract the chairman's attention"), reasons should be thought of as causing behavior. What a reason causes will have to be the behavior associated with the action if we are to elucidate "performs an action" in terms of "reasons." In addition to the circularity resulting if reasons were thought to cause actions, there is the problem of a vicious regress pointed out by Prichard. If acting is a reason causing something and if this something were an action, then in acting we would have to have a reason for the reason for . . . and so on *ad infinitum*.[16]

One argument against the view that reasons are causes has found particular favor.[17] A cause, it is claimed, is not logically tied to its effect; that is, it is logically possible that a cause occur and its presumed effect not occur. This view of causality as being a contingent, matter-of-fact relationship has roots in Hume and can be taken as the present orthodox view. But a reason (that is, a desire, or motive, or event, or so on) is logically tied to its effect. For reasons cannot be identified or described without referring to the resultant behavior. For example,

[15] In addition to Professor Davidson's "Actions, Reasons, and Causes" reprinted below, pp. 67–79, see David Pears, "Are Reasons for Actions Causes?" *Epistemology*, ed. Avrum Stroll (New York: Harper & Row, Inc., 1967); also see Raziel Abelson's review of Richard Taylor's *Action and Purpose*, in "Doing, Causing and Causing to Do," *Journal of Philosophy*, LXVI (1969), 178–192.

[16] Cf. Prichard, "Acting, Willing, Desiring," p. 45 below.

[17] See Davidson, pp. 75 f. below and Taylor, "Simple Action and Volition," pp. 58 ff. below. In addition to the sources cited by Davidson in footnote 6 (p. 75 below), cf. Pears, "Are Reasons for Actions Causes?" pp. 214 ff; and Keith Donnellan, "Reasons and Causes," *The Encyclopedia of Philosophy*, vol. 7, ed. Paul Edwards (New York: The Macmillan Company, 1967), 86 ff.

the only way to identify, or "pick out," a reason for one's arm rising is by referring to its effect, the arm's rising; and the only way to describe this volition is to call it "an arm-rising volition." Since reasons are not logically independent of their resultant behavior, reasons do not cause this behavior.

Davidson appears to refute this argument by taking the heroic line that cause and effect are not contingently related.[18] He says that the statement "Every true causal statement is empirical" is false. For him "causal statement" apparently refers to any statement that contains the words "cause" or "effect"; and hence, his claim is clearly correct: "The cause of B caused B" is indeed a nonempirical, true causal statement. But this claim does not refute the argument. The first premise says that it is logically possible that the event labeled "cause" occur and the event to be labeled "effect" not occur. It is logically possible, for example, that one billiard ball hit another and the second ball not move. Davidson has not shown that *this* or similar "causal" statements are false.[19]

One might continue to defend Davidson's tack and argue with Leibniz that causality is really a logical relation, but the argument can be refuted without any such appeal. The premise that a reason and its resultant behavior are not contingently related is unjustified. Supposing that reasons are causes, it is possible nevertheless to identify and describe them without referring to the resultant behavior. For a reason can be identified and described by referring to its *goal*. Suppose that I have a motive (reason) for signaling the chairman. Suppose also that just as I am about to signal, someone or something prevents me. I could nonetheless identify and describe my motive, not by the resultant behavior—which did not occur—but rather by the goal of having been recognized by the chairman. Sometimes in fact we identify or describe a motive by referring to the resultant behavior. We can do this, however, only when the goal and the resultant behavior coincide, that is, when we achieve our goal. Again, we recognize, identify, and describe motives (reasons) not by their actual outcomes, but rather by their expected or proposed outcomes. The reason for claiming that reasons and their resultant behavior are not contingently related is, then, unfounded.

Clearly this is not the end of the story. Other *prima facie* plausible objections can be raised against the volitional theory. (1) Singular causal statements entail general causal laws. But singular statements asserting that a person did something because of a reason cannot be generalized; for a person has it within his power to act contrary to his reason. (2) A person is somehow directly aware—he knows "without observation"—his reason for doing something. But in other causal situations a person is not directly aware of the cause. (3) The logic of the causal relation is different from the reason-behavior relation. The causal relation is transitive: if A caused B and B caused C, then A caused B. If one billiard ball caused a second to move, and the second a third, then the first caused the third to move. But the reason-behavior relation is either intransitive or nontransitive; in all (or some) cases, if a reason causes certain behavior, then the reason is not a reason for the effects of the behavior.[20] Suppose that I want to please Mary Smith. This desire leads me to have flowers sent to her. But unknown to me, she is dread-

18 "Actions, Reasons, and Causes," p. 75 below.
19 Cf. Raziel Abelson's "Doing, Causing and Causing to Do."
20 I was alerted to this problem by Mr. Holmes Rolston.

fully allergic to flowers and they cause her to have an allergy attack. Though I had a reason for sending her flowers, I had no reason for initiating an attack.

It may well be that these arguments, like the regress and logical relatedness arguments, are unsound. Davidson argues against (1) and (2). Against (1), if the claim that singular causal statements entail general laws is to obtain for ordinary causal situations, then it must be interpreted to mean that a singular causal statement entails some causal law or another. Indeed, in the simple case of a stone shattering a window, no one may now be aware of the exact causal laws involved. This interpretation of the claim also obtains for the reasons case. (2) Granting that we have special access to our reasons, that our knowledge of reasons is not inductive, it does not follow that reasons are not causes. In other cases of causal regularities our knowledge is not inductive; often one instance is sufficient to satisfy us that a causal law obtains. (3) A person can have a reason without knowing all that it is a reason for. I did not know that one of the consequences of giving Mary Smith flowers would be an allergy attack. Or if one claims that the total goal of the reason (desire, motive, or so on) is always known, the argument can be refuted by observing that reasons are *proximate* rather than remote causes. In the billiard-ball case, the first ball moving is the proximate, immediate cause of the second's moving, the second is the proximate cause of the third, but the first ball moving is not the proximate cause of the third—it is the remote cause.

Is Taylor's intuitive feeling that there are no volitions, or in other language, reasons, that cause the resultant behavior justified? The answer depends on the outcome of the current philosophical debate, on whether Davidson and others can adequately refute the arguments of their opponents. My own prejudice is that *if* human action can be analyzed as "behavior plus," the most likely candidate for the "plus" is reasons (volitions).

7. CONDITIONALS

Let us suppose that the volitional theory is not defensible. In that case we might return to what Ryle called "the ordinary man's" interpretation of "voluntary" and define "performs an action" in terms of conditionals, in terms of what would have happened *if* the agent had chosen differently, or had tried to act differently, or had different desires. The *prima facie* most plausible of these suggestions can be formulated—call it definition (D5)—by retaining the behavioristic conditions (i) and (ii) and adding:

(iii) (behavior) *b* would not have occurred if (person) *S* had chosen differently.

Consider the action of my buying a loaf of bread. The behavioral component of this action includes, for example, my hand extending toward the grocer with certain coins in it, my carrying the loaf out of the store, and so on. Presumably, if I had chosen otherwise, if I had chosen to buy cake, or not buy anything, these bits of behavior would not have occurred in just the way they did.

Definition (D5), however, is inadequate for at least three reasons. First, sometimes a person's body moves independently of the choices he could make. Suppose that Jones raises his hand at noon. Suppose also that for some reason Smith wants Jones' hand to rise at that time. Smith is very much stronger than Jones: and hence, Jones is unable to prevent Smith from lifting his hand. Accordingly, the definiendum is satisfied but not the definiens. Jones raised his hand. But condition (iii) is not satisfied: if Jones had chosen differently, his arm would nevertheless have risen—Smith would have lifted it.

Second, it is difficult to determine whether or not condition (iii) entails that the agent made a choice with respect to the behavior—but in either case definition (D5) is inadequate. Suppose, on the one hand, that condition (iii) does not entail that the agent made a choice with respect to the behavior. Definition (D5), then, is not adequate to distinguish between actions and nervous spasms. Sergeant Smith asks for volunteers for a dangerous mission. At that very moment Private Jones' hand rises because of a nervous spasm. Presumably if Jones had made a choice in this situation, he would have chosen not to have his hand rise. He would have taken precautions to ensure his hand's not rising, perhaps by placing it securely in his pocket. On the supposition that Jones made no choice with respect to the behavior of his hand's rising, then, all the conditions of the definiens are satisfied, but Jones did not perform the action of raising his hand. Now suppose on the other hand that condition (iii) entails that the agent made a choice with respect to the behavior. Since it follows from (D5) that "(person) S performed (action) a" entails condition (iii), "(person) S performed (action) a" entails that S made a choice with respect to (behavior) b. But persons sometimes perform actions without making a choice. No choice is made in habitual or absentminded actions or in mere pickings or takings or when some thing or person gets one to perform an action. A necessary condition for choosing is that the agent attentively believe that there are alternatives within his power.[21] I choose Scotch and soda only if I believe that I could have had some other drink, or perhaps no drink at all. But in cases of mere pickings and takings, I do not believe that there are alternatives within my power. I pick, without choosing, the Scotch and soda if I do not think that I could have had a different drink. And in performing a habitual action, the agent holds *no* attentive beliefs at the time about what he is doing (though he may hold beliefs about the *goal* of his action). I am not aware of, and hence do not believe anything about, what I am doing when I brush my teeth, walk, or type habitually. It follows, then, that persons do not choose to perform habitual actions or mere pickings. And since the false claim that each action is chosen validly follows from definition (D5), (D5) is inadequate.

The last charge against definition (D5) is circularity. If choosing is an action, then we have not defined "performs an action" in nonaction talk. But what is the nature of choosing? The Daveney and second Aristotle selections address themselves to this question, and to it we briefly turn our attention.

The claim that choosing is an action is usually interpreted to mean that choosing is identical with the action chosen. For example, "I chose to drink Scotch and soda" means that I drank Scotch and soda. Philosophers have, in

---

21 Cf. Taylor, *Action and Purpose* (Englewood Cliffs, New Jersey: Prentice-Hall, Inc., 1966), pp. 76–77.

general, rejected the view that choosing is an action.[22] They argue that this view leads to a vicious infinite regress and that it is open to counterexamples. Let us examine these two objections to the doing theory of choosing.

Assume that all choosings are actions. Since all actions are the results of choices, it follows that all choosings are the results of choices. Thus, a person chooses to perform an action only if he chooses to choose to . . . to perform it. But it is impossible that a person make and carry out an infinite number of choices. Hence, it is not the case that choosings are actions. However, it is not the assumption of this argument that is false, but rather the premise that all actions are the results of choices. As already indicated, habitual and absent-minded actions, as well as actions that another person or thing gets one to perform, are not the results of choices. If Brown gets me to order another Scotch and soda, then even though it is I who performed the action of ordering the drink, I did so without choosing.

Other versions of this argument have been proposed in which the conclusion is not that an infinite regress results, but rather the false (or meaningless) claim that persons can choose to choose. "It appears," says Professor Oldenquist, "that any action for which we can be held morally accountable is one we can choose. We *are* held morally accountable for our choices. Therefore, if choosing is an action it . . . follows that we can choose to choose." [23] But persons can, and sometimes do, choose to choose. Suppose that I were asked to judge the pie-baking competition at the County Fair. My chore would be to choose the winner. However, whether I accept this invitation is a difficult choice. Tasting the pies would certainly be pleasurable, but I already have commitments for that time. If I did judge the contest, then at an earlier time I would have chosen to choose the winner. The first premise of Oldenquist's formulation of the argument, in addition, is false. A person can be held morally accountable for an action he did not choose to perform. We can be held morally accountable for mere pickings and habitual actions; but persons do not choose to perform habitual actions or mere pickings or takings.

Turning to the counterexample attack against the doing theory of choosing, Daveney says, "If one considers . . . statements where the perfect or the plu-perfect of 'choose' is used, it becomes quite clear that the choosing is different from the doing. *Viz.* in the morning I say 'I have chosen to play cricket this afternoon' or 'I had chosen to play for the local team that afternoon, but something prevented me.' " [24] Unlike the regress attack, cases of unsuccessful or prevented choices and cases of choice involving no overt physical actions tell against the view that choosing is identical with the action chosen. But why restrict a doing analysis of choosing to such a naïve view?

[22] In addition to Daveney, the main rejecters are: W. D. Glasgow, "On Choosing," *Analysis,* XVII (1957), 135–139, and "The Concept of Choosing," *Analysis,* XX (1960), 63–67; P. H. Nowell-Smith, "Choosing, Deciding and Doing," *Analysis,* XVIII (1958), 63–69; and A. Oldenquist, "Choosing, Deciding, and Doing," *The Encyclopedia of Philosophy,* vol. 2, ed. Paul Edwards, 96–104. The main exceptions are: J. L. Evans, "Choice," *Philosophical Quarterly,* V (1955), 303–315; and Richard Taylor, *Action and Purpose,* pp. 72–77.

[23] Oldenquist, "Choosing, Deciding, and Doing," *The Encyclopedia of Philosophy,* vol. 2, 97.

[24] T. F. Daveney, "Choosing," p. 86 below; cf. Nowell-Smith, "Choosing, Deciding and Doing," p. 65.

A person chooses to perform an action only if he *commits* himself to performing it. Committing here is not tied to announcing a decision or promising; rather, it involves taking steps to bring about a certain outcome. More exactly, a person commits himself to performing an action just in case he performs all those actions he justifiably believes to be preliminaries to the action in question, or if he did not perform all those actions he justifiably believes to be preliminaries, he would have performed them if he had had the opportunity. Committing oneself in this sense is certainly an action; even if only the subjunctive disjunct of this definition obtains, an action has been performed. The agent has intentionally brought about a change in the world; he has set the stage, as it were, in such a way that certain other changes would be brought about if he is given the opportunity. This version of the doing theory of choosing meets Daveney's examples. If I chose to play cricket but am prevented, I nevertheless committed myself to playing it. I believed with good reason that gathering my equipment, putting myself in the proper frame of mind, and so on, is all I need do in order to play. However, in this case I did not have the opportunity to perform these preliminary actions. I chose to play cricket without performing any overt, physical action. In short, then, if an adequate doing analysis of choosing can be developed along these lines, including probably the condition that the agent prefers to perform the action in question more than the alternatives he believes to be within his power, then any explication of "performs an action" in terms of "choosing" would be circular.[25]

Conditionals other than "The behavior would not have occurred if the agent chose differently" might be suggested for the analysis of action, most prominently "The behavior would not have occurred if the agent tried to behave differently." However, formulating the conditional in terms of trying is inadequate for the same sorts of reasons as the choosing conditional. Taking the circularity charge, trying is to be understood in terms of action. Trying (or undertaking) is not some mysterious happening distinct from one's actions: trying to do something *is* doing one thing in order to, in the endeavor to, do something else.[26] Suppose that I am trying to raise my arm while it is tied to the chair. In trying to raise my arm, I perform certain actions, for example, pushing up with my fingers and pulling with my other arm, in order to have my hand rise. If I sat on the chair and did nothing, then I would not be trying to raise my arm. Or again, in trying to cough, I contract my throat muscles and breathe out in order to make a coughing sound. (Of course some things a person does, he does without trying. Normally I cough or wink without trying; there is nothing I do in order to cough or wink.) Trying, then, is to be understood in terms of action, and hence cannot be used to explicate "performs an action" in nonaction talk.

The arguments used against the choosing and trying conditionals can probably be used against conditionals that refer to motives, desires, wants, or so on. The reason for the qualification "probably" is that careful investigation is needed into

[25] This analysis of choosing is developed in detail in the author's paper "Choosing and Doing," *Ratio*, December 1969.

[26] For an extended defense of this position see Richard Taylor, *Action and Purpose*, pp. 77–85. Also cf. Prichard, ". . . what we call trying to do something is as much doing something as what we ordinarily call doing something, although the word 'trying' suggests that it is not" ("Acting, Willing, Desiring," p. 48 below). And cf. Roderick Chisholm, "Freedom and Action," p. 286 below; Arnold S. Kaufman, "Ability," pp. 200 ff. below.

the nature of desiring, wanting, and so on, before it can be categorically claimed that the circularity argument applies, before it can be claimed that they are correctly explicated only in terms of "performs an action."

8. RULE-FOLLOWING

Our failure to define "performs an action," it may be urged, results from taking a microscopic, rather than macroscopic, viewpoint. Human action can only be understood in the context of all human endeavors, or as Melden puts it in his paper "Action," ". . . in the context of practices in which rules are obeyed, criteria employed, [and] policies . . . observed." [27] Following Wittgenstein, Melden is appealing to the distinction between obeying or following a rule and acting in accordance with it. Suppose that a young child who knows nothing about the game of chess picked up a knight and put it down in the vacant square two forward and one to the left. Here the child would be *acting in accordance with* the rule for moving knights in chess, but he would not be *following* or *obeying* it. Only a person who at least partially knew how to play chess could follow this rule. An action, then, is performed only if a rule is followed. We can formulate Melden's view in "Action," which appeared prior to his *Free Action* from which the first two selections come, by retaining the naïve behavioristic conditions (i) and (ii) and adding:

(iii) (person) S followed or obeyed the appropriate rules.

However, this definition of "performing an action" in terms of "rule-following behavior"—call it (D6)—is also problematical. Granted that in order for one person to understand or interpret another person's behavior it is helpful or perhaps necessary to see that other person's behavior within a social context, viewing an action within the larger framework of many people acting does not specify what an action is. Knowing the customs, practices, and rules a person is following permits us to classify his action, to state what sort of action it is: but it does not permit us to say what an action *is*, which is the ontological question we have been trying to answer. To make the point differently, the notion of rule-following is to be understood in terms of action. To obey a rule is to act in a prescribed way. An explication of "performs an action" in terms of "rule-following behavior" is, then, viciously circular.

Further, definiton (D6) is problematical even if we ignore the charge of circularity. For a person can act without following any rule. In concluding his paper Melden claims that if a man's arm rises randomly, without reason, then he did not perform an action. Although Melden is probably right here, what of the case in which a man *deliberately* acts so that he obeys no rule? Artists, social reformers, inventors, and innovators in general, attempt and sometimes succeed in acting in this way. Granted that innovators often set new rules, or at least set the stage for new rules, the point remains that *at the time they are acting*, they obey no rule. And surely, actions were performed in these cases; things did not merely happen to these persons; they *did* something. Persons, in short, have the power to act deliberately contrary to established practices, traditions, and rules.

[27] P. 97 below.

They seldom do; and when they do, they might not be understood: but persons do in fact act without following rules.

A sympathetic reader of Melden might claim that he is maintaining that no definition of the kind we have been offering is adequate and that the best we can do is classify actions. Even if we accept this reading of the text, it remains to be seen whether something more enlightening than classification is forthcoming. Indeed, section III is devoted to showing that although the concept of action is not to be analyzed as "behavior plus," we can say some very enlightening things about it.

9. ACTION AND RESPONSIBILITY

Arguing from a point of view similar to Melden in his paper "Action," it might be maintained that human action *is* behavior to which responsibility can be ascribed. That is, "performs an action" is defined by retaining the naïve behavioristic conditions (i) and (ii) and adding:

(iii) responsibility is ascribable to (person) S for (behavior) b.

Thus according to this proposal [call it definition (D7)], Smith's shooting the girl is an action because he is responsible for her having been shot.

In favor of definition (D7) Professor H. L. A. Hart has argued that the concepts of action, like many legal concepts (in the law of contracts, for example), is defeasible; that is, claims of having performed an action, like claims of having entered into a contract, can be overridden (defeated) or weakened by excuses and mediating circumstances. Since defeasible concepts are not merely descriptive, but also *ascriptive*, Hart continues, no set of purely descriptive statements can explicate "performs an action." What is being ascribed to an agent in claiming that he has performed an action is responsibility for bringing about a certain state of affairs. In other words, in making the statement that a person performed an action, we ourselves are doing something; we are holding him responsible.[28]

What, however, does it mean to say that a person is responsible for something? On the occasion of a person's causing something to happen, we sometimes say that he is responsible for bringing about that state of affairs. Thus, for example, if I brought about the vase's breaking by dropping it, that is, if I am the *cause* of the vase's breaking, then I am responsible for its breaking. The causal sense of "responsibility," however, is not appropriate for (D7). Hart and others who hold the ascriptivistic thesis are claiming that the concept of human action is essentially a moral and social concept. Action is behavior interpreted within the context of moral and social rules and practices. To reduce responsibility to causation by the agent is, at best, to assert a volitional-type analysis.

In "Responsibility and Action," Professor Kurt Baier distinguishes within the social and moral context of bringing people to account five senses of "responsi-

---

28 See H. L. A. Hart, "The Ascription of Responsibility and Rights," *Proceedings of the Aristotelian Society,* 1948–1949, pp. 171–194; reprinted in *Logic and Language,* ed. A. G. N. Flew (New York: Doubleday & Company, Inc., 1965; first published 1951), pp. 151–174. Cf. Hart, *Punishment and Responsibility,* esp. chapters II, IV, and IX. Also cf. Joel Feinberg, "Action and Responsibility," *Philosophy in America,* ed. M. Black (London: George Allen and Unwin Ltd., 1965), pp. 134–160; reprinted in *The Philosophy of Action,* ed. A. White (Oxford: Oxford University Press, 1968), pp. 95–119.

bility."[29] First, to say that a person is responsible for something can mean that he is *accountable* for it; that is, he is fit to be brought to account, he is in possession of the psychologically necessary and sufficient conditions for having the ability to be guided by social rules and practices.[30] Presumably, young children and madmen are not fit to be brought to account. Second, "responsibility" can mean what Baier calls "task-responsibility." Whereas a person is accountable for anything and everything he does, he is task-responsible only for bringing about specific states of affairs (for example, mowing the lawn or feeding the dog). Having a task-responsibility is one sort of obligatory social requirement; other sorts are conformity to moral rules, fulfillment of commitments, and performance of duties.[31] Third, to say that a person is responsible for something can mean that he is *answerable* for it, that is, he has failed to satisfy an obligatory social requirement (for example, a task-responsibility). "Prior to the catastrophe the captain was (task-) responsible for the safety of the passengers and the crew and, therefore, after the catastrophe, became responsible-answerable"—without an adequate excuse. When we ask who is *to blame* for what occurred, we are asking who brought it about by breaking a social or moral rule without an exculpatory explanation.[32] Fifth, when a person is culpable for something, he is *liable* to unwanted treatment, such as punishment, condemnation, and payment of compensation. The "full-blown" sense of "responsibility" is liability.

Prima facie the sense of "responsibility" relevant to definition (D7) is "answerability," the sense in which a person failed to discharge an obligatory social or moral requirement. A normal person's mere reflexes satisfy the criterion of a person behaving who has social obligations and who is psychologically fit to fulfill these obligations. And since persons often perform actions "for good reasons," that is, have excuses for what they do, "culpability" and "liability" are too strong for definition (D7). However, even if condition (iii) is interpreted as saying that the agent is answerable for his behavior, the analysis is problematical. First, as Baier points out, there are counterinstances to the definition; and secondly, as Professor Geach indicates in his paper "Ascriptivism," there is a "radical flaw" in this approach to the problem.[33]

First the counterexamples.[34] There are actions that persons perform that are not contrary to any social or moral restrictions; for example, in ordinary circumstances, my scratching my head while alone in my room is value-neutral. Moreover, sometimes one agent is responsible (answerable) for another's actions. If I am a child or a member of an ideal Communistic communal, responsibility for what I do is ascribable not to me, but rather to my parents, or in the latter case, to the community as a whole. Or to take a specific case, suppose that Smith gets the emperor to signal for the execution. Smith convinces the emperor that the prisoner is deserving of this punishment and that a great amount of good will result from the execution. Moreover, Smith has been reliable in the past, and the emperor has taken reasonable steps to confirm Smith's claim in this case.

---

[29] See pp. 100–108 below.
[30] See pp. 103–104 below.
[31] See p. 104 below.
[32] See pp. 105–107 below.
[33] Reprinted pp. 117–120 below; see especially p. 119.
[34] Cf. Baier, "Responsibility and Action," pp. 112–113 below.

Smith, however, lied to the emperor. The execution is entirely unwarranted. Hence, the emperor performed the action of signaling for the execution. But the definiens is false. If someone were answerable for initiating the execution, then Smith, not the emperor, would be answerable for it. On the other side, the definiens is not sufficient for the truth of the claim that the agent performed an action. For a person is sometimes answerable not for his actions, but rather for the *consequences* of his actions.[35] Suppose that Brown is replenishing the oil supply. In lifting and carrying the drums, he is insufficiently cautious and unbeknownst to him, he spills some oil. The spilled oil then causes another person to fall and injure himself. Brown is answerable for the dangerous situation and ensuing accident, though the spilling of the oil was not an action of his; it was nothing he did intentionally, but rather it was a consequence of his replenishing the oil supply.

Let us turn now to Geach's attack on ascriptivism in action theory. Geach argues, if I understand him correctly, that ascriptivism assumes that the only use of the term "action," or any other action-term (e.g., "intentional," "done on purpose"), is in *calling* or labeling something an action. But this assumption is false. "Action" and action-terms in general are used in cases where no labeling is involved. Moreover, the primary use of "action" and action-terms is in predication, not in labeling. In conditional and disjunctive sentences, "action," for example, is not used to call or label something an action. In "If Jones' firing the gun is an action, then he is guilty of murder," "action" is predicated of "Jones' firing the gun." "Jones' firing the gun" has not been labeled an action; for the sentence "If Jones' firing the gun is an action, then he is guilty of murder" is consistent with it not being the case that Jones' firing the gun is an action—his firing the gun might have been the result of a nervous spasm. In declarative sentences, moreover, "action" and action-terms are used to predicate something of a subject, though this may not be their only use. If action-terms did not have a predicative use in declarative sentences, then inferences such as

(i) If Jones' firing the gun is an action, then he is guilty of murder.
(ii) Jones' firing the gun is an action.
   ergo
(iii) He is guilty of murder.

would be invalid because they commit the fallacy of equivocation. But these inferences are clearly valid. Though the ascriptivist's assumption that the *only* use of action-terms is in calling or labeling something an action is false, we sometimes do in fact call things actions. Taking a hint from Frege, we are able to call things actions by assertively using a sentence in which an action-term, especially "action," is predicated of a subject.[36] In short, since the primary use of action-terms is in predication, the calling of something an action must be explained in terms of

---

[35] G. Pitcher, in "Hart on Action and Responsibility," *Philosophical Review*, LXIX (1960), 226–235 and John Ladd, in "The Ethical Dimensions of the Concept of Action," *Journal of Philosophy*, LXII (1965), 633–645, hold the stronger position that in *all* cases a person is responsible for the consequences of his actions. Cf. J. B. Schneewind's reply to Ladd, "Responsibilities and Liability," *Journal of Philosophy*, LXII (1965), abstract pp. 649–650.

[36] See Gottlob Frege, "Der Gedanke," 1919, translated as "The Thought," by A. M. and Marcelle Quinton, *Mind*, LXV (1956), 289–311.

predicating action-terms of subjects. However, the problem of explaining what a sentence in which an action-term is predicated of a subject means is the problem with which we started, namely, finding an expression equivalent in meaning to "A person performs an action."

Although human action is not behavior to which we can ascribe responsibility, Baier argues, there is nevertheless an important conceptual link between action and responsibility.[37] Actions are performed by agents. An agent is a being who has the capacity to impose on his reactions to the environment a pattern conforming to his beliefs about what reactions will bring about the preferred moral and social states of affairs and prevent or terminate the rejected ones. Clearly, having this capacity presupposes the framework of bringing people to account. Only if there are obligatory requirements for which someone can receive unwanted treatment if he disregards them without excusing reasons, can we meaningfully talk about bringing one's behavior into conformity with these social and moral requirements. In short, one cannot understand what an agent is, what one of the *relata* in the two-place relation "performs" is, without understanding what it is to bring someone to account, that is, to ascribe responsibility in some sense to him.

Baier, it is important to note, is concerned with "agent" in its strictest sense, that is, "agent" in the sense of "moral agent." It is at least logically possible that there is an agent who, from birth, is completely isolated from other agents. Such an agent, however, would not be a *moral* agent. He would not be able to understand many ordinary action descriptions, namely, those that pertain to social and moral situations. He would not know what it is to steal or to murder, though he would know what it is to take things and to kill. A moral agent, moreover, is a *rational* agent. It is controversial, however, whether in all cases a rational agent is a moral agent. For it is unclear whether our isolated agent could be rational. If rationality of an agent depends solely on his seeing the consistency or inconsistency of beliefs, then it is conceivable that our isolated agent would be rational. But if rationality also depends on acting for "the general good"—if, for example, our isolated agent prefers to relieve an itch even if it means the horrendous annihilation of many other persons, then we would not say that our isolated agent is rational.

[37] See "Responsibility and Action," pp. 113 ff. below.

MERE BEHAVIOR

PHYSIOLOGICAL HAPPENINGS AND BODILY ACTIONS

A. I. Melden

Hume once complained about the careless procedure of philosophers who all too frequently, as he put it, began their discourses on morals with the familiar copulation "is" and then without explanation or justification employed the quite different locution "ought" (A Treatise of Human Nature, Bk. III, Pt. I, Sec. 2. See the concluding paragraph). But here too we seem to have a gap that needs to be bridged between things that happen, get done, and things that are done by persons when they raise their arms or perform any of the very many sorts of actions of which they are capable. And here, too, Moore's open question technique comes to mind (Principia Ethica, Ch. I). A very great number of physiological events take place, happen, get done when one raises one's arm; but it not only makes sense to ask whether these things are things that one does, it is in fact questionable that this is the case. If so, we cannot identify what happens, gets done, with what a person does. Here, corresponding to the familiar gaps that have plagued philosophers, not only in morals but also in aesthetics and in many another field of philosophy, is the gap between matters of physiological happening and matters of human action. And here as elsewhere the appearance of a gap is symptomatic of conceptual confusion.

In the present chapter I shall focus attention upon the question whether or not matters of physiological happenings can also be described legitimately as matters of action, things done by the agent. But first a word of warning is in order to guard against a familiar a priorism with respect to matters of physiology.

From Free Action by A. I. Melden (New York: Humanities Press, Inc., 1961), pp. 56–65. Reprinted by permission of Humanities Press, Inc., and Routledge & Kegan Paul Ltd.

The problem of how we may construe matters of bodily happening, whether these be the movements of muscles or limbs, as matters of human action has seemed to some philosophers to throw doubt upon the common assumption of physiologists that a complete causal account of such bodily happenings in terms of antecedent physiological occurrances is possible. Prichard, for example, remarks that if we are to think that by willing we expect some change in our bodies "we are implying the idea that in doing so, we are butting into, or interfering with, the physical system" (*Moral Obligation*, p. 193). For the act of volition, the willing, is construed as a causal factor in the absence of which in the given circumstances the bodily movement would not have occurred. And this seems to imply that in cases of human action there are gaps in the chain of physiological causes which are filled in by the doings of agents; whether these be willings or any other instances of causal efficacy of minds is of no matter. Now there is undoubtedly a difference between a matter of physiological happening and a bodily movement that is correctly describable as something done by the agent. We must be on our guard, however, against the conclusion we are too often invited to draw, namely, that the claims and aspirations of physiologists must be rejected since whenever a person acts, no complete physiological explanation of the bodily happening is possible. This surely is *a priorism* at its worst, recognition of which should warn us that there is something radically wrong with the picture we have in mind of the manner in which the gap between physiological happening and doing is to be bridged. According to this picture (often quite explicitly drawn in diagrammatic representations of the bodily mechanism in order to explain, for the benefit of laymen and children, how it is that human beings perceive and act in response to stimuli), the human body is an elaborate mechanism, in which extremely fine and complex controls in the nervous system determine the character of the bodily responses to stimuli from without. So far we have only the picture of an elaborate machine. In order, then, to provide verisimilitude, to give us the impression that the mechanism is that of a human being, we are invited to think of the controls in the central nervous system as somehow manipulated; and this is sometimes done by adding to the diagram, by representing a humanlike figure pulling levers and pushing buttons. Prichard's willings are precisely the equivalent of these manipulating activities and, like the sort of diagram I have described, imply that there is a gap in any possible physiological explanation of the observable physiological happenings—the movements of our limbs, the blinkings of eyes, the movements of lips and tongue, and so on. What has happened in effect is that the attempt to bridge the gap between physiological happening and human doing has been made only by introducing another gap, this one in the physiological chain of causes.

The course of Western philosophy is littered with the relics of philosophic doctrines that have attempted to legislate what science can or cannot do. The physiologist who envisages the possibility of a complete physiological explanation of bodily happenings surely has history on his side. Before we reject the possibility of such explanations we could do far worse than reexamine the model of the proceedings, a model that threatens once more a clash between philosophy and science. On this model, physiological happenings are construed as doings only by means of the peculiar order of causes involved—a happening is also a doing if and only if it is produced in a certain way, *e.g.* by willings—and, as we have seen, this approach, quite independently of its dubious *a priorism*, is less than auspicious.

Let us look more closely at the following: "One raises one's arm by contracting certain muscles—this is how one does it." This implies, of course, that one's muscles are under one's immediate control, that one causes one's arm to rise by moving one's muscles just as one causes the door to unlock by turning the key in the lock. On this picture of the proceedings it is the interior bodily events—certain muscle movements—that are under our immediate control; by moving those muscles we cause the arm to rise. I want to argue that this is a mistake.

Suppose this picture to be true. Then surely I must know which muscles to move. If I cause my arm to rise by moving certain muscles, just as I cause the door to unlock by turning the key in the lock, then just as I can give a true account of the bodily movement I perform in the latter case so I must be able to give a true account of something I do in the former case. When I turn the key in the lock, I may know very little if anything about the mechanism of locks or the manner in which keys inserted and turned in locks produce their familiar effect, but surely I can tell without inspecting or observing what I am doing, that I am executing a twisting maneuver with my hand as I firmly hold the key in the lock. But what true account of the movement of the muscles can I give? What I know about the muscle movements involved in the raising of my arm is very little indeed; and must I know *anything* about these muscle movements in order to raise my arm? But if I need know nothing about the physiology of arm movements, how is it possible for me to have learned how to raise my arm? For on the present view I can raise my arm only by doing something that causes my arm to rise, just as I can unlock the door only by turning the object called "a key" in the thing commonly described as a lock. So I must be aware of what I am doing in the former case just as I am aware of what I am doing in the latter. Must I learn the physiology of arm movements before I can get my arm to rise in the air? If there is a parallel between causing the door to unlock by turning the key in the lock and causing my arm to rise by moving certain muscles, I should be utterly helpless in the matter of getting my arm to rise in the air until I knew which muscles to move—just as a child is utterly helpless when confronted by a locked door, until it knows what action to perform in order to get the door to unlock. The whole idea that one causes one's arm to rise in the air by manipulating certain internal bodily pulleys and levers is an unwitting piece of philosophical humor.

Does this mean that one cannot move those muscles that do get moved, and in the very precise way in which it happens, when one raises one's arm? Not at all! Indeed, nothing is easier: all one need do is simply raise one's arm! Does this mean that any physiological happening, anything of this kind that gets done, is a case of an action, a doing? Not at all. Does this mean that the view that the contraction of muscles causes the elevation of the arm must be rejected, that it is the other way around since the raising of the arm causes the muscles to contract? Indeed not!

I remarked that nothing is easier than to move those muscles that do get moved in just the way in which they are moved when one raises one's arm, but here we must guard ourselves against misunderstanding. Suppose someone tells me, "Move those muscles that do get moved in just the way in which they are moved when you raise your arm." What is he telling me to do? Is he telling me merely to do this—move those muscles in that particular way, and nothing else? In that case my natural retort would be "Which muscles do you mean?" And if he replies, "Never mind which muscles they are, just move them in just the way in which . . . ," what on earth is he asking me to do? Is this merely a queer way of telling me to raise my arm? But in that case he does not want me merely to move those muscles, since the only way I can oblige is by raising my arm. Certainly I can get those muscles to move in that way by raising my arm, but equally well I can do it by grasping my arm and raising it just as in the case of an idle motor I can get the pistons to move up and down by manually operating the crankshaft. In ordinary circumstances and uttered out of the blue, so to speak, we should have difficulty in understanding someone who says, "Move those muscles that do get moved in just the way in which they are moved when you raise your arm."

Nevertheless, we can imagine circumstances in which this would be quite intelligible. Imagine someone teaching me something of the physiology of the arm. He shows me how the arm structure rises when this muscle contracts, that one relaxes, and so on. He shows me, in other words, how the muscles operate when I raise my arm. Now he connects electrodes to each of these muscles and arranges them in such a way that two meter needles will come together at a given point when these muscles are brought into play in the way described. When the muscles move in the way in which they move when I lower my arm, the needles will behave differently. I then learn how to bring the needles together, how to bring them apart, and so on, and I come to be able to read what is going on in my muscles by watching the movements of the needles, just as a mechanic can read what is going on in a motor by watching the results recorded on his test instruments. If under these circumstances, I am told, "Move those muscles that do get moved in just the way in which they are moved when you raise your arm," I can comply only by bringing the meter needles together, and this I can do only by raising my arm. Here the instruction is intelligibly different from "Raise your arm." For suppose that someone unfamiliar with the experiment watches me and notices that my instructor is satisfied every time I raise my arm in response to his "Move those muscles that do get moved in just the way in which . . ."; he may know that I can do what I must do only by raising my arm, but he will have no further knowledge of what I am required to do.

In special circumstances, the above being only one imaginable case, I can perform the required muscle movements that do take place normally when I raise my arm. But in such cases I do not raise the arm by moving those muscles—I move the muscles by raising the arm. The example should make it clear that my raising my arm is not the effect of some immediate interior bodily doing of mine. I get my muscles to move in the required way by getting the needles to move in a certain way and I do the latter by raising my arm. I do not calculate in any way how to move my arm by doing something that produces it; what occupies my attention is the movement of the needles and what this means for me. In short, the whole picture of bodily actions, such as the movement of our limbs, according to which these are produced by interior performances in which we engage, whether these be muscle movements or anything else, is a caricature of the actual situation. For similar considerations will apply equally well to other candidates for the title of "things immediately done by us" and which allegedly in their turn produce the motions of our limbs, whether these be the stimulation of the muscle fibers, the excitation of brain centers or what have you. We do not move our limbs by manipulating any sorts of interior levers or pulleys within the body.

It should be clear now that not every physiological happening in the chain of causes that issue in the motion of one's arm is a case of something done. For only in very special circumstances can such a happening be described as an action. Equally well, the contention that in such special circumstances the happening in question is an action accomplished by raising one's arm, in no way does violence to the familiar matter of physiological fact, namely, that such happenings are causes, not effects, of the motion of one's arm. Such cases are quite different from the one cited earlier in which one raises one's arm by lifting it by means of the other arm—by doing this the arm is flaccid as it is lifted and in the process of being lifted certain muscles will be moved, just as in the case of a motor one can reverse the causal sequence of the transmission of the motion of a piston to the crankshaft, by turning the crankshaft manually and forcing the pistons to move in the cylinders of the motor. In the very special case I have elaborated, in order to illustrate the fact that one can be said to move one's muscles by raising one's arm, one performs the *action* of raising one's arm. To say that one moves certain muscles by raising one's arm, is not to say that the physiological happening described as "muscle movements" is produced by the physiological happening described as "the elevation of one's arm." To suppose that it is the same thing is to confound what we have been at pains to emphasize, namely, that physiological happenings are not to be identified with human action. That I can be said to move certain muscles by raising my arm leaves unimpaired the matter of physiological fact that it is the motion of these muscles that causes the motion of the arm. Finally, it should be clear that no attempt to bridge the gap between the physiological happening described as the movement of one's arm and the action described as moving one's arm by any device such as the introduction of causes, mental or physiological, will do. One does not raise one's arm by performing another doing which has the motion of one's arm as effect—one simply raises one's arm.

BEHAVIOR PLUS SOME CONCURRENT EVENT

"ACTION EQUALS BODILY MOVEMENT PLUS MOTIVE"

A. I. Melden

I shall now very briefly review the course of the previous argument. In Chapter III, a number of questions were raised about the relations between the events described as "muscles in the arm moving in such-and-such ways," "raising one's arm" and "signalling." We have now seen that while ordinarily the muscle-movements referred to may be said to cause the arm to rise, it is by no means clear that they function as cause of that action described as "my raising my arm"—there is, as we have seen, a disparity between the description "one's arm rising" and "raising one's arm," the former being a matter of bodily happening, the latter a matter of human action. Yet it is true that when, in normal circumstances, my arm rises as I signal, the rising of the arm *is* also describable as my action of raising my arm. What we can say, therefore, is that the movement of muscles causes the bodily happening which is in some sense *involved in* the action of raising the arm. We have therefore to inquire into the nature of the relation between the bodily happening and the action of raising the arm. And since, as we have seen, an instance of my arm rising cannot be identified as an instance of my raising my arm on the ground that the former is produced by certain events, mental or physical —a bodily happening cannot be construed as a bodily action by reference to the order of causes—we must now ask how it is that something described as the rising of my arm may also be described as my raising my arm. Indeed, we shall have to get clear about the relations between the descriptions "raising my arm" and

From *Free Action* by A. I. Melden (New York: Humanities Press, Inc., 1961), pp. 73–82. Reprinted by permission of Humanities Press, Inc., and Routledge & Kegan Paul Ltd.

"signalling" since, as we remarked earlier in Chapter III, raising my arm *is*, in the appropriate circumstances, signalling. In short, we need to understand more clearly the relations between the events (I use this word as a neutral term for both matters of bodily happening and matters of human action) described as "muscle-movements of such-and-such a sort," "arm rising," "raising the arm" and "signalling." Evidently this matter is far more difficult than it appeared to be when we first considered the suggestion that just as one signals by raising one's arm, so one raises one's arm by having certain muscles move. The muscle-movements cause that bodily happening described as "the arm rising." But although the bodily happening needs to be distinguished from the action of raising the arm, the former, in appropriate circumstances, is the very same event as the latter. So, too, while "raising the arm" and "signalling" are different descriptions, a case of the former does not produce, but in appropriate circumstances is the very same thing as, a case of the latter. How is this possible?

First we need to consider more closely a suggestion mentioned in Chapter III that an action is no mere item of "overt behavior" but this together with something else, a motive. "Overt behavior," we are sometimes told, is something merely "physical," something less than an action. The formula, then, is that action equals "overt behavior" plus motive. What precisely can we make of this? "Overt behavior" would seem to mean behavior that is open to view, public, capable of being seen by an observer. And what can be meant by the statement that such behavior is something merely physical? If someone signals a turn as he is driving his car, surely his action of signalling no less than the motion of his arm as it rises is normally open to view, capable of being seen by other motorists on the road. Are we to say that no one ever sees anyone else raising his arm, signalling or doing any of the very many sorts of things people do in their daily activities? Or is it that "sees" is being used in some special technical sense so that in that special sense it is false that anyone ever sees anyone else ever doing anything at all? Or, that what we commonly speak of as seeing in such instances is not, strictly speaking, just seeing, but seeing together with something else, perhaps interpreting, inferring or what have you? The doctrine that "overt behavior" is something less than human action appears to be loaded with suggestions—epistemological overtones—that cry out for careful and detailed examination. Here is something merely physical: the consideration that no human being could be 150 feet tall, for this is wholly explicable in terms of the physical properties of bones, muscles, and other tissues. Again, that the arm rises when such-and-such muscles move is a physical matter wholly accountable in terms of the forces exerted together with certain elementary principles of mechanics. But when one sees someone raise his arm as he signals in what sense is he seeing something merely physical? Certainly he is seeing a bodily happening—the arm rising; but he is not observing the physical process of forces applied by muscle movements to such-and-such points in the arm structure. "Physical" would seem to be jargon for "bodily" and suggests in any case a contrast with "mental." The formula then is best understood as saying that an action is a bodily movement plus an interior mental occurrence—a motive. The rising of my arm is a case of my raising my arm if and only if there is this mental occurrence of a motive.

Now it is certainly true that wherever motives can be cited there at any rate is the arena in which actions may be performed. This is not to say that if a person has a motive for doing something, he will necessarily do it; a man may have a motive for killing his wife but excellent reasons for refraining from doing so. But where motives can be cited in order to explain behavior, there at any rate we have actions—the motives are then the motives for the actions thereby explained. The use of this preposition "for" following the term "motive" shows something important about the concept of a motive. And it is the use of this preposition that needs to be examined in connection with the view that an action consists of a bodily movement or happening plus some interior mental event identified as a motive. If what makes the rising of one's arm, for example, a case of the action described as "raising one's arm" is the presence of an interior mental event called the "motive," of what action is this alleged motive a motive? By hypothesis this motive cannot be the motive for the rising of the arm since this is only a bodily happening, and motives, whatever else they may be, are motives for actions. Can the action of which this constituent motive is the motive be the raising of the arm? This surely cannot be true; for if it were, the idea of the motive would presuppose the idea of the action to be explained. In that case the alleged explanation of the action of raising the arm is hopelessly circular. In other words, it is impossible to define the action of raising the arm in terms of a bodily movement plus motive, since the alleged motive, if it is really one, has to be understood as the motive for some action performed or performable by the agent; and if this motive is the motive for raising the arm, the motive, far from defining or constituting that action, presupposes it.

The formula under examination proposes to define "raising one's arm," for example, in terms of the rising of one's arm together with the presence of some mental occurrence labelled a "motive." Let it be granted for the moment that an action can be construed as a bodily happening plus some other interior occurrence —that this will not do at all I shall attempt to show in the sequel. What the argument presented above shows is that even if one could construe an action as a bodily happening plus some other factor, that factor cannot possibly be a motive. Here the logical feature of the term "motive," namely that a motive is the motive for an action, is of crucial importance. If the factor were a motive it must needs be the motive for an action. But of what action is this alleged motive a motive? The action cannot be the rising of the arm—that is merely a bodily happening. Can it be the action of raising the arm? If so, then the account is circular: it explains the conception of the action of raising the arm in terms of bodily happening plus motive, and then proceeds to explain the motive in terms of the very action of raising the arm for which an explanation was ostensibly given. But if the action of which the constituent motive is not the action of raising the arm, some other action must be cited, and the same difficulty breaks out once more. In short, on the present view, the expression "motive for an action" becomes unintelligible. No doubt there is an important logical connection between motives and actions, but that connection cannot be construed as that of part to whole.

But it is a mistake in principle to attempt to define an action as a bodily happening plus any other concurrent event, mental or bodily. Let the action of raising the arm be A, the bodily occurrence B, and the concurrent event C. Then any such definition alleges that A is B plus C. Now A is an action, hence the description of A must exhibit the logical features of an action. For one thing, given that A has taken place, it follows from the account of A that someone performed it.

Nothing of this sort follows from the description of B as a bodily happening. It must then follow from the description of B together with that of the interior occurrence C. But what sort of description of C can be given such that given it and the description of B, it follows that the action A has been performed? Only if a reference to the logical feature of A, as an action, is contained in the description of C, would this entailment hold. That is to say, C must be understood as that which makes such a bodily happening as the rise of one's arm a case of one's raising one's arm. But no concurrent event C distinct from B could have this logical property that it involves a logically necessary relation to any other event, specifically to event B. What alone can make the rising of my arm my action of raising my arm is that which makes it so; but that which makes it so cannot be another event distinct from the bodily event itself.

This is not to deny that we can offer descriptions of occurrences in terms of their relational, perhaps causal, properties. Certainly we very often do so. Let us then characterize C in terms of some relational property it has with respect to B and hence to A. In that case, however, I shall not know that I have performed the action A unless I am aware of the occurrence C and indeed of the bodily occurrence B. But that I am raising my arm I can vouch for no matter what goes on at the time my arm rises, whereas if A were B plus C, I could not know that a case of A occurred unless I knew that C occurred. What goes on in the way of interior events may be anything or nothing when I raise my arm. But suppose *per impossibile* that I must know that some C is taking place in order to be able to vouch for the occurrence of the action A. That C has some relational property with respect to B and hence with respect to A is after all a matter of fact that cannot be established by any inspection of C by itself. Hence even if in raising my arm I were aware of some interior occurrence C together with the bodily movement of my arm rising, it still would not follow that I could vouch for the fact that I am raising my arm. In addition, I must know that C has the required relational property. Grant, then, that A is B plus C, that in order to vouch for A I must be aware not only of C but also of the relational property that C has with respect to both B and A, what can this relational property be? If the property is a causal property, I must know then that the occurrence of C produces the occurrence of B. But unless C is something describable as my action (in which case we have moved in a full circle), nothing about any action performed is deducible from the knowledge of B and its production by another event C. And if the relational property is not a causal property, what on earth can it be? In short, the logical force of an action cannot be derived from any set of statements about happenings and their properties. The contention that my arm's rising is a case of my raising my arm because of the presence of some concurrent event simply will not do. No doubt *something* makes the rising of my arm the action of my raising my arm, but that *something* cannot be another event distinct from the mere bodily happening.

In one respect, moreover, the formula we have been considering is too strong. It asserts that the presence of a motive is a necessary condition of the occurrence of an action, but the presence of a motive is neither a necessary nor a sufficient condition. Not a sufficient condition, since a person may refrain from acting on a motive; a jealous person, aware of his jealousy, may for that very reason refrain from acting jealously—indeed he may go out of his way to benefit the person of whom he is jealous. Not a necessary condition, since a person may act without a motive. If I say, in reply to the question "Why did you do that?," "No reason at all; I just did," must I be lying or mistaken? Certainly a person may do something when he is well aware of what he is doing, when he is not acting from habit, on impulse or under hypnosis, and where he has no motive for what he does. Some of these cases are odd, others not. Suppose, for example, I wear a blue shirt rather than a white one; must I have a motive for putting on the blue one? I might have a motive: this one goes with my suit or my tie; but again I might have no motive at all and this sort of case is not infrequent. There are other cases in which something is amiss but in which no motive is present and the reply that can be given to the question "Why did you do it?" is something else again. In Camus' *The Stranger* a man kills an Arab on the sun-drenched beach. He had no intention of doing so and later when asked for the motive for his crime can only reply, "It was because of the sun." Is that a motive? The man's remark makes no sense although in some way we can understand the whole history of the incident for all its irrationality. (Indeed, we can understand someone who tells us, "Last night I dreamed that I bought five pounds of virtue at the flower shop," even though it is nonsensical to speak of virtue as this sort of purchaseable item.) The words are without sense, but the man and his action for all their strangeness are not altogether unintelligible; if they were we should be, as indeed we are not, appalled by his utter inhumanity. Or suppose, to consider the case posed by G. E. M. Anscombe, ". . . someone hunted out all the green books in his house and spread them out carefully on the roof" and when asked "Why?" replies "No particular reason; I just thought I would" (*Intention*, p. 26); here the words are intelligible, but not the man.

There would seem to be, therefore, various sorts of cases where things done are done without motive. And as Anscombe remarks about the general reply to the question "Why?," namely, "No particular reason; I just did," such answers "are often quite intelligible; sometimes strange; and sometimes unintelligible" (*loc. cit.*). The formula that an action is a bodily movement plus a motive, all other objections aside, is too simple to fit the wide variety of cases that need to be considered—that there is a motive for every action is altogether doubtful.

Does all of this mean that there is no logical connection between motives and action? Not at all. Does it mean that where no motive is present, the action is inexplicable? Certainly not. In order to resolve these matters it will be necessary to look more carefully at the character of motives and the manner in which these explain conduct.

VOLUNTARY BEHAVIOR

from ETHICA NICOMACHEA

Aristotle

30 Since virtue is concerned with passions and actions and on voluntary passions and actions praise and blame are bestowed, on those that are involuntary pardon, and sometimes also pity, to distinguish the voluntary and the involuntary is presumably necessary for those who are studying the nature of virtue, and useful also for legislators with a view to the assigning both of honors and of punishments.

1110a Those things, then, are thought involuntary, which take place under compulsion or owing to ignorance; and that is compulsory of which the moving principle is outside, being a principle in which nothing is contributed by the person who is acting or is feeling the passion, e.g. if he were to be carried somewhere by a wind, or by men who had him in their power.

 But with regard to the things that are done from fear of greater evils or for 5 some noble object (e.g. if a tyrant were to order one to do something base, having one's parents and children in his power, and if one did the action they were to be saved, but otherwise would be put to death), it may be debated whether such actions are involuntary or voluntary. Something of the sort happens also with regard to the throwing of goods overboard in a storm; for in the abstract no one 10 throws goods away voluntarily, but on condition of its securing the safety of himself and his crew any sensible man does so. Such actions, then, are mixed, but are more like voluntary actions; for they are worthy of choice at the time when they

From Book III, Chapter 1, of "Ethica Nicomachea," *The Oxford Translation of Aristotle*, Vol. IX, translated by W. D. Ross (Oxford, England: The Clarendon Press, 1963). Reprinted by permission of the Clarendon Press, Oxford.

Line numbers have been retained for purposes of cross-referencing.

are done, and the end of an action is relative to the occasion. Both the terms, then, "voluntary" and "involuntary," must be used with reference to the moment of action. Now the man acts voluntarily; for the principle that moves the instrumental parts of the body in such actions is in him, and the things of which the moving principle is in a man himself are in his power to do or not to do. Such actions, therefore, are voluntary, but in the abstract perhaps involuntary; for no one would choose any such act in itself.

For such actions men are sometimes even praised, when they endure something base or painful in return for great and noble objects gained; in the opposite case they are blamed, since to endure the greatest indignities for no noble end or for a trifling end is the mark of an inferior person. On some actions praise indeed is not bestowed, but pardon is, when one does what he ought not under pressure which overstrains human nature and which no one could withstand. But some acts, perhaps, we cannot be forced to do, but ought rather to face death after the most fearful sufferings; for the things that "forced" Euripides' Alcmaeon to slay his mother seem absurd. It is difficult sometimes to determine what should be chosen at what cost, and what should be endured in return for what gain, and yet more difficult to abide by our decisions; for as a rule what is expected is painful, and what we are forced to do is base, whence praise and blame are bestowed on those who have been compelled or have not.

What sort of acts, then, should be called compulsory? We answer that without qualification actions are so when the cause is in the external circumstances and the agent contributes nothing. But the things that in themselves are involuntary, but now and in return for these gains are worthy of choice, and whose moving principle is in the agent, are in themselves involuntary, but now and in return for these gains voluntary. They are more like voluntary acts; for actions are in the class of particulars, and the particular acts here are voluntary. What sort of things are to be chosen, and in return for what, it is not easy to state; for there are many differences in the particular cases.

But if some one were to say that pleasant and noble objects have a compelling power, forcing us from without, all acts would be for him compulsory; for it is for these objects that all men do everything they do. And those who act under compulsion and unwillingly act with pain, but those who do acts for their pleasantness and nobility do them with pleasure; it is absurd to make external circumstances responsible, and not oneself, as being easily caught by such attractions, and to make oneself responsible for noble acts but the pleasant objects responsible for base acts. The compulsory, then, seems to be that whose moving principle is outside, the person compelled contributing nothing.

Everything that is done by reason of ignorance is *not* voluntary; it is only what produces pain and repentance that is *in*voluntary. For the man who has done something owing to ignorance, and feels not the least vexation at his action, has not acted voluntarily, since he did not know what he was doing, nor yet involuntarily, since he is not pained. Of people, then, who act by reason of ignorance he who repents is thought an involuntary agent, and the man who does not repent may, since he is different, be called a not voluntary agent; for, since he differs from the other, it is better that he should have a name of his own.

Acting by reason of ignorance seems also to be different from acting *in* ignorance; for the man who is drunk or in a rage is thought to act as a result not of ignorance but of one of the causes mentioned, yet not knowingly but in ignorance.

Now every wicked man is ignorant of what he ought to do and what he ought to abstain from, and it is by reason of error of this kind that men become unjust
30 and in general bad; but the term "involuntary" tends to be used not if a man is ignorant of what is to his advantage—for it is not mistaken purpose that causes involuntary action (it leads rather to wickedness), nor ignorance of the universal (for *that* men are *blamed*), but ignorance of particulars, i.e. of the circumstances
1111a of the action and the objects with which it is concerned. For it is on these that both pity and pardon depend, since the person who is ignorant of any of these acts involuntarily.

Perhaps it is just as well, therefore, to determine their nature and number. A man may be ignorant, then, of who he is, what he is doing, what or whom he is acting on, and sometimes also what (e.g. what instrument) he is doing it with,
5 and to what end (e.g. he may think his act will conduce to some one's safety), and how he is doing it (e.g. whether gently or violently). Now of all of these no one could be ignorant unless he were mad, and evidently also he could not be ignorant of the agent; for how could he not know himself? But of what he is doing a man might be ignorant, as for instance people say "it slipped out of their mouths as they were speaking," or "they did not know it was a secret," as
10 Aeschylus said of the mysteries, or a man might say he "let it go off when he merely wanted to show its working," as the man did with the catapult. Again, one might think one's son was an enemy, as Merope did, or that a pointed spear had a button on it, or that a stone was pumice-stone; or one might give a man a draught to save him, and really kill him; or one might want to touch a man, as
15 people do in sparring, and really wound him. The ignorance may relate, then, to any of these things, i.e. of the circumstances of the action, and the man who was ignorant of any of these is thought to have acted involuntarily, and especially if he was ignorant on the most important points; and these are thought to be the circumstances of the action and its end. Further, the doing of an act that is called
20 involuntary in virtue of ignorance of this sort must be painful and involve repentance.

Since that which is done under compulsion or by reason of ignorance is involuntary, the voluntary would seem to be that of which the moving principle is in the agent himself, he being aware of the particular circumstances of the action. Presumably acts done by reason of anger or appetite are not rightly called
25 involuntary.[1] For in the first place, on that showing none of the other animals will act voluntarily, nor will children; and secondly, is it meant that we do not do voluntarily *any* of the acts that are due to appetite or anger, or that we do the noble acts voluntarily and the base acts involuntarily? Is not this absurd, when
30 one and the same thing is the cause? But it would surely be odd to describe as involuntary the things one ought to desire; and we ought both to be angry at certain things and to have an appetite for certain things, e.g. for health and for learning. Also what is involuntary is thought to be painful, but what is in accordance with appetite is thought to be pleasant. Again, what is the difference in

---

[1] A reference to Pl. *Laws* 863 B, ff., where anger and appetite are coupled with ignorance as sources of wrong action.

respect of involuntariness between errors committed upon calculation and those committed in anger? Both are to be avoided, but the irrational passions are thought not less human than reason is, and therefore also the actions which proceed from anger or appetite are the man's actions. It would be odd, then, to treat them as involuntary.

. . .

THE DISTINCTION BETWEEN VOLUNTARY AND INVOLUNTARY

Gilbert Ryle

It should be noticed that while ordinary folk, magistrates, parents, and teachers, generally apply the words "voluntary" and "involuntary" to actions in one way, philosophers often apply them in quite another way.

In their most ordinary employment "voluntary" and "involuntary" are used, with a few minor elasticities, as adjectives applying to actions which ought not to be done. We discuss whether someone's action was voluntary or not only when the action seems to have been his fault. He is accused of making a noise, and the guilt is his, if the action was voluntary, like laughing; he has successfully excused himself, if he satisfies us that it was involuntary, like a sneeze. In the same way in ordinary life we raise questions of responsibility only when someone is charged, justly or unjustly, with an offense. It makes sense, in this use, to ask whether a boy was responsible for breaking a window, but not whether he was responsible for finishing his homework in good time. We do not ask whether it was his fault that he got a long-division sum right, for to get a sum right is not a fault. If he gets it wrong, he may satisfy us that his failure was not his fault, perhaps because he had not yet been shown how to do such calculations.

In this ordinary use, then, it is absurd to discuss whether satisfactory, correct, or admirable performances are voluntary or involuntary. Neither inculpation nor exculpation is in point. We neither confess to authorship nor adduce extenuating circumstances; neither plead "guilty" nor plead "not guilty"; for we are not accused.

From *The Concept of Mind* by Gilbert Ryle (New York: Barnes & Noble, Inc., and London: Hutchinson & Co., Ltd., 1949), pp. 69–74. Reprinted by permission of the publishers.

But philosophers, in discussing what constitutes acts voluntary or involuntary, tend to describe as voluntary not only reprehensible but also meritorious actions, not only things that are someone's fault but also things that are to his credit. The motives underlying their unwitting extension of the ordinary sense of "voluntary," "involuntary," and "responsible" will be considered later. For the moment it is worth while to consider certain consequences which follow from it. In the ordinary use, to say that a sneeze was involuntary is to say that the agent could not help doing it, and to say that a laugh was voluntary is to say that the agent could have helped doing it. (This is not to say that the laugh was intentional. We do not laugh on purpose.) The boy could have got the sum right which he actually got wrong; he knew how to behave, but he misbehaved; he was competent to tie a reef knot, though what he unintentionally produced was a granny knot. His failure or lapse was his fault. But when the word "voluntary" is given its philosophically stretched use, so that correct as well as incorrect, admirable as well as contemptible acts are described as voluntary, it seems to follow by analogy with the ordinary use, that a boy who gets his sum right can also be described as having been "able to help it." It would then be proper to ask: Could you have helped solving the riddle? Could you have helped drawing the proper conclusion? Could you have helped tying a proper reef knot? Could you have helped seeing the point of that joke? Could you have helped being kind to that child? In fact, however, no one could answer these questions, though it is not at first obvious why, if it is correct to say that someone could have avoided getting a sum wrong, it is incorrect to say that he could have avoided getting it right.

The solution is simple. When we say that someone could have avoided committing a lapse or error, or that it was his fault that he committed it, we mean that he knew how to do the right thing, or was competent to do so, but did not exercise his knowledge or competence. He was not trying, or not trying hard enough. But when a person has done the right thing, we cannot then say that he knew how to do the wrong thing, or that he was competent to make mistakes. For making mistakes is not an exercise of competence, nor is the commission of slips an exercise of knowledge *how;* it is a failure to exercise knowledge *how.* It is true in one sense of "could" that a person who had done a sum correctly could have got it wrong; in the sense, namely, that he is not exempt from the liability to be careless. But in another sense of "could," to ask, "Could you have got it wrong?" means "Were you sufficiently intelligent and well trained and were you concentrating hard enough to make a miscalculation?," and this is as silly a question as to ask whether someone's teeth are strong enough to be broken by cracking nuts.

The tangle of largely spurious problems, known as the problem of the Freedom of the Will, partly derives from this unconsciously stretched use of "voluntary" and these consequential misapplications of different senses of "could" and "could have helped."

The first task is to elucidate what is meant in their ordinary, undistorted use by "voluntary," "involuntary," "responsible," "could not have helped," and "his fault," as these expressions are used in deciding concrete questions of guilt and innocence.

If a boy has tied a granny knot instead of a reef knot, we satisfy ourselves that it was his fault by first establishing that he knew how to tie a reef knot, and then by establishing that his hand was not forced by external coercion and that there were no other agencies at work preventing him from tying the correct knot. We establish that he could tie reef knots by finding out that he had been taught, had had practice, usually got them right, or by finding that he could detect and correct knots tied by others, or by finding that he was ashamed of what he had done and, without help from others, put it right himself. That he was not acting under duress or in panic or high fever or with numb fingers, is discovered in the way in which we ordinarily discover that highly exceptional incidents have not taken place; for such incidents would have been too remarkable to have gone unremarked, at least by the boy himself.

The first question which we had to decide had nothing to do with the occurrence or nonoccurrence of any occult episode in the boy's stream of consciousness; it was the question whether or not he had the required higher-level competence, that of knowing how to tie reef knots. We were not, at this stage, inquiring whether he committed, or omitted, an extra public or private operation, but only whether he possessed or lacked a certain intelligent capacity. What satisfied us was not the (unattainable) knowledge of the truth or falsity of a particular covert cause-overt effect proposition, but the (attainable) knowledge of the truth or falsity of a complex and partially general hypothetical proposition—not, in short, that he did tie a shadowy reef or granny knot behind the scenes, but that he could have tied a real one with this rope and would have done so on this occasion, if he had paid more heed to what he was doing. The lapse was his fault because, knowing how to tie the knot, he still did not tie it correctly.

Consider next the case of an act which everyone would decide was not the agent's fault. A boy arrives late for school and on inquiry it turns out that he left home at the usual time, did not dally on his way to the omnibus halt and caught the usual omnibus. But the vehicle broke down and could not complete the journey. The boy ran as fast as he could the rest of the way, but was still late. Clearly all the steps taken by the boy were either the same as those which normally bring him to school in time, or were the only steps open to him for remedying the effects of the breakdown. There was nothing else that he could have done and his teacher properly recommends him to follow the same routine on future occasions. His late arrival was not the result of a failure to do what he was capable of doing. He was prevented by a circumstance which was not in his power to modify. Here again the teacher is judging an action with reference to the capacities and opportunities of the agent; his excuse is accepted that he could not have done better than he did. The whole question of the involuntariness of his late arrival is decided without the boy being asked to report any deliverances of consciousness or introspection about the execution or nonexecution of any volitions.

It makes no difference if the actions with which an agent is charged either are or embody operations of silent soliloquy or other operations with verbal or nonverbal images. A slip in mental arithmetic is the pupil's fault on the same grounds as a slip made in written arithmetic; and an error committed in matching colors in the mind's eye may merit the reproach of carelessness in the same way as an error committed in matching colors on the draper's counter. If the agent could have done better than he did, then he could have helped doing it as badly as he did.

Besides considering the ordinary senses of "voluntary," "involuntary," "responsible," "my fault," and "could" or "could not help," we should notice as well the ordinary uses of such expressions as "effort of will," "strength of will," and "irresolute." A person is described as behaving resolutely when in the execution of difficult, protracted, or disagreeable tasks he tends not to relax his efforts, not to let his attention be diverted, not to grumble, and not to think much or often about his fatigue or fears. He does not shirk or drop things to which he has set his hand. A weakwilled person is one who is easily distracted or disheartened, apt to convince himself that another time will be more suitable or that the reasons for undertaking the task were not after all very strong. Note that it is no part of the definition of resoluteness or of irresoluteness that a resolution should actually have been formed. A resolute man may firmly resist temptations to abandon or postpone his task, though he never went through a prefatory ritual-process of making up his mind to complete it. But naturally such a man will also be disposed to perform any vows which he has made to others or to himself. Correspondingly the irresolute man will be likely to fail to carry out his often numerous good resolutions, but his lack of tenacity of purpose will be exhibited also in surrenders and slacknesses in courses of action which were unprefaced by any private or public undertakings to accomplish them.

Strength of will is a propensity the exercises of which consist in sticking to tasks; that is, in not being deterred or diverted. Weakness of will is having too little of this propensity. The performances in which strength of will is exerted may be performances of almost any sort, intellectual or manual, imaginative or administrative. It is not a single-track disposition or, for that and other reasons, a disposition to execute occult operations of one special kind.

By "an effort of will" is meant a particular exercise of tenacity of purpose, occurring when the obstacles are notably great, or the countertemptations notably strong. Such efforts may, but need not, be accompanied by special processes, often of a ritual character, of nerving or adjuring oneself to do what is required; but these processes are not so much ways in which resoluteness is shown as ways in which fear of irresoluteness manifests itself.

Before we leave the concept or concepts of voluntariness, two further points need to be made. (1) Very often we oppose things done voluntarily to things suffered under compulsion. Some soldiers are volunteers, others are conscripts; some yachtsmen go out to sea voluntarily, others are carried out to sea by the wind and tide. Here questions of inculpation and exculpation need not arise. In asking whether the soldier volunteered or was conscripted, we are asking whether he joined up because he wanted to do so, or whether he joined up because he had to do so, where "had to" entails "no matter what he wanted." In asking whether the yachtsman went out to sea of his own accord or whether he was carried out, we are asking whether he went out on purpose, or whether he would still have gone out as he did, even if he had meant not to do so. Would bad news from home, or a warning from the coastguard, have stopped him?

What is involuntary, in this use, is not describable as an act. Being carried out to sea, or being called up, is something that happens to a person, not something which he does. In this respect, this antithesis between voluntary and involuntary differs from the antithesis we have in mind when we ask whether someone's tying of a granny knot, or his knitting of his brows, is voluntary or involuntary.

A person who frowns involuntarily is not forced to frown, as a yachtsman may be forced out to sea; nor is the careless boy forced to tie a granny knot, as the conscript is forced to join the army. Even frowning is something that a person does. It is not done to him. So sometimes the question "Voluntary or involuntary?" means "Did the person do it, or was it done to him?"; sometimes it presupposes that he did it, but means "Did he do it with or without heeding what he was doing?" or "Did he do it on purpose or inadvertently, mechanically, or instinctively, etc.?"

(2) When a person does something voluntarily, in the sense that he does it on purpose or is trying to do it, his action certainly reflects some quality or qualities of mind, since (it is more than a verbal point to say) he is in some degree and in one fashion or another minding what he is doing. It follows also that, if linguistically equipped, he can then tell, without research or conjecture, what he has been trying to accomplish. But, as will be argued in Chapter V, these implications of voluntariness do not carry with them the double-life corollaries often assumed. To frown intentionally is not to do one thing on one's forehead and another thing in a second metaphorical place; nor is it to do one thing with one's brow muscles and another thing with some nonbodily organ. In particular, it is not to bring about a frown on one's forehead by first bringing about a frown-causing exertion of some occult nonmuscle. "He frowned intentionally" does not report the occurrence of two episodes. It reports the occurrence of one episode, but one of a very different character from that reported by "he frowned involuntarily," though the frowns might be photographically as similar as you please.

VOLITIONS

ACTING, WILLING, DESIRING

H. A. Prichard

The question "What is acting or doing something?" seems at first unreal, i.e. a question to which we already know the answer. For it looks as though everyone knows what doing something is and would be ready to offer instances. No one, for instance, would hesitate to say to another "You ought to go to bed," on the ground that neither he nor the other knows the kind of thing meant by "going to bed." Yet, when we consider instances that would be offered, we do not find it easy to state the common character which we think they had which led us to call them actions.

If, as a preliminary, we look for help to the psychologists, from whom we naturally expect to get it, we find we fail. We find plenty of talk about reflex actions, ideomotor actions, instinctive actions, and so on, but no discussion of what actions are. Instead, they seem to take for granted that our actions are physical processes taking place within our body, which they certainly are not.

We should at first say that to do something is to originate or to bring into existence, i.e. really, to cause, some not yet existing state either of ourselves or of someone else, or, again, of some body. But, for clearness' sake, we should go on to distinguish those actions in doing which we originated some new state directly from those in which we did this only indirectly, i.e. by originating directly some other state, by originating which we indirectly originated the final state. As instances of the former we might give moving or turning our head, and as in-

From *Moral Obligation* by H. A. Prichard (Oxford, England: The Clarendon Press, 1949), pp. 187–198. Reprinted by permission of the Clarendon Press, Oxford.

I

stances of the latter, curing our toothache by swallowing aspirin, and killing another by pressing a switch which exploded a charge underneath him. If challenged, however, we should have to allow that even in instances of the former kind we did not originate directly what the instances suggest that we did, since what we did originate directly must have been some new state or states of our nerve cells, of the nature of which we are ignorant. We should, however, insist that in doing any action we must have originated *something* directly, since otherwise we could not originate anything indirectly.

The view that to act is to originate something was maintained by Cook Wilson in a paper on *Means and End*. In the course of this paper he also maintained (1) that an action required the desire to do it, and (2) that it is important to avoid the mistake of thinking that the origination of something X is the willing of X, apparently on the ground that if it were, X would exist as soon as we willed it, and yet it usually does not. He also appeared to hold that the origination of X, though not identical with willing the origination, required it, so that when I originated a movement of my hand, this required as an antecedent my willing this origination, and this willing in turn required the desiring to originate the movement.

According to Cook Wilson, then, in considering an action we have to distinguish three things: first, the action itself, the originating something; second, the required willing to originate this; and third, the required desire to originate this. And according to him what we will and what we desire are the same, viz. the action.

Professor Macmurray, in a Symposium [1] on "What is action?", takes substantially the same view of what an action is. He says: "An action is not the concomitance of an intention in the mind and an occurrence in the physical world: it is the *producing* of the occurrence by the Self, the *making* of a change in the external world, the *doing* of a deed. No process which terminates in the mind, such as forming an intention, deciding to act, or willing, is either an action or a component of action." But he goes on to add: "In certain circumstances such a mental event or process may be followed *necessarily* by action."

Now, so far as I can see, this account of what an action is, though plausible and having as a truth underlying it that usually in acting we do cause something, is not tenable.

Unquestionably the thing meant by "an action" is an activity. This is so whether we speak of a man's action in moving his hand, or of a body's action such as that of the heart in pumping the blood, or that of one electron in repelling another. But though we think that some man in moving his hand, or that the sun in attracting the earth, causes a certain movement, we do not think that the man's or the sun's activity *is* or *consists in* causing the movement. And if we ask ourselves: "Is there such an activity as originating or causing a change in something else?," we have to answer that there is not. To say this, of course, is not to say that there is no such thing as causing something, but only to say that though the causing a change may require an activity, it is not itself an activity. If we then ask: "What is the kind of activity required when one body causes another to move?," we have to answer that we do not know, and that when we speak of a force of attraction or of repulsion we are only expressing our knowledge that there is some activity at

[1] Aristotelian Society, Supplementary Volume XVII (1938).

work, while being ignorant of what the kind of activity is. In the case, however, of a man, i.e., really, of a man's mind, the matter is different. When, e.g., we think of ourselves as having moved our hand, we are thinking of ourselves as having performed an activity of a certain kind, and, it almost goes without saying, a *mental* activity of a certain kind, an activity of whose nature we were dimly aware in doing the action and of which we can become more clearly aware by reflecting on it. And that we are aware of its special nature is shown by our unhesitatingly distinguishing it from other special mental activities such as thinking, wondering, and imagining. If we ask "What is the word used for this special kind of activity?" the answer, it seems, has to be "willing." (I now think I was mistaken in suggesting that the phrase in use for it is "setting oneself to cause.") We also have to admit that while we know the general character of that to which we refer when we use the word "willing," this character is *sui generis* and so incapable of being defined, i.e. of having its nature expressed in terms of the nature of other things. Even Hume virtually admits this when he says: "By the *will*, I mean nothing but *the internal impression we feel and are conscious of, when we knowingly give rise to any new motion of our body or new perception of our mind*," [2] and then goes on to add that the impression is impossible to define. Though, however, the activity of willing is indefinable, we can distinguish it from a number of things which it is not. Thus obviously, as Locke insisted, willing is different from desiring, and again, willing is not, as some psychologists would have it, a species of something called conation of which desiring is another species. There is no such genus. Again, it is not, as Green in one passage [3] implies, a species of desiring which is desiring in another sense than that ordinary sense in which we are said to desire while hesitating to act.

In addition, plainly, willing is not resolving, nor attending to a difficult object, as James holds, nor for that matter attending to anything, nor, again, consenting to the reality of what is attended to, as James also maintains, nor, indeed, consenting to anything, nor, once more, identifying ourself with some object of desire, as Green asserts in another passage.[4]

Consequently, there seems to be no resisting the conclusion that where we think of ourselves or of another as having done a certain action, the kind of activity of which we are thinking is that of willing (though we should have to add that we are thinking of our particular act of willing as having been the doing of the action in question, only because we think it caused a certain change), and that when we refer to some instance of this activity, such as our having moved our finger or given some friend a headache, we refer to it thus not because we think it was, or consisted in, the causing our finger to move or our friend's head to ache, but because we think it had a certain change of state as an effect.

If, as it seems we must, we accept this conclusion, that to act is really to will something, we then become faced by the question: "What sort of thing is it that we will?"

Those who, like Cook Wilson, distinguish between acting and willing, answer that what we will is an action, which according to him is the originating some

[2] Hume, *Treatise* (Selby-Bigge, p. 399).
[3] *Prolegomena*, §§ 140–2.
[4] *Prolegomena*, § 146.

change. Thus Green says: "To will an event" (i.e. presumably some change) "as distinguished from an act is a contradiction." And by this he seems to mean that, for instance, in the case which he takes of our paying a debt, what we will is the paying of our debt and not our creditor's coming into possession of what we owe him. Again, James and Stout, though they do not consider the question, show by their instances that they take for granted that what we will is an action. Thus James says: "I will to write, and the act follows. I will to sneeze and it does not." [5] And Stout illustrates a volition by a man's willing to produce an explosion by applying a lighted match to gunpowder.[6] But, unfortunately, James speaks of what he has referred to as, the act of writing which I will, as certain physiological movements, and similarly Stout speaks of, the production of an explosion which I will, as certain bodily movements. And, of course, the bodily movements to which they are referring are not actions, though they may be the effects of actions. Plainly, then, both are only doing lip service to the idea that what we will is an action. And James, at least, drops doing even this. For immediately after making the statement just quoted, viz. "I will to write, and the act follows. I will to sneeze and it does not," he adds: "I will that the distant table slide over the floor towards me; it also does not." Yet no one would say that the sliding of the table, as distinct from my sliding it, was an action.

In this connection it is well for clearness' sake to bear two things in mind. The first is that some transitive verbs used for particular actions are also used intransitively. Thus one not only speaks of turning one's head but also says that one's head turned. And the second is that, while the phrase "turning one's head" stands for an action and so for an activity of one's mind, yet when I say "my head turned" I am speaking simply of a movement of my head which is a change of place and not an action. The difference is made clear by considering what is plainly a mistake made by Professor Macmurray. He says that the term "action" is ambiguous. He says: "It may refer either to what is done or to the doing of it. It may mean either 'doing' or 'deed.' When we talk of 'an action' we are normally referring to what is done. . . . To act is to effect a change in the external world. The deed is the change so effected." And he emphasizes what he considers the ambiguity in order to indicate that it is doings and not deeds that he is considering. Obviously, however, there is no ambiguity whatever. When I move my hand, the movement of my hand, though an effect of my action, is not itself an action, and no one who considered the matter would say it was, any more than he would say that the death of Caesar, as distinct from his murder, was an action or even part of an action.

This difference between, e.g., my moving my hand and a movement of my hand, is one which James and Stout seem to ignore, as becomes obvious when James speaks of the sliding of a table as, like writing, an action. We find the same thing, too, in Locke. For though, e.g., he says that "we find by experience, that, barely by willing it, we can move the parts of our bodies," [7] yet in contrasting a human with a physical action he implies that what we will is a movement of our body. Probably, if pressed, he would have said that, strictly speaking, what

[5] James, *Psychology*, ii, p. 560.
[6] Stout, *Manual of Psychology*, iv, p. 641.
[7] Locke, *Essay*, ii, 21, § 4.

we will is a movement and so not an action. In addition, James and Stout seem to treat the distinction between an act of willing, or, as they prefer to call it, a volition, and what is willed, as if it were the same as the distinction between an act of willing and its effect, although they are totally different.

It should be clear from what I have just said that those who hold that what we will is an action must, to be successful, mean by an action something which really is an action. They may, of course, maintain that what we will is a physical process, such as a movement of my hand, but if they do they are really denying that what we will is an action.

It should also now be clear that if we face the question "What sort of thing do we will?," we have only two answers to consider: (1) that it is some change of state of some thing or person; and (2) that it is an action. If, however, we are forced to conclude, as we have been, that doing something is an act of willing, we seem forced to exclude the second answer, simply on the ground that if it were true, then whenever we think of ourselves as having done some action, we must be thinking of ourselves as having willed some action, i.e. as having willed the willing of some change X; and to think this seems impossible. By the very nature of willing, it seems, what we will must be something other than willing, so that to will the willing of a change X must be an impossibility. And if we even try to deny this, we find ourselves forced to admit that the willing of X, which (we are contending) is what we will, must in turn really be the willing the willing of something else, and so on, and thus become involved in an infinite regress. It is true that Cook Wilson, in a long unpublished discussion, tried to vindicate the analogous idea that in certain limiting cases, viz. those in which the desire moving us is not the desire of some change but the desire to cause it ourselves, as happens in playing golf or patience, what we originate is identical with our origination of something. But he never seems to me to succeed in meeting the objection that this identity must be impossible. Similarly, it seems to me, it is impossible for there to be a case in which the willing the willing of X is identical with willing X.

We are thus left with the conclusion that where we think we have done some action, e.g. have raised our arm or written a word, what we willed was some change, e.g. some movement of our arm or some movement of ink to a certain place on a piece of paper in front of us. But we have to bear in mind that the change which we willed may not have been the same as the change we think we effected. Thus, where I willed some movement of my second finger, I may at least afterwards think that the change I effected was a movement of my first finger, and, only too often, where I willed the existence of a certain word on a piece of paper, I afterwards find that what I caused was a different word. Again, in two cases of the act we call trying to thread a needle, what I willed may have been the same, though the changes I afterwards think I effected were very different, being in the one case the thread's going through the needle and in the other its passing well outside it.

Suppose now that it be allowed that so far I have been right. Then the following admissions must be made:

1. An action, i.e. a human action, instead of being the originating or causing of some change, is an activity of willing some change, this usually causing some change, and in some cases a physical change, its doing or not doing

this depending on the physical conditions of which the agent is largely ignorant.

2. Sometimes, however, we have performed such an activity without, at any rate so far as we know, having caused any physical change. This has happened when, e.g., we willed a movement of our hand, at a time when it was either paralyzed or numb with cold, whether we knew this or not. No doubt in such cases our activity would not ordinarily be called an action, but it is of the same sort as what we ordinarily call and think of as an action.

3. There is no reason to limit the change which it is possible to will to a movement of some part of our body, since, as James says in effect, we can just as much will the sliding of a table towards us as a movement of our hand towards our head. Indeed, we may, in fact, will this in order to convince ourselves or someone else that by doing so we shall not cause the table to slide. And it looks as though we sometimes will such things in ordinary life, as when in watching a football match we want some player's speed to increase, and will it to increase.

4. Where we have willed some movement of our body and think we have caused it, we cannot have directly caused it. For what we directly caused, if anything, must have been some change in our brain.

5. Where we think that by willing some change we effected some change in the physical world, we are implying the idea that in doing so, we are butting into, or interfering with, the physical system, just as we think of an approaching comet as effecting a breach in the order of the solar system, so long as we do not regard the comet as part of the system. This idea is, of course, inconsistent with our belief in the uniformity of nature unless we include in nature minds as well as bodies; and in any case it is inconsistent with our belief in the conservation of energy. But so long as we think, as we do, that at any rate on some occasions we really effect something in the physical world, we must admit this. And if we knew that such effecting was impossible, we should give up acting.

We have now to face another question, viz. "Does acting require a desire, and if it does, the desire of what?"

It is at least very difficult to avoid Aristotle's conclusion that acting requires a desire, if only for the reason he gives, viz. that διάνοια αὐτὴ οὐθὲν κινεῖ. It seems that, as Locke maintained, if we never desired something we should never do anything. But what is the desire required?

Here only one or other of two answers seems possible, viz. (1) that it is a desire of the change X which we will, and (2) that it is a desire of the willing of X. And when we try, we do not find it easy to decide between them. For on the one hand, the desire required seems to have to be the desire of X, on the ground that, if we are to will X, we must desire X. And on the other hand, it seems that it must be the desire to will X, since unless we *desired* to will X we could not will X. Indeed, just for this reason Plato seems to have gone too far in the *Gorgias* when he maintained that in acting we never desire to do what we do, but only that for the sake of which we do it. For, if acting is willing, it seems that the desire required must be a desire of the willing, even though the desire be a dependent desire, i.e. a desire depending on the desire of something else for its own sake, viz. that for the sake of which we do the action. And Plato's mistake seems to have been that of restricting desiring to desiring something for its own sake.

The two answers are, of course, radically different. For if the desire required is the desire of X, the thing desired and the thing willed will be the same, as indeed Green implies that they are when he maintains that willing is desiring in a special sense of "desiring." But if so, while the willing of X will require what for want of a better term we seem to have to call the thought of X, as being something involved in the desire of X, it will not require either the desire of the willing of X or, for that reason, even the thought of willing X. On the other hand, if the desire required is the desire to will X, the thing desired and the thing willed will necessarily be different, and while the willing of X will require the desire of willing X and so also the thought of willing X, it will not require the desire of X, though it will require the thought of X, as being something involved in the thought of willing X. It should, however, be noted that in the case of the latter alternative, the desire of X may in some cases be required indirectly as a condition of our desiring the willing of X.

To repeat here for clearness' sake what is central—if the desire required is the desire of X, the willing of X will not require either the desire of the willing of X or even the thought of willing X, while, if the desire required is the desire of willing X, the willing of X will not require the desire of X, though it will require the thought of X.

On consideration, however, we have to reject the idea that the desire required is the desire of X, on three grounds. First, if it were true, we should always will any change which we desired to happen, such as the sliding of the table, whether or not we thought that if we were to will it to happen we should thereby cause it to happen; and obviously we do not. Second, we occasionally will a change to happen without any desire for it to happen. This must occur, e.g., if a man ever does an act moved solely by the desire for revenge, willing, say, the movement of a switch which he is confident will result in the death of another, not from any desire for his death but solely from the desire to cause it by willing the movement. And even if there are no acts animated solely by the desire for revenge, there are certainly actions approximating to this. At all events, in the case of playing a game the desire at work must be not the desire of some change but the desire to cause it. A putter at golf, e.g., has no desire for the ball to fall into the hole; he only desires to cause it to fall in. This contention is, I think, not met by maintaining, as Cook Wilson in fact does, that the player desires the falling into the hole as caused by his action, and so desires the falling as part of, or an element in, his action. Its falling is neither a part of, nor an element in, his action; at best it is only an effect of it. And the player could only be said to desire the falling if, as he does not, he desired it to happen irrespectively of what would cause it to happen. And in this connection it may be added that if the desire required were the desire of X, it would be impossible to do any act as one which we think would or might fulfill some obligation, since *ex hypothesi* the desire required will be a desire for a change X and not a desire to *will* a change X. Then, third, there is a consideration which comes to light if we consider more closely what it is that we will in certain cases, and more especially in those in which we describe an action as one of trying to do so and so. Suppose, e.g., I have done what we describe as having tried to jump a ditch, and so imply that beforehand I was doubtful of success. Obviously I did not will a movement of my body which I was sure would land me, say, two clear yards on the other side, since if I had thought of willing this I should have realized that willing this would not result in my getting across. I willed that movement the willing of which, if I were to will it, I thought the most likely of all the willings of movements in my power to result in my landing on the farther bank. And in this connection it seems worth noting that what we call trying to do something is as much doing something as what we ordinarily call doing something, although the word "trying" suggests that it is not. It is the willing a change described in the way in which I have just described what I willed in trying to jump a ditch.

It therefore seems that the desire required must be the desire of the willing of a certain change X. Yet this conclusion is exposed to two objections. The first is that if it were true, it would be impossible to will something X for the first time. For in this context we mean by a desire to will X a desire we can only have in consequence of thinking that if we were to will X, our doing so would be likely to cause something else, and ultimately something which we desire for its own sake. But we cannot desire to will something X, unless we at least have a conjecture that if we were to will X, our willing X might cause some change which we desire for its own sake. And this conjecture requires the thought that on some previous occasion we have willed X and thence concluded from what we think followed this willing of X that it may have caused something else Y. Yet ex hypothesi we cannot have willed X on this previous occasion from the desire to will X, since then we had no idea of what willing X might cause. James expresses what is really this objection, though in a misleading way, when he says: "If, in voluntary action properly so-called" (i.e. in what is really an action), "the act must be foreseen, it follows that no creature not endowed with divinatory power can perform an act voluntarily for the first time." [8] The statement as it stands is, of course, absurd, because no one before acting *knows* what his act will be, or even that he will act. But it can be taken as an inaccurate way of expressing the thought that an act of will requires an idea of something which we may cause if we perform the act.

To this objection I have to confess that I cannot see an answer. Yet I think that there must be an answer, since, however it has come about, for us as we are now an act of will does seem to require the desire of it, and so some idea of something which it might effect. I need hardly add that it is no answer to maintain that the desire immediately required by willing something X is in some cases the desire of X, and in others the desire of willing X.

The second objection is one which seems to me, though insidious, an objection which can be met. It can be stated thus: "It is all very well to say that the desire immediately presupposed by willing X is the desire to will X. But to say this is not enough. For we often desire to will X, and yet do not, as when we hesitate to get out of bed or out of a warm bath, and when this is so, obviously something else is required, and this something can only be the willing to will X, so that after all there must be such a thing as willing to will." But to this the reply seems

[8] James, *Psychology*, ii, p. 487.

clear. Though it is possible to desire to desire, as when I desire to desire the welfare of my country more than I do, it is impossible to will to will, for the reason already given. And where we hesitate to will X, what is required is not the willing to will X but either a certain increase in our desire to will X or a decrease in our aversion to doing so. Certainly, too, we often act on this idea, hoping, e.g., that by making ourselves think of the coldness of our breakfast if we stay in bed we shall reach a state of desire in which we shall will certain movements of our body. And sometimes we succeed, and when we do, we sometimes, as James puts it, suddenly find that we have got up, the explanation of our surprise apparently being that we, having been absorbed in the process of trying to stimulate our desire to get up, have not reflected on our state of desire and so have not noticed its increase.

There is also to be noticed in this connection a mistake into which we are apt to fall which leads us to think that there must be such a thing as willing to will. We of course frequently want certain changes to happen and also want to will certain changes. But we are apt not to notice that the objects of these desires differ in respect of the conditions of their realization, and in consequence to carry the account of the process of deliberation described by Aristotle one step too far—as Aristotle did not. According to him, when we want the happening of something Z which is not an action of ours and which we think we cannot cause directly, we often look for something else Y from the happening of which the happening of Z would result, and then if necessary for something else X from the happening of which Y would result, until we come to think of something A from the happening of which X, Y, and Z would in turn result, and which we also think it in our power to cause by a certain act a. And when we have found A the process stops. We, however, are apt to carry the process one step farther, and apply to the act a, i.e. the willing of something β, the willing of which we think likely to cause A, the same process that we applied to Z, Y, X, and A, thus treating the willing of β as if it were not the willing of something (which it is), but a change which some act of willing might cause. As a result of doing this we ask "From what act of willing would the willing of β result?," and the answer has to be "The willing the willing of β." But the very question is mistaken, because the willing of β is not a change like Z, Y, X, and A. The only proper question at this stage must be not "From what *willing* would the willing of β result?" but "From what *something* would the willing of β result?" And the proper answer must be: "From a certain increase in our desire to will β."

SIMPLE ACTION AND VOLITION

Richard Taylor

In the last chapter I noted a difference in kind between mere motions and changes of my body, on the one hand, and such motions and changes of my body as represent actions of mine, on the other, even in those rather rare cases in which the two are behaviorally identical. I did not, however, consider the significance of that difference or the implications it has for a theory of human behavior, and that is my present concern.

ACTIONS AND MERE BODILY MOTIONS

Such things as the beating of my heart and the growth of my hair, for example, are motions and changes of my body, but in a familiar though somewhat baffling sense they are not things with which I have anything to do. So long as I am living at all these are just processes in the natural history of my body, or physiological processes which I am helpless either to make happen or to prevent from happening in any direct way. They are not, so far as I am concerned, much unlike the ticking of a clock or the growth of weeds around my window, except that I am apt to have a keener interest in them.

My arms and fingers sometimes move, on the other hand, or my body moves from place to place, carried hither and thither by my legs, and these motions seem clearly to be events of a wholly different kind. They are in some sense changes that are within my control, things that I am not helpless to make happen

Richard Taylor, *Action and Purpose* © 1966. Reprinted by permission of Prentice-Hall, Inc., Englewood Cliffs, New Jersey, pp. 57–72.

or to prevent from happening. Indeed, if they happen at all it is sometimes *because* I make them happen. And this seems manifestly different from my body, or my brain and nervous system, making them happen. The beating of my heart and innumerable other bodily processes are governed by my nervous system, though I nevertheless have nothing to do with them and they are no actions of mine. Some of these processes even occur without my being in the least aware of them, and some, such as certain of the processes involved in the homeostasis of my body, I am altogether ignorant of throughout my entire life. I am, moreover, occasionally surprised to find some part of my body, such as my finger or eyelid, moving or "twitching" in response, presumably, to some slight disorder in my nervous system, exactly to observation as though I had moved it myself. Sometimes, just as I am falling asleep, my body undergoes a convulsive jerk no different from what I could have done myself. I nevertheless somehow know that I had nothing to do with it, any more than with the motions of my hair in the wind.

There seems, further, to be a clear difference between the *thoughts* that merely occur within me and those which are within my control. For sometimes when I am daydreaming, or relaxing and waiting for sleep, thoughts and images just arise within me which I was not seeking, not trying to think, and for which I have no use, even thoughts that annoy me and which I try to dispel. But at other times thoughts come to me because I actively think them, or seek them, or bring them forth myself, as when I am trying to find my way out of some philosophical paradox, or solve a riddle, or complete a letter, or thinking through some projected course of action, or trying to recall a name. In the case of such thoughts, unlike the others, it seems to me that I am active or doing something, that I am bringing them forth, that what thoughts then occur to me are to some extent up to me, and that were it not for my actively thinking them they would be most unlikely to occur at all. Sometimes, moreover, the thoughts may be the same in either case; sometimes, for instance, someone's name, or a tune, runs through my mind, unsought, as when I am on the verge of sleep or otherwise not concentrating, whereas at other times the same name, or the same tune, may come to me because I call it forth.

We speak, however, not only of the actions or doings of men but of the actions or doings of inanimate things, like acids, explosives, and engines. Thus, it is perfectly intelligible to say of a given acid that it is dissolving zinc, or of a match that it started a forest fire, or of a tree that it shed its leaves, and so on. It looks like we might be expressing wholly different ideas of action in these cases, however, for it is certainly not obvious that I am saying the same sort of thing when I say of a match, for instance, that it started a forest fire, and when I say of a man that *he* started such a fire; or when I say that a tree is shedding its leaves, and that a man is shedding his clothes. In both cases I seem to be speaking of actions, and of men or things as doing these actions, but they are perhaps not actions in the same sense at all.

There is, nevertheless, one thing that actions of both kinds, if they are of different kinds, have in common; namely, that it is neither inappropriate nor misleading to use causal terminology in either case. Thus, we can say that I am moving my fingers, but not my heart, and the same idea would be suitably expressed by saying that I cause the motions of my fingers but not those of my heart. Similarly, we can say that a given acid is dissolving a piece of zinc, but not a piece of glass, and the same idea would be expressed by saying that the acid causes the zinc, but not the glass, to dissolve.

It is probably considerations of this sort that have, as noted earlier, led philosophers of other ages to attach great and fundamental importance to the concept of *action,* and the correlative notions of agency and active power, contrasting these with *passion* and such obvious correlates as *patient,* distinctions that have almost disappeared from philosophical literature, though they are still alive among the distinctions drawn by common sense and need only to be pointed out. When I am thinking or moving my limbs, I am acting—exhibiting agency or active power—according to this ancient conception, whereas when thoughts are merely occurring to me—as in dreams, or when someone is reading me a story— or when parts of my body are moving in a manner with which I have nothing to do—as in the case of my heart beating in response to internal impulses, or my hair being blown by the wind—I am passive, having something done *to* me. I suppose the common word *patience* has its origin here, as suggesting the idea of one who undergoes change not originated by himself, and without resistance. Certainly the clinical notion of a patient goes back to this distinction, as does the popular notion of a passion, and of suffering something as contrasted with doing something.

One way of putting the problems of the present chapter, then, is to ask whether such distinctions really apply to inanimate things; whether, that is, inanimate things are ever truly active beings in the sense in which men sometimes suppose themselves to be *agents,* or whether all the changes in such things can be regarded as passive, that is, as ordinary causal consequences of other changes. If, further, it should turn out that no concept of agency is needed for the description of the behavior of inanimate things, the question can be asked whether it is needed for the description of any human activity, or whether, on the contrary, human behavior cannot in every case be understood as passive—that is, as consisting of ordinary causal consequences of other changes, without the necessity of ever regarding men as agents in an irreducible sense.

SIMPLE ACTIONS

I shall be concerned here only with the simplest kinds of actions in order to bring into clear focus the concept of agency once deemed so elementary for the understanding of human nature. Consequently, I shall not consider such complex activities as piloting a ship, planning military strategy, writing a poem, and the like, but rather simple acts such as moving one's hand (as contrasted with having it moved) or recalling a name (as contrasted with being reminded of it). For surely if there is any act whose description is similar to that of ordinary changes in inanimate things, it would be such a simple act, perfectly familiar to everyone and requiring no special skill, training, strength, or wit. Everyone in a sense understands such simple actions perfectly well; yet, although they can be described, they remain unanalyzable. To derive such a conclusion philosophically, we must find, *first,* that an absolute distinction between acting and being acted upon can be drawn with precision, and, *second,* that the concept of an act cannot be analyzed in terms of the concepts sufficient for the description of inanimate behavior nor, in fact, in terms of any concepts either simpler or more clear. In this chapter I demonstrate the futility of certain more or less traditional kinds of analysis. In the chapter following I shall show why they were bound to be futile from the start and then outline what appears to be a more promising, though admittedly more metaphysical, approach to the basic understanding of human activity.

VOLUNTARY AND INVOLUNTARY ACTS

The distinction between voluntary and involuntary behavior is sometimes crucial, particularly in certain contexts of ethics but is not of significance in this inquiry. By a voluntary act I mean only what is done "on purpose," that is, intentionally, deliberately, and so on, and when I speak simply of an act I mean exactly the same thing. When a man does something under threat or in compliance with a command that can be enforced, he does it on purpose or intentionally, his purpose being to avoid the consequences of disobedience; to that extent he does it "voluntarily," despite the fact that, in the ordinary sense, his behavior illustrates perfectly what is meant by acting involuntarily. I do not, therefore, by any means intend to deny the important distinction between voluntary and involuntary actions. It is only a distinction that has no relevance to what I want to consider. The contrast I want to draw is between behavior which constitutes acting, like raising one's hand, and behavior which does not, like the beating of one's heart or perspiring under the influence of fear. When I speak of "voluntary" activity I mean only to contrast it with bodily movements and changes of this latter kind, which are strictly not acts, rather than with activity performed under coercion.

THE ELEMENTS OF A SIMPLE ACT

I shall restrict myself in this chapter to simple *observable* actions, that is, actions which involve or are expressed in *bodily movements*, leaving for later the consideration of mental activity.

Consider, then, a situation in which I make a mark with a pencil, a simple line for example. Now three facts can be discriminated in this perfectly commonplace situation, namely:

1. That I move my hand,
2. That my hand moves, and
3. That my hand moves a pencil.

Men often perform more complicated and interesting actions than these, to be sure, and sometimes actions extending over a considerable period of time, like running a race or directing a battle. They often perform simpler actions, too—one might simply move his hand without making any mark or moving any pencil, for instance. This, however, will serve as a paradigm of a fairly simple action, and it will be my purpose to elicit the complete difference in kind between these three simple facts contained in the action. To do this, I shall show first what a gulf separates the first fact, in which alone the notion of myself occurs as a subject, from the second, and then show what a similar gulf there is between the second and the third and, more significantly, between the first and the third. The first, as we shall see, involves the idea of an act of an active being, myself, while the second expresses only the idea of an event, change, or motion, without involving the notion of action or agency, and the third embodies only an ordinary causal relation, without agency, between two things.

ACTS AND EVENTS

It might seem that there is no absolute distinction between the first two facts, the one consisting of my moving my hand and the other of my hand's moving, but only a slight and insignificant difference in the way one and the same idea is expressed. The first statement does, indeed, suggest the idea of *doing* something, but we often speak of inanimate objects as doing things without suggesting any special element of agency—as for example, of the moon waxing and waning, of a tree shedding its leaves, a river rushing into the sea, and so on. And just as in these cases we are plainly not expressing anything except the occurrence of processes or events, there might seem to be no need to suppose that the act of a man is any special case. To say that a tree sheds its leaves is only to say that, under certain presupposed conditions, the leaves of that tree drop off. Similarly, it might seem, to say that I move my hand is only to say that, under certain conditions that are presupposed, my hand moves, this event being regarded as an act of mine only by virtue of the fact that it is *my* hand that moves.

Now if this were true there would not, contrary to what has been suggested, be any gulf between our first and second facts, for they would be one and the same fact. That this is not true, however, and that an act of an agent is therefore essentially different from the behavior of any inanimate thing, in which no agency is involved, follows from the consideration that the first fact, that I move my hand, logically entails, but is never entailed by, the second fact, that my hand moves. When I say that *I* move my hand I am saying something *more* than that my hand moves, for this latter might be true even though the former were not. This difference is, indeed, the very difference between an act and an event; for while every act is an event, or entails an event, not every event is an act, it being very common for things to occur, even in one's own body, which neither he nor anyone else makes occur.

To illustrate what this logic proves, it is possible that I should have a nervous spasm or disorder, such that my hand moves from time to time, or perhaps shakes, or twitches, without my having anything to do with it. We could not then say that I had moved my hand, simply in virtue of the fact that the motion had occurred and was unquestionably the motion of *my* hand, for by hypothesis I had nothing to do with it. It just moved, in spite of me. Evidently, then, its moving is not equivalent to my moving it. In the case of the tree, however, the fact that its leaves drop off, and that it sheds its leaves, *are* one and the same fact. Given that trees are the kinds of things they are, namely, passive beings, there are no circumstances under which it could be true that a tree's leaves drop off, without it also being true that the tree sheds its leaves. From the fact that either occurs we can infer that the other does too, simply because they are identically the same thing. Similar remarks can, of course, be made concerning the behavior of any inanimate and hence nonactive object whatever, such as the moon's waxing and waning, the river's rushing to the sea, and so on.

TRANSITIVE AND INTRANSITIVE MOTIONS

The difference between the second and the third facts that I have discriminated is fairly obvious, and not at all crucial to our inquiry, since neither involves any special notion or agency. The significant difference is simply a difference in the sense of "moves" involved in each. The second fact, consisting simply of my hand moving, amounts to nothing more than my hand undergoing motion, or change of place. It does not entail that anything else moves. The third fact, however, consists of my hand's imparting its motion to another thing, a pencil in this case, such that here the word "moves" occurs transitively. The second fact, accordingly, does not entail the third, but the third seems to entail the second; for the second could be true without the third being true, but it is difficult to see how the third could be true without the second being true too.

ACTS AND INTERNAL EVENTS

Aristotle sometimes spoke as though a voluntary act were distinguishable from other things by the fact that its cause is within the agent whose action it is. Most philosophers since have assumed that this is true, even obviously so, though perhaps in need of refinement. It has seldom been sufficiently appreciated what overwhelming difficulties there are in the idea of something's being "within" an agent.

If this were true, however—that is, if an act, as distinguished from a bodily motion that is not an act, were simply a bodily motion caused by something within the agent whose act it is—then there would be no radical difference in kind between the first of the three facts discriminated above, which is an act, and the third, which is not. The third fact, that my hand moves a pencil, involves only the idea that my hand, in moving, causes the motion of a pencil, a simple, straightforward causal relationship. If the first fact, that I move my hand, could be adequately expressed by saying that something within me causes my hand to move, then this, too, would be a simple and straightforward description of a causal relationship, and our first and third facts would accordingly be much the same.

This, however, is most assuredly *not* the proper description of an act, for there are numberless examples of things which manifestly are not acts, but which nevertheless fit that description perfectly. The causes of my heart beats are assuredly within me, for instance, in the clearest sense imaginable, yet these are no acts of mine, voluntary or otherwise. The phenomena of growth, too, like the growth of my hair and fingernails, have their causes within me, but these are never things that I *do*. They are merely changes that my body undergoes. Fear sometimes causes a man to perspire, but this is no act of his. It is merely something that his body does. But when a man raises his hand we cannot say that this is merely something that his body does. When a man's death is brought about by an internal disorder it is not thereby inferred that he killed himself, though that would follow if the suggestion before us were true. The spasms and convulsions to which some people are banefully subject arise from internal causes, yet these are as good examples as one could find of passive motions that are in no sense acts of those who are so afflicted.

SPIRITUAL EVENTS WITHIN THE MIND OR SOUL

In view of this obvious fact, that the mere *internal location* of its cause does not convert a bodily motion into an act, it has long been customary for philosophers to suppose that acts are distinguished from other events in having very special *kinds* of internal causes; namely, certain mental, or nonphysical events, in the mind or soul, called "acts of will" or, what is exactly the same, "volitions." Thus, in case the causal antecedents of any bodily change are entirely physical in nature, then, whether those causes occur within or without the body, or both, that change is no act, but a mere bodily change, no different in kind from the changes found in inanimate things. But if, on the other hand, that bodily change includes among its causal antecedents some event that is mental and therefore nonphysical in nature, and if in particular that nonphysical event is an act of will or a volition, and is such that the bodily change would not have occurred in its absence, then, according to this view, it is an act of an agent in whose mind that nonphysical event occurred. This theory, which I shall call "the volitional theory," simply describes acts as those bodily changes which have volitions as their remote or proximate causes.

I have already commented on this conception in the previous discussion of powers, and there is no need for repetition. Here it need only be noted that those who have embraced this opinion have not done so on the basis of any kind of experience whatever, whether "internal" or "external," "introspective" or "extrospective," nor has it been arrived at by psychological investigation, nor by the interpretation of any empirical data of psychology. The volitional theory is, in fact, nothing but the offspring of the marriage between a certain metaphysical presupposition, on the one hand, and the bewitchment of grammar, on the other. The metaphysical presupposition—which never has and never could be shown to be true—is that every event *must* have some other event as its cause, and hence, that there *must* be some internal event which is the cause of any bodily motion that is an act. If this internal cause of an act is not some bodily event—as it plainly cannot be, since it is just those bodily motions which have bodily causes that are *not* acts—then it must, of course, be some nonbodily event. Thus there arises the idea of "mental"—that is, nonbodily—causes. The grammatical trap with which this metaphysical presupposition has merged is the labeling in ordinary language of certain acts as "voluntary." The alleged internal causes thus receive a *name*, "volitions," suggested by the very word "voluntary"—and the illusion is thus complete that, there being this name, there *must* be some kind of event that it names.

I am not here suggesting that acts, or the bodily motions sometimes designated as acts, are uncaused. On the contrary, I shall later develop the idea that the cause of an act is, quite simply, the agent who performs it. This suggests, however, that the kind of causation involved in human behavior is the efficient causation of events by active beings, that is, by men, involving the exercise of active power. For the present, however, I mean to confine myself to showing—or, more accurately, to pointing out—that acts are not external effects of internal events, whether these are called "volitions," "acts of will," or whatnot.

THE NONEMPIRICAL CHARACTER OF THE VOLITIONAL THEORY

No one has ever arrived at a belief in volitions by observing them. They find no place in the data of empirical psychology, nor does it appear that anyone has ever found volitions occurring within himself, or within his mind, by any introspective scrutiny of his mental life. It is doubtful, in fact, whether any such thing as a volition, as construed by this theory, has ever occurred under the sun, and this would seem at least to be a defect in the volitional theory, whatever might be its philosophical merits.

Suppose it were otherwise. Let us suppose, in other words, that the volitional theory were true. What then would one actually *find* whenever he performed any simple act? He would, obviously, find not merely that he was performing an act, but that he was performing *two* of them, one of these being a private or internal act of willing, in his mind or soul, and the other an observable bodily act, which would be the causal consequence of this. Even this, however, is highly misleading, for according to the volitional theory an observable act simply *is* a bodily motion caused by a certain kind of change in the mind called a "volition." What, accordingly, one would find, or should certainly be able to find, anytime he performs an observable act, is both *events*—the internal alteration in his mind or soul, followed by the observable change of his body. But in fact one finds nothing like this at all. When I speak voluntarily, I do not find occurring within myself a volition to speak, and then forthwith find my tongue and other vocal organs moving in response to this inner mental change. When I move my finger I do not, and cannot, discover the occurrence within me of a special mental event, and later observe the finger moving in response to this. What I am actually aware of when I speak is that I am speaking—not merely that my tongue and lips are moving and making words, and not that these are moving in response to something else that is happening inside me. What I am aware of when I move my hand, and all that I seem able to become aware of, is that I am moving my hand —not just that my hand is moving, *nor* that it is moving as a causal consequence of something *else* that I find happening. I will to speak in speaking, and will to move my hand in moving it. There are not two things I do in each such case, nor two things that I find happening, but just one; or at least, that is all I can *find*.

It is said that those who are subject to epileptic convulsions are forewarned of an impending convulsion by a certain feeling. They sooner or later learn, upon the advent of this peculiar feeling, to expect their bodies to begin behaving in certain ways. All of us, moreover, know what it is like to feel a sneeze coming on. There is a certain feeling which, we have learned, is always or often followed by that convulsive exhalation called "sneezing." Hardly anything could be less like a voluntary act than things of this sort; indeed, they are good paradigms of involuntary behavior or automatic responses. And yet if the theory of volitions were true, voluntary behavior would not differ in kind at all from this kind of behavior—only in its underlying subjective cause. Voluntary sneezes, on this view, would only be sneezes caused by certain inner changes called "volitions," while involuntary ones would be caused by certain other inner changes—certain nasal tickles, and so on. The only trouble is, that one can *feel* a nasal tickle, can say when it begins and when it stops, can try to get rid of it, and so on, whereas no one, apparently, can actually *feel* any sneeze volition, can say when it begins and when it stops, or try to get rid of it. Indeed, we seem unable to say anything at all about volitions, except that they cause our bodies to move in this way and that—sneeze volitions causing our bodies to sneeze, arm-raising volitions causing our arms to go up, and so on. And because we *can* say this sort of thing, there are philosophers who have persuaded themselves that such inner causes do actually exist in their souls, and even some who have spoken as though they could *feel* them occurring there, or introspectively *discover* them occurring there, with as little doubt as that we *feel* an irritation that leads to sneezing. Now others may say what they please; they may solemnly affirm, if they wish, that they are perpetually aware, or can easily become aware by some simple "inward" glance, of volitions occurring within them, volitions of the greatest diversity, and some of the most incredible complexity—like the volition of the sort needed to spell out a word, for instance, or to pronounce a complete sentence. For myself, to paraphrase a philosopher of an earlier day, I am quite certain that no such thing ever occurred within me. I do not believe that I have merely *failed to find* things that are in fact occurring within me daily, nor that, finding them, I have failed to *recognize* them. They appear to be pure fictions, for my behavior seems not one whit less voluntary in the apparent absence of such alleged inner causes.

THE CHARACTERLESSNESS OF VOLITIONS

Quite apart from any introspective scrutiny of one's own mental life, one ought to suspect that volitions are fictional just from the way they are referred to in philosophical literature—and they are not, it is perhaps worth noting, ever referred to elsewhere. They are always referred to and described in terms of their *effects*, never in terms of themselves, leading one to suspect that perhaps they have no inherent characteristics by which they even can be identified.

Now in any true causal relationship one can always, in case he knows what both events are, describe them independently of each other. If, for instance, I know that a window was broken by the impact of a brick, I can describe this cause quite informatively without any reference to the breaking of the window, which is its effect. I can say, that is, that this cause was the motion of a brick of such and such description, having such and such weight and moving at such and such speed, striking the window in a specific way, and so on. Similarly, a physiologist can give some sort of description of the causes of my heartbeats, or the growth of my hair, without necessarily mentioning these effects at all. But it is quite *impossible* to describe any volition or act of will except in terms of its alleged effects. Can anyone, for instance, describe the volition to move one's index finger in the motion of a figure eight without reference to that finger and that motion? Can anyone describe such a volition, adequately to distinguish it from, say, the volition to make a similar motion of the middle finger without reference to either finger? Can any particular volition be described at all? Seemingly not. If we ask just what *is* the volition to move one's finger, we only get as a reply that it is the internal or mental cause of just such a motion. The only thing that distinguishes it from the volition to move another finger is that it in fact caused the motion of *this* finger. Such an alleged cause is, evidently, pure fiction. When we ask for some sort of description of the cause, we get the one-word reply, "volition," and when we ask what on earth this might be, we are merely told that it is the cause of the voluntary motion of the finger—as if by this kind of discourse we should somehow feel wiser! It is exactly as though a physiologist were to announce that he had discovered the cause of the heartbeat and, upon being asked what that cause is, replied that it is the heartbeat impulse and then filled out the description of this by saying that by heartbeat impulse he is, of course, referring to those events which are the causes of heartbeats. No one would imagine that he had learned anything about the causes of heartbeats by such a disquisition.

HEARTBEATS

The heartbeat provides a good example of an involuntary motion. One can, to be sure, control its rate to some rather slight extent by doing something *else* voluntarily—by exercising, for instance, or by resting—or one can stop it altogether by, say, putting a bullet through it, but the motions of the heart cannot be controlled in the same direct way that, for example, certain motions of the fingers can. In this respect the heart's behavior is as far "removed from the will" as, say, the motions of a clock pendulum—which, incidentally, can also be controlled in an indirect way, by voluntarily making adjustments, or perhaps smashing it. Indeed, were it not for my knowledge, which was at some time learned, that my very existence from one moment to the next depends upon this pulse, I would probably consider it with the same relative indifference and idle curiosity that I do the ticking of a clock.

Why, then, should we not regard those inner impulses which control the heartbeat as acts of will or volitions? This question, so far as I know, has never been asked, because no one has ever seen the point of it. But surely we know that the regular contractions and relaxations of the heart are individually caused by impulses of some kind or other, whether they be mental, physical, or whatever. Why, then, shall we not properly call these impulses volitions?

The answer to this certainly *cannot* be that we are not consciously aware of those impulses, the way that we are of such things as headaches and tickles, for it has been abundantly stressed that no man is ever consciously aware of any volition, either. No man can ever truly say anything like, "Ah! there is an arm-raising volition—now it is subsiding, but now it is recurring with slightly greater intensity, and now I shall try to suppress it or ignore it," and so on. Indeed, as we have seen, no one can even begin to describe any volition at all—which he should certainly be able to do if he were ever conscious of one—except in terms of its alleged effect, of which he is plainly conscious. All that one is ever consciously aware of in performing a voluntary act is, besides the act itself, certain feelings of muscular effort and resistance, and one is not always even aware of these. When I am cleaning out my pipe, for instance, I am conscious only of cleaning my pipe, together with the certain slight muscular effort and resistance involved in doing so. The motions that I then make are not each and every one accompanied by additional events, of which I am ever conscious, which are the volitions to make those motions. They are accompanied only by the feeling of the pipe and its resistance, which is an effect, and certainly no cause, of the motions I then make.

Nor can the answer to this question be that the heartbeat impulses are of a physical nature, whereas volitions are ("by definition") mental. No one could ever show that heartbeat impulses and volitions, if there are such things, are not of exactly the same nature, whether this be called mental or physical. One can indeed define volitions as nonphysical events, but one can as easily define heartbeat impulses in the same way; the question will still remain whether there are volitions and heartbeat impulses, as thus defined, and if so, whether they are any different. This, of course, can only be decided by examination and experience, not by inventing definitions of words. If, as is very doubtful, there are such events as volitions within us, of which any man can become intimately aware every time he acts voluntarily, then there is no philosophical reason for denying that these events are of the same sort as those heartbeat impulses of which, however, we are not intimately aware. Since, however, it is seriously doubtful whether any one is ever aware of a volition, and quite certain that no one is ever aware of the impulses that control heartbeats, then the two are apparently similar in this negative respect, at least, and may be identical in others. We are, to be sure, sometimes aware of our intentions, purposes, motives, and the like, but that is not the awareness of any inner event of long or short duration which one finds to be the cause of a bodily motion, in any way comparable to that in which fear, for instance, is sometimes the cause of perspiration. To be "aware of one's intention" is only to have made up one's mind what he is going to do, now or later, to have settled upon a course of action, and to remember it. It would be quite unbelievable to suppose that bodily motions are literally caused by anything like this, and absurd to suppose that every voluntary motion must be.

It is, however, quite obvious why philosophers are never tempted to think of heartbeat impulses as volitions; namely, that the heartbeats are not voluntary. This does *not* mean that they are not "caused by volitions" since, for all we know, they may be. What it does mean is that they are not within one's immediate control. They individually occur in their own way and at their own pace, and quite in spite of the agent in whose body they occur, disregarding here the in-direct ways that the pulse rate can be increased or decreased.

This good reason for excluding heartbeat impulses as examples of volitions is not, however, available to holders of the theory of volitions. For according to that theory, to say that something is "within one's immediate control" just *means* that it is caused by a volition. If, accordingly, there are such things as volitions, and it should turn out that heartbeat impulses are in fact the same sorts of things as these, then the holders of this theory would have to conclude that heartbeats are voluntary after all, which would be absurd. Nor can the holder of the volitional theory say that the heartbeat impulses themselves are involuntary and not within one's control, for again, all it means to say that something is voluntary, according to that theory, is that it is caused by a volition. Not knowing the cause of a heartbeat impulse, then, how can anyone say that it is not caused by a volition? If, to be sure, the heartbeat impulse should itself turn out to be a volition, then it might be meaningless either to affirm or to deny that it is caused by a volition, since the holders of the volitional theory often maintain that it is meaningless to speak of volitions as being either voluntary or involuntary. But it is certainly *not* meaningless to deny that the heartbeat impulses are voluntary or within our immediate control, for everyone knows perfectly well that they are not. Something's being voluntary or within one's immediate control cannot, therefore, be equivalent to its being caused by a volition.

· · ·

THE WILL

Gilbert Ryle

(1) FOREWORD

Most of the mental-conduct concepts whose logical behavior we examine in this book, are familiar and everyday concepts. We all know how to apply them and we understand other people when they apply them. What is in dispute is not how to apply them, but how to classify them, or in what categories to put them.

The concept of volition is in a different case. We do not know in daily life how to use it, for we do not use it in daily life and do not, consequently, learn by practice how to apply it, and how not to misapply it. It is an artificial concept. We have to study certain specialist theories in order to find out how it is to be manipulated. It does not, of course, follow from its being a technical concept that it is an illegitimate or useless concept. "Ionization" and "off side" are technical concepts, but both are legitimate and useful. "Phlogiston" and "animal spirits" were technical concepts, though they have now no utility.

I hope to show that the concept of volition belongs to the latter tribe.

(2) THE MYTH OF VOLITIONS

It has for a long time been taken for an indisputable axiom that the Mind is in some important sense tripartite, that is, that there are just three ultimate classes of mental processes. The Mind or Soul, we are often told, has three parts, namely, Thought, Feeling and Will; or, more solemnly, the Mind or Soul functions in

From *The Concept of Mind* by Gilbert Ryle (New York: Barnes & Noble, Inc., and London: Hutchinson & Co. Ltd., 1949), pp. 62–69. Reprinted by permission of the publishers.

three irreducibly different modes, the Cognitive mode, the Emotional mode and the Conative mode. This traditional dogma is not only not self-evident, it is such a welter of confusions and false inferences that it is best to give up any attempt to refashion it. It should be treated as one of the curios of theory.

The main object of this chapter is not, however, to discuss the whole trinitarian theory of mind but to discuss, and discuss destructively, one of its ingredients. I hope to refute the doctrine that there exists a Faculty, immaterial Organ, or Ministry, corresponding to the theory's description of the "Will" and, accordingly, that there occur processes, or operations, corresponding to what it describes as "volitions." I must however make it clear from the start that this refutation will not invalidate the distinctions which we all quite properly draw between voluntary and involuntary actions and between strong-willed and weak-willed persons. It will, on the contrary, make clearer what is meant by "voluntary" and "involuntary," by "strong-willed" and "weak-willed," by emancipating these ideas from bondage to an absurd hypothesis.

Volitions have been postulated as special acts, or operations, "in the mind," by means of which a mind gets its ideas translated into facts. I think of some state of affairs which I wish to come into existence in the physical world but, as my thinking and wishing are unexecutive, they require the mediation of a further executive mental process. So I perform a volition which somehow puts my muscles into action. Only when a bodily movement has issued from such a volition can I merit praise or blame for what my hand or tongue has done.

It will be clear why I reject this story. It is just an inevitable extension of the myth of the ghost in the machine. It assumes that there are mental states and processes enjoying one sort of existence, and bodily states and processes enjoying another. An occurrence on the one stage is never numerically identical with an occurrence on the other. So, to say that a person pulled the trigger intentionally is to express at least a conjunctive proposition, asserting the occurrence of one act on the physical stage and another on the mental stage; and, according to most versions of the myth, it is to express a causal proposition, asserting that the bodily act of pulling the trigger was the effect of a mental act of willing to pull the trigger.

According to the theory, the workings of the body are motions of matter in space. The causes of these motions must then be *either* other motions of matter in space *or*, in the privileged case of human beings, thrusts of another kind. In some way which must forever remain a mystery, mental thrusts, which are not movements of matter in space, can cause muscles to contract. To describe a man as intentionally pulling the trigger is to state that such a mental thrust did cause the contraction of the muscles of his finger. So the language of "volitions" is the language of the paramechanical theory of the mind. If a theorist speaks without qualms of "volitions," or "acts of will," no further evidence is needed to show that he swallows whole the dogma that a mind is a secondary field of special causes. It can be predicted that he will correspondingly speak of bodily actions as "expressions" of mental processes. He is likely also to speak glibly of "experiences," a plural noun commonly used to denote the postulated nonphysical episodes which constitute the shadow-drama on the ghostly boards of the mental stage.

The first objection to the doctrine that overt actions, to which we ascribe intelligence-predicates, are results of counterpart hidden operations of willing is this. Despite the fact that theorists have, since the Stoics and Saint Augustine, recommended us to describe our conduct in this way, no one, save to endorse the theory, ever describes his own conduct, or that of his acquaintances, in the recommended idioms. No one ever says such things as that at 10 A.M. he was occupied in willing this or that, or that he performed five quick and easy volitions and two slow and difficult volitions between midday and lunchtime. An accused person may admit or deny that he did something, or that he did it on purpose, but he never admits or denies having willed. Nor do the judge and jury require to be satisfied by evidence, which in the nature of the case could never be adduced, that a volition preceded the pulling of the trigger. Novelists describe the actions, remarks, gestures, and grimaces, the daydreams, deliberations, qualms, and embarrassments of their characters; but they never mention their volitions. They would not know what to say about them.

By what sorts of predicates should they be described? Can they be sudden or gradual, strong or weak, difficult or easy, enjoyable or disagreeable? Can they be accelerated, decelerated, interrupted, or suspended? Can people be efficient or inefficient at them? Can we take lessons in executing them? Are they fatiguing or distracting? Can I do two or seven of them synchronously? Can I remember executing them? Can I execute them, while thinking of other things, or while dreaming? Can they become habitual? Can I forget how to do them? Can I mistakenly believe that I have executed one, when I have not, or that I have not executed one, when I have? At which moment was the boy going through a volition to take the high dive? When he set foot on the ladder? When he took his first deep breath? When he counted off "One, two, three—Go," but did not go? Very, very shortly before he sprang? What would his own answer be to those questions?

Champions of the doctrine maintain, of course, that the enactment of volitions is asserted by implication, whenever an overt act is described as intentional, voluntary, culpable, or meritorious; they assert too that any person is not merely able but bound to know that he is willing when he is doing so, since volitions are defined as a species of conscious process. So if ordinary men and women fail to mention their volitions in their descriptions of their own behavior, this must be due to their being untrained in the dictions appropriate to the description of their inner, as distinct from their overt, behavior. However, when a champion of the doctrine is himself asked how long ago he executed his last volition, or how many acts of will he executes in, say, reciting "Little Miss Muffet" backwards, he is apt to confess to finding difficulties in giving the answer, though these difficulties should not, according to his own theory, exist.

If ordinary men never report the occurrence of these acts, for all that, according to the theory, they should be encountered vastly more frequently than headaches, or feelings of boredom; if ordinary vocabulary has no nonacademic names for them; if we do not know how to settle simple questions about their frequency, duration, or strength, then it is fair to conclude that their existence is not asserted on empirical grounds. The fact that Plato and Aristotle never mentioned them in their frequent and elaborate discussions of the nature of the soul and the springs of conduct is due not to any perverse neglect by them of notorious ingredients of daily life but to the historical circumstance that they were not acquainted with a special hypothesis the acceptance of which rests not on the discovery but on the postulation, of these ghostly thrusts.

The second objection is this. It is admitted that one person can never witness the volitions of another; he can only infer from an observed overt action to the volition from which it resulted, and then only if he has any good reason to believe that the overt action was a voluntary action, and not a reflex or habitual action, or one resulting from some external cause. It follows that no judge, schoolmaster, or parent ever knows that the actions which he judges merit praise or blame; for he cannot do better than guess that the action was willed. Even a confession by the agent, if such confessions were ever made, that he had executed a volition before his hand did the deed would not settle the question. The pronouncement of the confession is only another overt muscular action. The curious conclusion results that though volitions were called in to explain our appraisals of actions, this explanation is just what they fail to provide. If we had no other antecedent grounds for applying appraisal-concepts to the actions of others, we should have no reasons at all for inferring from those actions to the volitions alleged to give rise to them.

Nor could it be maintained that the agent himself can know that any overt action of his own is the effect of a given volition. Supposing, what is not the case, that he could know for certain, either from the alleged direct deliverances of consciousness, or from the alleged direct findings of introspection, that he had executed an act of will to pull the trigger just before he pulled it, this would not prove that the pulling was the effect of that willing. The connection between volitions and movements is allowed to be mysterious, so, for all he knows, his volition may have had some other movement as its effect and the pulling of the trigger may have had some other event for its cause.

Thirdly, it would be improper to burke the point that the connection between volition and movement is admitted to be a mystery. It is a mystery not of the unsolved but soluble type, like the problem of the cause of cancer, but of quite another type. The episodes supposed to constitute the careers of minds are assumed to have one sort of existence, while those constituting the careers of bodies have another sort; and no bridge-status is allowed. Transactions between minds and bodies involve links where no links can be. That there should be any causal transactions between minds and matter conflicts with one part, that there should be none conflicts with another part of the theory. Minds, as the whole legend describes them, are what must exist if there is to be a causal explanation of the intelligent behavior of human bodies; and minds, as the legend describes them, live on a floor of existence defined as being outside the causal system to which bodies belong.

Fourthly, although the prime function of volitions, the task for the performance of which they were postulated, is to originate bodily movements, the argument, such as it is, for their existence entails that some mental happenings also must result from acts of will. Volitions were postulated to be that which makes actions voluntary, resolute, meritorious, and wicked. But predicates of these sorts are ascribed not only to bodily movements but also to operations which, according to the theory, are mental and not physical operations. A thinker may ratiocinate resolutely, or imagine wickedly; he may try to compose a limerick and he may meritoriously concentrate on his algebra. Some mental processes then can, according to the theory, issue from volitions. So what of volitions themselves? Are they voluntary or involuntary acts of mind? Clearly either answer leads to absurdities.

If I cannot help willing to pull the trigger, it would be absurd to describe my pulling it as "voluntary." But if my volition to pull the trigger is voluntary, in the sense assumed by the theory, then it must issue from a prior volition and that from another *ad infinitum*. It has been suggested, to avoid this difficulty, that volitions cannot be described as either voluntary or involuntary. "Volition" is a term of the wrong type to accept either predicate. If so, it would seem to follow that it is also of the wrong type to accept such predicates as "virtuous" and "wicked," "good" and "bad," a conclusion which might embarrass those moralists who use volitions as the sheet anchor of their systems.

In short, then, the doctrine of volitions is a causal hypothesis, adopted because it was wrongly supposed that the question, "What makes a bodily movement voluntary?" was a causal question. This supposition is, in fact, only a special twist of the general supposition that the question, "How are mental-conduct concepts applicable to human behavior?" is a question about the causation of that behavior.

Champions of the doctrine should have noticed the simple fact that they and all other sensible persons knew how to decide questions about the voluntariness and involuntariness of actions and about the resoluteness and irresoluteness of agents before they had ever heard of the hypothesis of the occult inner thrusts of actions. They might then have realized that they were not elucidating the criteria already in efficient use, but, tacitly assuming their validity, were trying to correlate them with hypothetical occurrences of a paramechanical pattern. Yet this correlation could, on the one hand, never be scientifically established, since the thrusts postulated were screened from scientific observation; and, on the other hand, it would be of no practical or theoretical use, since it would not assist our appraisals of actions, depending as it would on the presupposed validity of those appraisals. Nor would it elucidate the logic of those appraisal-concepts, the intelligent employment of which antedated the invention of this causal hypothesis.

Before we bid farewell to the doctrine of volitions, it is expedient to consider certain quite familiar and authentic processes with which volitions are sometimes wrongly identified.

People are frequently in doubt what to do; having considered alternative courses of action, they then, sometimes, select or choose one of these courses. This process of opting for one of a set of alternative courses of action is sometimes said to be what is signified by "volition." But this identification will not do, for most voluntary actions do not issue out of conditions of indecision and are not therefore results of settlements of indecisions. Moreover it is notorious that a person may choose to do something but fail, from weakness of will, to do it; or he may fail to do it because some circumstance arises after the choice is made, preventing the execution of the act chosen. But the theory could not allow that volitions ever fail to result in action, else further executive operations would have to be postulated to account for the fact that sometimes voluntary actions are performed. And finally the process of deliberating between alternatives and opting for one of them is itself subject to appraisal-predicates. But if, for example, an act of choosing is describable as voluntary, then, on this suggested showing, it would have in its turn to be the result of a prior choice to choose, and that from a choice to choose to choose. . . .

The same objections forbid the identification with volitions of such other familiar processes as that of resolving or making up our minds to do something and that of nerving or bracing ourselves to do something. I may resolve to get out of bed or go to the dentist, and I may, clenching my fists and gritting my teeth, brace myself to do so, but I may still backslide. If the action is not done, then, according to the doctrine, the volition to do it is also unexecuted. Again, the operations of resolving and nerving ourselves are themselves members of the class of creditable or discreditable actions, so they cannot constitute the peculiar ingredient which, according to the doctrine, is the common condition of any performance being creditable or discreditable.

• • •

ACTIONS, REASONS, AND CAUSES *

Donald Davidson

What is the relation between a reason and an action when the reason explains the action by giving the agent's reason for doing what he did? We may call such explanations *rationalizations,* and say that the reason *rationalizes* the action.

In this paper I want to defend the ancient—and commonsense—position that rationalization is a species of ordinary causal explanation. The defense no doubt requires some redeployment, but not more or less complete abandonment of the position, as urged by many recent writers.[1]

I

A reason rationalizes an action only if it leads us to see something the agent saw, or thought he saw, in his action—some feature, consequence, or aspect of the action the agent wanted, desired, prized, held dear, thought dutiful, beneficial, obligatory, or agreeable. We cannot explain why someone did what he did

* Presented in a symposium on "Action" at the sixtieth annual meeting of the American Philosophical Association, December 29, 1963.

From *The Journal of Philosophy*, LX, No. 23 (November 7, 1963), 685–700. Reprinted by permission of the author and *The Journal of Philosophy.*

[1] Some examples: G. E. M. Anscombe, *Intention,* Oxford, 1959; Stuart Hampshire, *Thought and Action,* London, 1959; H. L. A. Hart and A. M. Honoré, *Causation in the Law,* Oxford, 1959; William Dray, *Laws and Explanation in History,* Oxford, 1957; and most of the books in the series edited by R. F. Holland, *Studies in Philosophical Psychology,* including Anthony Kenny, *Action, Emotion and Will,* London, 1963, and A. I. Melden, *Free Action,* London, 1961. Page references in parentheses will all be to these works.

simply by saying the particular action appealed to him; we must indicate what it was about the action that appealed. Whenever someone does something for a reason, therefore, he can be characterized as (*a*) having some sort of pro attitude toward actions of a certain kind, and (*b*) believing (or knowing, perceiving, noticing, remembering) that his action is of that kind. Under (*a*) are to be included desires, wantings, urges, promptings, and a great variety of moral views, aesthetic principles, economic prejudices, social conventions, and public and private goals and values in so far as these can be interpreted as attitudes of an agent directed toward actions of a certain kind. The word "attitude" does yeoman service here, for it must cover not only permanent character traits that show themselves in a lifetime of behavior, like love of children or a taste for loud company, but also the most passing fancy that prompts a unique action, like a sudden desire to touch a woman's elbow. In general, pro attitudes must not be taken for convictions, however temporary, that every action of a certain kind ought to be performed, is worth performing, or is, all things considered, desirable. On the contrary, a man may all his life have a yen, say, to drink a can of paint, without ever, even at the moment he yields, believing it would be worth doing.

Giving the reason why an agent did something is often a matter of naming the pro attitude (*a*) or the related belief (*b*) or both; let me call this pair the *primary reason* why the agent performed the action. Now it is possible to reformulate the claim that rationalizations are causal explanations, and give structure to the argument as well, by stating two theses about primary reasons:

1. For us to understand how a reason of any kind rationalizes an action it is necessary and sufficient that we see, at least in essential outline, how to construct a primary reason.
2. The primary reason for an action is its cause.

I shall argue for these points in turn.

II

I flip the switch, turn on the light, and illuminate the room. Unbeknownst to me I also alert a prowler to the fact that I am home. Here I do not do four things, but only one, of which four descriptions have been given.[2] I flipped the switch because I wanted to turn on the light, and by saying I wanted to turn on the light

---

[2] We would not call my unintentional alerting of the prowler an action, but it should not be inferred from this that alerting the prowler is therefore something different from flipping the switch, say just its consequence. Actions, performances, and events not involving intention are alike in that they are often referred to or defined partly in terms of some terminal stage, outcome, or consequence.

The word "action" does not very often occur in ordinary speech, and when it does it is usually reserved for fairly portentous occasions. I follow a useful philosophical practice in calling anything an agent does intentionally an action, including intentional omissions. What is really needed is some suitably generic term to bridge the following gap: suppose "A" is a description of an action, "B" is a description of something done voluntarily, though not intentionally, and "C" is a description of something done involuntarily and unintentionally; finally, suppose A=B=C. Then A, B, and C are the same—what? "Action," "event," "thing done," each have, at least in some contexts, a strange ring when coupled with the wrong sort of description. Only the question "Why did you (he) do A?" has the true generality required. Obviously, the problem is greatly aggravated if we assume, as Melden does (*Free Action*, 85), that an action ("raising one's arm") can be identical with a bodily movement ("one's arm going up").

I explain (give my reason for, rationalize) the flipping. But I do not, by giving this reason, rationalize my alerting of the prowler nor my illuminating of the room. Since reasons may rationalize what someone does when it is described in one way and not when it is described in another, we cannot treat what was done simply as a term in sentences like "My reason for flipping the switch was that I wanted to turn on the light"; otherwise we would be forced to conclude, from the fact that flipping the switch was identical with alerting the prowler, that my reason for alerting the prowler was that I wanted to turn on the light. Let us mark this quasi-intentional [3] character of action descriptions in rationalizations by stating a bit more precisely a necessary condition for primary reasons:

C1. *R* is a primary reason why an agent performed the action *A* under the description *d* only if *R* consists of a pro attitude of the agent toward actions with a certain property, and a belief of the agent that *A*, under the description *d*, has that property.

How can my wanting to turn on the light be (part of) a primary reason, since it appears to lack the required element of generality? We may be taken in by the verbal parallel between "I turned on the light" and "I wanted to turn on the light." The first clearly refers to a particular event, so we conclude that the second has this same event as its object. Of course it is obvious that the event of my turning on the light can't be referred to in the same way by both sentences, since the existence of the event is required by the truth of "I turned on the light" but not by the truth of "I wanted to turn on the light." If the reference were the same in both cases, the second sentence would entail the first; but in fact the sentences are logically independent. What is less obvious, at least until we attend to it, is that the event whose occurrence makes "I turned on the light" true cannot be called the object, however intensional, of "I wanted to turn on the light." If I turned on the light, then I must have done it at a precise moment, in a particular way—every detail is fixed. But it makes no sense to demand that my want be directed at an action performed at any one moment or done in some unique manner. Any one of an indefinitely large number of actions would satisfy the want, and can be considered equally eligible as its object. Wants and desires often are trained on physical objects. However, "I want that gold watch in the window" is not a primary reason, and explains why I went into the store only because it suggests a primary reason—for example, that I wanted to buy the watch.

Because "I wanted to turn on the light" and "I turned on the light" are logically independent, the first can be used to give a reason why the second is true. Such a reason gives minimal information: it implies that the action was intentional, and wanting tends to exclude some other pro attitudes, such as a sense of duty or obligation. But the exclusion depends very much on the action and the context of explanation. Wanting seems pallid beside lusting, but it would be odd to deny that someone who lusted after a woman or a cup of coffee wanted her or it. It is not unnatural, in fact, to treat wanting as a genus including all pro attitudes as

---

[3] "Quasi-intentional" because, besides its intensional aspect, the description of the action must also refer in rationalizations; otherwise it could be true that an action was done for a certain reason and yet the action not have been performed. Compare "the author of *Waverley*" in "George IV knew the author of *Waverley* wrote *Waverley*."

species. When we do this and when we know some action is intentional, it is empty to add that the agent wanted to do it. In such cases, it is easy to answer the question "Why did you do it?" with "For no reason," meaning not that there is no reason but that there is no *further* reason, no reason that cannot be inferred from the fact that the action was done intentionally; no reason, in other words, besides wanting to do it. This last point is not essential to the present argument, but it is of interest because it defends the possibility of defining an intentional action as one done for a reason.

A primary reason consists of a belief and an attitude, but it is generally otiose to mention both. If you tell me you are easing the jib because you think that will stop the main from backing, I don't need to be told that you want to stop the main from backing; and if you say you are biting your thumb at me because you want to insult me, there is no point in adding that you think that by biting your thumb at me you will insult me. Similarly, many explanations of actions in terms of reasons that are not primary do not require mention of the primary reason to complete the story. If I say I am pulling weeds because I want a beautiful lawn, it would be fatuous to eke out the account with "And so I see something desirable in any action that does, or has a good chance of, making the lawn beautiful." Why insist that there is any *step,* logical or psychological, in the transfer of desire from an end that is not an action to the actions one conceives as means? It serves the argument as well that the desired end explains the action only if what are believed by the agent to be means are desired.

Fortunately, it is not necessary to classify and analyze the many varieties of emotions, sentiments, moods, motives, passions, and hungers whose mention may answer the question "Why did you do it?" in order to see how, when such mention rationalizes the action, a primary reason is involved. Claustrophobia gives a man's reason for leaving a cocktail party because we know people want to avoid, escape from, be safe from, put distance between themselves and, what they fear. Jealousy is the motive in a poisoning because, among other things, the poisoner believes his action will harm his rival, remove the cause of his agony, or redress an injustice, and these are the sorts of things a jealous man wants to do. When we learn a man cheated his son out of greed, we do not necessarily know what the primary reason was, but we know there was one, and its general nature. Ryle analyzes "he boasted from vanity" into "he boasted on meeting the stranger and his doing so satisfies the lawlike proposition that whenever he finds a chance of securing the admiration and envy of others, he does whatever he thinks will produce this admiration and envy" (*The Concept of Mind,* 89). This analysis is often, and perhaps justly, criticized on the ground that a man may boast from vanity just once. But if Ryle's boaster did what he did from vanity, then something entailed by Ryle's analysis is true: the boaster wanted to secure the admiration and envy of others, and he believed that his action would produce this admiration and envy; true or false, Ryle's analysis does not dispense with primary reasons, but depends upon them.

To know a primary reason why someone acted as he did is to know an intention with which the action was done. If I turn left at the fork because I want to get to Katmandu, my intention in turning left is to get to Katmandu. But to know the intention is not necessarily to know the primary reason in full detail. If James goes to church with the intention of pleasing his mother, then he must have some pro attitude toward pleasing his mother, but it needs more information to tell whether his reason is that he enjoys pleasing his mother, or thinks it right, his duty, or an obligation. The expression "the intention with which James went to church" has the outward form of a description, but in fact it is syncategorematic and cannot be taken to refer to an entity, state, disposition, or event. Its function in context is to generate new descriptions of actions in terms of their reasons; thus "James went to church with the intention of pleasing his mother" yields a new, and fuller, description of the action described in "James went to church." Essentially the same process goes on when I answer the question "Why are you bobbing around that way?" with "I'm knitting, weaving, exercising, sculling, cuddling, training fleas."

Straight description of an intended result often explains an action better than stating that the result was intended or desired. "It will soothe your nerves" explains why I pour you a shot as efficiently as "I want to do something to soothe your nerves," since the first in the context of explanation implies the second; but the first does better, because, if it is true, the facts will justify my choice of action. Because justifying and explaining an action so often go hand in hand, we frequently indicate the primary reason for an action by making a claim which, if true, would also verify, vindicate, or support the relevant belief or attitude of the agent. "I knew I ought to return it," "The paper said it was going to snow," "You stepped on *my* toes," all, in appropriate reason-giving contexts, perform this familiar dual function.

The justifying role of a reason, given this interpretation, depends upon the explanatory role, but the converse does not hold. Your stepping on my toes neither explains nor justifies my stepping on your toes unless I believe you stepped on my toes, but the belief alone, true or false, explains my action.

III

In the light of a primary reason, an action is revealed as coherent with certain traits, long- or short-termed, characteristic or not, of the agent, and the agent is shown in his role of Rational Animal. Corresponding to the belief and attitude of a primary reason for an action, we can always construct (with a little ingenuity) the premises of a syllogism from which it follows that the action has some (as Miss Anscombe calls it) "desirability characteristic." [4] Thus there is a certain irreducible—though somewhat anemic—sense in which every rationalization justifies: from the agent's point of view there was, when he acted, something to be said for the action.

Noting that nonteleological causal explanations do not display the element of justification provided by reasons, some philosophers have concluded that the concept of cause that applies elsewhere cannot apply to the relation between reasons and actions, and that the pattern of justification provides, in the case of reasons, the required explanation. But suppose we grant that reasons alone justify

---

[4] Miss Anscombe denies that the practical syllogism is deductive. This she does partly because she thinks of the practical syllogism, as Aristotle does, as corresponding to a piece of practical reasoning (whereas for me it is only part of the analysis of the concept of a reason with which someone acted), and therefore she is bound, again following Aristotle, to think of the conclusion of a practical syllogism as corresponding to a judgment, not merely that the action has a desirable characteristic, but that the action is desirable (reasonable, worth doing, etc.).

in explaining actions; it does not follow that the explanation is not also—and necessarily—causal. Indeed our first condition for primary reasons (C1) is designed to help set rationalizations apart from other sorts of explanation. If rationalization is, as I want to argue, a species of causal explanation, then justification, in the sense given by C1, is at least one differentiating property. How about the other claim: that justifying is a kind of explaining, so that the ordinary notion of cause need not be brought in? Here it is necessary to decide what is being included under justification. Perhaps it means only what is given by C1: that the agent has certain beliefs and attitudes in the light of which the action is reasonable. But then something essential has certainly been left out, for a person can have a reason for an action, and perform the action, and yet this reason not be the reason why he did it. Central to the relation between a reason and an action it explains is the idea that the agent performed the action *because* he had the reason. Of course, we can include this idea too in justification; but then the notion of justification becomes as dark as the notion of reason until we can account for the force of that "because."

When we ask why someone acted as he did, we want to be provided with an interpretation. His behavior seems strange, alien, outré, pointless, out of character, disconnected; or perhaps we cannot even recognize an action in it. When we learn his reason, we have an interpretation, a new description of what he did which fits it into a familiar picture. The picture certainly includes some of the agent's beliefs and attitudes; perhaps also goals, ends, principles, general character traits, virtues or vices. Beyond this, the redescription of an action afforded by a reason may place the action in a wider social, economic, linguistic, or evaluative context. To learn, through learning the reason, that the agent conceived his action as a lie, a repayment of a debt, an insult, the fulfillment of an avuncular obligation, or a knight's gambit is to grasp the point of the action in its setting of rules, practices, conventions, and expectations.

Remarks like these, inspired by the later Wittgenstein, have been elaborated with subtlety and insight by a number of philosophers. And there is no denying that this is true: when we explain an action, by giving the reason, we do redescribe the action: redescribing the action gives the action a place in a pattern, and in this way the action is explained. Here it is tempting to draw two conclusions that do not follow. First, we can't infer, from the fact that giving reasons merely redescribes the action and that causes are separate from effects, that therefore reasons are not causes. Reasons, being beliefs and attitudes, are certainly not identical with actions; but, more important, events are often redescribed in terms of their causes. (Suppose someone was injured. We could redescribe this event "in terms of a cause" by saying he was injured.) Second, it is an error to think that, because placing the action in a larger pattern explains it, therefore we now understand the sort of explanation involved. Talk of patterns and contexts does not answer the question of how reasons explain actions, since the relevant pattern or context contains both reason and action. One way we can explain an event is by placing it in the context of its cause; cause and effect form the sort of pattern that explains the effect, in a sense of "explain" that we understand as well as any. If reason and action illustrate a different pattern of explanation, that pattern must be identified.

Let me urge the point in connection with an example of Melden's. A man driving an automobile raises his arm in order to signal. His intention, to signal, explains his action, raising his arm, by redescribing it as signaling. What is the pattern that explains the action? Is it the familiar pattern of an action done for a reason? Then it does indeed explain the action, but only because it assumes the relation of reason and action that we want to analyze. Or is the pattern rather this: the man is driving, he is approaching a turn; he knows he ought to signal; he knows how to signal, by raising his arm. And now, in this context, he raises his arm. Perhaps, as Melden suggests, if all this happens, he does signal. And the explanation would then be this: if, under these conditions, a man raises his arm, then he signals. The difficulty is, of course, that this explanation does not touch the question of why he raised his arm. He had a reason to raise his arm, but this has not been shown to be the reason why he did it. If the description "signaling" explains his action by giving his reason, then the signaling must be intentional; but, on the account just given, it may not be.

If, as Melden claims, causal explanations are "wholly irrelevant to the understanding we seek" of human actions (184) then we are without an analysis of the "because" in "He did it because . . . ," where we go on to name a reason. Hampshire remarks, of the relation between reasons and action, "In philosophy one ought surely to find this . . . connection altogether mysterious" (166). Hampshire rejects Aristotle's attempt to solve the mystery by introducing the concept of wanting as a causal factor, on the grounds that the resulting theory is too clear and definite to fit all cases and that "There is still no compelling ground for insisting that the word 'want' *must* enter into every full statement of reasons for acting" (168). I agree that the concept of wanting is too narrow, but I have argued that, at least in a vast number of typical cases, some pro attitude must be assumed to be present if a statement of an agent's reasons in acting is to be intelligible. Hampshire does not see how Aristotle's scheme can be appraised as true or false, "for it is not clear what could be the basis of assessment, or what kind of evidence could be decisive" (167). Failing a satisfactory alternative, the best argument for a scheme like Aristotle's is that it alone promises to give an account of the "mysterious connection" between reasons and actions.

IV

In order to turn the first "and" to "because" in "He exercised *and* he wanted to reduce and thought exercise would do it," we must, as the basic move,[5] augment condition C1 with:

C2. A primary reason for an action is its cause.

The considerations in favor of C2 are by now, I hope, obvious; in the remainder of this paper I wish to defend C2 against various lines of attack and, in the process, to clarify the notion of causal explanation involved.

[5] I say "as the basic move" to cancel the suggestion that C1 and C2 are jointly *sufficient* to define the relation of reasons to the actions they explain. I believe C2 can be strengthened to make C1 and C2 sufficient as well as necessary conditions, but here I am concerned only with the claim that both are, as they stand, necessary.

A. The first line of attack is this. Primary reasons consist of attitudes and beliefs, which are states or dispositions, not events; therefore they cannot be causes.

It is easy to reply that states, dispositions, and conditions are frequently named as the causes of events: the bridge collapsed because of a structural defect; the plane crashed on takeoff because the air temperature was abnormally high; the plate broke because it had a crack. This reply does not, however, meet a closely related point. Mention of a causal condition for an event gives a cause only on the assumption that there was also a preceding event. But what is the preceding event that causes an action?

In many cases it is not difficult at all to find events very closely associated with the primary reason. States and dispositions are not events, but the onslaught of a state or disposition is. A desire to hurt your feelings may spring up at the moment you anger me; I may start wanting to eat a melon just when I see one; and beliefs may begin at the moment we notice, perceive, learn, or remember something. Those who have argued that there are no mental events to qualify as causes of actions have often missed the obvious because they have insisted that a mental event be observed or noticed (rather than an observing or a noticing) or that it be like a stab, a qualm, a prick, or a quiver, a mysterious prod of conscience or act of the will. Melden, in discussing the driver who signals a turn by raising his arm, challenges those who want to explain actions causally to identify "an event which is common and peculiar to all such cases" (87), perhaps a motive or an intention, anyway "some particular feeling or experience" (95). But of course there is a mental event; at some moment the driver noticed (or thought he noticed) his turn coming up, and that is the moment he signaled. During any continuing activity, like driving, or elaborate performance, like swimming the Hellespont, there are more or less fixed purposes, standards, desires, and habits that give direction and form to the entire enterprise, and there is the continuing input of information about what we are doing, about changes in the environment, in terms of which we regulate and adjust our actions. To dignify a driver's awareness that his turn has come by calling it an experience, much less a feeling, is no doubt exaggerated, but whether it deserves a name or not, it had better be the reason why he raises his arm. In this case, and typically, there may not be anything we would call a motive, but if we mention such a general purpose as wanting to get to one's destination safely, it is clear that the motive is not an event. The intention with which the driver raises his arm is also not an event, for it is no thing at all, neither event, attitude, disposition, nor object. Finally, Melden asks the causal theorist to find an event that is common and peculiar to all cases where a man intentionally raises his arm, and this, it must be admitted, cannot be produced. But then neither can a common and unique cause of bridge failures, plane crashes, or plate breakings be produced.

The signaling driver can answer the question "Why did you raise your arm when you did?," and from the answer we learn the event that caused the action. But can an actor always answer such a question? Sometimes the answer will mention a mental event that does not give a reason: "Finally I made up my mind." However, there also seem to be cases of intentional action where we cannot explain at all why we acted when we did. In such cases, explanation in terms of primary reasons parallels the explanation of the collapse of the bridge from a structural defect: we are ignorant of the event or sequence of events that led up to (caused) the collapse, but we are sure there was such an event or sequence of events.

B. According to Melden, a cause must be "logically distinct from the alleged effect" (52); but a reason for an action is not logically distinct from the action; therefore, reasons are not causes of actions.[6]

One possible form of this argument has already been suggested. Since a reason makes an action intelligible by redescribing it, we do not have two events, but only one under different descriptions. Causal relations, however, demand distinct events.

Someone might be tempted into the mistake of thinking that my flipping of the switch caused my turning on of the light (in fact it caused the light to go on). But it does not follow that it is a mistake to take "My reason for flipping the switch was that I wanted to turn on the light" as entailing, in part, "I flipped the switch, and this action is further describable as having been caused by my wanting to turn on the light." To describe an event in terms of its cause is not to identify the event with its cause, nor does explanation by redescription exclude causal explanation.

The example serves also to refute the claim that we cannot describe the action without using words that link it to the alleged cause. Here the action is to be explained under the description: "my flipping the switch," and the alleged cause is "my wanting to turn on the light." What possible logical relation is supposed to hold between these phrases? It seems more plausible to urge a logical link between "my turning on the light" and "my wanting to turn on the light," but even here the link turned out, on inspection, to be grammatical rather than logical.

In any case there is something very odd in the idea that causal relations are empirical rather than logical. What can this mean? Surely not that every true causal statement is empirical. For suppose "A caused B" is true. Then the cause of B=A; so, substituting, we have "The cause of B caused B," which is analytic. The truth of a causal statement depends on *what* events are described; its status as analytic or synthetic depends on *how* the events are described. Still, it may be maintained that a reason rationalizes an action only when the descriptions are appropriately fixed, and the appropriate descriptions are not logically independent.

Suppose that to say a man wanted to turn on the light *meant* that he would perform any action he believed would accomplish his end. Then the statement of his primary reason for flipping the switch would entail that he flipped the switch—"straightway he acts," as Aristotle says. In this case there would certainly be a logical connection between reason and action, the same sort of connection as that between "It's water-soluble and was placed in water" and "It dissolved." Since the implication runs from description of cause to description of effect but not conversely, naming the cause still gives information. And, though the point is often overlooked, "Placing it in water caused it to dissolve" does not entail "It's water–soluble"; so the latter has additional explanatory force. Nevertheless, the explanation would be far more interesting if, in place of solubility, with its ob-

[6] This argument can be found, in one or more versions, in Kenny, Hampshire, and Melden, as well as in P. Winch, *The Idea of a Social Science*, London, 1958, and R. S. Peters, *The Concept of Motivation*, London, 1958. In one of its forms, the argument was of course inspired by Ryle's treatment of motives in *The Concept of Mind*.

vious definitional connection with the event to be explained, we could refer to some property, say a particular crystalline structure, whose connection with dissolution in water was known only through experiment. Now it is clear why primary reasons like desires and wants do not explain actions in the relatively trivial way solubility explains dissolvings. Solubility, we are assuming, is a pure disposition property: it is defined in terms of a single test. But desires cannot be defined in terms of the actions they may rationalize, even though the relation between desire and action is not simply empirical; there are other, equally essential criteria for desires—their expression in feelings and in actions that they do not rationalize, for example. The person who has a desire (or want or belief) does not normally need criteria at all—he generally knows, even in the absence of any clues available to others, what he wants, desires, and believes. These logical features of primary reasons show that it is not just lack of ingenuity that keeps us from defining them as dispositions to act for these reasons.

C. According to Hume, "we may define a cause to be an object, followed by another, and where all the objects similar to the first are followed by objects similar to the second." But, Hart and Honoré claim, "The statement that one person did something because, for example, another threatened him, carries no implication or covert assertion that if the circumstances were repeated the same action would follow" (52). Hart and Honoré allow that Hume is right in saying that ordinary singular causal statements imply generalizations, but wrong for this very reason in supposing that motives and desires are ordinary causes of actions. In brief, laws are involved essentially in ordinary causal explanations, but not in rationalizations.

It is common to try to meet this argument by suggesting that we do have rough laws connecting reasons and actions, and these can, in theory, be improved. True, threatened people do not always respond in the same way; but we may distinguish between threats and also between agents, in terms of their beliefs and attitudes.

[The suggestion is delusive, however, because generalizations connecting reasons and actions are not—and cannot be sharpened into—the kind of law on the basis of which accurate predictions can reliably be made.] If we reflect on the way in which reasons determine choice, decision, and behavior, it is easy to see why this is so. What emerges, in the *ex post facto* atmosphere of explanation and justification, as *the* reason frequently was, to the agent at the time of action, one consideration among many, *a* reason. Any serious theory for predicting action on the basis of reasons must find a way of evaluating the relative force of various desires and beliefs in the matrix of decision; it cannot take as its starting point the refinement of what is to be expected from a single desire. The practical syllogism exhausts its role in displaying an action as falling under one reason; so it cannot be subtilized into a reconstruction of practical reasoning, which involves the weighing of competing reasons. The practical syllogism provides a model neither for a predictive science of action nor for a normative account of evaluative reasoning.

Ignorance of competent predictive laws does not inhibit valid causal explanation, or few causal explanations could be made. I am certain the window broke because it was struck by a rock—I saw it all happen; but I am not (is anyone?) in command of laws on the basis of which I can predict what blows will break which windows. A generalization like "Windows are fragile, and fragile things tend to break when struck hard enough, other conditions being right" is not a predictive law in the rough—the predictive law, if we had it, would be quantitative and would use very different concepts. The generalization, like our generalizations about behavior, serves a different function: it provides evidence for the existence of a causal law covering the case at hand.

We are usually far more certain of a singular causal connection than we are of any causal law governing the case; does this show that Hume was wrong in claiming that singular causal statements entail laws? Not necessarily, for Hume's claim, as quoted above, is ambiguous. It may mean that "A caused B" entails some particular law involving the predicates used in the descriptions "A and B," or it may mean that "A caused B" entails that there exists a causal law instantiated by some true descriptions of A and B.[7] Obviously, both versions of Hume's doctrine give a sense to the claim that singular causal statements entail laws, and both sustain the view that causal explanations "involve laws." But the second version is far weaker, in that no particular law is entailed by a singular causal claim, and a singular causal claim can be defended, if it needs defense, without defending any law. Only the second version of Hume's doctrine can be made to fit with most causal explanations; it suits rationalizations equally well.

The most primitive explanation of an event gives its cause; more elaborate explanations may tell more of the story, or defend the singular causal claim by producing a relevant law or by giving reasons for believing such exists. But it is an error to think no explanation has been given until a law has been produced. Linked with these errors is the idea that singular causal statements necessarily indicate, by the concepts they employ, the concepts that will occur in the entailed law. Suppose a hurricane, which is reported on page 5 of Tuesday's *Times*, causes a catastrophe, which is reported on page 13 of Wednesday's *Tribune*. Then the event reported on page 5 of Tuesday's *Times* caused the event reported on page 13 of Wednesday's *Tribune*. Should we look for a law relating events of these *kinds*? It is only slightly less ridiculous to look for a law relating hurricanes and catastrophes. The laws needed to predict the catastrophe with precision would, of course, have no use for concepts like hurricane and catastrophe. The trouble with predicting the weather is that the descriptions under which events interest us—"a cool, cloudy day with rain in the afternoon"—have only remote connections with the concepts employed by the more precise known laws.

The laws whose existence is required if reasons are causes of actions do not, we may be sure, deal in the concepts in which rationalizations must deal. If the causes of a class of events (actions) fall in a certain class (reasons) and there is a law to back each singular causal statement, it does not follow that there is any law connecting events classified as reasons with events classified as actions—the classifications may even be neurological, chemical, or physical.

---

[7] We could roughly characterize the analysis of singular causal statements hinted at here as follows: "A caused B" is true if and only if there are descriptions of A and B such that the sentence obtained by putting these descriptions for "A" and "B" in "A caused B" follows from a true causal law. This analysis is saved from triviality by the fact that not all true generalizations are causal laws; causal laws are distinguished (though of course this is no analysis) by the fact that they are inductively confirmed by their instances and by the fact that they support counterfactual and subjunctive singular causal statements.

D. It is said that the kind of knowledge one has of one's own reasons in acting is not compatible with the existence of a causal relation between reasons and actions: a person knows his own intentions in acting infallibly, without induction or observation, and no ordinary causal relation can be known in this way. No doubt our knowledge of our own intentions in acting will show many of the oddities peculiar to first-person knowledge of one's own pains, beliefs, desires, and so on; the only question is whether these oddities prove that reasons do not cause, in any ordinary sense at least, the actions that they rationalize.

You may easily be wrong about the truth of a statement of the form "I am poisoning Charles because I want to save him pain," because you may be wrong about whether you are poisoning Charles—you may yourself be drinking the poisoned cup by mistake. But it also seems that you may err about your reasons, particularly when you have two reasons for an action, one of which pleases you and one which does not. For example, you do want to save Charles pain; you also want him out of the way. You may be wrong about which motive made you do it.

The fact that you may be wrong does not show that in general it makes sense to ask you how you know what your reasons were or to ask for your evidence. Though you may, on rare occasions, accept public or private evidence as showing you are wrong about your reasons, you usually have no evidence and make no observations. Then your knowledge of your own reasons for your actions is not generally inductive, for where there is induction, there is evidence. Does this show the knowledge is not causal? I cannot see that it does.

Causal laws differ from true but nonlawlike generalizations in that their instances confirm them; induction is, therefore, certainly a good way to learn the truth of a law. It does not follow that it is the only way to learn the truth of a law. In any case, in order to know that a singular causal statement is true, it is not necessary to know the truth of a law; it is necessary only to know that some law covering the events at hand exists. And it is far from evident that induction, and induction alone, yields the knowledge that a causal law satisfying certain conditions exists. Or, to put it differently, one case is often enough, as Hume admitted, to persuade us that a law exists, and this amounts to saying that we are persuaded, without direct inductive evidence, that a causal relation exists.[8]

E. Finally I should like to say something about a certain uneasiness some philosophers feel in speaking of causes of actions at all. Melden, for example, says that actions are often identical with bodily movements, and that bodily movements have causes; yet he denies that the causes are causes of the actions. This is, I think, a contradiction. He is led to it by the following sort of consideration: "It is futile to attempt to explain conduct through the causal efficacy of desire—all *that* can explain is further happenings, not actions performed by agents. The agent confronting the causal nexus in which such happenings occur is a helpless victim of all that occurs in and to him" (128, 129). Unless I am mistaken, this argument, if it were valid, would show that actions cannot have causes at all. I shall not point out the obvious difficulties in removing actions

---

[8] My thinking on the subject of this section, as on most of the topics discussed in this paper, has been greatly influenced by years of talk with Professor Daniel Bennett, now of Brandeis University.

from the realm of causality entirely. But perhaps it is worth trying to uncover the source of the trouble. Why on earth should a cause turn an action into a mere happening and a person into a helpless victim? Is it because we tend to assume, at least in the arena of action, that a cause demands a causer, agency an agent? So we press the question; if my action is caused, what caused it? If I did, then there is the absurdity of infinite regress; if I did not, I am a victim. But of course the alternatives are not exhaustive. Some causes have no agents. Primary among these are those states and changes of state in persons which, because they are reasons as well as causes, make persons voluntary agents.

① what is the action — the cause
② casual relationships + knowledge

CONDITIONALS

from ETHICA NICOMACHEA

Aristotle

. . .

Both the voluntary and the involuntary having been delimited, we must next
5 discuss choice; [1] for it is thought to be most closely bound up with virtue and
to discriminate characters better than actions do.

Choice, then, seems to be voluntary, but not the same thing as the voluntary;
the latter extends more widely. For both children and the lower animals share
in voluntary action, but not in choice, and acts done on the spur of the moment
we describe as voluntary, but not as chosen.

10 Those who say it is appetite or anger or wish or a kind of opinion do not seem
to be right. For choice is not common to irrational creatures as well, but appetite
and anger are. Again, the incontinent man acts with appetite, but not with
choice; while the continent man on the contrary acts with choice, but not with
15 appetite. Again, appetite is contrary to choice, but not appetite to appetite. Again,
appetite relates to the pleasant and the painful, choice neither to the painful nor
to the pleasant.

Still less is it anger; for acts due to anger are thought to be less than any others
objects of choice.

From Book III, Chapter 2, of "Ethica Nicomachea," *The Oxford Translation of Aristotle*, Vol. IX,
translated by W. D. Ross (Oxford, England: The Clarendon Press, 1963). Reprinted by permission of
the Clarendon Press, Oxford.

Line numbers have been retained for purposes of cross-referencing.

[1] Προαίρεσις is a very difficult word to translate. Sometimes "intention," "will," or "purpose"
would bring out the meaning better; but I have for the most part used "choice." The etymological
meaning is "preferential choice."

But neither is it wish, though it seems near to it; for choice cannot relate to   20
impossibles, and if any one said he chose them he would be thought silly; but
there may be a wish even for impossibles, e.g. for immortality. And wish may
relate to things that could in no way be brought about by one's own efforts,
e.g. that a particular actor or athlete should win in a competition; but no one   25
chooses such things, but only the things that he thinks could be brought about
by his own efforts. Again, wish relates rather to the end, choice to the means;
for instance, we wish to be healthy, but we choose the acts which will make us
healthy, and we wish to be happy and say we do, but we cannot well say we
choose to be so; for, in general, choice seems to relate to the things that are in our
own power.

For this reason, too, it cannot be opinion; for opinion is thought to relate to   30
all kinds of things, no less to eternal things and impossible things than to things
in our own power; and it is distinguished by its falsity or truth, not by its badness
or goodness, while choice is distinguished rather by these.

Now with opinion in general perhaps no one even says it is identical. But it   1112a
is not identical even with any kind of opinion; for by choosing what is good or
bad we are men of a certain character, which we are not by holding certain
opinions. And we choose to get or avoid something good or bad, but we have
opinions about what a thing is or whom it is good for or how it is good for him;
we can hardly be said to opine to get or avoid anything. And choice is praised   5
for being related to the right object rather than for being rightly related to it,
opinion for being truly related to its object. And we choose what we best know
to be good, but we opine what we do not quite know; and it is not the same
people that are thought to make the best choices and to have the best opinions,
but some are thought to have fairly good opinions, but by reason of vice to   10
choose what they should not. If opinion precedes choice or accompanies it, that
makes no difference; for it is not this that we are considering, but whether it is
identical with some kind of opinion.

What, then, or what kind of thing is it, since it is none of the things we have
mentioned? It seems to be voluntary, but not all that is voluntary [is] an object
of choice. Is it, then, what has been decided on by previous deliberation? At any   15
rate choice involves a rational principle and thought. Even the name seems to
suggest that it is what is chosen before other things.

．．．

CHOOSING

T. F. Daveney

1. INTRODUCTION

In this paper I am concerned to show what is involved when we choose something, or choose to do something. Part of what I have to say consists in an attack on the view that choosing is simply some kind of act; and this, I maintain, not only fails to do justice to the complexity of the concept, but also gives ground unnecessarily to the determinist. For if we hold that choosing is an act, we are unable at the same time to subscribe to the not uncommon view that the free act is one that is chosen. The reason is not far to seek. The act of choice itself, if free, must be the product of a further choice, and this further choice, if free, must be the product of yet another choice, and so *ad infinitum*. Such a conclusion is clearly untenable. My own explication of the concept, if it is valid, avoids this regress by showing that choice is not an act—or at least is not to be usefully described in this way. It would also follow that the statement "All choices are determined," is either innocuously true, or incomprehensible.

In the course of this article I examine three views on the nature of choosing: (1) That choosing is an action identifiable with the action chosen; [1] so that to say, "I chose to play cricket instead of golf," means, "I played cricket." (2) That choosing is an action, as far as choosing *objects* is concerned, but in the case of

From *Mind*, LXXIII (1964), 515–526. Reprinted by permission of the author and *Mind*.
[1] J. L. Evans, "Choice," *Philosophical Quarterly*, October 1955.

choosing *actions,* choosing is deciding.[2] (3) That choosing is, in all cases, the same as deciding, and is in fact the upshot of a process of deliberation.[3]

2. PRESUPPOSITIONS OF CHOOSING

In this section I discuss the presuppositions of choosing; that is to say, those conditions which require to be fulfilled for something to be correctly described as a choice.

1. There must be alternative courses open to the agent. If I take the one and only chocolate in the box, I cannot be said to have chosen it.

2. The agent must *know* that there are alternatives, and that the embracing of one involves the rejection of the others. If, for example, I *think* that there is only one chocolate in the box, when in fact there are more, I cannot be said to choose that chocolate in taking it.

3. I must believe that the alternatives are possible of attainment. I cannot choose between buying St. Paul's Cathedral or Westminster Abbey, if I am aware that these buildings are not for sale.

4. This condition, which is rather less obvious than the preceding three, I call the condition of aim or requirement. It is more easily seen if we consider cases in which an agent wants something, and considers a number of alternative means by which his want may be satisfied. The particular choice he makes can be seen as a fulfillment of a prior requirement, and it is this which guides his choice. For example, if it is my wish to arrive at a particular destination as quickly as possible, my choice of transport would be guided by this desire, and the choice I make would be comprehensible to others if it were explained in these terms. The requirement which my final selection satisfies acts as a principle of choice, and it is by reference to it that I choose the one alternative rather than the other. Let us consider a *prima facie* case of choice where this condition does not obtain. I pick up a stone from a heap on the beach, and say that I have chosen it. I am then asked what requirement the selection of this particular stone fulfills. I reply that there is not any requirement; I have chosen this stone, and I am going to take it home. Now this claim to have chosen the stone is very curious indeed. Normally it would be supposed that I had some aim that I wished to conceal; but failing this, it is surely nonsense.

A further point; of any choice it would seem possible to ask such questions as, "Was it good, bad, judicious, careless, stupid, thoughtful, etc.?" But they certainly would not be relevant in the above example. The point is that epithets such as these presuppose a criterion for judging the choice, and what criterion can there be apart from the choice's satisfying, or helping to satisfy, the agent's want?

It might be objected that on occasions when we are suddenly and unexpectedly confronted by a choice-situation, this condition of prior aim or requirement must surely be absent, simply because the alternatives thrust upon us are unforeseen. For example, I am offered, quite out of the blue, an attractive job in a foreign country, and I have to decide whether to take it or remain in my present post. What could be the aim that guides my present decision? In cases like these, the aim or requirement which the choice is judged to satisfy, becomes clear, and is

[2] P. H. Nowell-Smith, "Choosing, Deciding, Doing," *Analysis*, January 1958.
[3] W. D. Glasgow, "On Choosing," *Analysis*, June 1957.

adopted by the agent, in the process of reflecting on the alternatives. During the course of deliberation new features are discerned, consequences traced out in imagination, comparisons made, and disparate features pondered, *e.g.* large salary against alien environment. Finally the agent sees more or less clearly what it is he wants, and chooses that alternative which suits him best, or least ill, in the circumstances. But "suits us best" is only comprehensible in terms of what it is that we want, or want most, *vis-à-vis* the alternatives with which we are confronted. My choice to accept the foreign job is taken because, say, I come to see that what I really want is a large salary and scope for advancement, even when it has to be bought at the cost of desperately hard work and uprooting myself from a pleasant circle of friends. This view of the prior aim is reinforced by the consideration that afterwards, whatever my choice, it makes sense to ask, "What did you choose this course of action for? What did you have in mind when you chose in this way?" And these questions are answerable in terms of what the agent wanted in choosing as he did, and how his choice helped to achieve —more or less—what he wanted.

5. The alternative we choose is always considered that which suits us best. This is a familiar dictum of Socrates and Aristotle, and is understandable if we interpret it to mean that we always select what we consider to be the best alternative to realize some end we have in mind. It is this condition which differentiates choosing from merely seeking; for I cannot be said to choose, if I am merely looking for an object answering a certain description among a lot of other things.

To illustrate this distinction, suppose I am about to perform a certain operation in carpentry. The job can, I know, be done with any one of a number of tools, although not all the tools will do the job equally well. I pick the one that I think will do the job better than anything else, and my decision to use *this* one as the most suitable, and my rejection of all the others, is a genuine case of choosing. This is a different case from the one in which I merely look for a pair of long-nosed pliers among a heap of pliers on the bench. In choice I am guided by an end in view, and what is chosen is what I think will best bring about this end. I evaluate the alternatives in the light of my aim and select the best. And to say I select that which I think the best in these circumstances is to state a logical truth. For if my claim to have chosen what I considered to be the best alternative for the realization of an avowed end X, should be doubted, doubt is automatically cast on my profession that I intended X. It would then be natural for the doubter to impute to me some other aim more fitting to my choice. For example, let us suppose that Mr. Jones, to whom I owe a considerable sum of money, is leaving the country from a distant port. I profess that I am anxious to catch Mr. Jones before he leaves, in order to repay the debt. I therefore plan my route, which, I claim, will get me to Mr. Jones before he departs. Now suppose it is subsequently discovered that I have knowingly taken the longest and slowest route, *i.e.* that I have not taken the alternative which I judge best to achieve my professed aim; in this case serious doubts would be cast on my claim that I wanted to catch Mr. Jones before he leaves. We should almost certainly hold this view if we were Mr. Jones. My aim, it would be pointed out, had really been to avoid catching Mr. Jones, and the evidence put forward would be that the longest and slowest route was the best alternative for achieving the end of dodging payment. In other words, evidence for what the agent views as the best alternative, is evidence for the aim the agent wishes to achieve—logically. This is valid also for so-called "unconscious desires." "My dear fellow," says my friend, "I believe you when you say that you wanted to repay Mr. Jones, but I maintain that unconsciously there was a strong desire to bilk. You must have known that the shortest route to Liverpool was not via Bristol, and this lapse on your part argues an unconscious desire to arrive after the ship had departed. . . ."

I should like to consider an apparent objection to condition 5. Consider this example. Someone, anxious to perform a card trick, asks me to pick a card from a number lying on a table. I take one, or point one out. In these circumstances (a) I have no prior aim which my selection satisfies, and (b) as a consequence I cannot be said to have chosen the best alternative. Now I think that if the word "choice" can be used in these circumstances—and it seems to have an odd ring about it—then it is an extended use. It cannot be said that I chose carefully or carelessly, etc., and I cannot answer the question, "What did you choose that one for?" If I do give an answer to this question, then whatever it is, it will be construed in terms of some aim I had in mind which my selection best satisfies. For example, I might say, "It was the nearest." It will then be supposed that I had made up my mind to select that card which, say, caused me the least effort to pick up. If, however, there is no such aim which my selection satisfies, it would be more natural to describe an action such as this as *picking* a card rather than choosing a card.

3. CHOOSING AS BOTH DOING AND DECIDING

I should now like to examine the first of the three theories of choice mentioned in my introduction; that is the view that choosing is the same as *deciding*, if what is chosen is an action, but that it is *doing* in all other cases. What is chosen "in all other cases" would seem to be things. "I chose tea rather than coffee." "I chose the low road rather than the high road." The doing in these examples would presumably be drinking the tea, and walking along the road, or some such activity. Examples of choosing an action are, "I chose to walk home" and, "I chose to relinquish authority." These are to be taken as equivalent to, "I decided to walk home," and "I decided to relinquish authority."

Now in the first place the distinction seems to be a grammatical one—that is to say, if an infinitive follows "choose" then an *action* is chosen, and the choosing is deciding. On the other hand, if a substantive follows "choose," then a *thing* is chosen, and choosing is doing. However, it seems unlikely that this grammatical difference is based on a logical distinction. It is an easy matter to turn statements of the kind, "I chose to walk home rather than ride," into, "I chose the course of action which involved walking home." The infinitive becomes a substantive. But I think that the real objection is that we do not choose objects as such, but rather states of affairs in which objects feature; and it is these states of affairs which my choices commit me to bringing about. Thus, when I choose a house, this is to be understood in terms of my committing myself to some aim relating to the house, such as buying it, renting it, recommending it to a friend. This point may be brought out in the following way. Suppose I pick a certain flower in a meadow, and announce that I have chosen it. A friend remarks, "You are going to write a sonnet about it, or take it home to decorate a room?"

I reply, "No. I haven't chosen the flower for anything—there is nothing I am going to do with it. I have just chosen it, for it is possible to choose things, isn't it?" And I steadfastly refuse to agree that there is any state of affairs relating to the flower which I commit myself to in making the choice. My claim to have chosen it, in these circumstances, is meaningless and could only have been made by a person who thought that choosing a flower was an act on all fours with cutting it, smelling it, crushing it, and so on.

Quite frequently of course the context gives a clue to the kind of activity envisaged by the agent. If, on being confronted with a selection of drinks, I say, "I choose sherry," it would be understood that it is my intention to drink it—or if I am in a jolly mood, to pour it over someone's head, or something else. But in any case I aim at some state of affairs which involves the sherry. This of course follows from my view that choice is to be understood in terms of purpose, or end. The end of an envisaged action, or one that is actually being performed for that matter, can never be an object *per se*. Actions do not end in objects, but in states of affairs, or more actions. Briefly, then, it would seem that if it is not possible to choose objects as such, the view under consideration must be amended, *i.e.* all choosing is choosing actions or states of affairs, and choice consists in deciding to perform these actions, or bring about these states of affairs. This is almost the same as the third view mentioned in my introduction, and I will examine it later.

4. CHOOSING AS DOING

To say, "I chose to attend the meeting yesterday" (it is maintained), is to say, "I went to the meeting yesterday." The chief reason offered for this argument is that I cannot say, "I chose to go to the meeting, but didn't go." This is a contradiction. Now while agreeing that this is a contradiction, I maintain that the contradiction does not arise because choosing the action is the same as doing it. It arises because on those occasions when people use the past definite of "choose," in conjunction with an infinitive, *i.e.* I chose to do so and so, it is generally in answer to some such question as, "Did you have to do so and so, or did you choose to do it?" It is already implied in the question that the agent did the action, but what has to be settled is whether he did it under pressure, or because he merely wanted to. The emphasis falls on "chose." "I *chose* to go to the meeting." If one considers similar statements where the perfect or the pluperfect of "choose" is used, it becomes quite clear that the choosing is different from the doing. *Viz.* in the morning I say, "I have chosen to play cricket this afternoon," or, "I had chosen to play for the local team that afternoon, but something prevented me."

It may be argued that although the point I have made is valid, it is not generally valid, and that my objection holds only for those statements of choice where the action, so to speak, is taken for granted, and where the subject under consideration is whether it was performed because the agent felt so inclined, or because he had to. But, the argument continues; take a different case. "I chose the sherry rather than the beer." To add, "but I didn't take the sherry," is to contradict oneself, and this contradiction cannot be explained away in the fashion of the previous example. "I chose the sherry rather than the beer," is not about the fact that there was no compulsion or persuasion in my taking the sherry—

with the implied statement that I took it. I might take the sherry, which I find distasteful, under social pressure, and yet still be able to say truthfully, "I chose the sherry rather than the beer." It could be maintained, therefore, that as a consequence of this particular self-contradiction, *i.e.* "I chose the sherry rather than the beer, but I didn't take the sherry," "choosing the sherry" clearly means "taking it."

But this argument will not hold. The contradiction, if such it is, consists in announcing an intention, and then not carrying it out when the opportunity is present. It is rather like saying, "Ah! Here's Camden Town. Now I get out," and then not getting out. If I tell someone that yesterday I was offered sherry or beer, and chose sherry, then, in the absence of further information, it would be assumed that I took the sherry. If I added, "But I didn't take the sherry," then it would be assumed I had changed my mind. The point is, one just cannot say that choosing sherry is taking it, buying it, ordering it, or any other action one can think of. I can perform all these actions without choice entering into it. I might take, or buy, or order in contexts where there were no alternatives. It is no escape to say that the action should really be described as taking-the-sherry-rather-than-the-beer, thus implying the choice, because although there is an action called taking the sherry, there is no action, different in kind to this, called taking-the-sherry-rather-than-the-beer. Or if it is insisted that there is, then the difference can only be found in the intention of the agent, in the fact that he has made up his mind to take one to the exclusion of the other. In other words taking-the-sherry-rather-than-the-beer can only be understood in terms of the agent's having already made up his mind about one out of a number of alternatives confronting him.

I think there are two considerations which may have caused this error of identification of choice with action. Firstly there are what might be called "official" acts of choice. That is to say, there are situations in which a person will not be acknowledged to have chosen unless he performs some physical act. For example, if I receive my calling up papers, and I am instructed to tick off that branch of the forces I wish to serve with, unless I actually do the ticking, I will not—as far as the Ministry of Labour and National Service are concerned—have chosen. Yet it is plain I could already have made up my mind and just forgotten to tick.

The second consideration is more complex. Most of the choosing situations in which we find ourselves, involve some sort of physical act. For example, I choose the one red tie out of all the ties in the box. Now my decision in favor of the red tie might be cotemporal with my action of picking it up. And one might be tempted to suppose that the action actually constituted the choice, for any spectator apprised of the situation, could report that the choice was being made as soon as he saw my arm move. But of course the choice is not merely the picking up of the tie, as this is compatible with my having no choice at all. I might be carrying out a command, or taking the first thing to come to hand. Only if the spectator knows what I know about the alternatives, can he say, "And now he is choosing." Choice involves conscious acceptance and rejection, and no simple physical movement is equivalent to this. Nor could a mere movement take the place of the agent's judging that *this* was the best alternative in the circumstances.

5. CHOOSING AS DECIDING

According to this view, choice is the same as decision and decision is the upshot of a process of deliberation. Now although I think it is true to say that if I choose an object or an action, I also decide upon that object, or decide to do that action, it does not follow that choice and decision are to be identified. The following example makes this clear: "The instant I awoke, I decided to get up." Now it would be odd to describe this as a choice, for consider how curious it would sound if someone were to say, "A praiseworthy choice," or ask, "Was it a difficult choice?" The word "decide," in this context, merely means "determine," or "resolve." That fact that I made up my mind as soon as I awoke, shows that my decision did not involve passing alternatives under review, neither did it involve a previous state of indecision; yet these conditions must surely obtain if deliberation occurs. In one sense, then, decision is neither identifiable with choice, nor is it necessarily the product of deliberation.

However, the question arises whether choice itself, as a subclass of decision, always involves deliberation; and if this is the case, whether choice is the upshot of such a process. Now it seems to me that if deliberation consists in examining, comparing, and evaluating alternatives in the light of a general aim, and such deliberation is a process which endures for a certain time, then there are cases of choice where the *process* seems to be absent. The skilled carpenter does not necessarily deliberate about the tool best suited to a job that confronts him. He may choose without any preliminary brooding. Of course, he knows what it is that he wants, he also knows the alternatives with which he is confronted, and further, that the selection of one involves the rejection of all the others. He also believes that the particular choice he makes is best fitted to fulfill his want. Now if it is maintained that such knowledge and belief constitute minimal deliberation, I should not be inclined to argue the point. However, I think that deliberation of this kind can be distinguished from the self-conscious business of examining, comparing, and evaluating alternatives. The latter is a process in time, the former is having certain knowledge and holding a belief.

But having made this point, it is nevertheless important to recognize that in the example cited a transition from a state of indecision to one of decision has taken place, and that this transition occurred *at* a time, but not *for* a time. Because of this, the decision might be termed a culmination or upshot, although I think it is important to recognize that it is not the upshot of a temporal process. Perhaps the case could be likened to someone's solving a problem the instant it is presented to him. The solution could be termed an upshot, but there need not be implied any enduring activity, such as thinking it out, of which it is the culmination.

A further point which substantiates my view, although it is not, I think, a conclusive argument, is the logical possibility of sentences of the type, "Without deliberating I took the short cut across the meadow, rather than the long way round by road."

6. DELIBERATION AND CHOICE

The relationship between deliberation and choice, I think, can be explained in this way. One begins with the logically prior condition of aim; *e.g.* I decide to buy a motor car. But not just any car, for if this were the case, no choice would be involved. It must be a car answering certain requirements, and I say "answering certain requirements" advisedly, for if I could describe the car in terms of features it objectively possesses, *viz*. black saloon, 1500 cc., five-seater, the process of looking over a number of cars would merely amount to seeking, not choosing. My requirements, naturally enough, would be couched in subjective terms, *e.g.* soberly attractive (according to my lights), sufficiently roomy (using my criterion for what is roomy), easily maintained (I am the sole judge of what is easy maintenance), etc. Now deliberation consists in observing such objective features as black, saloon, 1500 cc. AND JUDGING WHETHER THEY FIT MY REQUIREMENTS. When I have discovered the car which seems to me to be most suitable, my choice is made. So deliberation is really a process of discovery which involves not only observing the objective features of objects, but also judging whether these features are fitting in relation to something that is wanted. It is in this sense that our choices are guided by some prior aim. All this fits neatly into an adaptation of Aristotle's practical syllogism.

(1) "I have made up my mind to buy a car for such and such purposes.
(2) *This* car best satisfies my requirements.
(3) Therefore (logically) I choose this.
(4) Therefore (logically) I will buy it."
(5) And I buy it.

(3) follows from (1) and (2), but we have to make allowance for the case in which none of the selections offered comes up to the minimum standard, and *all* are rejected. In this case (2) would read, "This car is the best of the lot, but it is just not good enough." No choice follows. (4) follows from (1), (2), and (3), because I have already stated that I will buy a car answering to certain requirements; and this car, since it is suitable, I commit myself to buying. The point here is that "choosing the car" in this case is just, "choosing the car to buy." My intention to buy the car gives meaning to the choice. Failure to commit myself after I had made my selection would imply a last minute change of mind.

To sum up, choosing consists in making up one's mind with regard to a particular object, action or state of affairs, in a context of alternatives, and the particular choice is made in the light of best fulfilling some aim or requirement the agent has in mind—in the sense that if the agent "chose" something, but claimed that no requirement or aim was fulfilled, we would conclude that he was either talking nonsense, or concealing his aim.

7. CHOICE AND DETERMINISM

In conclusion I should like to relate this exposition of choice to the hypothesis that all choices are determined. Now clearly, if what I have said about the nature of choosing is valid, there is a sense in which any particular choice is determined by the consideration that it best satisfies some aim entertained by the agent. In other words, if I want an attractive, hardwearing, and comfortable pair of shoes, and after due deliberation, make a selection, my choice is clearly determined by my judging that the pair in question best suits my purposes. But to say my selection is determined in this way is merely to make the logical point that it would be impossible for me to choose *other than* what I think best suits my purposes, in this, or any, choice-situation. But is anyone likely to be much bothered by the view that considerations of suitability to aims often determine what we do?

Of course the thesis could be interpreted as meaning that because other factors are at work, the prior aim or requirement has no part to play in determining choice. After all, without this particular condition obtaining, we cut loaves, drive cars, write letters; so why can we not just choose this or that object? But this is nonsense, as the case of choosing the stone shows, and only someone who thought that choosing was an act analogous to writing, driving, or cutting, could be misled in this way.

A third interpretation of the deterministic hypothesis is that all our deliberations are shadow play and are never efficacious in guiding us to that object which best satisfies our requirement. We select, and deliberation is really no more than going through the motions of choice. There are two points about this position.

1. If it is agreed, as I think it must be, that choice has as a necessary condition the prior requirement, then to say deliberation is shadow play is to commit oneself to the view that whenever a choice satisfies a requirement, it is purely fortuitous. Deliberation, because it is inefficacious, cannot guide us, and our choice is the result of whatever forces bind our action. But would not this be stretching our credulity to breaking point? It hardly seems plausible that all those purposes which are fulfilled daily by our choices, should be fulfilled purely by blind chance.

2. A different form of the same argument is that we choose, and then invent reasons for our choice. But this falls to an earlier objection. Unless choice is seen as fulfilling a prior requirement, it is not choice—at best it is picking out, and this alone does not constitute choice. Would the determinist go so far as to hold, then, that there is no such thing as choice, only picking out? If he does, he is hardly worth following.

I think that the reason why this question about the causation of choice has ever arisen, is because of the supposition that choice is some kind of act, and if choice is an act it may seem plausible to some to ask if it is caused. In this paper I have given what I consider to be strong reasons for supposing that choice is not some sort of doing, although things like picking up a tie or nodding at a car and saying "That one," may be contingently involved. If it is held that "making up one's mind" is an act, I would not contend for the word. What is important are the conditions in which "making up one's mind" occur; conditions which are notably absent in other acts.

If these arguments are valid, depending as they do on my own view of the nature of choice, the problem of determinism should be shifted from choosing to the wanting which lies behind. The question then becomes, "What makes us want, or aim at, the things we do want, or do aim at?" and not, "What makes us choose the things we do choose?" But this is quite another point.

RULE-FOLLOWING

ACTION

A. I. Melden

. . .

II

If one considered the question "What is a chess move?" it is easy to see that each of the kinds of answers considered and rejected in the preceding section will not do at all. It may be, when I move my chess piece during a game, that all that happens is that my fingers push a piece from one square to another. As long as we confine our attention to bodily and psychological processes, there may be nothing to distinguish a chess move from the mere change of position of chess men resulting from an infant's random movements. And, clearly, the appeals to absence of compulsion (but consider the many sorts of moves called "forced"), to "could have beens," "would have beens," and even to the use of elaborate disjunctive functions, such as we considered in the preceding section, would be greeted with amusement. Nevertheless, to make a move in a game of chess is after all to engage in a bodily movement of some sort, so whatever else one is doing in saying that a move was made, is one not saying that a certain bodily movement took place? And, similarly, in the case of other actions, is it not a part of what one is saying, in saying that an action has taken place, that certain relevant movements of fingers, arms or legs, and so on, have occurred? Plausible as this may be, it is in my opinion mistaken.

From *The Philosophical Review*, LXV (1956), 529–541. Reprinted by permission of the author and *The Philosophical Review*.

1. If there were such a so-called descriptive component, then in order that I might know what I was doing in any given case, I would need to know what bodily movements took place, and this I could know only by observing my own movements. But if someone asks me, "Do you know what you have done?" the affirmative answer I give is in no way predicated upon any observation I may have made of my bodily movements. If my answer is in error (I gave the clerk a five, instead of a one, dollar bill), the error is not one of observation. When I do something and know what I am doing, it is not that I observe myself in action, and if I were to watch my arms, legs, and so on as I performed many of the familiar actions in which I engage, I would very likely fumble. But even when I take care in what I do, it is not that I observe my bodily movements and guide them as I would my child's movements as she learns to write, ride a bicycle, or skate. If someone were to say to me reproachfully, "You did not watch what you were doing" as I drove my car, he would not be reproaching me for failing to observe my bodily movements, nor would he be urging me to watch them if he were to say, "Watch what you are doing!"

2. Consider third-person statements. Unless A had engaged in a bodily movement of some sort, he could not have done what he did, and unless I had used my eyes in observing what had gone on, I could not have described his action as I did. But from this it does not follow that in describing A's action I am describing his bodily movements. For there are descriptions and descriptions, the physiologist's descriptions of muscle movements, my descriptions of the movements of arms and legs, and our familiar descriptions of actions—passing the salt hastily, paying one's bill distastefully, and so forth. To say that John paid his bill distastefully is not to say two things, one of which is that his body moved in a certain way, any more than to say the latter is to assert in part at least that such-and-such muscles were brought into operation. And because the latter must be true if his arms and legs moved as they did, it simply does not follow that in offering my description of the bodily movement, I am, among other things, offering a physiological description of what took place. But there is just as much reason for saying this as for saying that a third-person action statement is a blend of diverse things, one of which is a descriptive component about the occurrence of a bodily movement.

The truth is that in saying as we do that A paid his bill, performed the castling maneuver, or passed the salt to his companion, we are in no way interested in the minutiae of bodily movements that may have taken place, just as one interested in the movements of arms, legs, and fingers, e.g., a dancer, may be sublimely ignorant of the physiological and biochemical changes that take place. Consider the example of the chess move. One who knows no chess may see only the movements of arms and fingers as odd-shaped objects are moved about on a checkered surface; one who knows the game may see a given offensive or defensive move taking place. The former simply does not know what takes place during the game, and the latter, far from offering a description that overlaps the former's curious description of what takes place, is saying something radically different in character.

3. But suppose a statement describing an action were a blend of diverse items, one being a description of a bodily movement. How must this "descriptive component" be supplemented in order that we may be provided with the force of a

statement about an action? It will be apparent that the attempt to provide a supplement by means of another "descriptive" statement, to the effect that the movement is voluntary, chosen, and so forth, must lead to one of two consequences. Either the crucial term (e.g., "voluntary," "chosen," "motivated") is much too restrictive or it is too broad, or if no change in the application of the term "action" is to ensue, a shift must be made in the use of the crucial term (e.g., voluntary) and all of the puzzles about action reappear once more in connection with this new usage. If, however, the supplementation is to be made by means of disguised contrary-to-fact conditionals, the same dilemma faces us in a new guise. It will not do to say, for example, that an action which took place is a certain kind of bodily movement that could have been other than what it was in the sense in which any physical occurrence could have been other than what it was, or in the sense appropriate to the familiar remark that a conscientious agent could not have acted otherwise. The sense of "could have been" required for the present purpose is just that sense involved in saying that the bodily movement counts as an action; but this does not help us.

It should not surprise us in view of these results to encounter even more drastic proposals. It has been agreed that the concept of an action is "fundamentally nondescriptive," [1] and among those to whom this proposal seems only to generate new paradoxes, it would not be unreasonable to expect to find representatives of the indefinability thesis. It would be dangerous to generalize, but the appearance of this familiar triad of theories is due to a familiar mistake—the failure to attend to the relevant context in which expressions have a use. The pattern of thought is as follows: "Actions are happenings. Statements describing actions are true or false. What happens is always some bodily movement and need be nothing more than this. Hence, whatever else a statement about an action may do, it describes such a movement." The underlying mistake is that what occurs when an action is performed can be understood independently of its context and hence need only be a bodily movement. How this is so I want to illustrate by reference to the analogous problem of the nature of a chess move.

III

Consider the relatively artificial situation in which a chess move is made. Here there is an obvious change of context from the ordinary situation in which conduct occurs. There is little temptation to define a chess move in terms of bodily and psychological phenomena or to argue that the concept is "nondescriptive" or "indefinable." The concept is obviously social in character, logically connected with the concept of rules. How does this connection with the notion of rules enable us to distinguish between the random movements of an infant pushing chess pieces about on a checkered board and the chess moves of players? I want to argue that this distinction is intelligible only by reference to the notion of *following* or *observing* the given rules.

Central to the concept of a rule is the idea of obeying or following it. The notion of disobeying is dependent upon the more fundamental idea of obeying. Infants who push chess pieces about on a chessboard do not disobey or violate the rules

[1] Cf. H. L. A. Hart, "The Ascription of Responsibility and Rights," in *Proceedings of the Aristotelian Society* (1948–1949). Although Hart does not discuss the relation between action and bodily movement, he seems to regard the term "descriptive" as properly applicable to bodily movements.

of chess—they do not play chess at all. A chess player may violate the rule only after he has learned to obey. Without obedience there can be no disobedience, just as without the telling of the truth there can be no lying. Further, a rule is no mere statement which we can understand independently of the practice that is the obeying or the following of the rule. To understand the rule is to understand the kind of thing that would be obeying it, and it is only because we have followed or obeyed rules that any statement of a new rule, one we have not so far learned to follow, is intelligible. Again, to follow or obey a rule is not to repeat to oneself what the rule requires, reflect upon the situation in which one finds oneself in order to determine that it is one to which the rule applies, and then decide to obey it. Such an account, if it were true, would only serve to create a doubt that the person in question had learned the rule, for at best it could only describe the learner's fumbling, hesitating procedure.[2] Once we have learned the rules, we do not interpret the rule to apply to the given situation and follow this with a decision to obey—we simply obey.[3] And if in any given situation we choose to disobey, such choice is only parasitic upon the general practice in which no choice is exercised at all. Finally, obeying a rule is not something that can occur only once.[4] I do not mean that there may not be such a thing as a new rule which is such that only one occasion arises to which it applies and such that after it has been obeyed only once it is then set aside. If such a case should ever arise, it would happen only because one had already learned what rules were in other situations and in learning these rules had engaged in the practice of obeying them. The point is that to obey a rule is to acquire a custom, habit, practice, and if only one instance suffices, this is owing to the derivative function of habits established with respect to other rules. Again, this is not to say that every instance of acting from habit or custom is a case of obeying a rule. "This is our practice," "this is what we do," need only express the things we do *as a rule*, in general, and through social habit, not the things we do in *following a rule*. Nevertheless, the familiar cases of obeying a rule are the cases in which the agent has acquired a habit, practice, custom—that way of thinking and doing that characterizes the man who knows his way about in situations by following the relevant rules. We need, therefore, to distinguish between the case in which what someone does *accords* with the rule and the case in which someone *follows* the rule. A child may push a piece called "the knight" from one square on a chessboard to another in such a way that what it does accords with the rule governing the piece, but in reporting this fact we need only observe the single item of behavior of the child. In saying of a child that it followed the rule, much more is at stake, namely, the question whether the child has learned the rules of the game (including the one concerning the knight) and in doing so has acquired the specific way of thinking and doing which is the playing of chess.

To attempt to understand a move in a game of chess in terms of bodily and psychological processes occurring at the time the agent makes his move is to

---

[2] Compare this account of obeying a rule with Prichard's account in "Duty and Ignorance of Fact," of coming to "know" that one has a duty. It is small wonder that in Prichard's account every claim that one has obeyed the rule is only problematical.

[3] See Wittgenstein's profoundly illuminating remarks in *Philosophical Investigations* on obeying rules, especially in § 219, "When I obey a rule, I do not choose, I obey *blindly*."

[4] Cf. Wittgenstein, *op. cit.*, § 199.

leave out what is essential to the move—the fact that what transpires in the way of such occurrent processes is a case of following the rules. Similarly, to attempt to understand the concept of a chess player in terms of occurrent psychological processes, the order of percepts, or some presumed psychical substance is once more to ignore that feature of the agent that consists in the fact that he has learned by repeated doings and hence has acquired the practice of acting as he does. In both cases the circumstances in which the bodily and psychological processes occur are crucial; for what makes the bodily movement a case of a move is the fact that movement of the piece on the board is a case of following a rule, and what makes the agent a chess player is that he has acquired that custom or practice—that way of thinking and doing—that characterizes those who follow the rules of chess. Chess player and chess move are thus correlative notions, and neither can be understood in terms of processes, bodily or psychological, viewed in isolation from the rules that have been learned and the characteristic ways of thinking and doing thereby achieved. Hence it is not that a piece has been pushed from one square to another that constitutes a chess move but that the bodily movement is that of an agent who, during the course of a game, exhibits the characteristic practice in thinking and doing that he has acquired. For someone who does not know what it is to make a move in a game, no report of what transpires at the times the moves were made would make any sense at all, and, observe as he would, such a being would have *no* idea of what was going on. For someone who knew no chess but did know what it was to follow the rules of *some* game, the reports of such activities would be understood only in the most fragmentary way; he might know that a game was being played but would not know what was going on. It is only because we ourselves have acquired that practice of following the rules of chess—the characteristic custom of doing things on a chessboard in a way that we understand because we share it with others who play chess—that the reports of a game are understood by us and recognized as true or false. The significance of the utterances we employ in reporting the activities on a chessboard is thus dependent upon the fact that we share with those involved in these activities the practices, in Wittgenstein's felicitous phrase, the form of life, of those who follow certain rules in the social transaction that is the playing of a game of chess.

Without this practice of obeying the rules, what we see is merely bodily movement. With it, we see this movement as a chess move, for we treat the physical movement made as a move in the play that takes place, and in our doing so, the physical movement that occurs takes on a wholly new aspect. It is because we supply this practical context of acquired skill that we can understand the descriptive accounts of those who report to us the progress of a game; without it such accounts are unintelligible.

All this may be granted; but it will be objected that a chess move is only one very special kind of action. We act in all sorts of ways, even in sweeping the chessmen off the board, thus bringing the play to an abrupt end. With this I should certainly agree, but the case of the chess move is nonetheless important, for the very artificiality of the example may serve to remind us of what is too easily forgotten in the case of other types of action, namely, the crucial importance of the practical context of common or shared practices involved in following rules, applying criteria, observing principles, acting on policies, and so on. Actions do constitute a whole family of cases, but in various respects this practical context is essential to an understanding of the distinction between a bodily movement and an action. *Observer?*

IV

Consider some of the things we commonly do: we purchase food, drive automobiles, play, work, help and hinder our fellows. In all such activities, we have learned by imitating or following the instructions of others in obeying rules, employing criteria, following policies in the practices in which we engage. Thus in purchasing food our selection is guided by criteria for excellence, ripeness, and so on, and in paying for the items selected, our behavior is guided by various criteria and rules governing the use of currency. We act in such instances without reflection precisely because we have acquired the requisite skills. Or consider the enormously complex set of practices acquired by those driving their automobiles through traffic, responding to a variety of cues—the condition of the road surface, the sound of the motor, the presence of pedestrians and vehicles blocking the way, the signals of other motorists, the road signs, the traffic lights, and the instructions of the traffic police. In this complex set of practices we may recognize the observance of rules, the application of criteria, the response to instructions, the following of policies of safe, economical, or efficient driving, and so on. These practices are supplemented by other complicating and even supervening practices. One may drive an automobile in order to make up one's mind whether to purchase it or in order to test it, and throughout one will be guided in general in one's thinking and doing by the observance of moral rules and principles. It is not that there are practices and practices, each independent of the other, so that at one time one is driving an automobile, at another making a purchase, at another responding to the moral requirements of the situation. It is rather that we have a blending of the practices we have acquired, in the activities in which we engage, where various practices are themselves affected by the general practice of observing moral rules and principles. It is this ability to carry out a complex and organized set of practices in which throughout the agent is guided without reflection by moral rules that marks the achievement of responsibility. Even in the relatively artificial case of a chess move, what takes place when the move is made has to be understood in terms of the practice of observing not only the rules of chess but also those of good conduct and good manners, for these are involved in the agent's way of thinking and doing.

It is equally important to bear in mind the enormous difference between the permissive rules of chess and the prescriptive and justifying rules of morality, between the justification of the rules of traffic and the justification of the rules of morality, between the inevitable conflicts of rules (and the resulting exceptions) in the field of morality and the occasional predicament that may arise when the ill-formed rules of a game are discovered to be in conflict. Understanding a moral rule does involve understanding the kind of cases which may be excepted, but there cannot be any exception to the rules governing the movement of the knight in chess. These differences are so important that it is misleading to speak of the term "rule" as univocal.

One more comment on important differences: If I do not play chess, I shall not understand what a chess player does as his fingers push a piece from one square to another, but if I do not drive a car, it does not follow that I am incapable of knowing what someone at the wheel is doing when I see his arm pulling at the handbrake. Here we need to recall the reference made earlier to the derivative effects of the mastery of rules in order to see that this difference, important as it is, is no objection to the general contention. For the practices we share with others need not coincide precisely, indeed they cannot if there is to be diversity in the activities of individuals, but there must be enough similarity between the practices involved in different activities in order to allow for an understanding of one kind of activity which derives from the practice involved in another. Where there is no such similarity, as in the case of one who has never seen or heard of any game or as in the case of a bushman who has never seen or heard of machines of any sort, there is no understanding of what is being done, no matter how carefully attention is paid by such individuals to the bodily movements of agents when they engage, respectively, in games of chess or in the driving of automobiles.[5]

It is impossible within the limits of this paper to guard against all of the misunderstandings to which the analogy I wish to draw between chess moves and other actions may give rise. Briefly, I am maintaining that just as in the case of the concept of a chess move, so in the case of the concept of any action the context of practices in which rules are obeyed, criteria [are] employed, policies are observed—a way of thinking and doing—is essential to the understanding of the difference between such bodily movements and actions. Just as this way of thinking and doing marks in the one case the chess player, so it marks in the other the responsible agent, one who has acquired a complex of practices, among others the practice of observing moral rules and principles. The concepts "action" and "moral agent" or "person" are thus correlative.[6] Because we share so largely in our ways of thinking and doing, because in particular we are guided by moral rules and principles, we treat each other's bodily movements as actions, items of behavior for which the agent is responsible. Just as we supply a background of skills in understanding the bodily behavior of those engaged in playing chess, so we supply a complex background of skills in which rules are obeyed, criteria are employed, policies are observed, and so on, in understanding each other's behavior as action. This practical context—our common form of life—is crucial to our understanding. Without it we notice only bodily movements, and with it we see actions as we observe each other's behavior. Without it we employ the cool language of those who like coroners and physiologists are concerned to describe and explain bodily movements and effects, and with it we are enabled to participate in the use of discourse by which we impute responsibility to individuals when we treat them as persons or moral agents and their bodily movements as actions.

But this, it will be objected, is in effect to succumb to the philosophic vice of

---

[5] It is for this reason that anthropologists often need to enter into the practices of primitive tribes in order to understand their activities, their language—in short, their culture.

[6] Locke wisely rejects any attempt to define "person" in terms of ideas and an underlying immaterial substance. The concept, he tells us, is forensic and applies "only to intelligent agents capable of a law" and hence "concerned and accountable" (*Essay*, bk. II, ch. xxvii, sec. 26). It is this same correlativity of voluntary bodily behavior (i.e., action) and moral agent that leads Aristotle to remark about the individual whose unfortunate action was done by reason of ignorance that the terms "voluntary" and "involuntary" should not be applied to him in the event he does not repent, since such a being is a different sort of man and "should have a name of his own" (*Nicomachean Ethics*, 1110b).

generalizing from very special cases—those actions performed in the social arena for which agents may be praised or blamed, such as cheating or dealing honestly in making purchases and driving with care or with unconcern for the safety of others. The very language employed for such conduct implies that the individuals referred to or treated are responsible moral agents and subject to praise or blame for what they do. But there are other cases of action, surely, with respect to which a specifically moral way of thinking and doing, the practice of observing moral rules, seems altogether out of bounds, so that the alleged correlativity of the terms "moral agent" and "person" is only evidence of unrestrained generalization from very special cases. My concluding remarks are directed at this objection.

In order to understand the concept of an action, we need to see how sentences in which typical action verbs are employed are used. Admittedly there is no single use. Some sentences are employed in praising or blaming (e.g., "He did it" uttered accusingly or "He *did* it" uttered exultingly by one watching a heroic rescue). Some sentences are employed with a view to determining whether blame is appropriate but where no blaming may actually occur (as in the hearings held in courts or during legislative fact-finding inquiries). Again, we may speak of actions where no verdict is anticipated, moral or legal. If my wife relates to me the various things she saw my neighbor doing, she might do so with a view to supporting the low opinion in which she holds him, but, equally, she may do so in order to make conversation or because she knows me to have a friendly interest in my neighbor's activities. And in giving me this information or in describing to me how he behaved, is she not speaking of just the sort of thing for which in appropriate circumstances any neighbor *can* be praised or blamed, action in the present sense of the term? For consider the remarks appropriate to such employments by my wife of sentences about the activities of my neighbor: "What on earth is he up to?" "I hope he will not leave the hole there; children may fall into it and hurt themselves," and so on. In reporting or describing as she does the actions of my neighbor, my wife does *not* employ the neutral language of those concerned to relate or describe bodily movements. It is rather to treat the bodily movements that did occur as behavior of a responsible agent, to impute to him not only the practices of those who have learned by imitation, following instructions, and so forth the ways in which tools are employed and activities of various sorts conducted but also the general practice of attending to the interests and well-being of others. If we consider the remarks appropriate to such employments of action sentences and contrast them with those appropriate to the behavior of lunatics, infants, and wild animals, it becomes clear that such normal uses of action sentences risk defeat on two quite distinct grounds: First, on learning that the individual engaged in the observed bodily movements is not responsible or morally competent and second, on learning that the alleged bodily movements did not occur (e.g., it was really someone else). For in such normal uses of action sentences, we ascribe responsibility to the individuals in question by treating the bodily behavior as action, and this we do by viewing it against the background of a set of practices, among others the practice of observing moral rules and principles. In short, we impute to the individual our common moral form of life.

There are cases, of course, in which sentences are employed in describing the behavior of our fellows and in which there is no ascription of responsibility. I have already mentioned the language of coroners and physiologists, in which a position of neutrality is taken with respect to the responsibility of the individual. But in what sorts of cases of an admittedly responsible agent would the question of common practices including that of observing moral rules be irrelevant? Would it be a case in which the individual raises his arm? But in that case we must not describe what the individual does as signaling, saluting, leading others in physical exercise drill, and so on. For these descriptions at once bring us within the social arena in which common forms of life have been achieved and by reference to which action statements can be understood and bodily movements treated as actions. No, we shall even have to deny that in raising his arm the individual was even pretending to engage in these activities, exercising, following the instructions of his physician, and so on. We shall have to rest content with the statement that he was simply raising his arm and never mind any further queries. But in that case, when the individual raises his arm what happens is that a bodily movement, not an action, occurs.

RESPONSIBILITY

RESPONSIBILITY AND ACTION

Kurt Baier

We ordinarily take it for granted that most adults are normal and that all normal adults are responsible for their actions. Yet, there are powerful arguments to show i) that responsibility is incompatible with determinism, since if determinism is true, no one can act differently from the way he does; but ii) that responsibility is also incompatible with indeterminism, since if human actions are not caused at all, not even by the agent, then no one is responsible for them; and iii) that there is no third alternative. In the face of these difficulties, philosophers have adopted a bewildering variety of solutions. We may divide them into two main groups. "Conservatives" (as I shall call them) uphold the legitimacy of ascribing to normal human beings responsibility for their actions. They then attempt to show that responsibility is compatible with determinism, with indeterminism, with either, or that there is a third possibility, e.g., agent-causation.[1] "Revisionists" argue for the illegitimacy of ascribing to any human being responsibility for any of his actions and advocate the abolition of the concept and all practices based on it. It seems to me that most of the difficulties in this field are due to an inadequate understanding of the concept of responsibility. I shall attempt, in the first section, to describe and sketch the justification of a social practice, which I call "bringing people to account," in the context of which ascriptions of responsibility are typically made. (I shall further sketch the other practices presupposed by the

Reprinted by permission of the author.
[1] Cf. R. M. Chisholm, "Freedom and Action," *Freedom and Determinism*, ed. Keith Lehrer (New York: Random House, 1966), p. 11.

practice of bringing people to account, and enumerate the assumptions we must make about life in society if the practice of bringing people to account is to be justified.) I shall then set out the various claims which can be made with the word "responsible" and the logical or linguistic relations which obtain between them. In the second and third sections, I shall examine the implications which a justifiable practice of bringing people to account and the ascription to people of responsibility for something, have for the idea of determinism, and the concept of action.

I

1.) The following outline of the activity of bringing people to account is a rational reconstruction of our present practices. The principle underlying this reconstruction is twofold: to assign to the practice a purpose which can justify it, and to exhibit its chief characteristics as at least conducive to that purpose.

Bringing people to account is a social practice which has three consecutive and connected phases or stages. First comes the determination whether anyone, and if so who, has broken one of the relevant obligatory social rules or directives. If the outcome is negative, the process comes to an end. If it is positive, then the next move is to ascertain whether the person has an excuse, that is, an exculpatory explanation why he broke the rule. If he has an excuse, the investigation ends. But if he has no excuse, we enter the third phase, the imposition on him of one or other of three main types of unwanted treatment: the infliction of a penalty, that is, some intrinsically undesirable treatment previously affixed to such breaches of a social rule as he has been found guilty of; the expression of condemnation; and where the breach of the rule has resulted in harm or damage to someone, the imposition of the task of repairing the harm or damage done or of paying compensation for it.

Bringing people to account can thus be construed as a composite of three component practices, each with its own purpose or purposes. Fixing a penalty for excuseless rule-breaking and inflicting it on such rule-breakers serves two distinct purposes: deterring those who would otherwise be tempted to break the rules, and persuading those who have obeyed the rules that their behavior was wise, that crime does not pay. The latter goal of this practice may be of greater psychological importance for persons of limited "goodwill," than for those who lack goodwill but can be deterred. By persons of limited goodwill, I mean those who acknowledge the legitimacy of the moral rules and are prepared to obey them, even in the absence of deterring sanctions, but who are prepared to do so only on condition that others are doing likewise. Such persons would resent those who reap a double advantage by relying on others keeping the rules while breaking them themselves. They are quite happy to play the game when all others play too, but are unhappy to play it alone or even in the company of only some. It would not, moreover, be sensible for them to try to improve things by breaking the rules themselves for, as they may understand quite well, the good life for a person depends on others keeping the social rules. Their main concern should therefore be to ensure that others keep these rules. This attitude must not be confused with vindictiveness or the desire for revenge. There is no personal element in this resentment. Their concern is rather the perfectly proper concern for justice, the insistence that all shoulder their (fair) share of the burdens necessary for the good life for each. The demand for retributive justice is thus a natural extension of the demand for distributive justice.

Condemning those who have broken rules without excuse has the purpose of reforming them. The theory involves a complicated psychological process, beginning with the reminder of the wrong they have done, the realization of the error of their ways, the feeling of remorse, and the resolve to mend their ways. Clearly, the effectiveness of this form of treatment must depend on the appropriate prior moral education, if indeed an effective and unobjectionable education of this sort is available. It hardly needs to be stressed that with the decline of Christian moral upbringing, large numbers in our society do not nowadays receive any suitable moral education. If moral condemnation, accompanying punishment or essentially involved in it, was ever effective as a means of reforming rule-breakers, it can hardly be expected to be so now, given the present state of moral education.

Making those rule-breakers with no excuse repair or pay for the harm or damage they have done has two connected purposes. One is to add some deterring force to the imposition of penalties. The other is to provide redress for members of the community who have suffered at the hands of those whom the existence of the practice of bringing people to account has not managed to deter.

The purposes of the three component practices—deterrence, reform, and compulsory redress—all serve one overall purpose, a higher degree of conformity with the obligatory social rules than would be accomplished by relying solely on the method which, were it successful, would be more desirable. I mean the method of formulating and promulgating such social rules and of educating the members of the society in such a way that they acquire an understanding of the need for these rules, a high respect for them, and a sufficiently high degree of goodwill to obey them. The last component purpose, compulsory redress, points to the main purpose of the described practice of enforcement and of this other more desirable practice, namely, to limit as much as possible the harm people suffer as a consequence of living in sufficient proximity to others to make available to them the advantages of social organization.

Bringing people to account is thus a practice which not only presupposes the practice of regulating the behavior of members of a society by the promulgation of obligatory social rules, but is auxiliary to it. A condition of its justification will therefore be the justifiability of the practice to which it is auxiliary, and it will have to meet its own specific conditions as well. Thus, a necessary condition of its justifiability will be that a high level of conformity with such rules at the cost of enforcing them be preferable to a lower level at no such cost.

Let us assume the justifiability of at least some practices of regulating behavior by rule-inculcation (along with teaching the rationale of the rules); that is, let us assume that to the average individual the gains in increased power, capability, and security can outweigh the cost in spontaneity. Let us further assume that whether or not the gains outweigh the cost depends in part on the level of rule-obedience maintained, and that for an adequate level to be maintained by men as we know them, more is needed than mere promulgation and ordinary teaching form. The question then becomes "How can we with least cost raise the level of obedience to the level required?" Holding people to account for breach of the rules will be justifiable if we can show that this procedure costs less than any other known way of raising the level of conformity (e.g., than brainwashing, which would sacrifice individual autonomy to conformity).

Here one feature of this practice is crucial, namely, that incorporated in the second phase: the ascertainment of whether a person who has broken an obligatory social rule has an exculpatory explanation, and the proviso that, if he has, he is not properly subject to any of the three types of undesirable treatment. For although we may regard the unwanted treatment imposed on rule-breakers as a very objectionable aspect of the practice, the practice is so designed that nobody needs to suffer such treatment except as a consequence of his own choice. The proviso relating to excuses makes it possible for each person to attain what we assume it rational for everyone to aim at, namely, that everybody should reap the benefits of a high level of conformity with the social rules, but without anyone *having* to suffer the unwanted treatment. For the proviso about excuses has the consequence that everyone who, for one reason or another, is *unable* to conform to the rules, has ipso facto an excuse. Thence it would seem that the practice of bringing people to account is also justifiable, as long as it incorporates the proviso about excuses. Thus, the retributivist principles that all and only those responsible (culpable, guilty, at fault) should be punished, can be derived from the purpose of a teleologically justifiable practice, that of bringing people to account.

2.) We can now look at the various types of ascribing responsibility within the framework of the practice of bringing people to account. In a recent paper, Hart constructs the following story to illustrate the most important types of ascription of responsibility:

> As captain of the ship, X was responsible for the safety of his passengers and crew. But on his last voyage he got drunk every night and was responsible for the loss of the ship with all aboard. It was rumored that he was insane, but the doctors considered that he was responsible for his actions. Throughout the voyage he behaved quite irresponsibly and various incidents in his career showed that he was not a responsible person. He always maintained that the exceptional winter storms were responsible for the loss of the ship, but in the legal proceedings brought against him he was found criminally responsible for his negligent conduct, and in separate civil proceedings he was held legally responsible for the loss of life and property. He is still alive and he is morally responsible for the deaths of many women and children.[2]

2.1) Accountability. In Hart's story the doctors considered the captain responsible for his actions. They ascribed to him responsibility in the sense of "accountability," being fit to be brought to account (the German *Zurechnungsfähigheit*), because of the possession of all those psychological powers which are necessary and sufficient for the ability to be guided by promulgated social rules. Minors and madmen lack these powers. They cannot be guided by social rules

[2] "Postscript: Responsibility and Retribution," Chapter IX in *Punishment and Responsibility* (Oxford: Oxford University Press, 1968), see p. 211.

any more than the blind can be guided by traffic lights. They are therefore unfit to be brought to account; they are not accountable. Certain mental disorders may not altogether destroy these psychological powers but merely significantly reduce or impair them. We then speak of "diminished or impaired responsibility" (i.e., accountability).

Accountability may be a necessary condition of the proper imposition of any of the types of unwanted treatment. For even if the imposition of such treatment on nonaccountable persons did have the effect of raising the level of conformity with the social rules, this could not (ex hypothesi) be due to their greater willingness to be guided by the promulgated rules. Bringing them to account would not, therefore, be practice auxiliary to that of rule-promulgation. Such a practice would lack an important safeguard and would therefore require additional and possibly less plausible assumptions for its justification.

2.2) Task-responsibility and other obligatory social requirements. In Hart's story, X as the captain of the ship was responsible for the safety of the passengers and the crew. Let us call this sense of "responsibility" "task-responsibility." Unlike accountability, task-responsibility is always *for* something specific. A person simply is or is not accountable; or if we insist that he must be accountable for something, he is accountable for *anything and everything* for which one could be brought to account, i.e., "responsible for his actions." However, he is not task-responsible for any and all of his actions, but only for certain specific tasks. Unlike accountability, task-responsibility can be deliberately assumed or refused.

We indicate what he is task-responsible for in two different ways. We can indicate it by specifying a state of affairs: "for the safety of the crew," "for getting the dogs fed." Or we can indicate it by the identification of creatures capable of a good or interest, such as humans or dogs: "for Mary" or "for his dobermans." Such specifications may mean two quite different things. If I am task-responsible for Mary or the dobermans, I am task-responsible either for their well-being or for their not doing anything which would constitute the violation of a social rule.

A task-responsibility is a certain sort of obligatory social requirement. Other sorts are moral rules, duties, obligations, and commitments. There are no sharp lines between these sorts, for they are not sorts based on the same principle of classification. Roughly, moral rules mark out the things that are wrong for anyone ("Killing is wrong"); duties, the recurring tasks attached to a social role or position ("One of the duties of a parent is to look after his children"); obligations, the specific tasks a given person is required to perform as a consequence of his dealings with others ("You have an obligation to pay for the car repairs since the accident was your fault"); and commitments, the specific tasks he has undertaken to perform ("I am afraid summer teaching is one of my commitments for next summer. I promised the chairman some time ago"); and responsibilities, those requirements whose fulfillment involves forethought, care, intelligence, and initiative. Cooking her husband's meals, but not obedience to him, may be a wife's responsibility. But since these classifications are cross-classifications, there is no reason why one and the same task, say, providing for a certain woman, should not be among someone's duties (as her husband), his obligations (because in saving his life she had suffered injuries making her incapable of earning her own living), his commitments (since he had undertaken to do so in the marriage contract), and a responsibility (since it involves care, foresight, and initiative).

2.3) Answerability. If a person is accountable and has failed to satisfy one of the obligatory social requirements, not necessarily a task-responsibility, then another type of ascription of responsibility is applicable. I shall call it ascription of "answerability." I call it that because to be held responsible in this sense is to be required, by the rules of the practice of bringing people to account, to answer the question why one failed to conform to the obligatory social rule or directive in question. Much depends on what sort of true explanation of his failure is available to him, as we shall see shortly.

It will be helpful to make clear the differences between task-responsibility and answerability. Since one may conscientiously perform all one's tasks, one may be task-responsible for many things without being answerable for any; and vice versa, when the obligatory requirement one fails to perform is not a task-responsibility. What one is answerable for, can be indicated in the same ways as what one is task-responsible for. Thus, prior to the catastrophe the captain was (task-)responsible for the safety of the passengers and the crew and, therefore, after the catastrophe, became responsible=answerable for the loss of their lives. And if Jones is (task-) responsible for his daughter Joan, then he is answerable for any harm or hurt she suffers, and/or for any breach by her of an obligatory social rule.

Unlike task-responsibility, answerability cannot be assumed, but is incurred. One becomes task-responsible when an obligatory social rule or directive comes to apply to one, but answerable when one fails to conform to it. One ceases to be task-responsible if that rule no longer applies to one, but one ceases to be answerable only when he has provided the appropriate answer.

2.4) Culpability. In Hart's story, the remarks "He was found criminally responsible for his negligent conduct," "He was held legally responsible for the loss of life and property," and "He is morally responsible for the deaths of many women and children" report the ascription to the captain of responsibility in yet another sense, which I shall call "culpability." To say that someone is responsible for something in this sense is to say that he failed to discharge an obligatory social requirement without adequate excuse. It is, in other words, to claim that he is answerable for something and that he has no exculpatory answer.

It should not be thought, however, that "responsible" and "culpable" mean exactly the same or are used in exactly the same way. All that can be said is that they can be used to ask and answer similar questions, all appropriate at the third stage or phase of the activity of bringing someone to account. Thus, the question "Is Jones responsible for this?" can be rendered either as "Was Jones' conduct culpable?" or "Was Jones culpable in doing this?" There are three linguistic differences between the two expressions. The first is that whereas only persons can be responsible in this sense, either persons or conduct can be culpable, and persons are culpable simply because their conduct is. But this seemingly important difference is purely verbal since the ground for saying that a person is responsible or that conduct is culpable is the absence of an excuse. A second difference is that whereas, typically, the object of responsibility, what a person is responsible *for*, is a state of affairs or a person, the corresponding object of culpability is conduct, someone's failing to obey a rule. But here again the difference is more apparent than real. For the states of affairs a person is responsible for are those states of affairs which a rule requires him either to prevent or at any rate not to bring about, such as harm to another, and which he has failed to keep, whence he is responsible. The third difference is more substantial. A person can only be responsible or not responsible; he cannot be more or less so, but he can be more or less culpable. Of course, he can be solely or partly (i.e., jointly) responsible, but that only means that he may either be or not be solely or jointly responsible for something, but he cannot be more or less so. Whether someone is responsible for something is the question of whether or not he has an *exculpatory* explanation, which allows of degrees, not all of which are sufficiently high to *amount* to exculpation.

Again, similar questions can be asked by means of "Who (if anyone) is (responsible)=to blame for this?" and "Is he *guilty* of this?" The first question arises only in cases where something undesirable has happened, but the answer "He is to blame" ("It is his fault") can be given only if that undesirable event or state of affairs has come about because someone broke a social rule and did so without exculpatory explanation. The second question is asked in reference to an actual accusation, which is formulated in such a way that the degree of culpability is already built into it. The accusation determines how extenuating the explanation must be to be exculpatory.

And what is an exculpatory, what an inculpatory explanation? The ground of this distinction is derivable from the object of the practice of bringing people to account. As we have seen, that object is by unobjectionable methods to eliminate or reduce in number those cases of rule-breaking which result from people's inadequate resolve to do what is obligatorily required. If there is no call to strengthen someone's resolve, then he need not be brought to account. The goal of the practice is just a stiffening of that resolve where necessary. Therefore those who have transgressed an obligatory social rule in conditions under which a person "with the best will in the world" would have done the same thing, need not be brought to account. Persons whose transgression has such an explanation, have an exculpatory explanation why they failed to conform. It may be true that the willingness of others to obey the social rules could be increased by inflicting undesirable treatment on all those who have transgressed them whether they have an excuse or not. The justification of this safeguard for the individual of goodwill then depends on whether the loss through greater rule-violation or the loss through reduced protection for persons of goodwill is the greater. The existence of so-called "strict liability" expresses the judgment that in those cases conformity to the rule is more important than the protection of the nonculpable individual. Exculpatory explanations are those which show that a person's failure to conform was not due to an inadequacy of his will, but occurred or would have occurred *despite its adequacy*. Such explanations fall into three main categories: i) inability, ii) compulsion, iii) and ignorance.

i) A person failed to accomplish what he was required to do, although he was set on doing it. The main cases are opposition by irresistible force (a policeman, a cramp in the leg); opposition by someone with superior gamesmanship (a more aggressive driver); prevention by circumstances from doing what is required (no vacant parking lot, a flat tire). In these cases, a man failing to keep an appointment has the exculpatory explanation that with the best will in the world he could not make it.

ii) A person fails to do what is required because he was set on something else, but was so set because of excessive pressure on his will. In these cases, although the failure is due to a misdirected will, it is not due to lack of goodwill because in the absence of the excessive pressure, the person's will would not have been set in the wrong direction. The explanation is exculpatory because it shows that what is needed is not the redirection of Jones' will but the elimination of the excessive pressure on it. The main cases are coercion (threat of death or pain or loss), compulsion by circumstances ("The storm compelled him to jettison the cargo"), and inner compulsion ("He was too frightened to do it"). In all these cases, the question of what constitutes excessive pressure on the will depends on how much pressure the person is (or can legitimately be) required to resist. It is conceivable that a soldier on active duty who under torture gives away military information cannot offer the torture as an exculpatory explanation since he may be required to withstand such torture. A bank clerk, on the other hand, may be able to claim that he was coerced to hand over the money if the holdup man threatened to shoot him.

iii) A person failed to do (accomplish) what he was required to do through ignorance. This, too, typically is not, though it may be, a case of lack of goodwill, because the person would do what is required of him if he were not ignorant. However, this may be a case of lack of goodwill, namely, if the ignorance itself is due to lack of goodwill in failing to make the required effort to acquire the relevant knowledge. The main cases are ignorance of the requirement ("He did not know there was a law against it"), ignorance of some necessary conditions of success ("He did not know it was not loaded," "He did not know it was rat poison"). In all these cases what he knew he was doing (pulling the trigger, pouring the liquid) had a feature he did not know it had, on account of which what he did constituted his failure to conform and would not have been done had he known that it had that feature.

If the explanation of a person's behavior does not belong to one of these exculpatory types, it is inculpatory. In that case, the person who is answerable has failed to answer, and therefore must be said to be responsible, in the sense of culpable. He is to blame for what happened. It is his fault. He is guilty of something, i.e., he culpably failed to conform to a relevant social directive.

2.5) Liability. When a person has been found culpable, then he becomes liable to one or more of the three types of unwanted treatment (punishment, condemnation, payment of compensation). It must be recalled that what we are giving is a rational reconstruction of actual practices. In fact not all culpable men are punished, and some are liable to punishment although not culpable. Nevertheless it should be clear that the point of the whole procedure would be lost if culpability did not entail prima facie liability to punishment, that is to entail such liability unless the particular case can be shown to be exceptional in a way for which the rules of the procedure could not allow.

Bearing in mind the stages of the process of bringing people to account we can now sum up the various senses of "responsible," taking the final cumulative sense, where responsible=prima facie liable, as the main sense. Ascriptions of accountability and task-responsibility (as well as other forms of obligatory requirements, e.g., duty) state that the *presuppositions* of responsibility in the main sense are satisfied; ascriptions of answerability that a *presumption* of responsibility in the main sense is satisfied, a presumption which may, however, be rebutted by providing an excuse; ascriptions of culpability that the sufficient conditions of responsibility in the main sense are satisfied, that is the sense in which it means the satisfaction of the sufficient conditions of prima facie liability (i.e., liability unless there is something exceptional about the case).

Thus, that our captain was responsible-for-his-actions=accountable, and that he was responsible=task-responsible for the safety of the passengers, means that the presuppositions of responsibility in the main sense are satisfied: the question of his responsibility in the main sense does not even arise unless both these preliminary claims are established. When we say that it is the captain who is responsible= answerable for the loss of life and property, we mean that there is a presumption that he is responsible in the main sense and that he is responsible in the main sense unless he has an excuse (or in cases of strict answerability, even if he has an excuse). Finally, that the captain is legally and morally responsible=to blame, for the deaths of many women and children, is to ascribe to him responsibility in the main sense, i.e., that prima facie he is liable to some form of undesirable treatment. To say that someone is responsible in the main sense is thus to say that all the conditions for saying that he is prima facie liable are satisfied.

II

3.) The distinction between the various senses of "responsibility" listed in section I enables us to see more clearly the invalidity of certain types of argument designed to show that no one could be responsible for anything if everything were determined.

3.1) **Argument from Ultimate Nonresponsibility.** The first argument, to be called the Argument from Ultimate Nonresponsibility, occurs frequently in the current literature. It goes:

i) A person's ability to discharge obligatory social requirements depends on whether he has the appropriate innate endowment or, failing that, the appropriate early environment and training or, failing that, the innate ability to overcome the effects of inappropriate early environment and training.

ii) Therefore, his responsibility or lack of it for failing to discharge such requirements depends on whether he happens to have acquired this ability.

iii) But he cannot be responsible for not having acquired this ability.

iv) Therefore he is not ultimately responsible for failing to discharge such requirements.

The argument is seen to be invalid, if we bear in mind the distinction between responsibility-accountability and responsibility-culpability. For, of course, a person cannot become culpable unless he is accountable; hence no sense can be attached to the question of whether he is "ultimately responsible" for his actions, i.e., whether he is to blame for not becoming accountable.

Hospers, in (sections I and II of) his influential article "What Means This Freedom?" [3] gives a sympathetic version of the Argument from Ultimate Non-

---

[3] *Determinism and Freedom,* ed. Sidney Hook (New York: Crowell Collier and Macmillan, Inc., 1958), pp. 126–142.

responsibility, but then (in section III, and in a somewhat different spirit) argues as follows: "We operate on two levels of moral discourse . . . that of action . . . and that of the springs of action"; [4] the concepts of "can," "freedom," and "responsibility" apply only at the level of action, not that of the springs of action; therefore what I call steps iii and iv in the Argument from Ultimate Nonresponsibility are meaningless; [5] all we can say is that whether a person is a so-called normal person is simply a matter of luck, not something for which he or anyone else can be responsible. However, this thesis, while close to the truth, is not quite correct. For it is not true that the concept of responsibility has no application at what he calls the level of the springs of action. As we have seen, the ability which madmen and children lack and neurotics have in only inadequate measure, constitutes one kind of responsibility, namely, accountability, and concerns the springs of action. Hence the concept of responsibility has application at the level of the springs of action.

Secondly, it is not true that whether a person has or does not have certain desires (something at the level of the springs of action) is never something for which he can be blamed. On the contrary, if he is accountable and if he knows how to eradicate or control such desires, and if he is obligatorily required to do so, then he is responsible=culpable if he does not. Hence even the concept of responsibility=culpability has application at the level of the springs of action.

Lastly, and most importantly, it is not quite correct that whether a person becomes accountable is just a matter of luck. Of course, as far as he himself is concerned, it is a matter of luck, but as far as his human environment, parents, teachers, social institutions, or psychoanalysts are concerned, it may not be. For they may know how to turn him into an accountable human being, and if so, then it may be their task-responsibility to do so, and if he does not become accountable, his human environment may be answerable and even culpable.

3.2) Argument from Ultimate Noncontrol. A slightly different version makes explicit an underlying assumption of the Argument from Ultimate Nonresponsibility. The assumption is that a person is responsible only for those things over which he has control or power. We may call it the argument from ultimate noncontrol. It goes like this:

i) If N was responsible for what he did, then it must have been in his power not to do what he did.

ii) It could not have been in his power not to do what he did if what he did was determined by anything that was not itself within his power either to bring about or not to bring about.

iii) But if determinism is true, then what a man does is determined by events prior even to his birth.

iv) Therefore what N did was determined by events which were not themselves within his power either to bring about or not to bring about, and so he cannot be responsible for what he did.[6]

---

[4] *Ibid.*, p. 129.
[5] *Ibid.*, p. 130.
[6] For recent defenders of this argument, cf., e.g., R. M. Chisholm "Freedom and Action," pp. 12–13 or Peter Caws, *Science and the Theory of Value* (New York: Random House, Inc., 1967), p. 84.

This version is vitiated by the same shift in meaning between "responsibility=accountability" and "responsibility=culpability." For premise it is true, when "responsibility" means "culpability." In that case, it must have been in N's power not to do what he did. But all that is necessary for that is that he should not have had a certain exculpatory explanation for failing to do what was required of him, the explanation that with the best will in the world, a person like him, with his knowledge and in his circumstances, would not have succeeded in doing what was required of him. If a person with the required goodwill but otherwise exactly like N would have succeeded then the condition is satisfied: N had it in his power not to do what he did; he does not have the relevant excuse; he is responsible=culpable. Responsibility=culpability does not require any power or control over things which happened before one's birth or conception. Of course, such events outside one's control, such as early environmental influences and education, determine whether one is or is not responsible for one's action in another sense, namely, accountability. But in that sense of "responsible for one's actions," it is simply not plausible to hold that in order to be responsible=accountable one must have control over events prior to one's birth. From one's own point of view, the acquisition of accountability is a matter of luck, not of responsibility, i.e., not of task-responsibility, answerability, or culpability, and not of liability either, of course.

3.3) "First Intervention Point." The Argument from Ultimate Noncontrol is important because the assumption which it makes explicit has played a crucial role in the controversy over the freedom of the will. The assumption is that a person does not now have control over events, does not now have it in his power to do things, if these events and these actions can be shown to have causes that go back to times prior to his conception, his birth, or more exactly, to a point in time prior to the earliest moment at which he can be said to have exercised control over events or to have done things. Let us call this moment his "First Intervention Point."

This assumption suggests that if *what* a person does or brings about has a cause at all—and there is good reason to think that it must have if he is to be responsible for it—then this cause must ultimately be the agent himself and can not be events prior to his First Intervention Point. Of course, what N brings about, say, the death of another, may have among its causes earlier events, say, the entering of poison into the bloodstream of the victim, his drinking the poison, or N's pouring poison in his drink. But this chain of causally connected events must be *originated* by the agent himself. *He* must be the first cause of them if it is to be true that it was in his power to do or not to do the act in question. He must be "a prime mover unmoved." [7]

But if the assumption made explicit by the Argument from Ultimate Noncontrol is false, then this train of reasoning lacks a sound starting point. It provides no ground for thinking that agent-causation and event-causation are not compatible; that it cannot be true both that N originated, initiated, or began the chain of events which led to the death of the other; and that this chain of events had earlier events as causes. Assuming that it does make sense to cut up the total cause sequence of events into distinguishable chains of events, then N's originating, or setting in motion, such a chain of events may then be simply a way

---

[7] Cf. Chisholm, "Freedom and Action," pp. 17–18, also p. 23.

of referring to a certain type of event-causation, namely, one involving N's having a certain *goal-directed operative propensity* (that is, one whose realization is modified by changes in N's beliefs about how his goal can be attained and about the consequences of attaining it), a propensity which he has come to have in one or other from a set of ways which includes deliberation and choice.

3.4) "N could have acted differently."   Here an objection may be raised which many philosophers have taken seriously.[8] It may be said that I have at best given reasons for thinking that certain arguments against the compatibility of determinism and responsibility are unsound. To show that determinism and responsibility are compatible, I would at least have to provide a new account of what it is to be able to act otherwise than one does, an account which is compatible with determinism. For the only prima facie plausible account, that given by Moore, is notoriously untenable. [See G. E. Moore, "Free Will," pp. 148 ff. below. Ed.] However, in reply to this objection, it can, I think, be shown that a few changes will render Moore's account adequate.

It will be remembered that one of the reasons why Moore's first analysis of "N could have acted differently" may well be false on certain occasions when Moore's first analysis of it, "N would have acted differently if he had chosen" is true, namely, on those occasions when N could not have chosen differently.[9] And Moore's second analysis which attempts to take care of the objection, "N would have acted differently if he had chosen *and N* could have chosen differently" is inadequate because Moore analyzed "could have chosen" as "would have chosen if he had chosen" which involves an unsatisfactory regress.

However, we can accept the pattern of Moore's second analysis, if we substitute for Moore's account a satisfactory account of "could have chosen differently." Now it is easy to see that whereas rational action is based on rational choice, rational choice itself is based, not again on rational choice, but on rational preference. Thus, "N could have chosen differently" must be analyzed as "N would have chosen differently (i.e., would have succeeded in making a different choice), if he had (but) thought some other choice preferable." If N could have chosen differently from the way he did choose means only this, then it is compatible with determinism because it requires only that if certain important factors had been different, N would have made a different choice. That this is all it means can be seen from the fact that the alternative interpretation, which is incompatible with determinism, is absurd. For suppose we insist that "N could have chosen differently" should mean that N *might* have chosen differently from the way he did even though everything had been just as it was, even though N thought the actually chosen alternative preferable. Then, far from demanding the ability to choose differently, as ordinarily understood and really presupposed by responsibility, we are insisting that a person's choices should not depend on what he thought preferable. On this view, the ability to choose differently would

---

[8] Cf. e.g., Chisholm, "Freedom and Action," pp. 14–16.

[9] Another reason is that a being (e.g., an animal) may act and be able to act differently from the way he does, although he lacks the ability to choose. For "N could have acted differently" does not mean "N would have acted differently if and only if he had chosen, and he could have chosen differently." It means, rather, "N would have acted differently if he had (but) chosen, or decided, or thought fit, or wanted to . . . etc., and he could have chosen, or decided . . . etc. (whichever is relevant)." The range of verbs in the *if*-clause includes all those which are normally sufficient conditions of his coming to have an operative propensity to act differently.

be tantamount to irrationality or random selection. But this is surely an absurd demand.

What is involved in a person's ability, on a particular occasion, to choose differently from the way he does in fact choose, are three things:

i) The general ability to choose, that is, the ability to recognize alternative ways of accomplishing aims, the ability to weigh these alternatives, and the ability to act in accordance with the outcome of such weighings; three abilities which very small children and madmen do not have.

ii) The opportunity to choose, that is, an occasion on which one has a choice to make, an occasion when there are alternatives open to him as there are not when he is compelled, say, at gunpoint, or by circumstances, to do something. When he can correctly say that he had no choice, it is still true that he could have acted differently, but not true that he could have chosen differently, since he had no choice to make.

iii) The absence of insuperable internal obstacles to making on this occasion the choice which, on the basis of his own evaluation of the alternatives before him, he would want to make, as when he is too frightened or too neurotic to make the kinds of choice now before him.

Thus, "*N* could at *t* have chosen differently" means more than that at *t* he had a certain empirically detectable skill which all normal adults, but not all human beings, have. It means also that the appropriate conditions for its exercise are satisfied, namely, the absence of external and internal obstacles to selecting certain courses of action which, if the obstacles were left out of account, would be thought preferable.

III

What can we learn about the concept of action from our analysis of the ascription of responsibility in the context of bringing people to account?

A once popular theory held that attributing to someone a certain deed, i.e., saying something of the form "He did it," is to ascribe to him two things: first, some bodily movement which was the cause of "it," or a causal factor in "its" coming about, or which "constituted it"; and secondly, responsibility for "it." However, as has frequently been pointed out, this theory is untenable.[10] There are many things people do for which they are in no sense responsible. In the first place, they do things which are not forbidden and so they cannot be answerable, hence not to blame for doing them, nor liable. Secondly, when one person is responsible=answerable for another, then the first is answerable for what the other does, hence to say of the other that he did something is not necessarily to attribute answerability to him nor necessarily responsibility in any other sense either. Lastly, a person may have done something which he is required not to do, yet not be responsible for it, because he is not responsible for any of his actions, i.e., not what I call *accountable*.

[10] Cf. H. L. A. Hart, "The Ascription of Responsibility and Rights," *Proceedings of the Aristotelian Society*, 1948–1949; P. T. Geach, "Ascription" [See pp. 117–120 below. Ed.] and George Pitcher, "Hart on Action and Responsibility," both *Philosophical Review*, LXIX (1960); and Joel Feinberg, "Action and Responsibility," *Philosophy in America*, ed. Max Black (Ithaca: Cornell University Press, 1964). Also, H. L. A. Hart, *Punishment and Responsibility* (Oxford: Oxford University Press, 1968).

But not only is to say "He did it" not necessarily to ascribe responsibility, but also to say "He did not do it" may well ascribe responsibility. A satisfactory account of the relation between responsibility and action must also accommodate responsibility for all the various forms of not acting, such as inaction, doing nothing, letting something happen, evading, avoiding, shirking, omitting, failing, neglecting, abstaining, refraining, forbearing.

A better way in which an understanding of responsibility can help us get at this central idea is to extract the implications of a proposition which would generally be regarded as a truism. I mean the proposition that bringing people to account and ascribing responsibility to them presupposes that they are "rational agents" in the philosophical sense of that term. In fact, these two practices presuppose something even stronger, namely, that all normal adults are rational agents and that most adults are normal. For ascribing responsibility, which makes sense only within the framework of the practice of bringing people to account, which in turn makes sense only as a subsidiary to regulating people's conduct by the promulgation of obligatory social rules, is itself an effective and justifiable practice only in a context in which those who are not rational agents are an insignificant minority.

How, then, does an understanding of responsibility help us isolate the central feature of agency? Why is it a truism that bringing people to account, or ascribing responsibility to them, makes sense only for rational agents, that is, rational beings who are also agents, if indeed there can be rational beings who are not agents? Clearly, these practices make sense only for beings whose behavior can be regulated by the promulgation of social rules, that is, for beings who can *follow* rules, orders, directives, that is, for people who can understand the action-descriptions contained in such directives, and can, *at will*, behave in ways to which such action-descriptions would apply. Now, as we have seen, the point of these practices is to produce social states of affairs which, taking into account the "evil" of being required to follow directives, are preferable to the states which would result from the absence of all rules, or from the presence of other rules. Therefore, what is presupposed by these practices is the capacity of beings subject to them to impose on their reactions to the environment a pattern conforming to their beliefs about which of their reactions will bring about or maintain the preferred social states of affairs and prevent or terminate the rejected ones. Can we then say that this capacity is or at least involves rational agency?

Consider how we would distinguish between a rational being who is an agent and one who is a *mere* observer. By the latter, we would understand a creature capable of observing what is going on around him, able to prophesy what will happen, to be elated or depressed by the prospects, and to predict what will happen *if* certain other things happen, when he has no idea *whether* or not these other things will happen, and where such other things may be his own reactions to earlier changes in his environment. Such a mere observer may, for instance, predict that, if she cries, her husband will give in to her on a disputed point. She may even be able to predict that, if thwarted by him on this matter, she will cry. But of such a mere observer it will not be true that her preferences ever determine what happens, not even what happens in her body. By contrast, of a rational agent we should want to say that his preferences often determine what happens in his body, and through that even what happens in his environment; that therefore his interactions with the environment are not mere reactions, but forwardlooking actions; that his body is so organized that his preference for one state of affairs over another will bring about suitable changes in his body if he believes that such changes bring about the preferred and prevent the rejected state of affairs.[11]

The practice of bringing people to account presupposes this very capacity. For it presupposes that the existence of this practice helps to incline people to prefer the state of affairs resulting from there being enforced rules of a certain content to there not being such rules, and that the existence of such enforced rules makes them prefer following the rules and being free of the sanction, to not following the rules and risk having the sanction imposed on them, and that their having these preferences is by and large sufficient for their following the rules.

Here it may be objected that having this capacity is a necessary but not a sufficient condition of being an agent rather than a *mere* observer. Suppose our observer knows that if she weeps he will give in, and suppose that she desperately wants him to give in, and suppose furthermore that this want and this knowledge are, in such circumstances, sufficient conditions of its happening that she weeps. Would not then my account make her weeping an action? And does not this show its inadequacy?

It must be admitted that weeping would not necessarily be an action even if a person were structured in the way described. It might still be true only that in such a person weeping occurs when that suits his end and he desperately wants to accomplish that end. Thus, it might well be the case, as perhaps in "functional disorders," that there are built into our body two types of "servo-mechanisms": those of a type like the control of body temperature through sweating and shivering whose effective functioning is unaffected by our awareness or unawareness of its function, or by its function being or not being our goal; and those of a type like the "functional weeping" just described, in which the functioning of the mechanism depends on its function being our goal, though it may not depend on our being fully aware that it is our goal—since we may have repressed that awareness. Clearly, the workings of such mechanisms would not naturally be called actions, even in cases where our awareness of our having the relevant goal is a necessary condition of the functioning of the mechanism.

What, then, is missing? For the functioning of such a mechanism to qualify as action, at least one other condition must be satisfied: the change in question must occur in a part of the body which the being whose body it is can "move at will" or as philosophers sometimes put it, "which is directly under his control," as, e.g., the liver or a paralyzed arm is not. Indirect control of the part of the body in question is not sufficient because it itself presupposes direct control. One has indirect control over the paralyzed arm if changes in it can be brought about but only by changes in something else, e.g., lifting the paralyzed arm by the good one. There are, it seems to me, two conditions of saying that some part of one's body is under one's direct control.

---

[11] I have said more about the difference between the concepts of agent and observer in an article entitled "Action and Agent," *The Monist*, XLIX (April 1965), 183–195.

The first is that changes of or in it are jointly determined by the being's operative goal (what he is set on accomplishing at that time) and by his beliefs about what changes in the part in question will tend to bring about the attainment of his goal, and that this will be true for a *range* of operative goals. It implies, in other words, that if the agent had a different goal from that range and the same beliefs, or had the same goal and different beliefs about what would realize them, the actual changes in the part under direct control would be *suitably* different also. Typically, doing something involves a series of such changes in one or several parts under the agent's direct control. Each of these occurs under the determining influence of beliefs about what would be effective goal-pursuit, which are continually and suitably modified by the agent's concurrent observation of the environment.

The second and more important condition of saying that some part of the body is under one's direct control is that the causal determination of the changes of or in it have been learned. Otherwise these changes will still be something that happens, not something the agent does: it will remain essentially surprising, however often it happens. This is not of course to deny that there are innate conditions relating to the structure of the parts without which direct control over these parts could never be acquired. It may be that the reason why we do not acquire direct control over the rectum is not merely that, unlike the hands for instance, such control would not be very useful in attaining important goals, but that its structure makes it ill-endowed for the acquisition of such control. Just how learning proceeds is a matter for empirical investigation to reveal. But if my account is correct, then we can say that the question whether the movements of someone's limbs (or any other changes in parts which through learning come to be under the agent's direct control) are actions, does not arise prior to his acquisition of such control. To think of these movements or changes as "something the agent does," or brings about "at will," is confused because the child is not yet an agent, and so has as yet no will, since it does not yet have direct control over any parts of its body. Perhaps the kicking of his legs feels to him different from the reflex kicks of the patellar reflex, and no doubt it is different since he can learn to make coordinated, goal-directed movements with the legs but cannot learn to modify the reflex kick. But the distinction between happening and action together with corresponding introspectively distinguishable feels does not properly apply until the child has developed into an agent, i.e., when he has acquired the know-how involved in making goal-seeking movements.

In the case of human beings, acquiring the necessary know-how goes hand in hand with learning a great variety of action-descriptions, and the ability to formulate, declare, and execute one's intentions in terms of such action-descriptions. The practices we have discussed, controlling individual behavior by the promulgation of obligatory rules or directives, and bringing people to account, would not make sense except for people with this ability.

We may usefully distinguish two fundamentally different ways of employing action-descriptions in attributing actions to someone. We may do so "from an agent's point of view" or "from an observer's point of view." To do so from an agent's point of view is to attribute to him action as he saw it, i.e., saying what he aimed at, what his goal was, or what his intention was in doing what he did. This is to hint at what I will call an action-explanation, i.e., one which says that the explicandum is a change of or in a part of someone's body over which he has a direct control, a change which is jointly determined by his operative goal and his beliefs about suitable changes in that part. The main question then is whether the agent was successful or unsuccessful, whether he accomplished or failed to accomplish what he set out to do. Speaking of what a person *can* do is speaking of what he would accomplish if he were set on it. Attributing an action to someone from an observer's point of view is characterizing what is going on by an action-description but leaving open the question of whether that occurrence has an action-explanation, i.e., whether it was done intentionally or unintentionally. Thus, as a result of the availability of action-descriptions, one may correctly attribute an action to someone, from an observer's point of view, even though what has happened has, under that description, no action-explanation. In fact, as we shall see, it may have no action-explanation under any description.

If my account is correct, then the reason why functional weeping is not acting, is that it is a rigid unmodifiable response of a part of the body over which the agent has not acquired direct control in the sense explained. If a person can learn to shed and to stop shedding tears, to cry copiously or a tear at a time, in immediate response to commands or according to previously declared intentions, then we would not be so disinclined to call his weeping an action.

In the light of this answer to the question "What is action?" namely, the exercise of the ability to seek and attain goals, we can distinguish two further questions which must be kept apart, if we are to avoid unnecessary puzzles. The first is "Did an action occur?" or "Was that something someone *did?*" or "Did someone *do* something?" If I am right, then this means, properly understood, "Does this occurrence have *an action-explanation?*"

The second question should arise only if the first is answered in the affirmative. For if no action has occurred, one can hardly ask what it was. Yet, this question seems to arise even when nothing has occurred that has an action-explanation. Thus, of the railroad guard who slept off a hangover instead of attending to his duties, we can say that he neglected his duties, that he failed to switch the point, thus causing an accident, and that he is responsible for this. Here again, an understanding of the concept of responsibility helps us understand why what has occurred is naturally called action even if it does not have an action-explanation. For since there are many things a person can, and may be required to, do which he does not do, and many things he does not do which he can, and may be required to, refrain from doing, we may introduce new action descriptions, "doing right" and "doing wrong," under which something which in the fundamental sense was not a case of acting, becomes action under this description. Hence we need an understanding of the practice of holding people to account, in order to understand the full complexity of the concept of action.

ASCRIPTIVISM

P. T. Geach

The statement that an act x was voluntary, or intentional, or done with intent, or the like, on the part of an agent A has often been analyzed as a causal statement that x was initiated by some act of A's mind that was an act of bare will—a volition, or an act of A's setting himself to do x, or an act of intending to do x, or the like. Latterly there has been a reaction against this type of analysis; it has been held (in my opinion, quite rightly) that the attempt to identify and characterize these supposed acts of bare will always run into insuperable difficulties. To avoid such difficulties, some Oxford philosophers, whom I shall call Ascriptivists, have resorted to denying that to call an act voluntary, intentional, and so forth, is any sort of causal statement, or indeed any statement at all. In this note I shall try to expound and to refute Ascriptivism.

Ascriptivists hold that to say an action x was voluntary on the part of an agent A is not to *de*scribe the act x as caused in a certain way, but to *a*scribe it to A, to hold A responsible for it. Now holding a man responsible is a moral or quasi-moral attitude; and so, Ascriptivists argue, there is no question here of truth or falsehood, any more than there is for moral judgments. If B agrees or disagrees with C's ascription of an act to A, B is himself taking up a quasi-moral attitude toward A. Facts may support or go against such a quasi-moral attitude, but can never *force* us to adopt it. Further, the Ascriptivists would say, there is no risk of an antinomy, because ascription of an act to an agent can never conflict with

From *The Philosophical Review*, LXIX (1960), 221–225. Reprinted by permission of the author and *The Philosophical Review*. Slightly revised by author.

a scientific account of how the act came about; for the scientific account is *de*scriptive, and *de*scriptive language is in quite a different logical realm from *a*scriptive language. Though it has not had the worldwide popularity of the distinction between *de*scriptive and *pre*scriptive language, the Ascriptivist theory has had quite a vogue, as is very natural in the present climate of opinion.

Now as regards hundreds of our voluntary or intentional acts, it would in fact be absurdly solemn, not to say melodramatic, to talk of imputation and exoneration and excuse, or for that matter of praise and reward. Ascribing an action to an agent just does not *in general* mean taking up a quasi-legal or quasi-moral attitude, and only a bad choice of examples could make one think otherwise. (As Wittgenstein said, when put on an unbalanced diet of examples philosophy suffers from deficiency diseases.)

Again, even when imputation and blame are in question, they can yet be distinguished from the judgment that so-and-so was a voluntary act. There are savage communities where even involuntary homicide carries the death penalty. In one such community, the story goes, a man fell off a coconut palm and broke a bystander's neck; the dead man's brother demanded blood for blood. With Solomonic wisdom the chief ordered the culprit to stand under the palm tree and said to the avenger of blood, "Now you climb up and fall off and break his neck!" This suggestion proved unwelcome and the culprit went free. Though the vengeful brother may still have thought the culprit ought to have been punished, his reaction to the suggested method of execution showed that he knew as well as we do the difference between falling-off-a-tree-and-breaking-someone-else's-neck *voluntarily* or *intentionally* and just having it happen to you. To be sure, on his moral code the difference did not matter—his brother's death was still imputable to the man who fell on him—but this does not show that he had no notion of voluntariness, or even a different one from ours.

I said that Ascriptivism naturally thrives in the present climate of opinion; it is in fact constructed on a pattern common to a number of modern philosophical theories. Thus there is a theory that to say "what the policeman said is true" is not to describe or characterize what the policeman said but to corroborate it; and a theory that to say "it is bad to get drunk" is not to describe or characterize drunkenness but to condemn it. It is really quite easy to devise theories on this pattern; here is a new one that has occurred to me. "To call a man happy is not to characterize or describe his condition; macarizing a man" (that is, calling him happy: the words "macarize" and "macarism" are in the O.E.D.) "is a special nondescriptive use of language. If we consider such typical examples of macarism as the Beatitudes, or again such proverbial expressions as 'happy is the bride that the sun shines on; happy are the dead that the rain rains on,' we can surely see that these sentences are not used to convey propositions. How disconcerting and inappropriate was the reply, 'Yes, that's true,' that a friend of mine got who cited 'happy are the dead that the rain rains on' at a funeral on a rainy day! The great error of the Utilitarians was to suppose that 'the greatest happiness of the greatest number' was a descriptive characterization of a state of affairs that one could aim at; but in fact the term 'happiness' is not a descriptive term: to speak of people's happiness is to macarize them, not to describe their state. Of course 'happy' has a secondary descriptive force; in a society where the rich were generally macarized, 'happy' would come to connote wealth; and then someone whose own standards of macarism were different from those current in his society might use 'happy,' in scare-quotes so to say, to mean 'what most people count happy, that is rich'. . . ." There you are; I make a free gift of the idea to anybody who likes it.

There is a radical flaw in this whole pattern of philosophizing. What is being attempted in each case is to account for the use of a term "P" concerning a thing as being a performance of some other nature than describing the thing. But what is regularly ignored is the distinction between calling a thing "P" and predicating "P" of a thing. A term "P" may be predicated of a thing in an *if* or *then* clause, or in a clause of a disjunctive proposition, without the thing's being thereby called "P." To say, "If the policeman's statement is true, the motorist touched 60 mph" is not to *call* the policeman's statement true; to say, "If gambling is bad, inviting people to gamble is bad" is not to *call* either gambling or invitations to gamble "bad." Now the theories of nondescriptive performances regularly take into account only the use of a term "P" to *call* something "P"; the corroboration theory of truth, for example, considers only the use of "true" to *call* a statement true, and the condemnation theory of the term "bad" considers only the way it is used to *call* something bad; predications of "true" and "bad" in *if* or *then* clauses, or in clauses of a disjunction, are just ignored. One could not write off such uses of the terms, as calling for a different explanation from their use to *call* things true or bad; for that would mean that arguments of the pattern "if *x* is true (if *w* is bad), then *p*; but *x is* true (*w is* bad); *ergo p*" contained a fallacy of equivocation, whereas they are in fact clearly valid.

This whole subject is obscured by a centuries-old confusion over predication embodied in such phrases as "a predicate is *asserted of* a subject." Frege demonstrated the need to make an absolute distinction between predication and assertion; here as elsewhere people have not learned from his work as much as they should. In order that the use of a sentence in which "P" is predicated of a thing may count as an act of *calling* the thing "P," the sentence must be used assertively; and this is something quite distinct from the predication, for, as we have remarked, "P" may still be predicated of the thing even in a sentence used nonassertively as a clause within another sentence. Hence, calling a thing "P" has to be explained in terms of predicating "P" of the thing, not the other way round. For example, condemning a thing by calling it "bad" has to be explained through the more general notion of predicating "bad" of a thing, and such predicating may be done without any condemnation; for example, even if I utter with full conviction the sentence, "If gambling is bad, inviting people to gamble is bad," I do not thereby condemn either gambling or invitations to gamble, though I do predicate "bad" of these kinds of act. It is therefore hopeless to try to explain the use of the term "bad" in terms of nondescriptive acts of condemnation; and, I maintain, by parity of reasoning it is hopeless to try to explain the use of the terms "done on purpose," "intentional," or the like, in terms of nondescriptive acts of ascription or imputation.

With this I shall dismiss Ascriptivism; I adopt instead the natural view that to ascribe an act to an agent is a causal description of the act. Such statements are indeed paradigm cases of causal statements: cf. the connection in Greek between αἰτία ("cause") and αἴτιος ("responsible"). Let us recollect the definition of will given by Hume: "the internal impression we feel and are conscious of when we knowingly give rise to any new motion of our body or new perception of our mind." Having offered this definition of will, Hume concentrates on the supposed "internal impression" and deals with the causal relation between this and the "new motion" or "new perception" on the same lines as other causal relations between successive events. Like a conjurer, Hume diverts our attention; he makes us forget the words "knowingly give rise to," which are indispensable if his definition is to have the least plausibility. If Hume had begun by saying, "There is a peculiar, characteristic, internal impression which we are sometimes aware *arises in us* before a new perception or new bodily motion; we call this volition or will," then his account would have had a fishy look from the outset. To say we *knowingly give rise to* a motion of mind and body is already to introduce the whole notion of the voluntary; an "internal impression" need not be brought into the account, and is anyhow, I believe, a myth. But without the "internal impression" Hume's account of causality cannot be fitted to voluntary causality; without it we no longer have *two* sorts of event occurring in succession, but only, on each occasion, *one* event to which "we knowingly give rise"—words that express a non-Humian sort of causality.

For an adequate account of voluntary causality, however, we should need an adequate account of causality in general; and I am far from thinking that I can supply one. To develop one properly would require a synoptic view of the methods and results of the strict scientific disciplines—a labor of Hercules that far exceeds my powers; and it would take a better man than I am to see far through the dust that Hume has raised. All I have tried to do here is to make it seem worthwhile to investigate non-Humian ideas of causality in analyzing the voluntary, instead of desperately denying, as Ascriptivists do, that voluntariness is a causal concept.

section **II**

ABILITY AND POSSIBILITY:

ON DEFINING "A PERSON *CAN* PERFORM AN ACTION"

INTRODUCTION

ABILITY, POSSIBILITY, AND POWER

1. THE PROBLEMS

We often make statements not about the performance of an action, but rather about the *possibility* of performance. We make true statements such as "I can drive a Volkswagen," "He is able to swim the Channel," "You could have turned the other cheek," and "I cannot budge the stone." That these statements are about the possibility and not the actual occurrence of action is evident from the fact that "He is able to swim the Channel," for example, can be true even if he never swam the Channel, whereas "He swam the Channel" is true only if he swam the Channel. In order to explicate fully the nature of human action, we must explain the locution "A person *can* perform an action" in addition to the locution "A person performed an action." We need to know what it means to say that a person *can do* something in addition to knowing what it means to say that he does something.

A difficulty arises in the case of "can perform" that was, essentially, absent from "performs." Suppose that our man is locked in a cell. *Can* he, at that time, play the piano? Yes; he has played the piano many times in the past and there is no reason to believe that he has lost this ability by being temporarily locked in the cell. But it is retorted, surely he can*not* play now. For there is no piano in the cell! Which reply is correct? The answer is: both. Unlike the case of "performs," there are a number of relevant meanings or senses of "can perform." Since the context is no help in this instance, the first reply is correct because "can" can mean "has the ability to" and the second reply is correct because "can"

can mean "has the opportunity to," "is in the position to." Part of the problem for this section is distinguishing between the various human action "cans."

Categorizing these "cans" is only part of the problem. Section I and its Introduction were concerned with the question whether "performs an action" is explicable solely in nonaction talk, in particular in terms of "behavior plus." In this section, and in this Introduction, discussion will center on whether the relevant senses of "can" are explicable in nonaction talk. Metaphorically speaking, we want to know whether "performs an action" and all (or some) senses of "can perform an action" belong together in a closed circle of concepts.

The discussion of human action "cans" is relevant not only to the descriptive aspect of action but also to the metaphysical aspect, especially to the complex of issues called the Free Will Problem. Causal determinism is the view that everything that happens is caused. Or alternatively, whatever happens could not have happened in any other way. Traditionally, two counterclaims are made. The libertarian maintains that causal determinism is false. Some events—and the occurrences of actions are usually cited—are not caused; they could have happened otherwise. The second reply is that although it is true that every event is caused, it is compatible with this claim that persons could have acted otherwise. A common thesis of (one form of) libertarianism and "soft determinism," which is William James' name for the second, compatibilistic view, is that some actions are free. Now traditionally again, a person performs an action *freely* if, and only if, he can perform it and he can refrain from performing it.[1] This definition of "acting freely" is helpful, however, only if we know what "*can* perform" and "*can* refrain from performing" mean. We can evaluate these counterproposals to causal determinism only if we know what sense of "could" is involved in saying "he could have acted otherwise." Again, the meaning of "free action," and hence the tenability of determinism, depends on whether a systemic or an extra-systemic account of "can perform" is adequate.

2. HUMAN ACTION "CANS"

In "Ifs and Cans," Professor J. L. Austin distinguishes between three human action "cans": the opportunity sense, the ability sense, and the "all-in" sense, that is, the opportunity plus ability sense.[2] If our man has a piano in his cell, and if his hands are not bound, and so on, then he *can*—has the opportunity to—play the piano. If he has the requisite skill to play, then he *can*—has the ability to—play. And if he is in a position to play and also has the ability, then he *can,* in the "all-in" sense, play the piano. We can immediately add a fourth sense to Austin's three "cans." A person sometimes can perform an action even though he has neither the ability nor the opportunity. A person may have the ability to gain the ability to perform an action: he may have a "second-order ability." Suppose again that our man is locked in a bare cell. Although he does not have the ability and is not now in a position to play the piano, he nevertheless *can* play it. Upon release, he can learn to read music, practice scales, and so on. In this sense, call it the "capacity" sense, a person can perform an action, say *a,*

[1] Cf., e.g., John Locke, *Essay,* Bk. II, chap. xxi, sec. 8. Also cf. Richard Taylor, *Action and Purpose* (Englewood Cliffs, New Jersey: Prentice-Hall, Inc., 1966), p. 200.
[2] Reprinted pp. 161–178 below.

if and only if there is a set of abilities he has such that if he exercises them, then at a later time he will have the ability to do a.[3]

These four "cans" of human action are not exhaustive.[4] First, there are senses derived from the ability and capacity senses. For example, a person might have the capacity to do something without having the opportunity to exercise the appropriate set of subsidiary abilities. After being released, a turn of events might prevent our man from learning to read music, practicing the scales, and so on. There is, then, a further "can," that might be labeled the "capability" sense, in which a person can perform an action just in case he has both the capacity and a reasonable opportunity to exercise the appropriate set of subsidiary abilities. Second, there is a family of senses that pertain to responsibility and permissibility. To say that Jones can play the piano can mean that his playing is not against the law or that there are no moral or social restrictions on his playing. For example, sometimes when we say that a person *can*not do something, we mean nothing more than he *ought* not do it. "You cannot continue to insult your mother!" means, in an ordinary context, that you ought not continue to insult her. Third, to say that a person can perform an action can mean that it is possible that he perform it. There are at least two kinds of possibility relevant here, namely, physical (or causal) possibility and logical possibility. In order to distinguish between these two kinds of possibility, consider the sentence "Jones can run faster than the speed of sound." This sentence is true if the "can" expresses logical possibility; for the sentence is logically consistent. However, "Jones can run faster than the speed of sound" is false if the "can" expresses physical possibility. For the sentence is inconsistent with a statement of the laws of nature and a statement describing the state of Jones' muscles and other initial conditions.

A fourth "can," a "can" that philosophers have paid particular attention to, is somewhat more difficult to explicate. According to this sense, "I can raise my hand at noon" means that *it is within my power to* raise my hand at noon. Although in ordinary discourse we often use "has the ability to" to express what is meant by "has it within his power to," something being within one's power is different from his having the ability to do it. To claim that I have the ability to play the piano is to make a claim about what I am able to do under certain general conditions and not necessarily what I am able to do now under the existing conditions. To claim that it is within my power to play the piano is to make a claim about what I am able to do now under the obtaining conditions. If it is within my power to perform an action, then I have the opportunity to perform it; however, it does not follow from my having an ability that I also have the opportunity to exercise this ability. Ontologically, we can distinguish between two kinds of actions, general (or generic) actions and individual actions. When a person does something in the world, he performs an individual action. General actions, on the other hand, do not depend for their existence on being performed. They are abstract, nonspatio-temporal. They exist in the weak sense that everything that can be named exists. Ability claims pertain to general actions; having an action within one's power pertains to individual actions.

[3] Cf. G. H. von Wright, *Norm and Action*, p. 317 below. Also cf. Austin, "Ifs and Cans," p. 177, note 17, below.
[4] Cf. Bruce Aune, "Can" in *The Encyclopedia of Philosophy*, vol. 2, ed. Paul Edwards (New York: The Macmillan Company, 1967), 18–20.

Philosophers who prefer sparsely populated universes might object to talk about general actions. "*Only* those actions that are (or can be) performed by persons exist." We can accommodate this uneasiness by linguistically distinguishing between ability claims and claims of having an action within one's power. An action description either individuates, or it does not. If spatio-temporal reference is a sufficient individuating condition for an action description—though it almost certainly is not—then "playing my piano at noon, August 1, 1968" is an individuating action description and "playing a piano" is not.[5] Let us stipulate, contrary to some ordinary usage, that "ability to" is followed by a nonindividuating action description, and "within his power to" is followed by an individuating action description. It is simpler to talk about individual and general actions, however, than it is to speak in the linguistic idiom, and hence we shall do so. The appropriate translations can be made by those who have pangs of ontological discomfort.

These senses of "can" are not independent. The opportunity sense, it will be suggested shortly, is explicable in terms of the physical possibility sense. The capacity, "all-in," and related senses are clearly explicable in terms of the ability and opportunity senses. And the ability sense, it will be argued, is explicable in terms of an action's being within one's power. (We will not discuss further the moral and logical possibility senses.)

3. PHYSICAL POSSIBILITY

Professor Storrs McCall's paper "Ability as a Species of Possibility" is well argued and demonstrates a clear understanding of the issues. Basically, McCall can be interpreted as maintaining two theses about human action "cans": (A) the basic human action "can," the "can" in terms of which *all* others are definable, is the "all-in" sense, that is, the ability plus opportunity sense; and (B) the "all-in" sense is identical with the physical possibility sense. It will be argued here, however, that thesis (A) is true but misleading as McCall develops it, and thesis (B) is false.

Let us consider (A) first. For McCall, ability claims pertain to individual (as opposed to general) actions and include more than mere physical skill and know-how.[6] When McCall talks about the ability "can," he appears to refer to what we have called the within-one's-power sense. He construes "ability" in this way because he thinks that there is no meaningful sense of "can" that pertains to general (or generic) actions. If one is to understand a sentence of the form "Person S has the ability to (can) A," McCall believes, one must be able to specify exhaustively the conditions under which the person is said to have the ability in question.[7] But this contention is false. The sentences "Mickey Mantle has the ability to (can) hit home runs," "Albert Einstein had the ability to solve (could have solved) complex problems," and "My neighbor does not have the ability to (cannot) remain silent" are true and, hence, meaningful. They are meaningful without exhaustively specifying the conditions under which each

---

[5] See pp. 222 f. of the Introduction to section III for a discussion about action descriptions, including individuating action descriptions. See, too, Nicholas Rescher's "On the Characterization of Actions," reprinted pp. 247–254 below.

[6] Cf. "Ability as a Species of Possibility," p. 142 below.

[7] *Ibid.*, p. 144 below.

person is said to have (or lack) the ability in question. For, in general, it is not possible to list exhaustively these conditions. Ability claims are "forward looking"; they concern not only what a person has done in the past under certain conditions, but also what he might do in the future under similar, but different, unknown, conditions. Moreover, even if we were to restrict ability claims to past and present actions, it is highly doubtful that it is humanly possible to specify in all its glorious detail the conditions under which a person performed an action, particularly if we include relational predicates in the specification of the conditions. A definition of the usual ability "can," the sense that pertains to general actions, in terms of the within-one's-power sense will be suggested later in this introduction. Thesis (A) is misleading as McCall develops it, then, because it excludes the usual ability sense of "can" from the sphere of meaningful action talk.

Thesis (B) is more important—and more controversial. It states that McCall's "all-in" "can," which is the opportunity sense plus his restricted sense of ability, is identical with the "can" of physical possibility. Since physical possibility is adequately explained in nonaction talk, it follows that a large and important segment of the language of action is explicable extra-systemically, namely, in physical language. Metaphorically speaking, if McCall is right, action locutions do not form a closed circle; rather, they are linked to the language of physics. Hence McCall says ". . . no special analysis of statements like 'I can catch the 3:15 bus,' or 'Nicholas can't yodel to save his life' is necessary over and above the analysis of statements like 'Radar can be bounced off the moon' which assert a purely physical possibility." [8]

Clearly, in order to evaluate McCall's claim, we need to know what "physically possible" means. Contemporary philosophers have generally distinguished between two senses of this expression, and to these McCall adds a third. The first sense is in terms of laws of nature: roughly, an event is physically possible if, and only if, a statement of the event's occurrence is consistent with a statement of the laws of nature that obtain and a statement of the initial conditions that obtain. The second definition, McCall's original proposal, is based on Leibniz' notion of possible worlds and has affinities to Carnap's notion of state descriptions. On this view, an event is physically possible if, and only if, it occurs in at least one possible future. [9] *Prima facie* this definition is viciously circular. By "possible future" McCall does not mean "logically possible future." For, as he correctly notes, some events are logically possible but physically impossible. There is a logically possible world, but not a physically possible one, in which an electron traveling alone in a constant gravitational and electromagnetic field can reverse its direction even if the field is not altered. McCall seems to mean "physically possible future" by "possible future." However, we cannot determine what a physically possible future is unless we know what it is for an event to be physically possible. The concept of possible futures, nevertheless, may be philosophically valuable, for example, in formulating a theory of truth. The third definition, and the one McCall favors, is in terms of physically sufficient conditions. Reformulating this view, an event is physically possible from time t_1 to

[8] *Ibid.,* p. 139 below.
[9] *Ibid.,* p. 140 below.

time t_2, where t_1 is earlier than t_2 if, and only if, there exists at time t_1 no condition physically sufficient for the nonoccurrence of the event at t_2.[10] For example, it is now possible that a specific surface electron will escape from my desk top in five minutes. Though it may not in fact escape, presumably there is now no condition physically sufficient for its not escaping.

Is McCall's basic "can," that is, the within-one's-power plus the opportunity senses, identical with the "can" of physical possibility defined in terms of physically sufficient conditions? *No.* Some actions are physically possible in the appropriate sense, but not *psychologically possible* to perform. An action is within a person's power to perform, moreover, only if it is psychologically possible for him to perform it. Therefore, some actions are physically possible in the appropriate sense, but they are not within a person's power to perform. It follows from this that the within-one's-power sense plus the opportunity sense is not identical with the physical possibility sense.

The crucial premise in this rebuttal of thesis (B) is that there are some actions that are physically possible in the appropriate sense but psychologically impossible. Suppose that I am confronted with a quantity of arsenic. It is now physically possible that I will shortly swallow a lethal dose. There is no physically sufficient condition for my not swallowing it: my arms are in good working order, my throat is clear, no person or device is about to stop me, and so on. Nevertheless, I am unable to bring myself to swallow it. It is psychologically impossible for me to do it because of, among other things, my overriding desire to live.[11] A person might train himself to swallow arsenic, as in McCall's case of the chemistry professor who swallowed the arsenic together with an antidote.[12] We are considering the case, however, in which the agent knows that swallowing a lethal dose will result in his death.

One might reply, as McCall does, that "physical conditions" includes what we mean by "psychological conditions." My desire to remain alive in the arsenic case "rests on" my physical state.[13] McCall's reply consists in a tacit appeal to a form of physicalism, namely, that the usual concepts of physics and those that pertain to ordinary physical objects are adequate to account for all phenomena, including so-called mental phenomena. However, we are not now in a position to pass judgment on the tenability of this form of physicalism. To date, psychology and neurophysiology have not successfully accounted for mental phenomena. More important, it can be forcefully argued that the physical sciences *cannot* account for all mental phenomena; for the introduction of teleological concepts, such as purposefulness and intentionality, which are excluded by the physical sciences, is required for an adequate account of some mental phenomena.[14] In short, since we are not now—and probably will never be—in a position to affirm physicalism, we are not justified in subsuming psychological conditions under physical conditions.

[10] *Ibid.,* p. 141 below.
[11] Cf. Timothy Duggan and Bernard Gert's analysis of "the ability to will," in "Voluntary Abilities," pp. 208 ff. below.
[12] McCall, "Ability as a Species of Possibility," p. 142, n. 13.
[13] *Ibid.,* pp. 142, 145 below.
[14] A detailed defense of this objection to physicalism is given by Charles Taylor in his important book *The Explanation of Behavior* (New York: Humanities Press, Inc., 1964).

Thesis (B), however, contains an element of truth. A person *has the opportunity to* perform an action if, and only if, it is physically possible that he perform it. If there are physical conditions that prevent a person from performing an action, then he does not have the opportunity to perform it. If a man is locked in a bare cell, he does not have the opportunity to play the piano; for there is a physical condition sufficient for his not playing, for example, there is no piano within his reach. There may be insurmountable objections to McCall's explication of "physical possibility" in terms of "physically sufficient conditions," though I can see none. If there are, then some other tenable definition of "physical possibility" should be used to explicate "opportunity."

In short, then, there is a human action "can" that is explicable in nonaction talk, namely, the opportunity sense. A fundamental human action "can," the within-one's-power sense (McCall's restricted sense of "ability"), is not explicable solely in terms of physical possibility. Our task now is to determine whether there is an extra-systemic account of this "can," whether, that is, "it is within one's power to perform an action" is explicable in nonaction talk.

4. CONDITIONALS

Two theses have often been held about "cans" and "ifs." The *first* is that "can" statements are incomplete, or elliptical, without an appended "if"-clause; that is, in Austin's words, "cans" are constitutionally iffy.[15] For example, "He could have holed the putt" is incomplete, whereas "He could have holed the putt if the caddie had not stepped in the way" is complete and meaningful. The *second* and, from our point of view, more important thesis is that "can"-statements are adequately analyzed into "will if"-statements; that is, "can" is explicable extra-systemically in terms of what will happen under certain conditions.

Austin maintains that both theses are false. He also holds that they are "quite distinct and incompatible." [16] Though Austin is correct in pointing out that these theses have not always been differentiated, they certainly cannot be both false and incompatible; for if one statement is incompatible with another, then one is true and the other false. Rather, these theses complement each other. If "can"-statements are disguised "can if"-statements, then in analyzing a locution in which "can" occurs, we must consider the entire, nonelliptical expression. It will be argued that Austin is correct in claiming that "can"-statements are not analyzable into "will if"-statements but that he has failed to show that "cans" are not constitutionally iffy.

Austin believes that Moore and others think "cans" are constitutionally iffy because they take "could have" to be a past subjunctive, "which," Austin says, "is practically as much as to say that it needs a *conditional* clause with it." [17] But "could have" can be a past indicative, in which case the temptation to add a conditional clause disappears. Though the temptation disappears, it is nevertheless an open question whether "could have" used as a past indicative requires an "if"-clause. It remains to be seen whether "He could have gone straight home" and "I could have sung 'Yankee Doodle' " are intelligible without supposing that

[15] Austin, "Ifs and Cans," p. 161 below.
[16] *Ibid.*, p. 167 below.
[17] *Ibid.*

there are suppressed conditionals. Austin then argues that the supposition that a language contain a verb that must always be completed by an "if"-clause leads to absurdity.[18] Let "to X" be the verb in question. According to the supposition, there would then be expressions of the form "I X if I Y" and "I X if Y obtains." Since there are cases in which I in fact perform action Y, or in which conditions Y in fact obtain, it follows that an expression of the form "I X" is true. Hence, the supposition that there is a language—in particular, a natural language such as English—that does not countenance an expression of the form "I X" for every verb in the language is false. This argument, however, is unsound. There is no reason to believe that the usual rule of detachment obtains for the "if"-clauses in question (for example, "if he chooses otherwise" and "if he tries to act differently"). Indeed, Austin's other comments on the logic of "I can if I choose" and "I could have if I had chosen" lead us to believe that detachment rules are not appropriate here.[19] It is probably best not to treat "I can if I choose," "I could have if I had chosen," and so on, as conditionals at all: they do not consist of antecedents and consequents; they are, rather, simple or atomic sentences.

Austin, then, is not justified in denying that "cans" are constitutionally iffy. Without attempting finally to adjudicate this issue, let us turn to the second thesis, namely, that "can" is analyzable as "will if." Stating the thesis in terms of "tries," a suggestion that Austin says has "some plausibility," [20] and in terms of the within-one's-power sense of "can,"

(D1)   For every person S and every individual action a, S can perform a (it is within S's power to perform a) if, and only if, S will perform a if he tries to perform a.

There are parallel definitions to (D1) in other tenses; for example, "(person) S could have performed (action) a" means that S would have performed a if he had tried to perform it. We can, however, restrict our attention to (D1); for the tensed definitions stand or fall with it.

Moore and Nowell-Smith can be interpreted as defending definition (D1), or some version of it in which "chooses" replaces "tries," and Austin can be interpreted as arguing against (D1). Moore's examples indicate that he is talking about a "can," other than the opportunity sense, that takes individuating action descriptions as its object. In making the distinction between unperformed actions that could have been performed and those that could not have been performed, he says

> I *could* have walked a mile in twenty minutes this morning, but I certainly could *not* have run two miles in five minutes. I did not, *in fact*, do either of these two things; but it is pure nonsense to say that the mere fact that I *did* not does away with the distinction between them, which I express by saying that one *was* within my powers, whereas the other was *not*.[21]

[18] *Ibid.*, p. 168 below.
[19] *Ibid.*, pp. 164–165 below.
[20] *Ibid.*, p. 169 below.
[21] G. E. Moore, "Free Will," p. 151 below.

The "can" (or "could have") Nowell-Smith is talking about is more difficult to isolate, though it appears that he too is concerned with the within-one's-power sense. He says "He could have read *Emma* in bed last night, though he actually read *Persuasion;* but he could not have read *Werther* because he does not know German." [22] (However, when Nowell-Smith presents his view abstractly, he seems to be talking about the opportunity plus usual ability sense.) He says "in order to establish the 'could have' statement we should have to show (a) that he has performed tasks of similar difficulty sufficiently often to preclude the possibility of a fluke, and (b) that nothing prevented him on this occasion." [23] In his objections to Moore and Nowell-Smith, Austin takes them both to be talking about the within-one's-power sense. The examples Austin discusses, such as a golfer being able to hole a putt on a particular occasion,[24] are cases of persons being able to perform individual actions.

Austin's main objection to definition (D1) is that being able to do something is consistent with trying and failing. Suppose that a golfer, say Arnold Palmer, tries but misses a very short putt. It is nevertheless true that Palmer could have made (that is, had it within his power to make) this putt. There is a great amount of evidence that Palmer could have made the putt. In the past, under circumstances similar in all relevant respects, Palmer made putts of this kind. Moreover, discouraged by missing the putt, he returns to the green and in circumstances purposely made to be similar in all relevant respects, he proceeds to sink twenty-five consecutive putts. Hence, the definiendum of (D1) is satisfied —it was within his power to have sunk the putt; but the definiens is not satisfied —Palmer tried but failed to sink the putt.

It might be objected that the claim that Palmer could have sunk the putt on this occasion is unjustified. This common objection, however, is unwarranted. If the only manner of justifying the claim that Palmer could have sunk the putt is that he did in fact sink it, then the sense of "could" involved is not the within-one's-power sense. For persons do not perform all the actions that are within their power to perform. It is within my power to hold my breath for the next fifteen seconds, and it is within my power to shout "Geronimo"; but I do neither. If there is a manner of justifying the claim that Palmer could have sunk the putt when in fact he did not sink it, then *by hypothesis* the evidence in this case is sufficient to justify the claim. Again, although "Palmer can (has the power to) sink this putt" does not follow logically from "Palmer many times sank putts similar in all relevant respects to the putt in question," the latter statement is justifying evidence for the former.[25]

In his article "Ifs, Cans, and Causes," Professor Lehrer states another reason for rejecting definition (D1). Basically, to say that a person can do something

---

[22] P. H. Nowell-Smith, "Freedom and Responsibility," p. 158 below.

[23] *Ibid.*, p. 158 below. Cf. Nowell-Smith's reply ["Ifs and Cans," *Theoria,* XXVI, Part 2 (1960), 85–101] to Austin, in which he is talking about the ability "can"—though Nowell-Smith is not always clear, cf. p. 93.

[24] Austin, "Ifs and Cans," pp. 169–170, n. 9 below.

[25] See Keith Lehrer, "An Empirical Disproof of Determinism," in *Freedom and Determinism,* ed. Lehrer (New York: Random House, Inc., 1966), pp. 175–202; and Chapter 3, "The Problem of Freedom and Determinism," by Keith Lehrer, in *Philosophical Problems and Arguments* by Lehrer and James Cornman (New York: The Macmillan Company, 1968), pp. 120–199, for discussions relevant to the claim that there is adequate empirical evidence for Palmer's being able to sink the putt when in fact he did not.

if he tries, Lehrer reasons, is not to say that he will do it if he tries. This true claim, however, is contradicted by definition (D1); and, hence, (D1) is inadequate. Excluding the quantifiers for simplicity and again having "S" range over individual persons and "a" range over individual actions, Lehrer's somewhat complex argument can be reformulated in the following manner:

(1) "S can perform a" is equivalent to "S will perform a, if S tries to perform a." (assumption)

(2) "S can perform a, if S tries to perform a" is equivalent to "S will perform a, if S tries to perform a, if S tries to perform a." [from (1)]

(3) "S will perform a, if S tries to perform a, if S tries to perform a" is equivalent to "S will perform a, if S tries to perform a."

(4) "S can perform a, if S tries to perform a" is equivalent to "S will perform a, if S tries to perform a." [from (2) & (3)]

(5) "S can perform a" is not equivalent to "S will perform a."

(6) "S can perform a, if S tries to perform a" is not equivalent to "S will perform a, if S tries to perform a." [from (5)]

Therefore, (7) "S can perform a" is not equivalent to "S will perform a, if S tries to perform a." [from (1)–(6)]

Premises (4) and (6) are contradictories. Thus, assuming that the argument is valid, if premises (3) and (5) are true, then (1), which is equivalent in meaning to definition (D1), is false.[26] Premise (5), clearly, is true. As has been said, some actions that persons have the power to perform, they do not perform. Lehrer's example is that to say Jones can eat arsenic is not to say that he will eat it.

The argument then turns on premise (3). In support of (3), Lehrer argues that an expression of the form "if p, then if p, then q" is equivalent to an expression of the form "if p, then q." Since "S will perform a, if S tries to perform a, if S tries to perform a" has the form "if p, then if p, then q," it is equivalent to "S will perform a, if S tries to perform a." The main premise of this argument for

[26] It is not clear, however, that the argument is valid; for the inference from (5) to (6) may not be warranted. In his rejoinder to Goldberg and Heidelberger, Lehrer agrees that in "Ifs, Cans, and Causes" he was assuming that the "if" in the argument is conditional (see pp. 184–186 below). However, if the "if" is conditional, the argument is invalid. Premise (5) then has the form "$p \equiv \sim q$" and (6) has the form "$(r \supset p) \equiv \sim (r \supset q)$"; and (5) can be true when (6) is false— if "r" is false and "p" and "q" have different truth-values. Moreover, even if the "if" is not conditional, the argument may well be invalid. Lehrer might have been thinking, with Austin, that "S can perform a, if S tries" entails "S can perform a." And he might have also accepted the view that "S will perform a, if S tries" entails "S will perform a." In that case, premise (5) has the form "$p \equiv \sim q$" and (6) and the additional premise have the form "$(r \equiv \sim s) \& [(r \rightarrow p) \& (s \rightarrow q)]$." This revision is not sufficient to make the argument valid: for (5), again, can be true when (6) (and the additional premise) are false—if "r" and "s" are each false and "p" and "q" have different truth-values. The argument would be valid if "S can perform a, if S tries," and "S will perform a" is identical to "S will perform a, if S tries"; for the inference from (5) to (6) would be warranted by the principle of substitutivity of identicals. It is doubtful, however, that these identities obtain. Suppose that the action is one I perform without trying (a "basic action")—say, winking. It is true, then, that I wink, but false that I wink if I try. Or for the former (alleged) identity, suppose that the action is not trying anything at all for five minutes. Hence, "I can try to do nothing at all for five minutes" is true, but "I can try to do nothing at all for five minutes, if I try" is false. Lehrer's best option appears to be that there is some true (and ad hoc) principle that warrants the inference from (5) to (6) as a whole.

(3), however, is false. If "if p, then if p, then q" and "if p, then q" are taken to express entailment relations, for example, they are not equivalent. These two statement-forms are equivalent if they express material implication. But as Goldberg and Heidelberger correctly observe, Lehrer is not entitled to assume that "S will perform a, if S tries to perform a, if S tries to perform a" and "S will perform a, if S tries to perform a" are material conditionals or behave as material conditionals.[27]

Lehrer, in "Cans and Conditionals: A Rejoinder," accepts Goldberg and Heidelberger's criticism of his defense of premise (3), and then suggests another argument for the conclusion (7).[28] Sentences of the form "S will perform a, if S tries to perform a, if S tries to perform a" are either meaningful or meaningless. If, on the one hand, these odd sentences are meaningful, then they are merely a redundant way of saying what is expressed by sentences of the form "S will perform a, if S tries to perform a." If this equivalence in meaning obtains, premise (3) is established; and since the controversial premise, (3), is established, (7) follows by the original argument. If, on the other hand, sentences of this form are meaningless, then (7), the conclusion, is again established. For if a meaningless expression follows from the assumption (1), then that is a *reductio ad absurdum* argument for (1). Hence, in either case (7), the denial of definition (D1), is established.

Definition (D1) cannot be "patched up" by construing the conditional analysis of "can" in terms of "choose" or "want" or so on; for variations of Lehrer's argument in "Cans and Conditionals: A Rejoinder" are applicable. Moreover, Austin's main objection to (D1) also applies to these proposed revisions. Being able to do something is consistent with choosing and failing, with desiring and failing, and so on.

In his study of Austin's philosophical papers, Professor Chisholm suggests a revision of definition (D1) that is not subject to these criticisms; namely,

(D2) For every person S and every individual action a, S can perform a (it is within S's power to perform a) if, and only if, there is some individual action b such that if S tried to perform b, then he would perform a.[29]

Concerning Austin's objection, there is some action such that if our golfer tried to perform it when putting—perhaps keeping his left foot stationary—then he would have sunk the putt. This definition, further, is not subject to Lehrer's argument.

Definition (D2) is also inadequate for a reason Chisholm himself suggests.[30] Consider the following two statement-forms:

(i) It is necessary that S perform a if and only if S tries to perform b;
(ii) S cannot try to perform b.

[27] B. Goldberg and H. Heidelberger, "Mr. Lehrer on the Constitution of Cans," pp. 182–183 below. This criticism of Lehrer was also made by Ann-Mari Henschen-Dahlquist, "Remarks to Austin's Criticism of Moore's Analysis of 'Can,' " *Theoria*, XXIX (1962–1963), 310. The relevant passage in Austin is pp. 163 ff.
[28] Lehrer, "Cans and Conditionals: A Rejoinder," pp. 185–186 below.
[29] See Chisholm, "J. L. Austin's Philosophical Papers," p. 190 below.
[30] *Ibid.*, p. 191 below.

It follows from (i) and (ii) that S cannot perform *a*. This conclusion is consistent with the definiens of (D2) but inconsistent with the definiendum. Since there is a conjunction of statement-forms consistent with the definiens and inconsistent with the definiendum, the definiens and definiendum are not equivalent in meaning. Chisholm claims, and apparently correctly, that any analysis of "can" in terms of "will if" is subject to a similar argument. For it will always be possible to construct a conjunction of statement-forms on the model of (i) and (ii) that is consistent with "he will if" but inconsistent with "he can." [31]

5. ABILITY

We have argued so far that the within-one's-power "can" is not definable extra-systemically and that the opportunity "can" is definable extra-systemically in terms of physical possibility. We will now consider the "can" of ability, the "can" that pertains to general actions, that is linguistically, the "can" that takes nonindividuating action descriptions as its object. The ability "can" is one that frequently occurs in ordinary discourse; we might say, for example, "Mantle can hit home runs" or "Fisher can checkmate me."

In his paper "Ability," Professor Arnold Kaufman attempts to define "A person has the ability to A" at least partially in nonaction talk, in particular, in terms of physiological states. His proposal can be rephrased as follows: [32]

(D3)   For every person S and every general action A, S can A (S has the ability to A) just in case: if S is in the appropriate physiological state P at various times and for an appropriate number of these times S has the opportunity and tries to perform instances of A, then P causes S to succeed in performing A an appropriate number of times, as determined by the relative complexity of P.

A person has the ability to hit home runs, for example, provided that if he tries and has the opportunity, the physiological state of his body causes him to succeed in hitting a home run.

Definition (D3) is Kaufman's attempt to incorporate the following two *alleged* facts into the analysis of "ability." First, ability-statements are, in some sense, dispositional. They are not, however, analyzable as mere "summary dispositions," as cumulative reports about the conditions under which persons exercise their abilities. Second, we ordinarily think that, and our ordinary talk reflects that, internal, physiological states are causally relevant to the exercise of abilities.[33]

There is a preliminary difficulty for this definition. Persons have abilities to perform mental as well as bodily actions. They can decide on names, remember telephone numbers, and construct completeness proofs. As is well known, it is highly controversial whether any physiological state can cause a mental action, at least if "cause" is taken in its ordinary sense. The seriousness of this objection, however, depends in part on the outcome of the current philosophical debate concerning the identification of mental states with brain states. If mental states *are*

[31] *Ibid.*, p. 191 below.
[32] See p. 196; cf. p. 199 below.
[33] Cf. p. 196 below.

brain states, then there is nothing odd in claiming that a bodily state causes a mental one.[34]

However, definition (D3) is inadequate even if we restrict its range to bodily abilities. Assuming that S has the opportunity and tries to A on a number of occasions, (D3) entails

(K)   For every person S and every general action A, if S has the ability to A, then *if S is in the appropriate physiological state P, then P causes S to succeed in performing instances of A an appropriate number of times.*

The italicized "if-then" in (K) is either a logical "if-then" or it is not. If it is logical, then (K) is subject to counterexamples. Suppose that by hypothesis our golfer has the ability to sink short putts. Assume also that on numerous occasions he tries and has the opportunity to sink short putts: he is on a golf course, club in hand, facing the hole, and so on. Moreover, he is in the appropriate physiological state on these occasions: his blood pressure is normal, his heart is beating regularly, his nerves have not been severed, and so on. However, on each and every one of these occasions, a sudden and miraculous gust of wind pushes the ball aside immediately after it has been stroked. In this case, then, the agent has the ability to sink short putts and he is in the appropriate physiological state, but he never succeeds in sinking the putts. Being in the appropriate physiological state under the most favorable conditions is compatible with never successfully exercising one's abilities. If, on the other hand, the italicized "if-then" is not logical, then (K) states an empirical hypothesis, namely, that physiological states cause certain patterns of behavior (for example, chess-playing behavior, English-speaking behavior, and high-jumping behavior). In addition to the criticism that this hypothesis is at present unconfirmed, it can be replied that it is a mistake to offer an empirical hypothesis as the basis of a definition or analysis of "ability." It is one thing to do conceptual analysis; it is quite another to devise scientific hypotheses.[35] In short, if the italicized "if-then" in (K) is logical, then (K) is false; and if the "if-then" is not logical, then (K) states an empirical hypothesis. Since definition (D3) and some reasonable assumptions entail (K), it follows that either (D3) is false or it entails (with reasonable assumptions) an empirical hypothesis—and in either case, (D3) is not an adequate definition of "A person has the ability to A."

In "Voluntary Abilities," a paper with which I have great sympathy, Professors Duggan and Gert suggest another analysis of "ability." Duggan and Gert divide ability claims into three kinds: physical and intellectual abilities, abilities to will, and voluntary abilities. Abilities to will are abilities to bring oneself, as it were, to exercise one's physical or intellectual abilities. A person may have the physical ability to stand on a narrow slab of concrete; but if he has acrophobia, he will not be able to exercise this ability if, say, the slab is a ledge twelve stories high.

---

[34] Perhaps Kaufman attempted to forestall this objection by suggesting that "S is in the appropriate physiological state P" can be replaced by "S is in a certain condition C (C being the appropriate state of the organism brought to a certain pitch of development)" (p. 199 below). But this alternative formulation, and the context in which it occurs, retains an essentially physiological character.

[35] See George Thomas, "Abilities and Physiology," *Journal of Philosophy*, LXI (1964), 321–328, esp. 323–325.

Duggan and Gert define the ability to will in terms of the inducements or incentives that would make a person exercise the appropriate physical or intellectual ability. More exactly,

> To say that S can will to do x (a kind of action) is to say that it is possible to describe some state of affairs such that S would believe there were reasonable incentives for doing x and believing this would will to do x; and it is possible to describe some state of affairs such that S would believe there were reasonable incentives for not doing x and believing this, would will not to do x.[36]

A person has the voluntary ability to do something, according to Duggan and Gert, if and only if he has the physical or intellectual ability and also the ability to will to do it.

We are here concerned with the ordinary kind of ability, what Duggan and Gert have labeled "physical or intellectual ability," and which they define as follows:

(D4) For every person S and every general action A, S can A (S has the ability to A) just in case: if S wills to A, then simply given a reasonable opportunity S will A a reasonable number of times.[37]

Since some actions are done unintentionally, without willing to do them, the qualification that willing to A is not a necessary condition for A-ing is added to (D4).[38] The concept of willing, clearly, is fundamental to this and other analyses Duggan and Gert propose. S *wills to* A, they say, *if and only if S tries to* A *or S A's intentionally.*[39] "Willing," it is important to note, is itself analyzed in action talk. In this respect Duggan and Gert's discussion of "cans" has a strong systemic element in it.

Definition (D4), however, is subject to some of the same difficulties as Kaufman's definition, (D3). Suppose, again, that by hypothesis our golfer has the ability to sink short putts. He has a reasonable opportunity to sink them: on a number of occasions, he is on the golf course, putter in hand, facing the cup, and so on. Suppose also that on these occasions he tries to sink the putts: he strokes the balls in order that they fall into the cup. Now since he tries to sink the putts, it follows via Duggan and Gert's explication of "willing" that he wills to sink them. (Indeed, we can add that on any adequate explication of "willing," our golfer wills to sink the putts.) Suppose, finally, that on each occasion a sudden and miraculous gust of wind pushes the ball past the hole after it has been stroked. Hence, the antecedent of the definiens of (D4) is satisfied but not the consequent: our golfer wills to sink the putts, but because of miraculous gusts of wind *after* he has stroked the balls, he fails to sink them. It follows, then, that the agent does not have the ability to sink short putts; but this conclusion is contrary to our original hypothesis. A similar *reductio* argument can be used to show that the definiens is not sufficient for the definiendum. Suppose now that our golfer does

---

[36] See Duggan and Gert, "Voluntary Abilities," pp. 208–209 below.
[37] *Ibid.*, p. 207 below.
[38] *Ibid.*, pp. 206–207 below.
[39] *Ibid.*, p. 206 below.

not have the ability to sink short putts. Again he has reasonable opportunity when he hits the balls, and again he tries to sink them. Since he tries to sink the putts, it follows that he wills to sink them. Suppose, finally, that in these cases sudden and miraculous gusts of wind redirect the balls so that they in fact fall into the cup. Hence, the definiens of definition (D4) is satisfied. It follows, then, that contrary to the hypothesis, our golfer has the ability to sink short putts.

The source of the difficulty with Duggan and Gert's proposal, and in part with that of Kaufman, is that the epistemic concern of deciding and knowing whether someone has an ability has been confounded with the question of what it means to say that a person has an ability. Whether a person succeeds in exercising his ability under certain conditions is relevant, and perhaps necessary, for determining whether he has that ability. But a person can have an ability without ever successfully exercising it. Success, in short, plays no role in *defining* or *analyzing* "ability," though it plays an essential role in *knowing* whether a person has an ability.

Contrary to Kaufman and to Duggan and Gert, the "can" of physical and intellectual ability belongs wholly to the conceptual circle of action talk. For "ability" is definable primarily in terms of the within-one's-power sense of "can," and that in the following way:

(D5)   For every person S, every general action A, and every time duration t, S can A (S has the ability to A) during t just in case: if S were to have the opportunity to perform instances of A on certain occasions during t, then on those occasions that it is psychologically possible for S to perform instances of A, it would be within S's power to perform instances of A.

Thus, for example, to say that Mantle has the ability to hit home runs or that Fisher has the ability to checkmate me is to say that if Mantle were at bat and able to bring himself to swing for a home run or if Fisher were to play chess with me and able to bring himself to defeat me, then Mantle could (has it within his power to) hit a home run and Fisher could (has it within his power to) checkmate me. The concept of being psychologically able to do something, as before, is left at the intuitive level, though it bears a close resemblance to Duggan and Gert's notion of the ability to will.

Now it might be objected that definition (D5) fails to distinguish between cases of ability and cases of luck. Suppose that, for example, I tossed fair dice many times and that each time I rolled "7." Since in fact I rolled "7," it follows that it was within my power to have rolled "7." Hence, the definiens of (D5) is satisfied. It follows, then, that if (D5) is adequate, I had the ability to roll "7" with fair dice. Since I certainly do not have this ability, the objection continues, definition (D5) is not tenable.

This objection fails to differentiate actions from their consequences. What is within my power to do—what I can do—is to perform actions, not to bring about the occurrences of consequences of actions. The dice showing "7" is not an action, but rather the consequence of an action, namely, throwing the dice. Hence, throwing the dice on these occasions was within my power, though the dice showing "7" was not within my power. Thus, I did not have the ability to roll "7" with fair dice. One mark of a consequence of an action is that the agent did not *intentionally* bring it about. Although I did not intentionally bring it about that the dice showed "7," I nevertheless might have thrown them *with the intention* that they show "7"—but this is another matter. For, basically, doing something intentionally is doing it in a certain way or manner, whereas doing something with the intention that some state of affairs obtain is having that state of affairs obtain in the presence of a certain kind of mental event.[40] In short, then, the objection that agents have the ability to do what can only happen by luck is groundless. This sort of objection, perhaps, results from our habit in ordinary conversation of describing an action (here, throwing the dice) by describing its consequence (the dice showing "7").[41]

[40] This point strongly suggests that "intentional doing" can be given an adverbial rendering in much the same way as "appearing" and "believing." Cf. Wilfrid Sellars, *Science and Metaphysics* (New York: Humanities Press, Inc., 1967), pp. 176 ff. and his Lindley Lecture at the University of Kansas, April 1967, "Form and Content in Ethical Theory," published for the Department of Philosophy, University of Kansas.

[41] See Eric D'Arcy, *Human Acts* (Oxford: Oxford University Press, 1963), pp. 1–39.

PHYSICAL POSSIBILITY

ABILITY AS A SPECIES OF POSSIBILITY

Storrs McCall

In this paper I shall argue that human ability is a species of physical possibility. If this view is correct, then no special analysis of statements such as "I can catch the 3:15 bus," or "Nicholas can't yodel to save his life," is necessary over and above the analysis of statements like "Radar can be bounced off the moon" which assert a purely physical possibility. Furthermore, it is my contention that the meaning of "A is physically possible" is analyzable in terms of yet simpler concepts, so that *ipso facto* the expression "X can do A" is too. If this be so, then it is a mistake to regard statements of human ability as ultimately resting upon some unique, *sui generis* concept such as the "can" of human action or the notion of "being within one's power." At the end of the paper I shall consider the views of four philosophers [1] who hold that human ability *is* something over and above physical possibility; the first part of the paper will be devoted to arguing that it is not. [2]

To begin with, what is needed is a clear understanding of physical possibility and its twin, physical necessity. [3] These two, though often thought to be related to the concepts of logical possibility and necessity, are in reality barely on speaking terms with the latter. The main difference is that physical possibility and necessity are relative notions, while the others are not. For example, it is meaningless to ask whether a particular event such as the explosion of a can of tomato

Reprinted by permission of the author.

[1] Stuart Hampshire, Bruce Aune, Richard Taylor, and Roderick Chisholm.

[2] Some of my views on human action "cans" resulted from discussions with Myles Brand.

[3] These notions are discussed at length in "Time and the Physical Modalities," forthcoming in *The Monist*, and only the main thread of the argument is presented here.

soup is physically possible, but only whether that event is physically possible *relative to a set of initial conditions*. Relative to the can of soup's resting on the shelf it is doubtless not possible, but the case is different if it is put in the fire. On the other hand, it is always logically possible for a can of soup to explode, or to change into a Nile crocodile, without any reference to initial conditions at all.

To reinforce this point, which is vital for the argument of the whole paper, let us consider the question whether anything can be logically possible but physically impossible. It is true that recent advances in physics have undermined our confidence in the inherent impossibility of many happenings. For example, sitting in a bath, it is physically possible though extremely unlikely that our head should boil and our feet freeze in a block of ice.[4] But examples such as these should not convince us that, with the advent of modern physics, absolutely anything can happen. On the contrary, many things are physically impossible. It is physically impossible for instance that an electron, traveling alone in a constant gravitational and electromagnetic field, should reverse its motion and start to travel backwards. Of course it is *logically* perfectly possible for the electron to do this, and this example shows the necessity of regarding the physical modalities as inherently relative rather than unconditioned, for under a different set of initial conditions it *is* physically possible for an electron to reverse its motion.[5] Again it is physically necessary, relative to my jumping out the window at time t_1, that I hit the ground at time t_2, it being part of the initial conditions that no fireman's net is ready to receive me. This kind of possibility and necessity is sometimes called "causal."

There are two main ways in which the notions of physical possibility and physical necessity may be analyzed. The first of these is by means of the notion of a "possible future." Roughly and broadly, event A at time t_2 is necessary relative to time t_1 if and only if A occurs in all possible futures relative to t_1. For example, if I jump out the window at t_1, then there will in general be many different possible futures relative to t_1: one in which passerby X looks up, one in which he looks down, one in which my left foot crushes forty blades of grass, one in which it crushes fifty, etc. But these possible futures will all be alike in containing the event of my hitting the ground at some time t_2, and therefore this event is necessary in what might be called the Leibnizian sense: what is necessary is what is true in all possible futures. Similarly, what is physically possible is what is true in at least one possible future. This is the first way of defining the physical modalities.[6]

The second way is to speak not of possible futures but of necessary and sufficient conditions. Then A at t_2 is necessary relative to t_1 if and only if there exists at t_1 some condition sufficient for the occurrence of A at t_2. Thus if Tom is bitten prior to t_1, Tom's being shy at some time later than t_1 is necessary relative to t_1.[7] In the case of possibility, A at t_2 is physically possible relative to t_1 if and only if there exists at t_1 no condition sufficient for the nonoccurrence of A at t_2. Relative to August 1940, for example, the defeat of England in 1941 was possible, for al-

---

[4] The example is borrowed from Adolf Grünbaum.

[5] E.g., in a suitably altered electrical field.

[6] How many possible futures are there? Well, if at each instant in time at least two alternatives present themselves, the number of possible futures over a finite interval will have a cardinality greater than that of the continuum. See the author's abstract, "The cardinality of possible futures," forthcoming in *The Journal of Symbolic Logic*.

[7] Assuming that having once been bitten is sufficient for being subsequently shy.

though this event did not in fact occur there existed in August 1940 no state of affairs sufficient to ensure its nonoccurrence. An alternative way of defining physical possibility is to say that A at t_2 is possible relative to t_1 if and only if there is lacking at t_1 no necessary condition for A at t_2: a forest fire can start at 5 P.M. if at 4 P.M. a frustrated hunter with matches and pipe in his pocket is wandering through bone-dry undergrowth, dying for a smoke.[8] On the other hand, if at t_1 a necessary condition of A at t_2 *is* lacking, then A not only *does not* happen, it *cannot*. Poison gases in cylinders, and prisoners in gaol, not only do not escape when their valves are closed and their cells padlocked; they cannot. The reason is, that a necessary condition of their escaping is lacking.[9]

Let us now turn to the question of human ability. What I shall try to show is that there is a basic sense of "X can do A" which is identical with "it is physically possible for X to do A," and that other senses of "X can do A" are either definable in terms of the basic sense, or else have no clear meaning attached to them.

Suppose that a foursome has reached the eighteenth green, and that Black has a six-foot putt for hole and match. Can he sink it? Well, that depends. Under normal circumstances we should certainly say he could, since six-foot putts are regularly sunk on miniature golf courses by old ladies of ninety and babes in arms who have never held a club before. But in this case the circumstances may not be normal. Black may be very tired, or the match may be finishing in such darkness that he cannot see the hole, or he may be putting with his two iron, having wrapped his putter round a tree on the sixteenth. Still, this may not entail that Black *cannot* sink the putt, but only that it is unlikely that he will. The way of establishing whether he can or cannot is to determine whether, say at 7:12 P.M., there exists any condition sufficient for bringing it about that Black's ball miss the hole at 7:13 P.M. Let us suppose that there is not. Then, at 7:12, Black can hole the putt at 7:13, meaning that it is physically possible for him to do so. Note that the full specification of this ability of Black's requires a *double time reference*:[10] not only must we know the time of the action Black is reputedly able to perform, but we must also know the time at which he reputedly has the ability to perform it.

At 7:12, then, Black can sink the putt at 7:13. Let us now imagine him addressing the ball. The seconds tick by and Black becomes more and more nervous. His hands shake. At 7:12:58 he draws back his putter, stubs the ground and leaves the ball two feet short. At some point in this process what had previously been possible becomes impossible:[11] once the ball has stopped short at 7:12:59 it is impossible for Black to sink the putt, whereas at 7:12:00 it was possible. At what

[8] Note that it doesn't follow that if no necessary condition for A at t_2 is lacking at t_1, a sufficient condition is present at t_1, so that A becomes necessary relative to t_1. Although it may be true that the sum of all necessary conditions equals a sufficient condition, it is the sum of all necessary conditions *at all times* that is required for this, not just the sum of all necessary conditions at t_1.

[9] Care is called for in this connection, however, since though nothing can happen, a past or present necessary condition of which is lacking, the same does not hold true if a future necessary condition is lacking. This point is of importance for some recent arguments for fatalism. See the author's paper referred to above, and his review of Steven Cahn's *Fate, Logic and Time* in The *Journal of Philosophy*, LXV, No. 22 (November 21, 1968), 742–746.

[10] This phrase comes from Keith Lehrer and Richard Taylor, "Time, Truth and Modalities," *Mind*, LXXIV (1965), 395.

[11] *Pace* Diodorus Cronus, who (in a different context) maintained that the impossible does not follow from the possible [William Kneale and Martha Kneale, *The Development of Logic* (Oxford: Clarendon Press, 1962), p. 119].

point did it become impossible? Presumably once the blade of Black's putter had finished making contact with the ball, and failed to give it sufficient impetus. If on the other hand the ball had been struck correctly (allowing for lie, slowness, wormcasts etc.), then from that point on it would have been impossible for Black's putt not to drop, i.e., it would have been necessary for it to drop. It is significant that what was (at 7:12:00) neither impossible nor necessary can become (at 7:12:59) either impossible or necessary, whereas what was not previously possible can never become possible. This asymmetry of the physical modalities is not accurately reflected in the way we commonly think and talk about human abilities, since although we frequently speak of a man's being able to do something which he is not able to do at a later time, we also speak of a man's not being able to do something which he is able to do at a later time. But this is an imprecise way of talking, as will be seen upon examination.

Suppose Black tells us that he nurses a secret ambition to drive the green on the 250-yard twelfth, but cannot because of the water hazard which extends right up to the apron of the green. Suppose though that one day, as a result of Black's pleas to the Greens Committee, the pond is reduced in size, enabling Black's drives to roll up to the pin. Does this mean that Black was able at time t_2 to do something which at t_1 he was not able to do? No. Presumably if he *does* drive the green at t_3, $t_3 > t_2 > t_1$, then at t_1 he *was* able to drive the green at t_3 despite the presence of the pond. What he was not able at t_1 to do, of course, was to drive the green at any time prior to t_2, but then at t_2 he was not able to do *that* either.

The purpose of these golfing examples is to render plausible the thesis that what "X can do A" basically means is "it is physically possible for X to do A." There are various subsidiary meanings of "X can do A," but before turning to these I want to examine two minor consequences of the thesis just stated.

The first consequence is that a man can do things for the doing of which no skills can be developed. For example, rolling a seven blindfolded with fair dice, or turning the two dials of a safe by luck to the correct combination.[12] These things are physically possible under certain conditions, hence men can do them under those conditions. The second minor consequence is that we must be careful about the word "physical" as qualifying human abilities, since we occasionally speak of a man as being at once "physically capable" and "psychologically incapable" of doing one and the same thing. What does this mean? In a concrete case it might mean something like this: a man is incapable of swallowing arsenic when he knows that it is arsenic. This does not at first sight seem to be a case of physical incapacity, since if the man is given arsenic concealed in a chocolate, he swallows it readily enough. When he knows it is arsenic, however, his throat gags and he cannot swallow even if he wills to do so.[13] In such cases, as well as in neurotic cases such as compulsive washing of hands, it would be natural to speak of *psychological* incapacity, resting nevertheless on what we have called *physical* impossibility.

---

[12] See R. Chisholm, " 'He Could Have Done Otherwise,' " *The Journal of Philosophy,* LXIV (1967), 415–416. [Cf. pp. 298 ff. below. Ed.] See also the end of the present paper for a fuller discussion of this example.

[13] The body can, of course, be disciplined. There was a famous professor of chemistry at McGill who would swallow a lethal dose of arsenic followed by the antidote in front of his class.

Turning now to subsidiary senses of "X can do A," a common distinction is that which exists between ability and opportunity. That is to say, we often speak of a man having the ability to do A (though he does not have the opportunity), and we often speak of a man having the opportunity to do A (though he does not have the ability). Brown, for example, has the ability to drink two quarts of beer without taking a breath, though he rarely has the opportunity, and Peter frequently has the opportunity of beating his father at chess, but has never done so because he lacks the ability. In neither of these cases, however, is the agent able, in the basic sense we have been considering, to perform the action in question. If Brown lacks the beer, he cannot perform his drinking feat any more than Peter can beat his father at chess. X can properly do A, therefore, only if he has *both* the "ability" and the opportunity,[14] and it is only by courtesy that we assert "X can do A" if one of these is lacking. Nor is it clear in all cases whether the boundary between "ability" (in this courtesy sense) and opportunity can be drawn—is there for instance such a thing as the "ability" to roll a seven with fair dice over and above the opportunity? To sum up, although nothing is more natural than to distinguish between ability and opportunity, the temptation to erect a corresponding distinction between an "ability" and "opportunity" sense of "can" should probably be resisted, since one without the other always implies "can*not*."

A yet more common use of the word "can" is to be found in its application to *types* of actions ("generic" actions), rather than to individual actions. If, for instance, it is said that Tim can run a mile in four minutes, or milk a cow, or whistle through his teeth, it is simply asserted that he can perform actions of these types, without any particular occasion of his performing them being alluded to. The word "can" has not, however, been used in this way in the discussion up to now. In what I have called the "basic" sense of "X can do A," the variable "A" must be replaced by an expression referring to a particular action at a particular time. Thus "Black can hole his putt at 7:13," "Tim can milk Daisy tomorrow morning," etc.[15] Hence it remains to be seen whether the admittedly common use of the word "can" in connection with action-types rather than individual actions can be given any precise meaning in terms of the "basic" use discussed in this paper.

There are at least five things that could be meant by "Tim can run a mile in four minutes." First, "Tim can run a mile now," where the "can" has its customary application to individual actions; second, "Tim can run a mile at some future time t";[16] third, "If Tim were now starting to run a mile, he could [17] run it in four minutes"; fourth, "If at some future time t Tim were starting to run a mile, he could [18] run it in four minutes"; and fifth, "Tim has succeeded in running a mile in four minutes in a significantly large number of trials in the past." Although in each of these cases the word "can" is used in its "basic" sense, none of them con-

---

[14] Cf. J. L. Austin's "all-in" sense of "can." [Pp. 176–177 below. Ed.]

[15] It is true that in "Time and the Physical Modalities" a formal system of these modalities is constructed in which the variables range over event-types rather than over particular events. But in that system an assertion of physical possibility is always of the form Mxt_1t_2, i.e., "Event of type x, occurring at time t_1, is possible with respect to time t_2," and never of the form Mxt_1 or Mxt_2.

[16] Meaning "Tim can (run a mile at some future time t)," not "Tim (can run a mile) at some future time t."

[17] Note "could," not "would."

[18] See note 17.

stitutes a really satisfactory analysis of "Tim can run a mile in four minutes," as will be seen.

First, if they assert anything at all, those who assert that Tim can run a mile in four minutes would not wish to assert that he can do so *now*. For Tim might have just finished an exhausting race, or be fast asleep in bed. Second, they would not wish to assert that Tim can do so at some future time t, for Tim might in 1969 be only three years old, and even though he actually can (and does) run a four-minute mile in 1989, people would be unwilling to say that in 1969 he can. (One might perhaps get closer to what seems to be the intuitive meaning of "X can do things of type A" by analyzing this as "X can do things of type A at some future but proximate time t," but this is hopelessly vague.) Third, our statement cannot mean "If Tim were now starting to run a mile, he could run it in four minutes," for as before Tim might be exhausted, or might have just finished emulating Brown's feat of drinking two quarts of beer without a breath. Nor can it mean, fourthly, that if at some future time t Tim were starting to run a mile, he could run it in four minutes, for the Tim of time t is *not* the Tim of now or of the past, but the (future) Tim of time t, and it is quite possible to conceive of circumstances in which Tim loses the capacity to run a four-minute mile. Tim might have strained his heart from exhaustion in the last race, for example, or he might fall over when drunk and become concussed, in which case it would not be true of any future time t that if he started to run a mile at t, he could run it in four minutes. This leaves only the fifth possibility, that to say that Tim can run a four-minute mile is to say (in effect) that he has performed well in the past. But this alternative suffers from the converse defect of alternative four, since there are conceivable cases in which we might feel inclined to agree that Tim had performed well in the past, but because of subsequent incapacitation deny that he was now capable of running a four-minute mile.

The upshot seems to be that all attempts to analyze "X can do A," where A is an action-type, in terms of "X can do B," where B is a particular action, fail. This conclusion should not alarm us, for it is my contention that no clear meaning can be attached to the expression "X can do A" without exhaustively specifying the conditions under which X is alleged to have the ability in question, and to do this is to convert A into an individual action. Thus Tim can run a four-minute mile *if* he is rested, *if* the track is level and fast, *if* he has the right kind of competition, etc. But if these conditions are not satisfied then there are no two ways about it, he *cannot* run a four-minute mile, and to assert that he can is a mistake.

In conclusion, I should like briefly to consider the views of four philosophers unfriendly to the idea that the "can" of human ability is analyzable in terms of physical possibility.

In the first chapter of *Freedom of the Individual*, Stuart Hampshire calls attention to what he regards as important differences between pairs of propositions such as the following:

(1) The gas cannot escape now.
(2) Jones cannot escape now.

Hampshire regards (1) as a stronger version of

(3) The gas will not escape now.

On his view, it would be quite appropriate to deny (1) by saying: "I agree with you that in fact it will not happen now; but, all the same, it might; it is not altogether impossible. Your statement is too strong." [19] To assert that it cannot happen is, according to Hampshire, "at least to assert that there are grounds for believing that it will not happen, which are strong enough to justify the assertion that it cannot happen." The case of human ability, on the other hand, is different. To say that Jones cannot escape now is not a stronger way of saying that he will not: it does not consist in asserting that we have conclusive evidence that he will not. Instead, (2) asserts that Jones lacks the ability or the means or the opportunity to escape.

What Hampshire's position comes down to is an epistemic interpretation of the physical modalities, coupled with a nonepistemic interpretation of human ability. Given perfect information about the state of the gas and its container at time t_1, Hampshire would, I think, have to maintain that there was no difference between stating that the gas *cannot* escape at time t_2 and stating that it *will not*. Now this position is what one would expect of a determinist, since perfect information at t_1 enables one to predict what will happen at t_2 with complete accuracy if determinism is true. But, in an indeterministic situation, there is a very great difference between asserting (say) that an individual atom of carbon 14 *cannot* decay in the next year and asserting that it *will not* decay, since the first assertion is false and the second may well turn out to be true.[20] The difference between the two is not to be sought in the *grounds for believing* one rather than the other. Hence it does not seem to me that Hampshire's epistemic analysis of the physical modalities does justice to them, and if we reject his analysis, the differences he finds between physical possibility and human ability disappear.

Bruce Aune, in an article entitled "Can" in the *Encyclopaedia of Philosophy*, makes clear his discontent over identifying the "can" of human action with what he calls "conditional physical possibility." The discontent seems to amount to this. The notion of conditional physical possibility is an aseptic scientific one, ill-fitted to capture any of the morally important aspects of such a claim as "he could have done otherwise" when this claim is made of criminals, heroes, and others on whom moral judgment is being passed. But is this so? If a bank clerk pleads that it was physically impossible for him to refrain from putting ten dollars in his pocket every day he left work, do we believe him? No. Instead we seek psychiatric advice to establish that it *was* physically possible for him to refrain, e.g., that he was not a kleptomaniac. Here the notion of physical possibility seems exactly suited to be the basis for establishing moral responsibility. It is true, as Aune says, that the vocabulary of action description is "intentional" in a way in which scientific language is not. But there is no need to let this intentional element creep into the meaning of the word "can." In the total expression "X can do A" it represents a gain in clarity to confine the intentional element to the "A," and let the "can" be as precise and coldly scientific as possible.

Richard Taylor, in at least two places, argues against identifying the "can" of

---

[19] *Freedom of the Individual* (New York: Harper & Row, Inc., 1965), p. 12.

[20] Though not at the time it was made, but later. See the author's "Temporal Flux," *American Philosophical Quarterly*, III (1966), 273.

human agency with physical possibility.[21] Taking the example "I can move my finger to the left, and I can move it to the right," Taylor demonstrates convincingly that this form of words does not mean that my finger can move to the left or to the right, i.e., that it is physically possible for it to do so. For my finger might be entirely out of my control (its tendons might be cut, for example), and yet it might still be true to say that it could move to the left and that it could move to the right. The doctor might be able to move it, for example. Yet it would be false to say in this case that *I* could move my finger to the left or right. However, although Taylor's arguments are correct, we find in them no reason not to identify "X can do A" with "It is physically possible for X to do A," granted that the latter must be distinguished from "It is physically possible for A to occur."

Finally, we find in a recent paper by Chisholm an argument designed to show that the "could" of "He could have done otherwise" is not the "could" of physical possibility.[22] Chisholm's example is this. Suppose we say to X, "This morning you could have arranged things so that you would be in Boston by noon, but you didn't." Chisholm asks whether this statement could mean the following: there was a time this morning, say 10 o'clock, when there was no sufficient causal condition for X's not being in Boston by noon, though it turned out in the end that X was not in Boston by noon. Chisholm argues that the original statement could not mean this. For suppose that X in fact tried to get to Boston by noon, but was prevented from doing so by an entirely fortuitous event: another man, Y let us say, met X at 11 o'clock and held X back, without there being at 10 o'clock any causally sufficient condition for Y's doing so. This state of affairs is, as Chisholm points out, quite compatible with there being at 10 o'clock no sufficient causal condition for X's not being in Boston by noon. But it is *not* compatible with our original statement, namely that X could have arranged things so that he would be in Boston by noon. Hence the original statement does not mean that at, say, 10 o'clock there was no sufficient condition for X's not being in Boston by noon, i.e., that it was physically possible for him to be there.

Chisholm's example is not, however, convincing. No doubt it is quite correct to say that at 10 o'clock X could not have "arranged things" so that he would be in Boston by noon, for at 11 o'clock he was forestalled. But this means no more than that at 10 o'clock X could have done otherwise (i.e., could have been in Boston by noon), whereas at 11 o'clock X could not have done otherwise (i.e., could not be in Boston by noon). What was possible at 10 o'clock became impossible at 11 o'clock. What tends to mislead in Chisholm's example is the suggestion that if it was possible at 10 o'clock for X to get to Boston by noon (as indeed it was), then there ought to have been something which X could do at 10 o'clock which *ensured* that he reach Boston by noon. But this of course does not follow, and normally when we say "At t_1, X can do A at t_2," we do not mean "There is something X can do at t_1 to ensure that he do A at t_2." I say "normally" here, because there *are* cases in which we could conceivably mean just this. In Chisholm's example of the safecracker, for example, X might be able by luck to turn the knobs to the one correct combination out of 10,000 within 10 seconds, but this is not

21 "I Can," *The Philosophical Review*, LXIX (1960), 78–89; *Metaphysics* (Englewood Cliffs, New Jersey: Prentice-Hall, Inc., 1963), p. 39.
22 R. M. Chisholm, " 'He Could Have Done Otherwise,' " p. 412. [See pp. 295–296 below. Ed.]

usually what we have in mind when we say "X can open the safe in 10 seconds." Instead we have in mind the picture of a man who either knows the combination, or can detect what it is by listening to the safe's mechanism with a stethoscope, or can blow the safe open with dynamite. That is, X can do something to *make* or *force* the safe open in 10 seconds' time. In cases such as these, "At t_1, X can do A at t_2" admittedly does mean "($\exists B$) (It is physically possible for X to do B at t_1 & X's doing A at t_2 is physically necessary relative to X's doing B at t_1)." But this, although a variant on the basic sense of "can" discussed above, is once more an analysis of the latter in terms of physical possibility and physical necessity.

CONDITIONALS

FREE WILL

G. E. Moore

Throughout the last three chapters we have been considering various objections which might be urged against the theory stated in Chapters I and II. And the very last objection which we considered was one which consisted in asserting that the question whether an action is right or wrong does *not* depend upon its *actual* consequences, because whenever the consequences, *so far as the agent can foresee,* are *likely* to be the best possible, the action is always right, even if they are not *actually* the best possible. In other words, this objection rested on the view that right and wrong depend, in a sense, upon what the agent *can know.* And in the present chapter I propose to consider objections, which rest, instead of this, upon the view that right and wrong depend upon what the agent *can do.*

Now it must be remembered that, *in a sense,* our original theory does hold and even insists that this is the case. We have, for instance, frequently referred to it in the last chapter as holding that an action is only right, if it produces the best *possible* consequences; and by "the best *possible* consequences" was meant "consequences at least as good as would have followed from any action which the agent *could* have done instead." It does, therefore, hold that the question whether an action is right or wrong does always depend upon a comparison of its consequences with those of all the other actions which the agent *could* have done instead. It assumes, therefore, that wherever a voluntary action is right or wrong (and we have throughout only been talking of *voluntary* actions), it is true that

From *Ethics* by G. E. Moore (Oxford, England: The Clarendon Press, 1912), Chapter VI, pp. 122–137. Reprinted by permission of the Clarendon Press, Oxford.

the agent *could*, in a sense, have done something else instead. This is an absolutely essential part of the theory.

But the reader must now be reminded that all along we have been using the words "can," "could," and "possible" *in a special sense*. It was explained in Chapter I, that we proposed, purely for the sake of brevity, to say that an agent *could* have done a given action, which he didn't do, wherever it is true that he could have done it, *if* he had chosen; and similarly by what he *can* do, or what is *possible*, we have always meant merely what is possible, *if* he chooses. Our theory, therefore, has not been maintaining, after all, that right and wrong depend upon what the agent absolutely *can* do, but only on what he can do, *if* he chooses. And this makes an immense difference. For, by confining itself in this way, our theory avoids a controversy, which cannot be avoided by those who assert that right and wrong depend upon what the agent absolutely *can* do. There are few, if any, people who will *expressly* deny that we very often really could, *if* we had chosen, have done something different from what we actually did do. But the moment it is asserted that any man ever absolutely *could* have done anything other than what he did do, there are many people who *would* deny this. The view, therefore, which we are to consider in this chapter—the view that right and wrong depend upon what the agent absolutely *can* do—at once involves us in an extremely difficult controversy—the controversy concerning Free Will. There are many people who strenuously deny that any man ever *could* have done anything other than what he actually did do, or ever *can* do anything other than what he *will* do; and there are others who assert the opposite equally strenuously. And whichever view be held is, if *combined* with the view that right and wrong depend upon what the agent absolutely *can* do, liable to contradict our theory very seriously. Those who hold that no man ever *could* have done anything other than what he did do, are, if they *also* hold that right and wrong depend upon what we *can* do, logically bound to hold that no action of ours is ever right and none is ever wrong; and this is a view which is, I think, often actually held, and which, of course, constitutes an extremely serious and fundamental objection to our theory: since our theory implies, on the contrary, that we very often do act *wrongly*, if never quite rightly. Those, on the other hand, who hold that we absolutely *can* do things, which we don't do, and that right and wrong depend upon what we thus *can* do, are also liable to be led to contradict our theory, though for a different reason. Our theory holds that, provided a man could have done something else, *if* he had chosen, that is sufficient to entitle us to say that his action really is either right or wrong. But those who hold the view we are considering will be liable to reply that this is by no means sufficient: that to say that it *is* sufficient, is entirely to misconceive the nature of right and wrong. They will say that, in order that an action may be *really* either right or wrong, it is absolutely essential that the agent should have been *really able* to act differently, able in some sense quite other than that of merely being able, *if* he had chosen. If all that were really ever true of us were merely that we could have acted differently, *if* we had chosen, then, these people would say, it really would be true that none of our actions are ever right and that none are ever wrong. They will say, therefore, that our theory entirely misses out one absolutely essential condition of right and wrong—the condition that, for an action to be right or wrong, it must be *freely* done. And moreover, many of them will hold also that the class of actions which we absolutely *can* do is often not identical with those which we can do, *if* we choose. They may say, for instance, that very often an action, which we *could* have done, *if* we had chosen, is nevertheless an action which we *could not* have done; and that an action is always right, if it produces as good consequences as any other action which we really *could* have done instead. From which it will follow that many actions which our theory declares to be *wrong*, will, according to them, be right, because these actions really are the best of all that we *could* have done, though *not* the best of all that we could have done, *if* we had chosen.

Now these objections seem to me to be the most serious which we have yet had to consider. They seem to me to be serious because (1) it is very difficult to be sure that right and wrong do not really depend, as they assert, upon what we *can* do and not merely on what we can do, *if* we choose; and because (2) it is very difficult to be sure in what sense it is true that we ever *could* have done anything different from what we actually did do. I do not profess to be sure about either of these points. And all that I can hope to do is to point out certain facts which do seem to me to be clear, though they are often overlooked; and thus to isolate clearly for the reader's decision, those questions which seem to me to be really doubtful and difficult.

Let us begin with the question: Is it ever true that a man *could* have done anything else, except what he actually did do? And, first of all, I think I had better explain exactly how this question seems to me to be related to the question of Free Will. For it is a fact that, in many discussions about Free Will, this precise question is never mentioned at all; so that it might be thought that the two have really nothing whatever to do with one another. And indeed some philosophers do, I think, definitely imply that they *have* nothing to do with one another: they seem to hold that our wills can properly be said to be free even if we *never* can, in any sense at all, do anything else except what, in the end, we actually do do. But this view, if it is held, seems to me to be plainly a mere abuse of language. The statement that we have Free Will is certainly ordinarily understood to imply that we really sometimes have the power of acting differently from the way in which we actually do act; and hence, if anybody tells us that we have Free Will, while at the same time he means to deny that we ever have such a power, he is simply misleading us. We certainly have *not* got Free Will, in the ordinary sense of the word, if we never really *could*, in any sense at all, have done anything else than what we did do; so that, in this respect, the two questions certainly are connected. But, on the other hand, the mere fact (if it is a fact) that we sometimes *can*, in *some* sense, do what we don't do, does not necessarily entitle us to say that we *have* Free Will. We certainly *haven't* got it, *unless* we can; but it doesn't follow that we *have* got it, even if we *can*. Whether we have or not will depend upon the precise sense in which it is true that we can. So that even if we do decide that we really *can* often, in *some* sense, do what we don't do, this decision by itself does not entitle us to say that we have Free Will.

And the first point about which we can and should be quite clear is, I think, this: namely, that we certainly often *can*, in *some* sense, do what we don't do. It is, I think, quite clear that this is so; and also very important that we should realize that it is so. For many people are inclined to assert, quite without qualification: No man ever *could*, on any occasion, have done anything else than what he actually did do on that occasion. By asserting this quite simply, without qualification, they imply, of course (even if they do not mean to imply), that there is *no* proper sense of the word "could," in which it is true that a man *could* have acted differently. And it is this implication which is, I think, quite certainly absolutely false. For this reason, anybody who asserts, without qualification, "Nothing ever *could* have happened, except what actually did happen," is making an assertion which is quite unjustifiable, and which he himself cannot help constantly contradicting. And it is important to insist on this, because many people do make this unqualified assertion, without seeing how violently it contradicts what they themselves, and all of us, believe, and rightly believe, at other times. If, indeed, they insert a qualification—if they merely say, "In *one* sense of the word '*could*' nothing ever *could* have happened, except what did happen," then, they may perhaps be perfectly right: we are not disputing that they may. All that we are maintaining is that, in *one* perfectly proper and legitimate sense of the word "could," and that one of the very commonest senses in which it is used, it is quite certain that some things which didn't happen *could* have happened. And the proof that this is so, is simply as follows.

It is impossible to exaggerate the frequency of the occasions on which we *all* of us make a distinction between two things, neither of which *did* happen—a distinction which we express by saying, that whereas the one *could* have happened, [the] other could *not*. No distinction is commoner than this. And no one, I think, who fairly examines the instances in which we make it, can doubt about three things: namely (1) that very often there really is *some* distinction between the two things, corresponding to the language which we use; (2) that this distinction, which really *does* subsist between the things, is *the* one which we mean to express by saying that the one was possible and the other impossible; and (3) that this way of expressing it is a perfectly proper and legitimate way. But if so, it absolutely follows that one of the commonest and most legitimate usages of the phrases "could" and "could not" is to express a difference, which often really does hold between two things *neither* of which did actually happen. Only a few instances need be given. I *could* have walked a mile in twenty minutes this morning, but I certainly could *not* have run two miles in five minutes. I did not, *in fact,* do either of these two things; but it is pure nonsense to say that the mere fact that I *did* not, does away with the distinction between them, which I express by saying that the one *was* within my powers, whereas the other was *not. Although* I did neither, yet the one was certainly *possible* to me in a sense in which the other was totally *im*possible. Or, to take another instance: It is true, as a rule, that cats *can* climb trees, whereas dogs *can't.* Suppose that on a particular afternoon neither A's cat nor B's dog *do* climb a tree. It is quite absurd to say that this mere fact proves that we must be wrong if we say (as we certainly often should say) that the cat *could* have climbed a tree, though she didn't, whereas the dog *couldn't.* Or, to take an instance which concerns an inanimate object. Some ships *can* steam 20 knots, whereas others *can't* steam more than 15. And the mere fact that, on a particular occasion, a 20-knot steamer *did* not *actually* run at this speed certainly does not entitle us to say that she *could* not have done so, in the sense in which a 15-knot one *could* not. On the contrary, we all can and should distinguish between cases in which (as, for instance, owing to an accident to her propeller) she did not, *because* she could not, and cases in which she did not, *although* she could. Instances of this sort might be multiplied quite indefinitely; and it is surely quite plain that we all of us do *continually* use such language: we continually, when considering two events, neither of which *did* happen, distinguish between them by saying that whereas the one *was* possible, though it didn't happen, the other was *im*possible. And it is surely quite plain that what we mean by this (whatever it may be) is something which is often perfectly true. But, if so, then anybody who asserts, without qualification, "Nothing ever *could* have happened, except what did happen," is simply asserting what is false.

It is, therefore, quite certain that we often *could* (in *some* sense) have done what we did not do. And now let us see how this fact is related to the argument by which people try to persuade us that it is *not* a fact.

The argument is well known: it is simply this. It is assumed (for reasons which I need not discuss) that absolutely everything that happens has a *cause* in what precedes it. But to say this is to say that it follows *necessarily* from something that preceded it; or, in other words, that, once the preceding events which are its cause had happened, it was absolutely *bound* to happen. But to say that it was *bound* to happen, is to say that nothing else *could* have happened instead; so that, if *everything* has a cause, *nothing* ever could have happened except what did happen.

And now let us assume that the premise of this argument is correct: that everything really *has* a cause. What really follows from it? Obviously all that follows is that, in *one* sense of the word "could," nothing ever *could* have happened, except what did happen. This really *does* follow. But, *if* the word "could" is ambiguous— if, that is to say, it is used in different senses on different occasions—it is obviously quite possible that though, in *one* sense, nothing ever could have happened except what did happen, yet in *another* sense, it may at the same time be perfectly true that some things which did not happen *could* have happened. And can anybody undertake to assert with certainty that the word "could" is *not* ambiguous? that it may not have more than one legitimate sense? *Possibly* it is not ambiguous; and, *if* it is not, then the fact that some things, which did not happen, *could* have happened, really would contradict the principle that everything has a cause; and, in that case, we should, I think, have to give up this principle, because the fact that we often *could* have done what we did not do, is so certain. But the assumption that the word "could" is *not* ambiguous is an assumption which certainly should not be made without the clearest proof. And yet I think it often is made, without any proof at all; simply because it does not occur to people that words often are ambiguous. It is, for instance, often assumed, in the Free Will controversy, that the question at issue is solely as to whether everything is caused, or whether acts of will are sometimes uncaused. Those who hold that we *have* Free Will, think themselves bound to maintain that acts of will sometimes have *no* cause; and those who hold that everything is caused think that this proves completely that we have not Free Will. But, in fact, it is extremely doubtful whether Free Will is at all inconsistent with the principle that everything is caused. Whether it is or not, all depends on a very difficult question as to the meaning of the word "could." All that is certain about the matter is (1) that, if we have Free Will, it must be true, in *some* sense, that we sometimes *could* have done, what we did not do; and (2) that, if everything is caused, it must be true, in *some* sense, that we *never could* have done, what we did not do. What is very *un*certain, and what certainly needs to be investigated, is whether these two meanings of the word "could" are the same.

Let us begin by asking: What is the sense of the word "could," in which it is so certain that we often *could* have done, what we did not do? What, for instance, is the sense in which I *could* have walked a mile in twenty minutes this morning, though I did not? There is one suggestion, which is very obvious: namely, that what I mean is simply after all that I could, *if* I had chosen; or (to avoid a possible complication) perhaps we had better say "that I *should, if* I had chosen." In other words, the suggestion is that we often use the phrase "*I could*" simply and solely as a short way of saying "I *should, if* I had chosen." And in all cases, where it is certainly true that we *could* have done, what we did not do, it is, I think, very difficult to be quite sure that this (or something similar) is *not* what we mean by the word "could." The case of the ship may seem to be an exception, because it is certainly not true that she would have steamed twenty knots if *she* had chosen; but even here it seems possible that what we mean is simply that she *would, if the men on board of her* had chosen. There are certainly good reasons for thinking that we *very often* mean by "could" merely "would, *if* so and so had chosen." And if so, when we have a sense of the word "could" in which the fact that we often *could* have done what we did not do, is perfectly compatible with the principle that everything has a cause: for to say that, *if* I had performed a certain act of will, I should have done something which I did not do, in no way contradicts this principle.

And an additional reason for supposing that this *is* what we often mean by "could," and one which is also a reason why it is important to insist on the obvious fact that we very often really *should* have acted differently, *if* we had willed differently, is that those who deny that we ever *could* have done anything, which we did not do, often speak and think as if this really did involve the conclusion that we never should have acted differently, even *if* we had willed differently. This occurs, I think, in two chief instances—one in reference to the future, the other in reference to the past. The first occurs when, because they hold that nothing *can* happen, except what *will* happen, people are led to adopt the view called Fatalism—the view that *whatever we will,* the result will always be the same; that it is, therefore, *never* any use to make one choice rather than another. And this conclusion will really follow if by "can" we mean "*would* happen, even *if* we were to will it." But it is certainly untrue, and it certainly does not follow from the principle of causality. On the contrary, reasons of exactly the same sort and exactly as strong as those which lead us to suppose that everything has a cause, lead to the conclusion that if we choose one course, the result will *always* be different in *some* respect from what it would have been, if we had chosen another; and we know also that the difference would *sometimes* consist in the fact that *what* we chose would come to pass. It is certainly often true of the future, therefore, that whichever of two actions we *were* to choose, *would* actually be done, although it is quite certain that only one of the two *will* be done.

And the second instance, in which people are apt to speak and think, as if, *because* no man ever *could* have done anything but what he did do, it follows that he would not, even *if* he had chosen, is as follows. Many people seem, in fact, to conclude directly from the first of these two propositions, that we can never be justified in praising or blaming a man for anything that he does, or indeed for making any distinction between what is right or wrong, on the one hand, and what is lucky or unfortunate on the other. They conclude, for instance, that there is never any reason to treat or to regard the voluntary commission of a crime in any different way from that in which we treat or regard the involuntary catching of a disease. The man who committed the crime *could* not, they say, have helped committing it any more than the other man could have helped catching the disease; both events were equally inevitable; and though both may of course be great *misfortunes,* though both may have very bad consequences and equally bad ones—there is no justification whatever, they say, for the distinction we make between them when we say that the commission of the crime was *wrong,* or that the man was morally to blame for it, whereas the catching of the disease was *not* wrong and the man was not to blame for it. And this conclusion, again, will really follow if by "*could* not" we mean "*would* not, even if he had willed to avoid it." But the point I want to make is, that it follows *only* if we make this assumption. That is to say, the mere fact that the man *would* have succeeded in avoiding the crime, *if* he had chosen (which is certainly often true), whereas the other man would *not* have succeeded in avoiding the disease, *even* if he had chosen (which is certainly also often true) gives an ample justification for regarding and treating the two cases differently. It gives such a justification, because, where the occurrence of an event *did* depend upon the will, there, by acting on the will (as we may do by blame or punishment) we have often a reasonable chance of preventing similar events from recurring in the future; whereas, where it did *not* depend upon the will, we have no such chance. We may, therefore, fairly say that those who speak and think, as if a man who brings about a misfortune *voluntarily* ought to be treated and regarded in exactly the same way as one who brings about an equally great misfortune *involuntarily,* are speaking and thinking *as if* it were not true that we ever should have acted differently, even *if* we had willed to do so. And that is why it is extremely important to insist on the absolute certainty of the fact that we often really *should* have acted differently, *if* we had willed differently.

There is, therefore, much reason to think that when we say that we *could* have done a thing which we did not do, we *often* mean merely that we *should* have done it, *if* we had chosen. And if so, then it is quite certain that, in *this* sense, we often really *could* have done what we did not do, and that this fact is in no way inconsistent with the principle that everything has a cause. And for my part I must confess that I cannot feel certain that this may not be *all* that we usually mean and understand by the assertion that we have Free Will; so that those who deny that we have it are really denying (though, no doubt, often unconsciously) that we ever *should* have acted differently, even if we had willed differently. It has been sometimes held that this *is* what we mean; and I cannot find any conclusive argument to the contrary. And if it is what we mean, then it absolutely follows that we really have Free Will, and also that this fact is quite consistent with the principle that everything has a cause; and it follows also that our theory will be perfectly right, when it makes right and wrong depend on what we *could* have done, *if* we had chosen.

But, no doubt, there are many people who will say that this is *not* sufficient to entitle us to say that we have Free Will; and they will say this for a reason, which certainly has some plausibility, though I cannot satisfy myself that it is conclusive. They will say, namely: Granted that we often *should* have acted differently, *if* we had chosen differently, yet it is not true that we have Free Will, unless it is *also* often true in such cases that we *could* have *chosen* differently. The question of Free Will has been thus represented as being merely the question whether we ever *could* have chosen, what we did not choose, or ever *can* choose, what, in fact, we shall not choose. And since there is some plausibility in this contention, it is, I think, worth while to point out that here again it is absolutely certain that, in two different senses, at least, we often *could* have chosen, what, in fact, we did not choose; and that in neither sense does this fact contradict the principle of causality.

The first is simply the old sense over again. If by saying that we *could* have done, what we did not do, we often mean merely that we *should* have done it, *if* we had chosen to do it, then obviously, by saying that we *could* have *chosen* to do it, we may mean merely that we *should* have so chosen, *if* we had chosen *to make the choice*. And I think there is no doubt it is often true that we should have chosen to do a particular thing *if* we had chosen to make the choice; and that this is a very important sense in which it is often in our power to make a choice. There certainly is such a thing as making an effort to induce ourselves to *choose* a particular course; and I think there is no doubt that often if we *had* made such an effort, we *should* have made a choice, which we did not in fact make.

And besides this, there is another sense in which, whenever we have several different courses of action in view, it is *possible* for us to choose any one of them; and a sense which is certainly of some practical importance, even if it goes no way to justify us in saying that we have Free Will. This sense arises from the fact that in such cases we can hardly ever *know for certain* beforehand, *which* choice we actually *shall* make; and one of the commonest senses of the word "possible" is that in which we call an event "possible" when no man can *know for certain* that it will *not* happen. It follows that almost, if not quite always, when we make a choice, after considering alternatives, it *was* possible that we should have chosen one of these alternatives, which we did not actually choose; and often, of course, it was not only possible, but highly probable, that we should have done so. And this fact is certainly of practical importance, because many people are apt much too easily to assume that it is quite certain that they *will not* make a given choice, which they know they ought to make, if it were possible; and their belief that they *will* not make it tends, of course, to prevent them from making it. For this reason it is important to insist that they can hardly ever know for certain with regard to any given choice that they will *not* make it.

It is, therefore, quite certain (1) that we often *should* have *acted* differently, if we had chosen to; (2) that similarly we often should have *chosen* differently, *if* we had chosen so to choose; and (3) that it was almost always *possible* that we should have chosen differently, in the sense that no man could know for certain that we should *not* so choose. All these three things are facts, and all of them are quite consistent with the principle of causality. Can anybody undertake to say for certain that none of these three facts and *no* combination of them will justify us in saying that we have Free Will? Or, suppose it granted that we have not Free Will, unless it is often true that we *could* have chosen, what we did not choose:—Can any defender of Free Will, or any opponent of it, show conclusively that what he means by "*could* have chosen" in this proposition, is anything different from the two certain facts, which I have numbered (2) and (3), or some combination of the two? Many people, no doubt, will still insist that these two facts alone are by no means sufficient to entitle us to say that we have Free Will: that it must be true that we were *able* to choose, in some quite other sense. But nobody, so far as I know, has ever been able to tell us exactly what that sense is. For my part, I can find no conclusive argument to show either that some such other sense of "can" is necessary, or that it is not. And, therefore, this chapter must conclude with a doubt. It is, I think, possible that, instead of saying, as our theory said, that an action is only right, when it produces consequences as good as any which would have followed from any other action which the agent *would* have done, *if* he had chosen, we should say instead that it is right whenever and only when the agent *could not have done* anything which would have produced better consequences: and that this "*could not* have done" is *not* equivalent to "would not have done, *if* he had chosen," but is to be understood in the sense, whatever it may be, which is sufficient to entitle us to say that we have Free Will. If so, then our theory would be wrong, just to this extent.

FREEDOM AND RESPONSIBILITY

P. H. Nowell-Smith

. . .

The most difficult and important of the items on our list of moral judgments is "He could have acted otherwise" (2).* The facts about its logical connections with the others are tolerably clear. It is a necessary condition of all except (1) and it is also a necessary condition of (1) if "He broke a law" is taken to imply that he broke it voluntarily. What is not so clear is what (2) means or why it should be a necessary condition of the other items.

A man is not considered blameworthy if he could not have acted otherwise; and, although it is often easy to decide in practice whether he could have acted otherwise or not, it is not clear how we do this or why we should think it necessary to do it. Let us first examine the use of "could have" in some nonmoral cases.

"Could have" is a modal phrase, and modal phrases are not normally used to make straightforward, categorical statements. "It might have rained last Thursday" tells you something about the weather, but not in the way that "It rained last Thursday" does. It is sometimes said that it is used to express the speaker's ignorance of the weather; but what it expresses is not just this but his ignorance of any facts that would strongly tend to rule out the truth of "It rained." It would be a natural thing to say in the middle of an English, but not of a Californian summer.

From *Ethics* by P. H. Nowell-Smith (London: Penguin Books Ltd., 1954, 1964), pp. 239–243. Reprinted by permission of the publisher.
* The list of moral judgments is: (1) He broke a law or moral rule; (2) He could have acted otherwise; (3) He deserves censure (or punishment); (4) It would be just to censure (or punish) him; (5) He is a bad (cruel, mean, dishonest, etc.) man.—Ed.

But, whatever it does express, what it does *not* express is a belief in a third alternative alongside "it rained" and "it did not rain." Either it rained or it did not; and "it might have rained" does not represent a third alternative which excludes the other two in the way that these exclude each other.

But these modal phrases are also sometimes used in cases in which they cannot express ignorance since they imply a belief that the event concerned did not occur. It would be disingenuous for a rich man to say "I might have been a rich man"; but he could well say "I might have been a poor man" while knowing himself to be rich. The puzzle here arises from the fact that, if he is rich, he cannot be poor. His actual riches preclude his possible poverty in a way that would seem to imply that we could have no use for "he might have been poor." But this is only puzzling so long as we try to treat these modal expressions in a categorical way.

"Would have" and "might have" are clearly suppressed hypotheticals, incomplete without an "if . . ." or an "if . . . not . . . ." Nobody would say "Jones would have won the championship" unless (a) he believed that Jones did not win and (b) he was prepared to add "if he had entered" or "if he had not sprained his ankle" or some such clause.

It is not so obvious that "could have" sentences also express hypotheticals; indeed in some cases they obviously do not. If a man says "It could have been a Morris, but actually it was an Austin," it would be absurd to ask him under what conditions it could or would have been a Morris. "Could have" is here used to concede that, although I happen to know it was an Austin, your guess that it was a Morris was not a bad one. But "could have" also has a use which is more important for our purpose and in which, as I shall try to show, it is equivalent to "would have . . . if . . . ." It refers to a tendency or capacity. Consider the following examples:

(1) He could have read *Emma* in bed last night, though he actually read *Persuasion*; but he could not have read *Werther* because he does not know German.

(2) He could have played the *Appassionata*, though he actually played the *Moonlight*; but he could not have played the *Hammerklavier*, because it is too difficult for him.

These are both statements, since they could be true or false; and to understand their logic we must see how they would be established or rebutted. Neither could be established or rebutted in the way that "He read *Persuasion*" could, by observing what he actually did; and it is partly for this reason that we do not call them categorical. But, although they could not be directly verified or falsified by observation of what he did, this might be relevant evidence. It would be almost conclusive evidence in the first case, since it would be very odd if a man who actually read *Persuasion* was incapable of reading *Emma*. On the other hand, his having played the *Moonlight* is only weak evidence that he could have played the *Appassionata*, since the latter is more difficult and also because he might never have learnt it.

In each of these cases, in order to establish the "could have" statement we should have to show (a) that he has performed tasks of similar difficulty sufficiently often to preclude the possibility of a fluke, and (b) that nothing prevented him on this occasion. For example we should have to establish that there was a copy of *Emma* in the house.

Statements about capacities, whether of the "can" or of the "could have" kind, contextually imply unspecified conditions under which alone the person might succeed; and "could have" statements can be refuted either by showing that some necessary condition was absent (there was no copy of *Emma*) or by showing that the capacity was absent. The first point could be established directly. How could the second be established? In practice we do this either by appealing to past performances or failures or by asking him to try to do it now. It is clear that neither of these methods could be applied directly to the occasion in question. We know that he did not read *Emma,* and it is nonsense to ask him to try to have read *Emma* last night. And the very fact that evidence for or against "could have" statements must be drawn from occasions other than that to which they refer is enough to show that "he could have acted otherwise" is not a straightforward categorical statement, at least in the type of case we have been considering. Whether it is possible or necessary to interpret it categorically in moral cases is a point which I shall examine in the next section.

It might be argued that the sort of evidence by which "could have" statements are supported or rebutted is never conclusive; and this is true. The argument used is an inductive one, with a special type of conclusion. We might use an ordinary inductive argument to predict his future performance from known past performances or in support of a statement about an unknown past performance. But in this special case we know that he did not do the thing in question, because we know that he did something else; so we put our conclusion in the form "he could have done X."

Whatever the evidence, it is always open to a skeptic to say "I know he has always succeeded (failed) in the past; but he *might* have failed (succeeded) on this occasion." Now this sort of skepticism is not peculiar to "could have" statements; it is one variety of general skepticism about induction. It is *possible* that if I had tried to add 15 and 16 last night (which I did not) I should have failed; but it is also possible that if I tried now I should fail. Our use of "could have" statements, like our use of predictions and generalizations, always ignores such refined skepticism; and it would be absurd to try to base either freedom or responsibility on the logical possibility of such contingencies. In practice we ignore the skeptic unless he can produce reasons for his doubt, unless he can say why he believes that a man who has always succeeded might have failed on just that occasion. If no such reason is forthcoming we always allow inductive evidence which establishes the existence of a general capacity to do something to establish also the statement that the man could have done it on a particular occasion. Nor is this practice due to the fact that (the world being what it is) we are unfortunately unable to find better evidence and must fall back on probabilities. Our practice lies at the heart of the logic of "can" and "could have." For the skeptic is, here as elsewhere, asking for the logically impossible; he is asking us to adopt a criterion for deciding whether a man could have done something on a particular occasion which would make the words "can" and "could have" useless. What would be the result of accepting this suggestion? We should have to say that the only conclusive evidence that a man can do (could have done) X at time t is his actually doing (having done) X at time t. Thus the evidence that entitles us to say "He could have done X at time t" would also entitle us to say "He did X at time t," and the "could have" form would be otiose.

Capacities are a subclass of dispositions. To say that a man "can" do something is not to say that he ever has or will; there may be special reasons why the capacity is never exercised, for example that the occasion for exercising it has never arisen. A man might go through his whole life without ever adding 15 and 16; and we should not have to say that he couldn't do this. Yet a man cannot be said to be able to do something if all the necessary conditions are fulfilled and he has a motive for doing it. It is logically odd to say "Smith can run a mile, has had several opportunities, is passionately fond of running, has no medical or other reasons for not doing so, but never has in fact done so." And, if it is true that this is logically odd, it follows that "can" is equivalent to "will . . . if . . ." and "could have" to "would have . . . if . . . ." To say that Smith could have read *Emma* last night is to say that he would have read it, if there had been a copy, if he had not been struck blind, etc., etc., and if he had wanted to read it more than he wanted to read anything else. Both the "etc." and the last clause are important; we cannot specify all the necessary conditions; and, granted that the conditions were present and that he could have read it, he might still not have read it because he did not want to. But if he did not want to do anything else more than he wanted to read *Emma*, he could not in these conditions be said to have *chosen* to do something else. He might have *done* something else, but not in the important sense of "done" which implies choosing.

. . .

IFS AND CANS

J. L. Austin

Are *cans* constitutionally iffy? Whenever, that is, we say that we can do some-thing, or could do something, or could have done something, is there an *if* in the offing—suppressed, it may be, but due nevertheless to appear when we set out our sentence in full or when we give an explanation of its meaning?

Again, if and when there *is* an *if*-clause appended to a main clause which con-tains a *can* or *could* or *could have*, what sort of an *if* is it? What is the meaning of the *if*, or what is the effect or the point of combining this *if*-clause with the main clause?

These are large questions, to which philosophers, among them some whom I most respect, have given small answers: and it is two such answers, given recently by English philosophers, that I propose to consider. Both, I believe, are mistaken, yet something is to be learned from examining them. In philosophy, there are many mistakes that it is no disgrace to have made: to make a first-water ground-floor mistake, so far from being easy, takes one (*one*) form of philosophical genius.[1]

Many of you will have read a short but justly admired book written by Pro-fessor G. E. Moore of Cambridge, which is called simply *Ethics*. In it, there is a point where Moore, who is engaged in discussing Right and Wrong, says that if we are to discuss whether any act that has been done was right or wrong then we are bound to discuss what the person concerned *could have* done instead of

J. L. Austin, "Ifs and Cans" from *Proceedings of the British Academy*, XLII, published by Oxford University Press, 1956.

[1] Plato, Descartes, and Leibnitz all had this form of genius, besides of course others.

what he did in fact do. And this, he thinks, may lead to an entanglement in the problem, so-called, of Free Will: because, though few would deny, at least expressly, that a man could have done something other than what he did actually do *if he had chosen,* many people would deny that he *could* (absolutely) have done any such other thing. Hence Moore is led to ask whether it is ever true, and if so in what sense, that a man could have done something other than what he did actually do. And it is with his answer to this question, not with its bearings upon the meanings of *right* and *wrong* or upon the problem of Free Will, that we are concerned.

With his usual shrewdness Moore begins by insisting that there is at least *one* proper sense in which we can say that a man can do something he doesn't do or could have done something he didn't do—even though there may perhaps be *other* senses of *can* and *could have* in which we cannot say such things. This sense he illustrates by the sentence "I could have walked a mile in 20 minutes this morning, but I certainly could not have run two miles in 5 minutes": we are to take it that in fact the speaker did not do either of the two things mentioned, but this in no way hinders us from drawing the very common and necessary distinction between undone acts that we could have done and undone acts that we could not have done. So it is certain that, at least in *some* sense, we often could have done things that we did not actually do.

Why then, Moore goes on to ask, should anyone try to deny this? And he replies that people do so (we may call them "determinists") because they hold that everything that happens has a *cause* which precedes it, which is to say that once the cause has occurred the thing itself is *bound* to occur and *nothing* else *could* ever have happened instead.

However, on examining further the 20-minute-mile example, Moore argues that there is much reason to think that "could have" in such cases simply means "could have *if* I had chosen," or, as perhaps we had better say in order to avoid a possible complication (these are Moore's words), simply means "*should* have if I had chosen." And if this *is* all it means, then there is after all no conflict between our conviction that we often could have, in this sense, done things that we did not actually do and the determinist's theory: for he certainly holds himself that I often, and perhaps even always, should have done something different from what I did do *if I had chosen* to do that different thing, since my choosing differently would constitute a change in the causal antecedents of my subsequent act, which would therefore, on his theory, naturally itself be different. If, therefore, the determinist nevertheless asserts that in *some* sense of "could have" I could *not* ever have done anything different from what I did actually do, this must simply be a second sense [2] of "could have" different from that which it has in the 20-minute-mile example.

In the remainder of his chapter, Moore argues that quite possibly his first sense of "could have," in which it simply means "could or should have if I had chosen," is all we need to satisfy our hankerings after Free Will, or at least is so if conjoined in some way with yet a third sense of "could have" in which sense "I could have done something different" means "I might, for all anyone could know for certain beforehand, have done something different." This third kind of "could have"

---

[2] About which Moore has no more to tell us.

might, I think, be held to be a vulgarism, "could" being used incorrectly for "might": but in any case we shall not be concerned with it here.

In the upshot, then, Moore leaves us with only one important sense in which it can be said that I could have done something that I did not do: he is not convinced that any other sense is necessary, nor has he any clear idea what such another sense would be: and he is convinced that, on his interpretation of "could have," even the determinist can, and indeed must, say that I could very often have done things I did not do. To summarize his suggestions (he does not put them forward with complete conviction) once again:

1. "Could have" simply means "could have if I had chosen."
2. For "could have if I had chosen" we may substitute "should have if I had chosen."
3. The *if* clauses in these expressions state the causal conditions upon which it would have followed that I could or should have done the thing different from what I did actually do.

Moore does not state this third point expressly himself: but it seems clear, in view of the connections he alleges between his interpretation of "could have" and the determinist theory, that he did believe it, presumably taking it as obvious.

There are then three questions to be asked:

1. Does "could have if I had chosen" mean the same, in general or ever, as "should have if I had chosen"?
2. In either of these expressions, is the *if* the *if* of causal condition?
3. In sentences having *can* or *could have* as main verb, are we required or entitled always to supply an *if*-clause, and in particular the clause "if I had chosen"?

It appears to me that the answer in each case is No.

1. Anyone, surely, would admit that in general *could* is very different indeed from *should* or *would*.[3] What a man *could* do is not at all the same as what he *would* do: perhaps he could shoot you if you were within range, but that is not in the least to say that he would. And it seems clear to me, in our present example, that "I could have run a mile if I had chosen" and "I should have run a mile if I had chosen" mean quite different things, though unfortunately it is not so clear exactly what either of them, especially the latter, does mean. "I should have run a mile in 20 minutes this morning if I had chosen" seems to me an unusual, not to say queer, specimen of English: but if I had to interpret it, I should take it to mean the same as "If I had chosen to run a mile in 20 minutes this morning, I should (jolly well) have done so," that is, it would be an assertion of my strength of character, in that I put my decisions into execution (an assertion which is, however, more naturally made, as I have now made it, with the *if*-clause preceding the main clause). I should certainly not myself understand it to mean that if I

---

[3] Since Moore has couched his example in the first person, he uses "should" in the apodosis: but of course in the third person, everyone would use "would." For brevity, I shall in what follows generally use "should" to do duty for both persons.

had made a certain choice my making that choice would have caused me to do something. But in whichever of these ways we understand it, it is quite different from "I *could* have walked a mile in 20 minutes this morning if I had chosen," which surely says something rather about my opportunities or powers. Moore, unfortunately, does not explain why he thinks we are entitled to make this all-important transition from "could" to "should," beyond saying that by doing so we "avoid a possible complication." Later I shall make some suggestions which may in part explain why he was tempted to make the transition: but nothing can justify it.

2. Moore, as I pointed out above, did not discuss what sort of *if* it is that we have in "I can if I choose" or in "I could have if I had chosen" or in "I should have if I had chosen." Generally, philosophers, as also grammarians, have a favorite, if somewhat blurred and diffuse, idea of an *if*-clause as a "conditional" clause: putting our example schematically as "If *p*, then *q*," then it will be said that *q* follows from *p*, typically either in the sense that *p entails q* or in the sense that *p* is a *cause* of *q*, though other important variations are possible. And it seems to be on these lines that Moore is thinking of the *if* in "I can if I choose." But now, it is characteristic of this general sort of *if*, that from "If *p* then *q*" we *can* draw the inference "If not *q*, then not *p*," whereas we can *not* infer either "Whether or not *p*, then *q*" or "*q*" simpliciter. For example, from "If I run, I pant" we *can* infer "If I do not pant, I do not run" (or, as we should rather say, "If I am not panting, I am not running"), whereas we can *not* infer either "I pant, whether I run or not" or "I pant" (at least in the sense of "I am panting"). If, to avoid these troubles with the English tenses, which are unfortunately prevalent but are not allowed to matter, we put the example in the past tense, then from "If I ran, I panted" it *does* follow that "If I did not pant, I did not run," but it does *not* follow either that "I panted whether or not I ran" or that "I panted" period. These possibilities and impossibilities of inference are typical of the *if* of causal condition: but they are precisely reversed in the case of "I can if I choose" or "I could have if I had chosen." For from these we should not draw the curious inferences that "If I cannot, I do not choose to" or that "If I could not have, I had not chosen to" (or "did not choose to"), whatever these sentences may be supposed to mean. But on the contrary, from "I can if I choose" we certainly should infer that "I can, whether I choose to or not" and indeed that "I can" period: and from "I could have if I had chosen" we should similarly infer that "I could have, whether I chose to or not" and that anyway "I could have" period. So that, whatever this *if* means, it is evidently not the *if* of causal condition.

This becomes even clearer when we observe that it is quite common *elsewhere* to find an ordinary causal conditional *if* in connection with a *can*, and that then there is no doubt about it, as for example in the sentence "I can squeeze through if I am thin enough," which *does* imply that "If I cannot squeeze through I am not thin enough," and of course does *not* imply that "I can squeeze through." "I can if I choose" is precisely different from this.

Nor does *can* have to be a very special and peculiar verb for *ifs* which are not causal conditional to be found in connection with it: all kinds of *ifs* are found with all kinds of verbs. Consider for example the *if* in "There are biscuits on the sideboard if you want them," where the verb is the highly ordinary *are*, but the *if* is more like that in "I can if I choose" than that in "I panted if I ran": for we can certainly infer from it that "There are biscuits on the sideboard whether you want them or not" and that anyway "There are biscuits on the sideboard," whereas it would be folly to infer that "If there are no biscuits on the sideboard you do not want them," or to understand the meaning to be that you have only to want biscuits to cause them to be on the sideboard.

The *if*, then, in "I can if I choose" is not the causal conditional *if*. What of the *if* in "I shall if I choose"? At first glance, we see that this is quite different (one more reason for refusing to substitute *shall* for *can* or *should have* for *could have*). For from "I shall if I choose" we clearly cannot infer that "I shall whether I choose to or not" or simply that "I shall." But on the other hand, can we infer, either, that "If I shan't I don't choose to"? (Or should it be rather "If I don't I don't choose to"?) I think not, as we shall see: but even if some such inference can be drawn, it would still be patently wrong to conclude that the meaning of "I shall if I choose" is that my choosing to do the thing is sufficient to cause me inevitably to do it or has as a consequence that I shall do it, which, unless I am mistaken, is what Moore was supposing it to mean. This may be seen if we compare "I shall ruin him if I choose" with "I shall ruin him if I am extravagant." The latter sentence does indeed obviously state what would be the consequence of the fulfillment of a condition specified in the *if*-clause—but then, the first sentence has clearly different characteristics from the second. In the first, it makes good sense in general to stress the "shall," but in the second it does not.[4] This is a symptom of the fact that in the first sentence "I shall" is the present of that mysterious old verb *shall*, whereas in the second "shall" is simply being used as an auxiliary, without any meaning of its own, to form the future indicative of "ruin."

I expect you will be more than ready at this point to hear something a little more positive about the meanings of these curious expressions "I can if I choose" and "I shall if I choose." Let us take the former first, and concentrate upon the *if*. The dictionary tells us that the words from which our *if* is descended expressed, or even meant, "doubt" or "hesitation" or "condition" or "stipulation." Of these, "condition" has been given a prodigious innings by grammarians, lexicographers, and philosophers alike: it is time for "doubt" and "hesitation" to be remembered, and these do indeed seem to be the notions present in "I can if I choose." We could give, on different occasions and in different contexts, many different interpretations of this sentence, which is of a somewhat primitive and *loose-jointed* type. Here are some:

I can, quaere do I choose to?
I can, but do I choose to?
I can, but perhaps I don't choose to.
I can, but then I should have to choose to, and what about *that*?
I can, but would it really be reasonable to choose to?
I can, but whether I choose to is another question.
I can, I have only to choose to.
I can, in case I (should) choose to,
and so on.

---

[4] In general, though of course in some contexts it does: e.g. "I may very easily ruin him, and I *shall* if I am extravagant," where "shall" is stressed to point the contrast with "may."

These interpretations are not, of course, all the same: which it is that we mean will usually be clear from the context (otherwise we should prefer another expression), but sometimes it can be brought out by stress, on the "if" or the "choose" for example. What is common to them all is simply that the *assertion*, positive and complete, that "I can," is linked to the *raising of the question* whether I choose to, which may be relevant in a variety of ways.[5]

Ifs of the kind I have been trying to describe are common enough, for example the *if* in our example "There are biscuits on the sideboard if you want them." I don't know whether you want biscuits or not, but in case you do, I point out that there are some on the sideboard. It is tempting, I know, to "expand" our sentence here to this: "There are biscuits on the sideboard *which you can (or may) take* if you want them": but this, legitimate or not, will not make much difference, for we are still left with "can (or may) if you want," which is (here) just like "can if you choose" or "can if you like," so that the *if* is still the *if* of doubt or hesitation, not the *if* of condition.[6]

I will mention two further points, very briefly, about "I can if I choose," important but not so relevant to our discussion here. Sometimes the *can* will be the *can*, and the choice the choice, of legal or other *right*, at other times these words will refer to practicability or feasibility: consequently, we should sometimes interpret our sentence in some such way as "I am entitled to do it (if I choose)," and at other times in some such way as "I am capable of doing it (if I choose)." We, of course, are concerned with interpretations of this second kind. It would be nice if we always said "I *may* if I choose" when we wished to refer to our rights, as perhaps our nannies once told us to: but the interlocking histories of *can* and *may* are far too chequered for there to be any such rule in practice.[7] The second point is that *choose* is an important word in its own right, and needs careful interpretation: "I can if I like" is not the same, although the "can" and the "if" may be the same in both, as "I can if I choose." Choice is always between alternatives, that is between several courses to be weighed in the same scale against each other, the one to be *preferred*. "You can vote whichever way you choose" is different from "You can vote whichever way you like."

And now for something about "I *shall* if I choose"—what sort of *if* have we here? The point to notice is, that "I shall" is not an assertion of *fact* but an expression of *intention*, verging towards the giving of some variety of undertaking: and the *if*, consequently, is the *if* not of condition but of *stipulation*. In sentences like:

I shall | marry him if I choose.
I intend | to marry him if I choose.
I promise | to marry him if he will have me.

[5] If there were space, we should consider other germane expressions: e.g. "I can do it or not as I choose," "I can do whichever I choose" (*quidlibet*). In particular, "I can whether I choose to or not" means "I can, but whether I choose to or not is an open question": it does *not* mean "I can on condition that I choose and likewise on condition that I don't," which is absurd.

[6] An account on these lines should probably be given also of an excellent example given to me by Mr. P. T. Geach: "I paid you back yesterday, if you remember." This is much the same as "I paid you back yesterday, don't you remember?" It does not mean that your now remembering that I did so is a condition, causal or other, of my having paid you back yesterday.

[7] Formerly I believed that the meaning of "I can if I choose" was something like "I can, I have the choice," and that the point of the *if*-clause was to make clear that the "can" in the main clause was the "can" of right. This account, however, does not do justice to the role of the "if," and also unduly restricts in general the meaning of "choice."

the *if*-clause is a part of the object phrase governed by the initial verb ("shall," "intend," "promise"), if this is an allowable way of putting it: or again, the *if* qualifies the *content* of the undertaking given, or of the intention announced, it does *not* qualify the giving of the undertaking. Why, we may ask, is it perverse to draw from "I intend to marry him if I choose" the inference "If I do not intend to marry him I do not choose to"? Because "I intend to marry him if I choose" is not like "I panted if I ran" in this important respect: "I panted if I ran" does not assert anything "categorically" about me—it does not assert that I did pant, and hence it is far from surprising to infer something beginning "If I did not pant": but "I intend to marry him if I choose" (and the same goes for "I shall marry him if I choose") *is* a "categorical" expression of intention, and hence it is paradoxical to make an inference leading off with "If I do *not* intend."

3. Our third question was as to when we are entitled or required to supply *if*-clauses with *can* or *could have* as main verb.

Here there is one thing to be clear about at the start. There are *two* quite distinct and incompatible views that may be put forward concerning *ifs and cans*, which are fatally easy to confuse with each other. One view is that wherever we have *can* or *could have* as our main verb, an *if*-clause must always be understood or supplied, if it is not actually present, in order to complete the sense of the sentence. The other view is that the meaning of "can" or "could have" can be more clearly reproduced by *some other verb* (notably "shall" or "should have") with an *if*-clause appended to *it*. The first view is that an *if* is required to *complete* a *can*-sentence: the second view is that an *if* is required in the *analysis* of a *can*-sentence. The suggestion of Moore that "could have" means "could have if I had chosen" is a suggestion of the first kind: but the suggestion also made by Moore that it means "should have if I had chosen" is a suggestion of the second kind. It may be because it is so easy (apparently) to confuse these two kinds of theory that Moore was tempted to talk as though "should have" could mean the same as "could have."

Now we are concerned at this moment solely with the *first* sort of view, namely that *can*-sentences are not complete without an *if*-clause. And if we think, as Moore was for the most part thinking, about "could have" (rather than "can"), it is easy to see why it may be tempting to allege that it always requires an *if*-clause with it. For it is natural to construe "could have" as a past subjunctive or "conditional," which is practically as much as to say that it needs a *conditional* clause with it. And of course it is quite true that "could have" *may* be, and very often is, a past conditional: but it is *also* true that "could have" may be and often is the *past* (*definite*) *indicative* of the verb *can*. Sometimes "I could have" is equivalent to the Latin "Potui" and means "I *was* in a position to": sometimes it is equivalent to the Latin "Potuissem" and means "I *should have been* in a position to." Exactly similar is the double role of "could," which is sometimes a conditional meaning "should be able to," but also sometimes a past indicative (indefinite) meaning "was able to": no one can doubt this if he considers such contrasted examples as "I could do it 20 years ago" and "I could do it if I had a thingummy." It is not so much that "could" or "could have" is ambiguous, as rather that two parts of the verb *can* take the same shape.

Once it is realized that "could have" can be a past indicative, the general temptation to supply *if*-clauses with it vanishes: at least there is no more temptation to supply them with "could have" than with "can." If we ask how a Roman would have said "I could have ruined you this morning (although I didn't)," it is clear that he would have used "potui," and that his sentence is complete without any conditional clause. But more than this, if he had wished to add "if I had chosen," and however he had expressed that in Latin, he would still not have changed his "potui" to "potuissem": but this is precisely what he *would* have done if he had been tacking on some other, more "normal" kind of *if*-clause, such as "if I had had one more vote." [8]

That is to say, the "could have" in "could have if I had chosen" is a past indicative, *not* a past conditional, despite the fact that there is what would, I suppose, be called a "conditional" clause, that is an *if*-clause, with it. And this is, of course, why we can make the inferences that, as we saw, we can make from "I could have if I had chosen," notably the inference to "I could have" absolutely. Hence we see how mistaken Moore was in contrasting "I could have if I had chosen" with the "absolute" sense of "I could have": we might almost go so far as to say that the addition of the "conditional" clause "if I had chosen" makes it certain that (in Moore's language) the sense of "could have" is the absolute sense, or as I should prefer to put it, that the mood of "could have" is indicative.

It might at this point be worth considering in general whether it makes sense to suppose that a language could contain any verb such as *can* has been argued or implied to be, namely one that can never occur without an *if*-clause appended to it. At least if the *if* is the normal "conditional" *if* this would seem very difficult. For let the verb in question be *to X*: then we shall never say simply "I X," but always "I X if I Y": but then also, according to the accepted rules, if it is true that "I X if I Y," and *also* true (which it must surely sometimes be) that "I do, in fact, Y"; it must surely follow that "I X," simpliciter, without any *if* about it any longer. Perhaps this was the "possible complication" that led Moore to switch from the suggestion that "I could have" (in one sense) has always to be *expanded* to "I could have if" to the suggestion that it has always to be *analyzed* as "I should have if": for of course the argument I have just given does not suffice to show that there could not be some verb which has always to be *analyzed* as something containing a conditional *if*-clause: suggestions that this is in fact the case with some verbs are common in philosophy, and I do not propose to argue this point, though I think that doubt might well be felt about it. The only sort of "verb" I can think of that might always demand a conditional clause with it is an "auxiliary" verb, if there is one, which is used solely to form subjunctive or conditional moods (whatever exactly they may be) of other verbs: but however this may be, it is quite clear that *can*, and I should be prepared also to add *shall* and *will* and *may*, are not in this position.

To summarize, then, what has been here said in reply to Moore's suggestions in his book:

(*a*) "I could have if I had chosen" does not mean the same as "I should have if I had chosen."

---

[8] If the *if*-clause is "if I had chosen," then I *was* able, *was* actually in a position, to ruin you: hence "potui." But if the *if*-clause expresses a genuine *unfulfilled condition*, then plainly I was *not* actually in a position to ruin you, hence not "potui" but "potuissem." My colleague Mr. R. M.

(b) In neither of these expressions is the *if* clause a "normal conditional" clause, connecting antecedent to consequent as cause to effect.

(c) To argue that *can* always requires an *if*-clause with it to complete the sense is totally different from arguing that *can*-sentences are always to be analyzed into sentences containing *if*-clauses.

(d) Neither *can* nor any other verb always requires a conditional *if*-clause after it: even "could have," when a past indicative, does not require such a clause: and in "I could have if I had chosen" the verb is in fact a past indicative, not a past subjunctive or conditional.

Even, however, if all these contentions are true so far, we must recognize that it may nevertheless still be the case that *can, could,* and *could have,* even when used as indicatives, are to be analyzed as meaning *shall, should,* and *should have,* used as auxiliaries of tense or mood with another verb (i.e. so as to make that other verb into a future or subjunctive), followed by a conditional *if*-clause. There is some plausibility,[9] for example, in the suggestion that "I can do X" means "I shall succeed in doing X, if I try" and "I could have done X" means "I should have succeeded in doing X, if I had tried."

It is indeed odd that Moore should have plumped so simply, in giving his account whether of the necessary supplementation or of the analysis of "could have," for the one particular *if*-clause "if I had chosen," which happens to be particularly exposed to the above objections, without even mentioning the possibility of invoking other *if*-clauses, at least in some cases. Perhaps the reason was that *choose* (a word itself much in need of discussion) presented itself as well fitted to bridge the gulf between determinists and free-willers, which *try* might not so readily do. But as a matter of fact Moore does himself at one point give an analysis of "I could have done X" which is different in an interesting way from his usual version, although confusable with it. At a crucial point in his argument, he chooses for his example "The ship could have gone faster," and the suggestion is made that this is equivalent to "The ship *would* have gone faster *if her officers had chosen.*" This may well seem plausible, but so far from being in line, as Moore apparently thinks, with his general analysis, it differs from it in two important respects:

(a) The subject of the *if*-clause ("her officers") is different from the subject of the main clause ("the ship"), the subject of the original sentence;

Nisbet has pointed out to me the interesting discussion of this point in S. A. Handford, *The Latin Subjunctive,* pp. 130 ff. It is interesting that although this author well appreciates the Latin usage, he still takes it for granted that in English the "could have" is universally subjunctive or conditional.

[9] Plausibility, but no more. Consider the case where I miss a very short putt and kick myself because I could have holed it. It is not that I should have holed it if I had tried: I did try, and missed. It is not that I should have holed it if conditions had been different: that might of course be so, but I am talking about conditions as they precisely were, and asserting that I could have holed it. There's the rub. Nor does "I can hole it this time" mean that I shall hole it this time if I try or if anything else: for I may try and miss, and yet not be convinced that I couldn't have done it; indeed, further experiments may confirm my belief that I could have done it that time although I didn't.

But if I tried my hardest, say, and missed, surely there *must* have been *something* that caused me to fail, that made me unable to succeed? So that I *could not* have holed it. Well, a modern belief in science, in there being an explanation of everything, may make us assent to this argument. But

(b) the verb in the *if*-clause following "chosen" is different from the verb in the main clause, the verb in the original sentence. We do not readily observe this because of the ellipsis after "chosen": but plainly the verb must be, not "to go faster," but "to make her go faster" or, e.g., "to open the throttle."

These two features are dictated by the fact that a ship is inanimate. We do not wish seriously to ascribe free will to inanimate objects, and the "could" of the original sentence is perhaps only justifiable (as opposed to "might") because it is readily realized that some person's free will is in question.

If we follow up the lines of this new type of analysis, we should have to examine the relations between "I could have won" and "I could, or should, have won if I had chosen to lob" and "I could, or should, have won if he had chosen to lob." I will do no more here than point out that the difference between "could" and "should" remains as before, and that the sense of "I could have won," if it really is one, in which it means something of the sort "I should have won if he had chosen to lob" or "to let me win" (the parallel to the ship example), is of little importance—the "if" here is of course the conditional *if*.

It is time now to turn to a second discussion of *ifs* and *cans*. Quite recently my colleague Mr. Nowell-Smith, in another little book called *Ethics*, also reaches a point in his argument at which he has to examine the sentence "He could have acted otherwise," that is, could have done something that he did not in fact do. His reason for doing so is that, unless we can truly say this of people, we might find ourselves unable to blame people for things, and this would be generally regretted. This reason is not unrelated to Moore's reason for embarking on his earlier discussion, and Nowell-Smith's views show some resemblances to Moore's: perhaps this is because Nowell-Smith, like Moore at the time he wrote his book, is willing, if not anxious, to come to terms with determinism.

Nowell-Smith begins his discussion by saying (p. 274) that " 'could have' is a modal phrase, and modal phrases are not normally used to make categorical statements." I am not myself at all sure what exactly a "modal phrase" is, so I cannot discuss this assertion: but I do not think this matters, because he proceeds to give us two other examples of modal phrases, viz. "might have" and "would have," [10] and to tell us first what they are not (which I omit) and then what they are:

> "Would have" and "might have" are clearly suppressed hypotheticals, incomplete without an "if . . ." or an "if . . . not . . . ." Nobody would say "Jones would have won the championship" unless (a) he believed that Jones did not win and (b) he was prepared to add "if he had entered" or "if he had not sprained his ankle" or some such clause.

Here (a) is actually incorrect—we can say "Jones would (still) have won the championship, (even) if Hagen had entered"—but this does not concern us. (b),

such a belief is not in line with the traditional beliefs enshrined in the word *can*: according to them, a human ability or power or capacity is inherently liable not to produce success, on occasion, and that for no reason (or are bad luck and bad form sometimes reasons?).

[10] Also perhaps "may have," for he discusses "It *might* have rained last Thursday" in terms that seem really to apply to "It *may* have rained last Thursday."

however, seems to be fairly correct, at least as far as concerns "would have" (in the case of "might have" it might well be doubted).[11] So we have it that, when Nowell-Smith says that "would have" is a "suppressed hypothetical" he means that it requires the addition of an *if*-clause to complete the sense. And he goes on to say that "could have" sentences also (though not so obviously) "express hypotheticals," if not always at least in important cases, such as notably those where we say someone could have done something he didn't actually do: in these cases "could have" . . . is equivalent to "would have . . . if . . . ."

It will be clear at once that Nowell-Smith, like Moore, is not distinguishing between the contention that "could have" *requires supplementation by* an *if*-clause and the quite different contention that *its analysis contains* an *if*-clause.[12] On the whole it seems plain that it is the second (analysis) view that he wishes to argue for: but the argument he produces is that "could have" is (in important cases) like "would have," the point about which is that it needs an *if*-clause to complete it— as though this, which is an argument in favor of the *first* view, told in favor of the second view. But it cannot possibly do so: and in any event *could have* is liable, as we have already seen, to be in important cases a past indicative, so that the contention that it is like *would have* in requiring a conditional *if*-clause is unfounded.

Nevertheless, it must be allowed that Nowell-Smith may still be right in urging that "could have" *means* "would have if" and that, as he eventually adds, "can" means "will if." What has he to say in support of this?

He propounds two examples for discussion, which I think do not differ greatly, so I shall quote only the first. Here it is:

> He could have read *Emma* in bed last night, though he actually read *Persuasion*; but he could not have read *Werther*, because he does not know German.

This is evidently of the same kind as Moore's 20-minute-mile example. The first thing that Nowell-Smith urges is that such a "could have" statement is not a categorical, or a "straightforward" categorical, statement. And his argument in

---

[11] I refrain here from questioning it in the case of "would have." Yet "would" is agreed to be often a past indicative of the old verb *will*, requiring no *if*-clause: and I think myself that in, say, "X would have hanged him, but Y was against it" "would have" is likewise a past indicative— indeed it is from this sort of example that we can see how the past tenses of *will* have come to be used as auxiliaries of mood for forming the conditionals of other verbs.

To state what seem to be some grammatical facts (omitting all reference to the use of the words concerned in expressing wishes):

Could have is sometimes a past indicative, sometimes a past subjunctive of the verb *can*. When it is the main verb and is a subjunctive, it does require a conditional clause with it. *Can* and its parts are *not* used as auxiliaries of tense or mood to form tenses or moods of other verbs.

Would have, whether or not it is used as a past indicative or subjunctive of the verb *will*, is now commonly used (*should have* in the first person) as an auxiliary for forming the past subjunctive of other verbs: hence if it is the main verb it does in general require a conditional clause with it.

[12] It is true that he uses two different expressions: "would have" *is* a (suppressed) hypothetical, while "could have" sentences *express* hypotheticals. But it does not look as if any distinction is intended, and if it is, the protracted initial analogy between "could have" and "would have" seems irrelevant and misleading. Moreover, discussing the (unimportant) case of "It could have been a Morris," he writes that "it would be absurd to ask under what conditions it *could* or *would* have been a Morris" (my italics): this seems to show an indifference to the distinction that I am insisting on.

favor of this view is derived from the way in which we should establish its truth or falsity. No inspection of what the man actually did will, he says, verify directly that he could have done something else (here, read *Emma*) which he didn't do: rather, we should, to establish this, have to show

> (*a*) that he has performed tasks of similar difficulty sufficiently often to preclude the possibility of a fluke, and (*b*) that nothing prevented him on this occasion. For example, we should have to establish that there was a copy of *Emma* in the house.

To refute it, on the other hand, we should have to show either "that some necessary condition was absent" (there was no copy of *Emma*) or "that the capacity was absent." That is, let us say, we have to show on the one hand that he had both the ability and the opportunity to read *Emma,* or on the other hand that he lacked either the ability or the opportunity.

Nowell-Smith seems, at least at first, to be less interested in the matter of opportunity: for he says that we can establish "directly," i.e. by considering what the facts at the time actually were, at least that he did *not* have the opportunity, that is, that something did prevent him, and he does not seem daunted by the obviously greater difficulty of establishing, in order to establish that he *could* have done it, the general negative that *there was nothing* to prevent him. At any rate, it is at first upon our manner of establishing that he had (or had not) the *ability* to do this thing that he did not do that Nowell-Smith fastens in order to support his assertion that the "could have" statement is not categorical. That the man had the *ability* to read *Emma* can *not,* he says, be established "directly," i.e. by observing what happened on that past occasion, but only by considering what prowess he has displayed in the face of similar tasks in the past on other occasions, or displays now when put to the test: the argument that we have perforce to use is an "inductive" one (and, he adds, none the worse for that).

Now let us pass all this, at least for the sake of argument.[13] What interests us is to discover why Nowell-Smith thinks that these considerations show that "He had the ability to read *Emma*" is not a categorical statement. I confess I fail to follow the argument:

> The very fact that evidence for or against "could have" statements must be drawn from occasions other than that to which they refer is enough to show that "He could have acted otherwise" is not a straightforward categorical statement.

But do we really know what is meant by a "straightforward categorical statement"? Certainly it is not the case that statements made on the strength of inductive evidence are in general not categorical—for example, the statement that the next mule born will prove sterile: this seems categorical enough. Perhaps this

---

[13] Yet I think it is not hard to see that we cannot establish "directly," at least in many cases, that something "prevented" him: he was drugged or dazzled, which prevented him from reading, which establishes that he could not have read—but how do we know that being drugged or dazzled "prevents" people from reading? Surely on "inductive" evidence? And, in short, to be prevented is to be rendered unable.

example should be ruled out as not in point, on the ground that here there *will some day* be "direct" evidence relevant to the assertion, even if it is not available at the moment. Could the same, I wonder, be said of the inductive conclusion "All mules are sterile"? Or is that not categorical? I know that this has been interpreted by some philosophers to mean "If anything is a mule then it is sterile," but I see no reason to support that curious interpretation.

The situation becomes still more puzzling when we remember that Nowell-Smith is about to generalize his theory, and to assert, not merely that "could have" means "would have . . . if," but also that "can" means "shall or will . . . if." Suppose then that I assert "I can here and now lift my finger," and translate this as "I shall lift my finger if . . .": then surely this will be "directly" verified if the conditions are satisfied and I do proceed to lift the finger? If this is correct, and if the theory is indeed a general one, then there seems to be no point in insisting on the nonavailability of "direct" evidence, which is only a feature of certain cases. Incidentally, it is not in fact the case that to say "He could have done it" is always used in a way to imply that he did not in fact do it: we make a list of the suspects in a murder case, all of whom we think could have done it and one of whom we think did do it. True, this is not Nowell-Smith's case: but unless we are prepared to assert that the "could have" in his case differs in meaning from that in the murder case, and so to rule out the latter as irrelevant, we are in danger of having to admit that even "could have" sentences can be "directly" verified in favorable cases. For study of the facts of that past occasion can prove to us that he did it, and hence that our original "He could have" was correct.[14]

However, to proceed. Whether or not we should describe our conclusion here as "categorical" it seems that it should still be a conclusion of the form "he *could* have done so and so," and not in the least a conclusion concerning what he *would* have done. We are interested, remember, in his abilities: we want to know whether he could have read *Emma* yesterday: we ascertain that he did read it the day before yesterday, and that he does read it today: we conclude that he could have read it yesterday. But it does not appear that this says anything about what he *would* have done yesterday or in what circumstances: certainly, we are now convinced, he *could* have read it yesterday, but *would* he have, considering that he had read it only the day before? Moreover, supposing the view is that our conclusion is not of the "could have" but of the "would have if" form, nothing has yet been said to establish this, nor to tell us what follows the "if." To establish that he would have read it yesterday if . . ., we shall need evidence not merely as to his abilities and opportunities, but also as to his character, motives, and so on.

It may indeed be thought, and it seems that Nowell-Smith does at least partly think this, that what follows the "if" should be suppliable from the consideration that to say he could have, in the full sense, is to say not merely that he had the ability, which is what we have hitherto concentrated on, but also that he had the *opportunity*. For to establish *this*, do we not have to establish that certain *conditions* were satisfied, as for instance that there was a copy of *Emma* available? Very well. But here there is surely a confusion: we allow that, in saying that he

[14] There are, I should myself think, good reasons for not speaking of "I can lift my finger" as being directly verified when I proceed to lift it, and likewise for not speaking of "He could have done it" as being directly verified by the discovery that he did do it. But on Nowell-Smith's account I think that these would count as direct verifications.

could have, I do assert or imply that certain *conditions,* those of opportunity, *were satisfied:* but this is totally different from allowing that, in saying that he could have, I *assert something conditional.* It is, certainly, entirely possible to assert something conditional such as "he could have read *Emma* yesterday if there had been a copy available," *could* being then of course a subjunctive: but to say this sort of thing is precisely not to say the sort of thing that we say when we say "He could have acted otherwise," where "could have" is an indicative—implying, as we now do, that there was no copy available, we imply that *pro tanto* he could *not* have acted otherwise. And the same will be true if we try saying "He would have read *Emma* yesterday if there had been a copy available": this too certainly implies that he could not in fact have read it, and so cannot by any means be what we mean by saying that he could have read it.

In the concluding paragraph of his discussion, Nowell-Smith does finally undertake to give us his analysis not merely of "could have," but also of "can" (which he says means "will if"). And this last feature is very much to be welcomed, because if an analysis is being consciously given of "can" at least we shall at length be clear of confusions connected with the idea that "could have" is necessarily a subjunctive.[15]

The argument of the last paragraph runs as follows. It is "logically odd" to say something of this kind (I am slightly emending Nowell-Smith's formula, but only in ways that are favorable to it and demanded by his own argument):

Smith has the ability to run a mile, has the opportunity to run a mile, has a preponderant motive for running a mile, but does not in fact do so.

From this it follows directly, says Nowell-Smith, that "can" means "will if," that is, I suppose, that "Smith can run a mile" *means* "If Smith has the opportunity to run a mile and a preponderant motive for running it, he will run it."

It seems, however, plain that nothing of the kind follows. This may be seen first by setting the argument out formally. Nowell-Smith's premise is of the form

Not (p and q and r and not -s)

that is

Logically odd (ability+opportunity+motive+nonaction).

Now from this we can indeed infer

$p \supset ((q \text{ and } r) \supset s)$,

that is that

---

[15] It must, however, be pointed out once again that if we are to discuss the assertion that somebody can (now) do something, the previous arguments that our assertions are not categorical because they are based on induction and cannot be verified directly, whether they were good or not, must now be abandoned: because of course it *is* possible to verify this "directly" by the method Nowell-Smith has specified in another connection earlier, viz. by getting the man to try and seeing him succeed.

If he has the ability, then, if he has the opportunity and the motive, he will do it.

But we can*not infer* the converse

$$((q \text{ and } r) \supset s) \supset p,$$

or in other words that

If, when he has the opportunity and the motive, he does it, he has the ability to do it.

(I do not say this last is not something to which we should, when so put into English, assent, only that it does not follow from Nowell-Smith's premise: of course it follows merely from the premise that he does it, that he has the ability to do it, according to ordinary English.) But unless this second, converse implication *does* follow, we cannot, according to the usual formal principles, infer that p is *equivalent* to, nor therefore that it means the same as, $(q \text{ and } r) \supset s$, or in words that ability *means* that opportunity plus motive leads to action.

To put the same point nonformally. From the fact that, if three things are true together a fourth must also be true, we cannot argue that one of the three things *simply means* that if the other two are true the fourth will be true. If we could argue indeed in this way, then we should establish, from Nowell-Smith's premise, not merely that

"He has the ability to do X" simply means that "If he has the opportunity and the motive to do X, he will do X"

but also equally that

"He has the opportunity to do X" *simply means* that "If he has the ability and the motive to do X, he will do X"

and likewise that

"He has a preponderant motive to do X" *simply means* that "If he has the ability and the opportunity to do X, he will do X."

For clearly we can perform the same operations on q and r as on p, since the three all occupy parallel positions in the premise. But these are fantastic suggestions. Put shortly, Nowell-Smith is pointing out in his premise that if a man both can and wants to (more than he wants to do anything else), he will: but from this it does not follow that "he can" *simply means* that "if he wants to he will." Nowell-Smith is struggling to effect a transition from *can* to *will* which presents difficulties as great as those of the transition from *could* to *would*: he puts up his show of effecting it by importing the additional, and here irrelevant, concept of motive, which needless to say is in general very intimately connected with the question of what "he will" do.

When, in conclusion, Nowell-Smith finally sets out his analysis of "Smith could have read *Emma* last night," it is this:

> He would have read it, if there had been a copy, if he had not been struck blind, &c., &c., and if he had wanted to read it more than he had wanted to read (this should be "do") anything else.

But so far from this being what we mean by saying he could have read it, it actually implies that he could *not* have read it, for more than adequate reasons: it implies that he was blind at the time, and so on. Here we see that Nowell-Smith actually does make the confusion I referred to above between a statement which implies or asserts that certain conditions *were* fulfilled and a conditional statement, i.e. a statement about what would have happened if those conditions had been fulfilled. This is unfortunately a confusion of a general kind that is not uncommon: I need only mention the classic instance of Keynes, who confused asserting on evidence *h* that *p* is probable with asserting that on evidence *h p* is probable, both of which can be ambiguously expressed by "asserting that *p* is probable on evidence *h*," but only the former of which asserts that *p* is (really) probable. Here similarly there is a confusion between asserting on the supposition (or premise) that he had a copy that he could/would have read it, and asserting that on the supposition that he had a copy he could/would have read it, both of which can be ambiguously expressed by "asserting that he could/would have read it on the supposition that he had a copy," but only the former of which asserts that he (actually) could have read it.

To some extent, then, we learn from studying Nowell-Smith's arguments lessons similar to those that we learned in the case of Moore. But some are new, as for instance that many assertions about what a man *would have* done or *will do* depend, in critical cases, upon premises about his *motives* as well as, or rather than, about his abilities or opportunities: hence these assertions cannot be what assertions about his abilities *mean*.[16]

On one point I may perhaps elaborate a little further. It has been maintained that *sometimes* when we say "He could have done X" this is a conditional: it requires completion by an *if*-clause, typically "if he had had the opportunity," and so does *not* require us, if we are to establish its truth, to establish that he did in fact have the opportunity. Sometimes on the other hand it is a past indicative, implying that he did have the opportunity: in which case we do, to establish its truth, have to establish that certain conditions were satisfied, but the assertion is *not* to be described as a conditional assertion.

Now while I have no wish to retract this account in general or in all cases, I doubt whether it is the whole story. Consider the case where what we wish to assert is that somebody had the opportunity to do something but lacked the ability —"He could have smashed that lob, if he had been any good at the smash": here the *if*-clause, which may of course be suppressed and understood, relates not to

---

[16] Yet here it must be pointed out once more that it has not been shown that *all* assertions about what he would have done are so dependent, so that this particular argument against the analysis of "could have" as "would have if" is not conclusive: in particular, it does not dispose of the possible suggestion that "could have" means "would have if he had *tried*," for here considerations of motive may be irrelevant.

opportunity but to ability. Now although we might describe the whole sentence as "conditional," it nevertheless manages to assert, by means of its main clause, something "categorical" enough, viz. that he did have a certain opportunity. And in the same way Nowell-Smith's "He could have read *Emma*, if he had had a copy," does seem to assert "categorically" that he had a certain ability, although he lacked the opportunity to exercise it. Looking at it in this way, there is a temptation to say that "could have" has, besides its "all-in" *sense* several more *restricted senses*: this would be brought out if we said "He could have smashed it, *only* he is no good at the smash" or "He could have read *Emma but* he had no copy," where, we should say, "could have" is being used in the restricted senses of opportunity or of ability [17] only, and is a past indicative, not a past conditional.

This view might be reinforced by considering examples with the simple "can" itself. We are tempted to say that "He can" sometimes means just that he has the ability, with *nothing said* about opportunity, sometimes *just* that he has the chance, with nothing said about ability, sometimes, however, that he really actually *fully can* here and now, having both ability and opportunity. Now nobody, I think, would be tempted to say that "can," where it means one of the two lesser things, e.g. "has the opportunity," i.e. "can in the full sense if he has the ability," is grammatically a subjunctive or conditional. Perhaps, then, it was not correct to describe "He could have," either, as always a conditional where it asserts ability or opportunity only, with nothing said about the other, or even where the other is denied to have existed.

The verb *can* is a peculiar one. Let us compare it for a moment with another peculiar verb, *know*, with which it shares some grammatical peculiarities, such as lack of a continuous present tense. When I say that somebody *knows* what the thing in my hand is, I may mean merely that he has the ability to identify it given the opportunity, or that he has the opportunity to identify it if he has the ability, or that he has both. What do we say about *know* here? Certainly we are not prone to invoke the idea of a conditional, but rather that of different senses, or perhaps the still obscure idea of the dispositional. I must be content here merely to say that I do not think that the old armory of terms, such as "mood" and "sense," is altogether adequate for handling such awkward cases. The only point of which I feel certain is that such verbs as *can* and *know* have each an all-in, paradigm use, around which cluster and from which divagate, little by little and along different paths, a whole series of other uses, for many of which, though perhaps not for all, a synonymous expression ("opportunity," "realize," and so on) can be found.

It is not unusual for an audience at a lecture to include some who prefer things to be important, and to them now, in case there are any such present, there is owed a peroration. Why, in short, does all this matter? First, then, it needs no emphasizing that both *if* and *can* are highly prevalent and protean words, perplexing both grammatically and philosophically: it is not merely worth while, but essential, in these studies to discover the facts about *ifs* and *cans*, and to remove the confusions they engender. In philosophy it is *can* in particular that we seem

---

[17] I talk here and throughout of "ability" and "opportunity" only: but I realize that other abstract nouns like "capacity," "skill," and even "right" are equally involved. All these terms need listing and elucidating before we really get to grips with "can."

so often to uncover, just when we had thought some problem settled, grinning residually up at us like the frog at the bottom of the beer mug. Furthermore and secondly, we have not here been dissecting these two words in general or completely, but in a special connection which perhaps no one will hold trivial. It has been alleged by very serious philosophers (not only the two I have mentioned) that the things we ordinarily say about what we can do and could have done may actually be consistent with determinism. It is hard to evade all attempt to decide whether this allegation is true—hard even for those who, like myself, are inclined to think that determinism itself is still a name for nothing clear, that has been argued for only incoherently. At least I should like to claim that the arguments considered tonight fail to show that it *is* true, and indeed in failing go some way to show that it is *not*. Determinism, whatever it may be, may yet be the case, but at least it appears not consistent with what we ordinarily say and presumably think. And finally there is a third point. Reflecting on the arguments in this lecture, we may well ask ourselves whether they might not be as well assigned to grammar as to philosophy: and this, I think, is a salutary question to end on. There are constant references in contemporary philosophy, which notoriously is much concerned with language, to a "logical grammar" and a "logical syntax" as though these were things distinct from ordinary grammarian's grammar and syntax: and certainly they do seem, whatever exactly they may be, different from traditional grammar. But grammar today is itself in a state of flux; for fifty years or more it has been questioned on all hands and counts whether what Dionysius Thrax once thought was the truth about Greek is the truth and the whole truth about all language and all languages. Do we know, then, that there will prove to be any ultimate boundary between "logical grammar" and a revised and enlarged *Grammar?* In the history of human inquiry, philosophy has the place of the initial central sun, seminal and tumultuous: from time to time it throws off some portion of itself to take station as a science, a planet, cool and well regulated, progressing steadily towards a distant final state. This happened long ago at the birth of mathematics, and again at the birth of physics: only in the last century we have witnessed the same process once again, slow and at the time almost imperceptible, in the birth of the science of mathematical logic, through the joint labors of philosophers and mathematicians. Is it not possible that the next century may see the birth, through the joint labors of philosophers, grammarians, and numerous other students of language, of a true and comprehensive *science of language?* Then we shall have rid ourselves of one more part of philosophy (there will still be plenty left) in the only way we ever can get rid of philosophy, by kicking it upstairs.

IFS, CANS AND CAUSES

Keith Lehrer

In a recent article J. L. Austin [1] has criticized a view that he attributes to G. E. Moore, and, more specifically, to Moore's discussion of free will in his book *Ethics*.[2] Moore, according to Austin, holds the view that "I can, if I choose" and "I could have, if I had chosen" are expressions that express causal connections between their antecedents and consequents.

Austin argues that if a sentence of the form "If p, then q" expresses a causal connection between p and q, then from

> . . . "If p, then q" we can draw the inference "If not q, then not p" whereas we cannot infer either "whether or not p, q," or "q" simpliciter.[3]

He continues,

> These possibilities and impossibilities of inference are typical of the *if* of causal condition: but they are precisely reversed in the case of "I can if I choose" or "I could have if I had chosen." For from these we should not draw the curious inferences that "if I cannot, I do not choose to" or that "If I could not have, then I had not chosen to" . . . But on the contrary, from "I can, if

From *Analysis*, XX (1960), 122–124. Reprinted by permission of Basil Blackwell & Mott Ltd.

[1] *Editor's Note.* Mr. Lehrer's paper was received before the news of Professor Austin's death.

[2] J. L. Austin, "Ifs and Cans," contained in *Proceedings of The British Academy*, Vol. XLII, 1956, pp. 107–132. [See pp. 161–178 above. Ed.]

[3] *Ibid.*, pp. 112–113. [P. 164 above. Ed.]

I choose" we certainly should infer that "I can, whether I choose to or not" and indeed that "I can" period: and from "I could have if I had chosen" we should similarly infer that "I could have, whether I chose to or not" and that anyway "I could have" period. So that, whatever this *if* means, it is evidently not the *if* of causal condition.[4]

Thus Austin claims to have shown that Moore is mistaken in holding the view that "I can, if I choose" and "I could have, if I had chosen" express causal connections, and it seems evident to me that his argument is conclusive.

Assuming this argument to be correct, we can show that a very important view that Austin also attributes to Moore, and that has been held by many others as well, is certainly mistaken. Most simply the view is that "I can" is analyzable as "I shall, if I choose" and that "I could have" is analyzable as "I should have, if I had chosen" where "I shall, if I choose" and "I should have, if I had chosen" express causal connections between their antecedents and consequents.[5]

I shall first show, using Austin's argument as a premise, that if "I can" is analyzed as "I shall, if I choose," then the latter does *not* express a causal connection, and secondly, I shall show, independently of Austin's argument, that "I can" must not be analyzed as "I shall, if I choose." Similarly, I shall show that if "I could have" is analyzed as "I should have, if I had chosen," then the latter does not express a causal connection, and that "I could have" must not be analyzed as "I should have, if I had chosen." Finally, I shall show that "I can" and "I could have" must not be analyzed by any expressions of the form "I shall, if" and "I should have, if."

Let us suppose that "I can" is analyzed as "I shall, if I choose." If "I can" and "I shall, if I choose" are thus equivalent, we may substitute "I shall, if I choose" for "I can" in "I can, if I choose" and the result will be equivalent to the original expression, that is, to "I can, if I choose." By performing this substitution we arrive at the expression "I shall, if I choose, if I choose." Now the latter is of the form "If p, then if p, then q" and any expression of this form is equivalent to an expression of the form "If p, then q"—the extra antecedent is wholly redundant. For example, the sentence "If I run, then if I run, I sweat" is equivalent to simply "If I run, I sweat."

Thus "I shall, if I choose, if I choose" is equivalent to simply "I shall, if I choose." But we have arrived at "I shall, if I choose, if I choose" by substituting "I shall, if I choose" for "I can" in "I can, if I choose." Since "I shall, if I choose, if I choose" is equivalent to "I can, if I choose," and since "I shall, if I choose, if I choose" is equivalent to "I shall, if I choose," "I can, if I choose" is equivalent to "I shall, if I choose." However, by Austin's argument "I can, if I choose" does not express a causal connection, and since "I can, if I choose" is equivalent to "I shall, if I choose" the latter does not express a causal connection either.

We have seen that if "I can" is analyzed as "I shall, if I choose," then "I shall, if I choose" is equivalent to "I can, if I choose," and it should be clear from this that "I can" must not be analyzed as "I shall, if I choose." For "I can, if I choose"

[4] *Ibid.*, p. 113. [See p. 164 above. Ed.]
[5] *Ibid.*, pp. 110, 118. [See pp. 163 ff. above. Ed.]

is clearly not equivalent to "I shall, if I choose" because "I can" is not equivalent to "I shall." [6] To say that I can eat arsenic is not to say that I shall.

Similarly, if "I could have" is analyzed as "I should have, if I had chosen," then by substituting the latter for the former in "I could have, if I had chosen" we arrive at "I should have, if I had chosen, if I had chosen" which is equivalent to "I should have, if I had chosen." Since "I could have, if I had chosen" does not express a causal connection, neither does "I should have, if I had chosen." Again, since "I could have, if I had chosen" is not equivalent to "I should have, if I had chosen," because "I could" is not equivalent to "I should," "I could have" must not be analyzed as "I should have, if I had chosen."

Finally, a similar argument could be used to show that "I can" must not be analyzed as "I shall, if I want to" or "I shall, if I wish to" etc., and that "I could have" must not be analyzed as "I should have, if I had wanted to" or "I should have, if I had wished to" etc. For any attempt to analyze "I can" as "I shall, if" or "I could have" as "I should have, if" will lead to the absurd result that "I shall, if" is equivalent to "I can, if" or that "I should have, if" is equivalent to "I could have, if."

[6] *Ibid.,* pp. 111–112. [See pp. 163–164 above. Ed.]

MR. LEHRER ON THE CONSTITUTION OF CANS

Bruce Goldberg and Herbert Heidelberger

Mr. Keith Lehrer, in a recent issue of this journal,[1] attempts to demonstrate that if "I can" is analyzed as "I shall, if I choose" then "I shall, if I choose" does not express a causal relationship between the antecedent and the consequent. We shall not, in this paper, take issue with Lehrer's conclusion, viz., that "I shall, if I choose" is not causal; what we shall try to show is that his argument does not establish that conclusion. We shall do this by showing that in his demonstration Lehrer makes inferences which are forbidden by his initial supposition.

The supposition is that "I can, if I choose" is not causal. (This, as Lehrer points out, was proved by Austin in "Ifs and Cans." [2]) Lehrer's argument, briefly, is this. If "I can" is equivalent to "I shall, if I choose," then this last expression may be substituted for "I can" in "I can, if I choose." We thus get "I shall, if I choose, if I choose," which is transformed into simply "I shall, if I choose." The argument thus shows that "I shall, if I choose" is equivalent to "I can, if I choose," if "I can" is analyzed as "I shall, if I choose." But now since "I can, if I choose" is not causal, "I shall, if I choose" cannot be causal either.

However, the deduction is valid only if it is assumed that the "if"-clause in "I can, if I choose" is a conditional clause. But this is an assumption to which Mr. Lehrer is not entitled, if he accepts Austin's argument—as in fact he does. Austin shows that "I can, if I choose" is not a causal conditional, since it is not a conditional at all; for, he argues, if it were, "If I cannot, I do not choose to" would be

From *Analysis*, XXI (1961), 96. Reprinted by permission of Basil Blackwell & Mott Ltd.

[1] *Analysis*, 20.6 (June 1960), pp. 122–124. [See pp. 179–181 above. Ed.]

[2] In *Proceedings of The British Academy*, Vol. XLII, 1956, pp. 109–132. [See pp. 161–178 above. Ed.]

inferable from it, and plainly it is not. But if "I can, if I choose" is not a conditional, then none of the steps in Mr. Lehrer's argument can be taken, since they are founded upon the rules of inference sanctioned by the treatment of "I can, if I choose" as a conditional.

What Mr. Lehrer has established is that if one construes both "I can, if I choose" and "I shall, if I choose" as causal, where the latter constitutes an analysis of "I can," then one is committed to their equivalence. But if one takes only "I shall, if I choose" as causal, then this view is not at all affected by Mr. Lehrer's argument.

CANS AND CONDITIONALS: A REJOINDER

Keith Lehrer

In a recent issue of *Analysis*,[1] Bruce Goldberg and Herbert Heidelberger have taken issue with an article of mine that also appeared in *Analysis*.[2] In that article I had assumed that Austin's argument,[3] to the effect that "I can if I choose" is not a causal conditional, was conclusive. I then attempted to show that the view, attributed by Austin to Moore, that "I can" is analyzable as "I shall if I choose," where the latter is a causal conditional, is mistaken. The following quotation from my article expresses quite clearly, I believe, what I set out to do:

> I shall first show, using Austin's argument as a premise, that if "I can" is analyzed as "I shall, if I choose," then the latter does *not* express a causal connection, and secondly, I shall show, independently of Austin's argument, that "I can" must not be analyzed as "I shall, if I choose." [4]

In the first paragraph of their article, Messrs. Goldberg and Heidelberger say,

> We shall not, in this paper, take issue with Lehrer's conclusion, viz., that "I shall, if I choose" is not causal; what we shall try to show is that his argument does not establish that conclusion.[5]

From *Analysis*, XXII (1962), 22–24. Reprinted by permission of Basil Blackwell & Mott Ltd.

[1] "Mr. Lehrer on the Constitution of Cans," *Analysis*, 21.4 (March 1961), p. 96. [See pp. 182–183 above. Ed.]
[2] "Ifs, Cans and Causes," *Analysis*, 20.6 (June 1960), pp. 122–124. [See pp. 179–181 above. Ed.]
[3] "Ifs and Cans," *Proceedings of The British Academy*, Vol. XLII, 1956, pp. 107–132. [See pp. 161–178 above. Ed.]
[4] Lehrer, p. 123. [P. 180 above. Ed.]
[5] Goldberg and Heidelberger, p. 96. [P. 182 above. Ed.]

Now this is a very puzzling thing to say; for I did not present any argument to establish that conclusion. Nowhere in my article did I argue that "I shall, if I choose" is not causal, though I am convinced that it is not. I argued that *if* "I can" is analyzed as "I shall, if I choose," *then* "I shall if I choose" is not causal: which is quite different. Furthermore, as is clear from the quotation above, I went on to deny that "I can" *is* to be analyzed as "I shall, if I choose." So I do not see how they could have thought that I had presented an argument to show that "I shall, if I choose" is not causal.

However, their remarks are relevant to my argument to establish the conclusion that *if* "I can" is analyzed as "I shall, if I choose," *then* the latter is not a causal conditional, and I want to consider them in detail. Having summarized my argument, they correctly point out,

> Austin shows that "I can, if I choose" is not a causal conditional, since it is not a conditional at all. . . .

and conclude,

> But if "I can, if I choose" is not a conditional, then none of the steps in Mr. Lehrer's argument can be taken, since they are founded upon the rules of inference sanctioned by the treatment of "I can, if I choose" as a conditional.[6]

The conclusion of their argument seems to me to be plainly false. The first step in my argument simply consists in substituting "I shall, if I choose" for "I can" in "I can, if I choose," supposing that "I can" is analyzed as "I shall, if I choose," that is supposing that "I can" and "I shall, if I choose" are synonymous,[7] and surely this step can validly be taken whether "I can, if I choose" is a conditional or not. The valid substitution of synonyms is not subject to a restriction that such substitutions can only occur in conditional sentences!

My critics are thus mistaken in saying that none of the steps in my argument can validly be taken if "I can, if I choose" is not a conditional; but it is still possible that *some* of the steps in my argument cannot validly be taken if "I can, if I choose" is not a conditional. Let us consider this possibility. By substituting "I shall, if I choose" for "I can" in "I can, if I choose," we get "I shall, if I choose, if I choose." I then concluded that "I shall, if I choose, if I choose" is equivalent to simply "I shall, if I choose." Now this step from "I shall, if I choose, if I choose" to "I shall, if I choose" is clearly valid if we assume that "I shall, if I choose, if I choose" is a conditional; but, as Goldberg and Heidelberger point out, I am not entitled to that assumption, since I have assumed that "I can, if I choose" is not a conditional.

However, I still do think that the step is valid, though on rather informal grounds, because I do not see what "I shall, if I choose, if I choose" could mean unless it is just a redundant way of saying "I shall, if I choose." Thus, if "I shall, if I choose,

---

[6] *Ibid.* [Pp. 182–183 above. Ed.]

[7] I did not say in my article that if "I can" is analyzed as "I shall, if I choose," then they are synonymous; but, since it was an analysis in Moore's sense that was being discussed, this should have been obvious. See, G. E. Moore, "A Reply to My Critics" in *The Philosophy of G. E. Moore*, edited by P. A. Schilpp (Tudor Publishing Company, New York), p. 663.

if I choose" is meaningful, it must, I think, be equivalent to the simple "I shall, if I choose."

If it is objected that "I shall, if I choose, if I choose" is meaningless, that is not at all damaging to my argument. In fact, it would establish the conclusion. For we arrived at "I shall, if I choose, if I choose" by substituting "I shall, if I choose" for "I can" in the meaningful sentence "I can, if I choose"; this step is valid on the supposition that "I can" is analyzed as "I shall, if I choose"; and if we have arrived at a meaningless sentence, then that is a *reductio* of the supposition, that is, of the supposition that "I can" is analyzed as "I shall, if I choose." But if it is false that "I can" is analyzed as "I shall, if I choose," then the view mentioned above, which Austin attributes to Moore, *is* mistaken.

Though the principal contentions of Goldberg and Heidelberger are, I believe, mistaken, I am grateful to them for raising the question whether the validity of my argument depends on treating "I can, if I choose" as a conditional. For that is an important question, and I am glad to have had the opportunity to explain why I think the answer is negative.

J. L. AUSTIN'S PHILOSOPHICAL PAPERS

Roderick M. Chisholm

．．．

At the beginning of "Ifs and Cans" (1956), Austin states that he intends to discuss two large questions:

(1) "Whenever . . . we say that we can do something, or could do something, or could have done something, is there an *if* in the offing—suppressed, it may be but due nevertheless to appear when we set out our sentence in full or when we give an explanation of its meaning?"

And (2) "if and when there *is* an *if*-clause appended to a main clause which contains a *can* or *could* or *could have*, what sort of an *if* is it? What is the meaning of the *if*, or what is the effect or the point of combining this *if*-clause with the main clause?"

With respect to the first of these questions, he notes that it is one thing to say (*a*) that categorical sentences beginning with "I can," "He could have," etc., carry with them an implicit *if*-clause which is always understood and capable of being supplied, and that it is quite another thing to say (*b*) that such sentences may be paraphrased or explicated by means of other sentences which contain *if*-clauses. If, for example, we said that "I can" means the same as "I can if I try" we would be affirming (*a*), and if we said that "I can" means the same as "I will succeed if I try," we would be affirming (*b*).

What Austin says about *ifs* in connection with (2) is very important, it seems to me. He points out that the *ifs* of such sentences as "I can if I choose," "There are

From *Mind*, LXXIII, no. 289 (1964), 20–25. Reprinted by permission of the author and *Mind*.

biscuits on the sideboard if you want them," "I paid you back yesterday if you remember," and "You may exercise your rights if you want to," are not the *ifs* of causal (or other) conditions. For sentences of the form "if *p* then *q*," in which the *if* is the *if* of condition may be contraposed to "if not-*q* then not-*p*"; but none of the sentences just cited may be so contraposed. It is relevant to note that these nonconditional *if* sentences are not *if-then* sentences; even if we put the *if*-clause first, it would be unnatural to begin the other clause with *then*. Austin gives us a plausible positive account of the uses of these nonconditional *ifs* and shows how they may be used to express, or to assert, hesitation, doubt, or stipulation. For example, the *if* of "I shall marry him if I choose," provided the sentence is one in which the *shall* may be stressed, "qualifies the *content* of the undertaking given, or of the intention announced, it does *not* qualify the giving of the undertaking."

This account does not hold of all nonconditional *ifs*, however. There are some which are simply vulgarisms; *e.g.* "That's poisonous if you drink it" and "I hope you have a good time in Paris if I don't see you again." And there is another type of nonconditional *if* which Austin does not mention—those *ifs*, namely, that may be replaced by *even ifs*. "If it rains I will go," when the statement is intended in such a way that "even" may be inserted at the beginning, or "just the same" at the end, cannot be contraposed to "If I do not go it will not have rained." Here, too, "then" is inappropriate. (The nonconditional "even if *p*, *q*" seems to be equivalent to "*q* whether or not *p*" and to "*q* and it is false that if *p* then not-*q*.")

Austin's first question—"When we say 'I can,' 'He could,' etc., is there an *if* in the offing?"—arises in connection with the treatment of the problem of free will (Austin says "the problem, so-called, of Free Will") in G. E. Moore's *Ethics*. Moore had answered the question affirmatively in trying to show that the thesis of determinism is compatible with saying that people can, or could, do things that they do not do. Moore said:

> There are certainly good reasons for thinking that we *very often* mean by "could" merely "would, *if* so and so had chosen." And if so, then we have a sense of the word "could" in which the fact that we often *could* have done what we did not do, is perfectly compatible with the principle that everything has a cause: for to say that, *if* I had performed a certain act of will, I should have done something which I did not do, in no way contradicts this principle.

Austin intimates that, in the course of this discussion, Moore made a "first-water, ground-floor mistake," but it is not clear to me just what the mistake is that Moore is supposed to have made.

It *would* be a mistake to say that the *ifs* in "I can if I choose" and "He could have if he had chosen" are conditional *ifs*, for, as Austin points out, these sentences cannot be contraposed and their *ifs* ordinarily perform quite a different function. In the first chapter of his *Ethics* Moore did repeatedly use such expressions as "can if I choose" and "could have if he had chosen," but in chapter six, in which the discussion of free will occurs (and from which the above quotation is taken) he does not use these expressions. He says there that "could" means "would, if so and so had chosen," and he says "I could have" means "if I had performed a certain act of will, I should have," he does not suggest there that "can" and "could" are accompanied by implicit *if*-clauses, much less that they are accompanied by *if*-clauses containing conditional *ifs*.

Moore's point, in showing that the thesis of free will might be reconciled with that of determinism, was to indicate that certain sentences in which "can" or "could" occur may be replaced by certain *if-then* sentences in which "can" or "could" do not occur. It was unfortunate that he used the particular verb "choose" in his *if*-clauses, for, as Austin notes, there are objections applying to "choose" which do not apply to other verbs which Moore might have used instead. (Note that Moore does use another verb in his example at the end of the passage quoted.) If Austin is right, *if*-clauses containing "choose" or one of its variants as the principal verb are almost always nonconditional, in the sense just described. Was Moore's mistake simply that of interpreting "choose" in a way in which it is not ordinarily interpreted? This would be a mistake, but not a "first-water, ground-floor mistake." [1]

What Austin took to be Moore's basic mistake may have been that of supposing that "can" may be expressed in terms of "will if," or "would if," and that the indicative "could have" may be expressed in terms of "would have if." This may well be a mistake, but Austin's objections to it can be met, I think. He considers two ways of rendering "can" in terms of "will if," etc., and he shows that one of these is unsatisfactory, but I do not think that he shows the other to be unsatisfactory.

The first of these is the account of "could have" in P. H. Nowell-Smith's *Ethics*. Nowell-Smith considers the sentence (*C*) "Smith could have read *Emma* last night" and says that what it means could also be expressed by (*W*): "Smith would have read *Emma* last night, if there had been a copy, if he had not been struck blind, etc., etc., and if he had wanted to read it more than he wanted to read anything else." (This statement, which has the form "if *p*, if *r*, and if *s*, then *q*," may also be put as "if *p* and *r* and *s*, then *q*.") Austin offers several objections, the most telling of which seems to me to be the following: To establish *W* we need evidence, not merely as to Smith's abilities and opportunities, but also as to his character, motives, and the like; to establish *C* we do not need such evidence. But Austin also says this of *W*: So far from *W* being what we mean by saying Smith could have read the book, "it actually implies that he could *not* have read it, for more than adequate reasons: it implies that he was blind at the time, and so on." Unless I have seriously misunderstood Austin at this point, there would seem to be *two* mistakes underlying this remark. It is a mistake, first, to suppose that subjunctive conditionals, such as *W*, are necessarily contrary-to-fact—to suppose that they assert, imply, or presuppose that their antecedents are false. A man may assert *W*, for example, in the course of trying to decide whether its antecedent is true. ("Did he read *Emma* last night? I don't have the whole picture yet. But if there had been a copy . . . etc.") Or he may know that the antecedent is true and use the subjunctive in order to be noncommittal. ("I'm not saying, one way or the other. But this much is true: if there had been a copy . . . etc.") And the second

---

[1] "Then you agree, I said, that the pleasant is the good and the painful evil. And here I would beg my friend Prodicus not to introduce his distinction of names, whether he is disposed to say pleasurable, delightful, joyful. However, by whatever name he prefers to call them, I will ask you, most excellent Prodicus, to answer in my sense of the words.

"Prodicus laughed and assented, as did the others." *Protagoras* 358.

mistake is that of supposing that, from the fact that the antecedent of "if p and r and s, then q" is false, it follows that p is false and r is false and s is false.

There is still another possible way of expressing "can" in terms of "will if," or "would if," and expressing "could have" in terms of "would have if." Austin concedes that there is some plausibility in the "suggestion that 'I can do X' means 'I shall succeed in doing X, if I try' and 'I would have done X' means 'I should have succeeded in doing X if I had tried' "—plausibility, he says, "but no more," and he rejects the suggestion.

Among the objections to saying that "He can" means the same as "He will if he tries" are the following, all indicating possible cases in which "He can" is true and "He will if he tries" is not true. (i) A man who can do X may try to do X and because of an unexpected diversion or intrusion abandon the enterprise before he finishes; he gives up the puzzle because of a call to dinner. (Here we may say "He can but he wants his dinner" but not "He could if he did not want his dinner.") (ii) The man may try halfheartedly—*i.e.* he may not try as hard as he *can* try— and thus not complete the task. (iii) I can close my eyes, but it makes no sense to speak of me, now, *trying* to close my eyes. (iv) Austin suggests (this seems to be his principal objection to the formula) that "He can" is consistent with failure and "He will if he tries" is not. He says of the case where he misses a very short putt: "I may try and miss, and yet not be convinced that I could not have done it; indeed further experiments may confirm my belief that I could have done it that time although I did not." And finally (v) there may be things a man can do only if he does *not* try to do them. The golfer landed the ball at a certain place p; hence landing it at p was something which, at that time, he could do ("does" implies "can"); but had he tried to land the ball precisely at the place p where he did land it, then, in all probability, he would have failed.

These are valid objections to saying that "He can" means the same as "He will if he tries." But we may replace "He will if he tries" by a longer formula and then, I believe, they no longer apply. Suppose we say: "He can do X" means that there is something such that if he tried to do *it* then he would do X—*i.e.* that there is something Y such that if he tried to do Y then he would do X.

Then (i) we may say, of the man who could do the puzzle but gave it up in order to have his dinner, that there was something—*e.g.* doing the puzzle without having dinner—which was such that, had he tried to do *that*, he would have done the puzzle. (ii) Or if doing the puzzle required only a little more effort than he cared to put into it, then there was something—putting more effort into the puzzle —which was such that had he tried to do it he would have done the puzzle. (iii) Perhaps it makes no sense to say of me, now, that I may try to close my eyes; but there are other things I can be said to try to do—I can try to look the way I do when I'm asleep—which are such that if I do try to do them I will close my eyes. (iv) If Austin's golfer really could have holed it that time, then there was something such that, had he tried to do it along with the other things he did do, then the absent condition (*e.g.* applying more pressure with the thumb) would have been supplied, and he would have holed the ball. And (v) we may say of the man who landed the ball at p and who would not have done it had he tried to do it, that there were things such that had he tried to do *them* he would have landed the ball at p; they were just the things he did try to do. (We cannot say, however, that landing it at p is something that he can do "at will," or something he "knows how to do," for landing it at p is not itself something he can do if he tries.)

But there is still another possible difficulty: the statements "He does X if and only if he tries to do Y" and "He *cannot try* to do Y" are inconsistent with "He can do X," but they are not inconsistent with our *analysans*—they are not inconsistent with "There is a Y such that if he tries to do Y he will do X." (There are, of course, many acts which one cannot even *try* to perform.) This is the serious difficulty, I think. If it is a genuine one, then it applies not only to the present formula, but also to those which Austin mentions and, in all probability, to any attempt to define "can" in terms of "will if." For any such attempt will presumably introduce a verb of which "he" may be made the subject; it will then be grammatically permissible to insert "can not" between the subject "he" and the verb; and then it will be possible to describe a situation in which the *analysans* is true and "He can" is false. To overlook this possibility *is* a "first-water, ground-floor mistake."

All of which confirms Austin's profound remark: "In philosophy it is *can* in particular that we seem so often to uncover, just when we had thought some problem settled, grinning residually up at us like the frog at the bottom of the beer mug."

∙ ∙ ∙

ABILITY

ABILITY *

Arnold S. Kaufman

I

One of the ways we typically try to absolve a person from moral responsibility for some action is by claiming that he lacked some ability. A sees B drowning. He does not jump into the water in an effort to save B. When the question of his culpability arises, he pleads for exemption on the grounds that he is unable to swim. C sees that a boiler is about to explode. He tries to relieve the pressure, but fails. Just before the boiler does explode, he runs from the scene. The resulting disaster takes three lives. When the question of C's culpability arises, he pleads that he is unable to operate boilers. D accidentally witnesses a murder. In an effort to save the victim, he grabs a pistol which happens to be at hand and tries to shoot the murderer. Unfortunately, he misses. In excusing himself from responsibility, he claims that he does not have the ability to shoot a gun accurately.

The attempt to excuse someone on grounds of inability is not always accepted. If, for example, A had represented himself as a powerful swimmer in order to get a job as lifeguard and if it was in his role as lifeguard that inability resulted in failure to save the drowning man, B, then A's plea would seem insufficient to warrant exemption. Nevertheless, inability is one of the typical grounds of exemp-

From *The Journal of Philosophy*, LX, No. 19 (September 12, 1963), 537–551. Reprinted by permission of the author and *The Journal of Philosophy*. © Copyright 1963 by Journal of Philosophy, Inc.

* This paper was written while I was a Fellow at the Center for Advanced Study in the Behavioral Sciences. Professors Donald Davidson and Richard Wasserstrom helpfully commented on earlier versions of my arguments.

tion from moral responsibility. My aim is to analyze the concept of "ability" as it figures in situations such as those I have just described. My ultimate concern is to be clear about concepts crucial to an adequate theory of moral responsibility.

It seems reasonable to suppose that, if someone has the ability and the opportunity to do something, then, if he tries to do it, he will succeed. But this is not always the case. For example, suppose that, in the illustration cited above, D had had the ability to shoot a gun accurately. He might still have tried and failed. But either this outcome contradicts the assumption that it seemed reasonable to make, or one of the conditions specified in that assumption *must,* in fact, not be satisfied. Let us consider the possibility that one of the conditions is not satisfied.

D did fail. There is no doubt about that. Perhaps, however, he did not try as hard as he might have. That is why he failed. But then the original premise is false: ability and opportunity and effort are *not* enough; the effort has to be of a certain magnitude. So let us amend the assumption in the indicated way. "If someone has the ability and opportunity to do something, then, if he tries as hard as he might, he will succeed." But let us suppose that D did try as hard as he might, and he still failed to thwart the murderer.

Perhaps, then, he did not really have the opportunity. But a reasonably objective assessment of the circumstances makes it quite clear that he had all the opportunity he could ever hope to have. Visibility and weather conditions were good. There were no distractions. Unless one is inclined to argue that, given ability, effort, and failure, one is bound not to have had ample opportunity, it must be conceded that D did have the opportunity to shoot the murderer. As I am confident that the solution to the problem lies elsewhere, I will assume that there was no lack of opportunity.

That leaves D's ability to be questioned. Perhaps, after all, he did not really have the ability to shoot accurately. But he had shot accurately from that distance many times in the past. Moreover, shaken by his failure, he tests himself the next day and hits a comparable target in nineteen out of twenty tries. So he does seem to have the ability.

But perhaps abilites are things that come and go. Perhaps he did not have the ability on the particular occasion of his failure. He momentarily lost it, recovering it the next day. There is no evidence of this apart from his failure. In the case of an ability like shooting accurately, it seems plausible to suppose that a consistent record of success is ample evidence of the presence of the ability, even on those infrequent occasions of failure.[1] It is somehow absurd to suppose that the fact that Maris does not hit a home run every time he comes to bat, or that Chamberlain does not sink a basket every time he shoots from inside the foul line, indicates that they momentarily lose abilities only to recover them just before success. Abilities of this sort do not seem to be the sorts of things which, like graduate students and pangs of delight, come and go—at least not in the way that this attempt to resolve the inconsistency would require. They seem to be the sorts of things that are, on occasion, liable to failure.

---

[1] As Austin argues in "Ifs and Cans" (in *Philosophical Papers*, Warnock and Urmson, eds., Oxford, 1961), p. 166. All quotations or views attributed to Austin in this essay occur in the article cited. [See p. 169 above. Ed.]

Nowell-Smith, in responding to one of Austin's criticisms, insists upon this feature of having an ability, and proposes the following analysis. "A has the ability to x" means, he maintains, "A usually succeeds, if he tries" (96).[2] The analysis, of course, assumes the existence of opportunity. If one accepts this analysis, then one must reject the original assumption. It would have to be revised in the following way: "If someone has the ability and the opportunity to do something, then, if he tries as hard as he might to do it, he will usually succeed." Unfortunately, this resolution of the difficulty has two important defects.

First, there are some abilities that seem to require invariable success, others that seem to require only occasional success. The ability to move one's finger is an example of the first, the ability to hit home runs of the second. Maris does not have to hit home runs very often to be said to have the ability. And if someone had the opportunity to move his finger, tried, yet failed, we should deny that he had had the ability on that occasion. If we were convinced that he really had tried, we should insist that this was conclusive proof that his finger was, in fact, momentarily paralyzed. If it is reasonable to talk of momentarily losing one's ability in this instance, why not in the case of any other ability? Or, more generally, why should we admit one criterion of performance in the case of one ability, but another criterion in the case of some other ability? We could, of course, reformulate the analysis as well as the original assumption to take account of this variability (e.g., "A at least occasionally succeeds, if he tries"). But this would leave the fact of that variation shrouded in mystery. Any sound analysis should have something to say about this aspect of ability.

Second, it is at least logically possible to suppose that someone performed in a certain way by luck and not because he had the ability. A sensible person will not attribute to someone who throws ten sevens in a row an extraordinary ability to throw dice. He may suspect the dice thrower of cheating, but not of possessing some special skill. (Failure to be sensible about such things often results in large gambling losses.) Similarly, in the case of D's shooting, it is at least logically possible that his frequent record of success was due to luck (or, perhaps, divine intervention—which is, on certain theological principles, a sign of Divine luck—sometimes called Divine Grace). Admittedly, in the case of accurate shooting, the possibility is far-fetched. But this farfetched conjecture suggests a far less implausible point, viz., that some action is to count as an exercise of an ability only if it is reasonable to suppose that the ability was causally relevant to success. Austin talks of abilities producing success, but Nowell-Smith explicitly rejects this suggestion. "It would" he asserts in a way which I sincerely hope will soon become inimitable, "certainly be odd to suggest that abilities are causally connected with successes." He continues, "Austin talks of an ability as producing success or failure, as if it were a tool or a part of the body with which we do something and without which we cannot (contingently) do it. The metaphor of 'producing' can hardly be seriously intended . . ." (96). I do not know whether Austin seriously intended what he wrote. But I shall argue not only that abilities are normally thought to be causally connected with success, but that it is quite reasonable so to regard them. The very fact that we do often talk of abilities as enabling success suggests

2 "Ifs and Cans," Theoria, 26, 2 (1960). All quotations and views attributed to Nowell-Smith in this essay occur in the article cited.

this. Clearly, Nowell-Smith's proposed analysis is inconsistent with such a view. For on his dispositional analysis, the claim that someone has an ability is just a way of summarizing past success and forecasting future success. (I shall call dispositional notions that can be analyzed in this way "summary dispositions.")

Austin suggested a criticism of any attempt to analyze abilities in terms of the sort of hypothetical proposed by Nowell-Smith, which ought also to be considered. His criticism was primarily contained in a footnote which promises to become as famous as Hume's concluding footnote in the "Dialogues concerning Natural Religion." Austin there contended that, though such a hypothetical analysis has some plausibility, it is no more than plausible. For consider the assertion, "I can hole the putt." It surely does not mean "I shall hole the putt, if I try." For I may try and fail, and yet "further experiments may confirm my belief that I could have done it that time although I did not" (166). I take it that, when Austin uses the expression "could have" in this last statement, he means it in the ability sense. For, with uncharacteristic lack of precision, he goes on to talk of "human ability or power or capacity."

Austin is correct to claim that, if I try and fail, it does not follow that "I could have holed the putt" is false, when "could have" is being used in the ability sense. But as Nowell-Smith claims, all that is required is that "ability" be defined in such a way as to take into account this logical possibility of failure. In the case of putting, the most that can be embedded in the analysis is, "I *usually* hole the putt, if I try." Once this modification is admitted, the hypothetical analysis becomes immune to Austin's criticism. (That is, given the analysis, if I try and fail, it does not follow that I lack the ability.)

It is interesting to note that it is this argument that Austin has in mind when, at the end of his essay, he asserts that his arguments "go some way to show" that "Determinism, whatever it may be, may yet be the case, but at least it appears not consistent with what we ordinarily say and presumably think" (179). For, in the aforementioned footnote, after having tried to dispose of hypothetical analyses of "ability," he went on to assert:

> But if I tried my hardest, say, and missed, surely there *must* have been *something* that caused me to fail, that made me unable to succeed? So that I *could not* have holed it. Well a modern belief in science, in there being an explanation of everything, may make us assent to this argument. But such a belief is not in line with the traditional beliefs enshrined in the word *can:* according to *them,* a human ability or power or capacity is inherently liable not to produce success, on occasion, and that for no reasons (or are bad luck and bad form sometimes reasons?) (166).

One need not admit to this "modern belief in science" in order to deny that "the traditional beliefs enshrined in the word *can*" are inconsistent with belief in Determinism. For on the analysis I shall propose, which is, for what it is worth, not inconsistent with common usage, *some* abilities (not all) are indeed inherently liable not to produce success; but it is argued that there is no reason to think that such failure is not subject to scientific explanation. Whether or not denial of Determinism is enshrined in other parts of common usage is not thereby settled. All

I shall here argue is that Austin has not, as he cautiously supposed, gone some way toward showing that the belief is there enshrined.

Another approach to the analysis of "ability" is suggested by the defects of Nowell-Smith's proposal. The supposition that abilities are causally relevant to success as well as to variation in the appropriate percentage of success can be accounted for if "ability" is defined in terms of physiological states. Being in such and such a physiological state would be a cause of certain movements. For example, being in such a physiological state is a cause of a finger's moving (not someone's moving his finger) or a person's finger motions' resulting in a hit upon a target (not his hitting the target). Moreover, the difference in criteria can be accounted for in terms of the varying degrees of relevant physiological complexity. The ability to move one's finger is defined in terms of a physiological state that is relatively uncomplicated in a way which guarantees that, given opportunity and intention, success is assured. But marksmanship involves physiological conditions which are complex in ways that account for occasional failure. The fact that we do not presently have a very good idea of just what the causally relevant physiological states are does not preclude our assuming that they occur and that they have the required causal relevance. (For example, it may be that the more complex the physical or mental act, the higher the probability of neurological misfiring.)

But an analysis in terms of physiological states alone ignores the fact that abilities are, as Nowell-Smith and many others point out, dispositional properties. That is, to assert that someone has a certain ability entails that, if he tries to exercise his ability, he will meet with at least occasional success. From ability, opportunity, and effort we can deduce at least occasional success; but we cannot deduce such behavioral conformance from opportunity and effort alone. Any analysis must express the logical relatedness of ability and performance. If to attribute dispositional properties to an object is, logically, merely to summarize past behavior and forecast future behavior, then analysis in terms of physiological states is not permissible.

Some philosophers have argued that, if two terms are logically related, they cannot essentially refer to things that are causally related.[3] If this thesis is true, then reference to causally relevant physiological states cannot be part of the analysis of dispositional notions like "ability." The thesis is, however, false.

Consider the following analysis of "A is able to x": "A is in the appropriate physiological state, P, such that, given opportunity, P causes A to succeed in x'ing an appropriate number of times (as determined by the relevant complexity of P), if he tries to x." If this were an accurate description of usage, it would entail both that at least occasional success is, logically, a necessary criterion of the ability to x, and that the ability is causally relevant to the movements that constitute success. The situation is this. Ability means P and B (B being the behavioral criterion), where P tends to cause B. "P tends to cause B" is not a deterministic law. Hence, it does not entail that all behavior produced by ability is determined. On the other

---

[3] As A. Melden has put it: "The very notion of a causal sequence logically implies that cause and effect are intelligible without any logically internal relation of the one to the other. . . . (T)his surely is one lesson we can derive from a reading of Hume's discussion of causation" (Free Action, pp. 52–53). From this Melden goes on tacitly to infer that, if two things are logically related, they cannot be causally related. But the tacit inference is invalid.

hand, it is, like all tendency generalizations, *consistent* with determinism. I do not want to argue that this form of analysis is true for all dispositional terms. But the contention that it cannot be the form appropriate to any analysis of a dispositional notion is an entirely arbitrary judgment. Ryle, in his *Concept of Mind,* stresses the analogy between psychological dispositions and the brittleness of glass. But the very analogy should have cautioned him against occasional remarks which made it seem as if he believed that all dispositional notions were mere summary dispositions. For it is quite clear that when ordinary men impute brittleness to glass they mean not only to summarize what happens to glass under various conditions, but also to impute to glass *internal* properties, albeit unspecified, which are causally relevant to what happens to the glass under those conditions.

It is not enough to establish the mere possibility of such an analysis of "ability." I must now argue that the proposed analysis is, in fact, sound.

One objection to the proposal is that ordinary talk about abilities does not involve reference to physiological states in any clear and definite way. This may be admitted. But to this objection there are two replies. First, usage may involve reference to unspecified internal properties that are akin to physiological properties. Second, even if usage did not involve such reference, the fact should not be taken as a decisive reason for rejecting the proposed analysis.

Many philosophers have pointed out that satisfactory analysis of dispositions must support contrafactuals. To assert that "glass is brittle" is not simply to assert "glass will break under such and such conditions"; it is to make the much stronger assertion, "Glass would break, should such and such conditions occur." No doubt, if one were to ask the ordinary man how he would explain the fact that glass would break under these conditions, we are not likely to get anything much more informative than "That's the sort of thing glass is," or "Glass has some sort of structural property that accounts for the fact that it is likely to break under such and such conditions." But I am not arguing that the causal reference embedded in ordinary usage is very specific, only that there is reference to causally relevant internal or structural properties. The ordinary man might go on to say that scientists have discovered a great many things about the internal properties that account for the tendency glass has to break under such and such conditions. But that is another story. My contention is that usage of the term "ability" may also embody such reference. The fact that it supports contrafactuals suggests this; other facts tend to confirm it.

I shall mention just a couple of examples of the sort of supporting facts I have in mind. But these should suffice to exhibit the generality of my claim. Suppose a father who claims that his two-year-old son is potentially able to become a good football player is challenged. What kind of evidence would he adduce in defense of his claim? He might cite his son's large frame, the boy's sturdiness, his exceptional degree of muscular coordination, his healthy appetite, and so on. In citing such facts as relevant considerations, he is certainly expressing his general belief that certain physical properties of a human organism are causally relevant to acquisition of the ability to be a good football player. Given this belief, it would not be surprising if, in imputing that ability to someone, the father also imputed to that person certain relatively unspecified physical properties.

Or consider this example. I am listening to a lecture. It is boring. My eyes begin to close. I try as hard as possible to keep them open; but they irresistibly close. I am unable to keep my eyes open. Someone notices and asks, "Why did you close your eyes during the lecture?" I reply, "I was unable to keep them open." Surely this is not an unresponsive answer to the question. For I might have replied, "I closed them in order better to concentrate," or "I closed them because I had had some eye drops, and found the light painful." In citing my inability I am at least claiming that I was in that state, in this instance whatever state it is that underlies boredom, which caused my eyes to close no matter how hard I tried to keep them open.

Another feature of ordinary talk about abilities bears mention at this point. We distinguish potential abilities from capacities and capacities from abilities. An infant may have the potential ability to speak a language, but lack the capacity to do so. After a certain period of maturation he may acquire the capacity, and then the ability. I take it that the child's capacity is in this instance a certain sort of ability—the ability to learn something. Thus, in denying that the infant has the capacity to speak, we mean that it cannot now learn to speak. In order for him to be able to learn, the capacities he does possess must be brought to a certain pitch of development. This is, in a sense, what is involved in learning a language, or, for that matter, in the process of acquiring any ability. Consider another example. A large and muscular person cannot, despite his considerable muscular development, lift a weight of 300 lbs. But he has the capacity to lift such a weight. For, through a training process, his capacities can be brought to the appropriate pitch of development. First he lifts 100-lb. weights. They are easy. Then he tries his hand at 200-lb. weights. They are more difficult, but he manages. And before very long he is able, through training, to lift 200 lbs. as easily as he previously lifted 100 lbs. He then tries 250 lbs. Eventually, he acquires that ability. He is now ready for 300 lbs. His capacity to lift weights of that magnitude has, through training, been brought to the proper pitch of development. What these illustrations suggest is that an analysis of "ability" that expresses the view that abilities are causally relevant to success must surely be a plausible description of much usage.

In a sense, what emerges from this discussion is a natural history of the development of an ability—a natural history which is, however, quite extraordinary in one respect. That is, though causal relationships are assumed, they are often not specified. Ordinary men have long quite reasonably supposed that the fact that we are ignorant of the causal conditions of specifically human powers did not preclude one's supposing that there were such conditions; that these conditions were, so to speak, located "within the skin"; and that they did vary in ways that accounted for those human properties about which they lacked precise knowledge. Contrary to what Ryle and others sometimes seem to suppose, ordinary men have not assumed that human beings are empty sausage skins who, quite miraculously, seemed to be possessed of dispositional properties. Built into their dispositional terms or implicit in their discussion of abilites is reference to unspecified properties of the organism that are causally relevant to the disposition. And so, without any more embarrassment than I have already felt at my attempts to fill the empty sausage skin with unspecified internal states, let me round out this prolegomenon to an analysis of "ability" by marshaling the considerations previously adduced in a way that makes sense of the mysterious fact that different abilities have different criteria of success. Abilities may differ with respect to the complexity of the properties that underlie them. The physiological properties necessary for the ability to move one's finger are less complex than those which are necessary for the ability to hole putts in golf in a way which precisely accounts for the fact that we expect invariable success in the case of the former, but not in the case of the latter. Thus we can acknowledge, in an admittedly unspecified way, that performance and variation in the consistency of performance are causally related to specific states of the organism. So much seems to me to be implicit in much ordinary talk about abilities.

Of course, whatever allusion to underlying physiological states we may, in our ordinary remarks, make, it is so lacking in specific content that one might criticize these assertions as unscientific. And so, in a sense, they are. But one cannot have it both ways. Either one must admit that these unscientific distinctions are often drawn in ordinary talk about abilities; or one must, by giving ordinary talk scientific content, depart from its neutrality. That we do, in ordinary discourse, invoke the causally related properties of the organism when we talk of abilities seems to me to be quite clear. If one purports to be describing usage, one should not depart from it because criteria irrelevant to it—that is, criteria of what is or is not scientific —are involved.

On the other hand, I see no reason why philosophers, as well as ordinary men, cannot acknowledge what scientific investigation is making increasingly clear, viz., that human abilities are conditioned by physiological states of varying complexity. But, as the insistence on physiological reference raises issues that go beyond the scope of my thesis, I will be content to withdraw the reference to physiological states if others are content to permit me to draw the vague and unscientific distinction, embedded in much ordinary usage, between some condition of the organism which is causally relevant to having an ability, and the actual abilities to which it is causally related. The revised analysis, purged of explicit physiological reference, that thus emerges is: "A has the ability to x" means "A is in a certain condition, C (C being the appropriate state of the organism brought to a certain pitch of development), such that, given opportunity, C causes A to succeed in x'ing an appropriate percentage of the time (where the appropriate percentage is determined by the unspecified complexity of C), if he should try to x."

If, however, one insists on purging the analysis of all reference to internal causes, on the grounds that ordinary usage does not support such an account, there is no need for lengthy disputation. It seems to me that talk about abilities producing success is not a misleading metaphor and that this fact is sufficient to warrant the claim that the proposed analysis does not depart from ordinary usage. But the important thing is that much thought and action indicates that men do believe that there are such causally relevant conditions of the exercise of abilities. In general, our beliefs do tend to be reflected in usage. Yet there is nothing sacrosanct about usage; and if one insists in defining "ability" so that it is a summary disposition, treating the facts to which I have tried to call attention as indications of the beliefs men have regarding the causal conditions of abilities, this would not affect the bearing that the argument of this paper has on the problem of developing an adequate account of moral responsibility.

II

The proposed analysis (perhaps the older expression "rational reconstruction" would be better) consists of two clauses. The first specifies that the agent is in a certain condition which is causally relevant to success. I have already said as much as I shall say in this paper in defense of this provision. The second clause consists of the hypothetical, "A succeeds in x'ing an appropriate percentage of the time, if he tries." The proposal that an analysis of "ability" includes or consists of such a hypothetical has been criticized on a variety of grounds.

It has been argued that "A succeeds, if he tries" is either analytically true or opaque, that *trying* is certainly not an empirical condition of *success*. The "if," it is argued, is not the "if" of causal conditional. In the rest of this paper I shall consider the arguments for these conclusions.

Richard Taylor holds that "A succeeds in x'ing an appropriate percentage of the time, if he tries" is analytically true. He considers the statement, "I will move my finger, if I try," and asserts:

> Our entire criterion for saying what he wanted (or tried, or intended, or whatnot) to do, is what he in fact did; we do not infer the former from the latter on the basis of what we have in fact found, but we regard the former as something entailed by what we now find, namely, just his moving that finger.[4]

Thus, Taylor concludes, if the hypothetical is true at all, it rests "only on a conventional equivalence of meaning, and as such cannot be a causal relationship between states or events" (88). But his argument is unsound in at least two basic respects.

First, it is simply not true that "I tried to move my finger" is *entailed* by "I moved my finger." Nor is the statement, "He tried to move his finger" entailed by "He moved his finger." In the case of the third-person utterance, it may well be that he moved his finger while asleep. If we saw him do so, we would have no warrant for concluding that he *tried* to move his finger. (Even if he moved it while fully awake, we would not be deductively entitled to claim that he *tried* to do so; nor even that he intended to do so. At most we would be entitled to claim that he did so intentionally. And even this *entailment* is dubious if we hold that all we are really entitled to claim is that we saw his finger move and did not see him moving his finger.) However, it is true that if we saw him move his finger while he was fully conscious, then, if the situation is such that he might be expected to try to move his finger, we would normally be entitled to infer that he had tried to move it. What sort of situation is that? Well, he might be a patient whose right arm had been paralyzed down to the finger tips. Then, if his doctor said, "Try to move your finger," and we saw his finger move, we would be entitled to infer that he had indeed tried to move his finger. Of course, if we saw his fingers move, but also knew that an electric vibrator lying under the bed had accidentally been set into operation, we should not be in a position to know whether he had moved his finger and, hence, could not infer that he had tried to do so. Of course, we might have independent evidence. He might, for example, have said, in a tone of great excitement, "I tried to move my finger and succeeded!" He himself might

4 "I Can" (reprinted in *Free Will*, Walsh and Morgenbesser, eds., Prentice-Hall, 1962), p. 86. All quotations and views attributed to Taylor in this essay occur in the article cited.

mistakenly have supposed that the observed motion was the result of his having tried, and not the result of the motions of the electric vibrator. But at least we should have good reason to believe that he had, following his doctor's instructions, tried. The first-person case is more complex. But, broadly speaking, the remarks I have just made for the third-person case hold. So what he in fact did is not our "entire criterion" for inferring what he tried to do; but it is, in the appropriate circumstances, *one* fairly reliable criterion.

Perhaps Taylor was misled into making this exaggerated claim by the following considerations. From the fact that he has the opportunity, has the ability, does try, and does not stop trying, we can deduce that he will move his finger. We cannot deduce this fact from ability and opportunity alone. Hence, his moving his finger is not a criterion for his having tried in the way that the light's going on is a criterion for my having pushed the switch. The latter two occurrences are not logically related. But trying and moving one's finger are logically related. And he might further have accepted the dogma that I criticized a moment ago, viz., that if two things are logically related they cannot be causally related. And if they cannot be causally related, then either the hypothetical is analytically true, or it stands for nothing clear. But the dogma is as mistaken in this connection as it was in connection with ability. "Try," like "ability," is not used merely to summarize actions.

Which brings me to the second criticism mentioned a moment ago, viz., that if "trying" is not construed as a summary of action, then it is an opaque notion that refers to "internal hokus pokus" (in Taylor's words) or "a ghost in the machine" (in Ryle's).[5]

As I have already suggested, the thesis of Ryle's that is relevant is that those dispositional terms which are normally called "psychological" are mere summary dispositions, and never the kind of complex causal and summary dispositions which I have claimed "ability" to be, and now wish to claim "trying" to be. Put forward as a conceptual proposal, this claim can be discussed on its merits. Put as a general account of usage, it will not do for reasons that I have already given. It may, however, still be the case that "trying" is such a summary disposition. Taylor seems to think that either it is this, or it is opaque. By way of giving my reasons for rejecting the thesis that "trying" is a summary disposition, let me propose an analysis of what it means to say, "A tried to x." For it will be much easier to consider Ryle's thesis as it bears on "trying" if we have some concrete proposal before us.

Consider a situation in which a subject in a psychological experiment is pressing a button. His aim is to cause a red light to flash for ten seconds, the bulb being hidden from his view. He is not certain that he is succeeding. In fact, he is succeeding; the red light is flashing. Suppose he asserted, "I am making the red light flash." This statement is true. But, given his uncertainty, he should not have made that assertion. For anyone who hears the subject make this assertion is, under normal circumstances, entitled to infer that the subject is certain about what he is doing. Hence, either he is misdescribing what he is doing, or he is deliberately misleading those who happen to hear his statement. Let us assume that it is not his intention to mislead others. What would be a correct description of what he

[5] In fact, all Taylor does by way of defending this claim is to cite Ryle's arguments in *The Concept of Mind*.

is doing? Clearly, he could correctly describe what he is doing in the following terms, "I am *trying* to make the red light flash." But he is pressing a button. How can that be an instance of "trying to make a red light flash"? Suppose he happened to be pressing the button, though he firmly believed that it was unconnected to the light. Then, though his movements are identical with those described previously, he could not correctly describe what he is doing as "trying to make the red light flash"; (except, of course, if he intended to deceive). He must, in other words, believe that the pressing of the button *may* result in the red light's flashing. If he believes this, then, given his purpose, he is pressing the button *in order to* make the red light flash. These preliminary remarks suggest the following analysis of "A tried to x," (where A is a human being): "A is doing something in order to do or achieve x; but he is not certain that he will do or achieve x." The definition embodies both features to which my discussion has called attention; i.e., the fact that the actor does something *in order to* achieve something else, and the fact that he is *uncertain* about whether he is successful.

There is no "internal hokus pokus" or "ghost in the machine" involved in this analysis. It exhibits the dispositional features of trying in at least two respects. First, being uncertain is itself a dispositional property. That a person is uncertain about something means, among other things, both that he will not do certain things inconsistent with his uncertainty and that he will normally express the fact that he does not fully believe something. Second, to do one thing *in order to* do or achieve something else is dispositional. For it means, among other things, that the person will under normal conditions express a certain intention when asked and that he will normally give a certain reason for what he is doing.

But in virtue of what feature of the proposed analysis can trying be said to be causally relevant to some action? The agent is doing one thing (*y*) in order to do or achieve x. That is, he believes that his doing *y* is a means of doing or achieving x, and he takes this purported fact to be a reason for doing *y*. But if *y*'s being a means to x is his reason for his doing *y*, then *that* he takes this as a reason is causally relevant to his doing *y*. That is, in claiming that a person is trying to do something else, we are claiming that certain considerations are a reason for his doing what he is doing; and in claiming that, we are also citing a cause of his doing what he is doing, viz. that he takes those considerations as reasons for what he is doing.

I know that the view that reasons are not causes is another dogma encountered in much recent philosophy of mind. Taken in a certain way, the thesis is true. But there is another sense in which the view is seriously misleading. It is only this misleading thesis that the proposed analysis of "trying" contradicts. Whenever a certain consideration is a reason for someone, that fact supports a further causal claim, viz. *that* it is a reason for someone may be causally relevant to that person's action.

How does the proposed analysis of "ability" bear on the problem of providing an adequate theory of moral responsibility?

First, though it does not presuppose determinism, it is certainly consistent with a deterministic account of human thought and action.

Second, it clarifies a notion that is an important constituent of an adequate theory of moral responsibility. For absence of ability is an important ground of exemption from moral responsibility.

Finally, the analysis implies that, for most abilities, given ability, opportunity, and reasonable effort, one may still fail to do what he ought; and it suggests that this failure is not therefore blameworthy. That is, ability, opportunity, and reasonable effort do not imply that one *can* do something. For if one does make a reasonable effort and fails, that he made the effort may be a ground for exemption from moral responsibility. All we can reasonably require of a person is that he try reasonably hard to be in a position to do what he ought; and that, when in that position, he try reasonably hard to do what he ought. For we should not hold a person morally responsible if his neurological mechanisms happen to be misfiring. Yet there is no way to handle such grounds for exemption from responsibility in terms of the conventional notions of "opportunity" and "ability."

VOLUNTARY ABILITIES

Timothy Duggan and Bernard Gert

We are concerned with a particular sense of "can" that we propose to call the "can" of voluntary ability. The concept of a voluntary ability is a complex one. It includes both the concept of a physical or intellectual ability, and the concept of the ability to will to do a particular kind of action. These two concepts are themselves complex and stand in need of analysis. The terms "physical or intellectual ability," "voluntary ability," and "the ability to will" are technical terms. We believe, however, that they stand for familiar concepts which are actually employed though not fully articulated. Our discussion will be divided into three parts: the first will be devoted to an analysis of physical or intellectual abilities. The second will be devoted to an analysis of the ability to will. The third section will be devoted to an examination of certain consequences of our analysis of voluntary abilities for the traditional problems of freedom of the will and the nature of voluntary action.

I

Throughout we consistently distinguish between a *kind of action* and a *particular act,* and when we discuss physical abilities and the ability to will we are always concerned with *kinds* of action.[1] What will count as the same kind of action

From *American Philosophical Quarterly*, IV (April 1967), 127–135. Reprinted by permission of the authors and the *American Philosophical Quarterly*. Slightly revised by the authors.

[1] For the sake of brevity, in what follows we shall speak simply of physical abilities rather than physical or intellectual abilities although we intend that our analysis apply equally well to such abilities as the ability to recite a poem, solve crossword puzzles, and so on.

will depend upon which type of ability we are considering. When considering physical abilities, we say A and A' are the same kind of action if, and only if, from the fact that one has the physical ability to do A it follows that he has the physical ability to do A', and conversely.

Before we can present our analysis of the "can" of physical ability it is advisable to distinguish this sense of "can" from several other distinct, though related, senses of "can." There is, for example, that sense of "can" used in the sentence "Anyone can win the prize" in which "can" means simply that there are no restrictions put on who is allowed or permitted to win the prize; we shall not be concerned with this sense of "can" at all, nor with the sense of "can" which is used to express logical possibility. But there are several senses of "can" which are more closely related to the "can" of physical ability.

The abilities enjoyed by inanimate objects, like the ability of a machine to go a hundred miles an hour, we call *capabilities*. For these we give the following analysis: "S can do x" means: Given reasonable opportunity, S will do x a reasonable number of times. There is no mention of the order in which successes and failures must occur, provided that there is a reasonable number of successes. But there are some abilities of inanimate objects, such as the ability of titanium to withstand extremely high temperatures without melting, to which this analysis of capabilities does not apply. When we say, "This piece of titanium can withstand temperatures of over 1500 degrees," we do not mean given reasonable opportunity it will do so a reasonable number of times. For of this sort of ability, which we call a *capacity*, there is no point in talking of a *reasonable* opportunity, and even more important, when put to the test, a thing must not fail to manifest its capacities even once. To say that this piece of titanium can withstand temperatures of over 1500 degrees is to say that it will withstand such temperatures *whenever subjected to them*. If, on one occasion it does not withstand such a temperature, it can no longer be said to have that capacity. An automobile, on the other hand, may have the capability of going a hundred miles an hour, even if one day given reasonable opportunity it does not do so.

We are now in a position to distinguish between three kinds of abilities—capacities, capabilities, and physical abilities—and thus between three significantly different senses of "can" or "is able to." [2] Consider the following formulas:

(1) "S can do x," means "S will never fail to do x." This holds of such abilities as the ability of titanium to resist high temperatures, the ability of a sheet of plate glass to flex without shattering, etc. These kinds of abilities we call *capacities*.

(2) "S can do x," means: Simply given reasonable opportunity S will do x a reasonable number of times. This formula holds for such abilities as that of the refrigerator to make ice cubes (the abilities that machines have) or the ability of a person to digest fatty foods (*some* of the abilities that persons have). These kinds of abilities we call *capabilities*.

What we call physical abilities do not fit either of the above analyses. For physical abilities, "S can do x" does not entail "S will never fail to do x." Further, if given reasonable opportunity S fails to do x a reasonable number of times, it does

[2] We do not claim that this distinction accurately reflects ordinary usage. A glance at the dictionary is sufficient to show that "capacity," "capability," and "ability" are often used interchangeably. Our claim is simply that in philosophical discourse these distinctions will prove to be useful.

not follow that S cannot do x. A person may have the physical ability to run a mile in four minutes, have ample opportunity, and yet not do so a reasonable number of times simply because he does not will to do so.

"Choose," "try," "intend," "attempt," "decide," "resolve," etc., express related though different ideas. We make use of the term "will" in our analysis since it has a less circumscribed meaning than "choose," "try," "intend," etc. For example, it is a matter of debate whether or not a man who hands over his purse when threatened with physical violence can be said to choose to do so. But, as we use "will" it is correct to say that he wills to do so. In our use of "will" there is no suggestion of one's *wanting* to do the action in question, only that one did it intentionally. However, "S intends to do x" does not entail that S wills to do x because a person may intend to do this or that but when the time comes he neither does it nor does he try to do it, perhaps simply because he has changed his mind. In our sense of "will" there is no temporal gap between one's willing to do something and doing or trying to do it. If there is such a gap between "making up one's mind" to do something and doing or trying to do it, then this would be a case of intending or resolving rather than willing. The following relations hold between willing to do an action and doing it intentionally or trying to do it.

(1) If S tries (is trying) to do x, then S wills (is willing) to do x.

(2) If S does (is doing) x intentionally, then S wills (is willing) to do x.

(3) "S wills (is willing) to do x" if and only if "S tries (is trying) to do x, or S does (is doing) x intentionally." [3]

An analysis of the "can" of physical abilities must allow for the possibility that S *can* do x even though when given reasonable opportunity he does not do x. Consequently, we add to our analysis the phrase "if S wills to do x." But in order that our analysis not be too restrictive we add the phrase "But willing to do x is not a necessary condition for doing x." Thus, our analysis of physical ability does not exclude those kinds of actions which sometimes are done unintentionally. Without this addition our analysis would exclude everything that we wish to call physical abilities, e.g., the ability to walk or to talk. For one can do these things without willing to do them, e.g., in one's sleep or out of habit. However, this addition *does* rule out as physical abilities those for the exercise of which willing to do so is a logically necessary condition for doing so. Since one cannot commit murder unintentionally, the ability to commit murder is not a physical ability for willing to do so is a necessary condition for doing so. Although it sounds paradoxical to say that the ability to commit murder is not a physical ability, the paradox evaporates when it is realized that committing murder necessarily involves the exercise of physical abilities, i.e., involves doing kinds of actions which *might* be done without one's willing to do them. These same considerations apply to the ability to commit suicide and all other abilities for the exercise of which willing to do so is a necessary condition for doing so. To say of a person that he is capable of committing murder or suicide is not to say of him that he has certain physical

---

[3] This is not intended to be a philosophical analysis of willing, though we do provide an analysis of the *ability* to will, and consequently we are not subject to the criticism that we provide an analysis which makes essential use of the problematic notions of trying and intending. Whatever these might turn out to be, our account of willing would remain the same.

abilities but to say something about his *character*. And in general, statements about those abilities for which willing to exercise them is a necessary condition for doing so, will be found to be statements about character.

Our proposed analysis of the "can" of physical ability is: "S can do *x*" means: if S wills to do *x* then simply given a reasonable opportunity S will do *x* a reasonable number of times. But willing to do *x* is not a necessary condition for doing *x*.

We now turn to objections to the analysis as a whole.

Objection 1.   The analysis is too vague, i.e., the term "reasonable" which occurs several times does not admit of precise definition, whereas the statement "he can do *x*" seems to be perfectly precise.

Reply 1.   This vagueness is a valuable feature of our analysis, for "he can do *x*" as expressing physical ability is only superficially precise. This is apparent from the fact that equally well-informed observers, including the person claiming (or claimed) to have the ability, will differ on what shows that he can or cannot do *x*. Analyses of "S can do *x*" as "S will do *x* if he chooses" are inadequate just because they are too precise. If I have a reasonable opportunity, it may be, and often is, that even though I fail in one or more attempts, later attempts, if successful, do indeed show that I had the ability.[4] For example, there are a number of trials or opportunities for one to demonstrate his ability to high jump, pole vault, recite a poem from memory, etc. What counts as a reasonable number of times depends on the ability claimed. If I claim to be able to swim the English Channel, one success is enough to prove me right, though I may have failed ten times previously. But if I claim to have the ability to sink short putts, one success out of ten attempts or even one out of one is not enough to show that I can. Thus from the fact that a person does something it does not follow that he has the ability to do it. But if given reasonable opportunity, I will to do *x* and consistently fail to do it, then it would be correct to say that I cannot do it. Yet, even if I fail in all my attempts, it would be a mistake to conclude that I cannot do *x* if I never, in fact, have a reasonable opportunity. And, of course, what counts as a reasonable opportunity will sometimes be an undecidable issue.

Objection 2.   Granted that what will count as a reasonable number of times depends on the ability in question, even when we specify the ability, often there is no specific number of times which is *the* reasonable number of times. Yet according to the analysis any person who performs a reasonable number of times must be said to have the ability in question. Thus, there is no distinction between two people, both of whom perform a reasonable number of times, though one is more frequently successful than the other. That is, the analysis fails to account for different degrees of ability and thus for such expressions as "S can do *x* better than J."

---

[4] But not always. In the meantime I may have acquired the ability. In our analysis we say "simply given reasonable opportunity" in order to exclude this kind of case. Abilities, like capabilities, can be developed, lost, and regained. Our analysis concerns a person's abilities given the condition he is in at the time, not the condition he was or will be in. Thus we distinguish physical abilities from what we call "natural abilities." "S has the natural ability to do *x*" means: With natural development and/or a reasonable amount of training, S will acquire the physical ability to do *x*. The less training required the greater the natural ability.

Reply 2. On the contrary, a valuable feature of our analysis is that it does allow for degrees of ability. It is precisely because we do not equate ability with *consistent* success but only with *reasonable* success, that we can distinguish between different degrees of ability. If both Jones and Smith do x a reasonable number of times given the same number of attempts, and if Smith is successful a significantly greater number of times, we say that Smith can do x better than Jones. This, of course, is not a complete account of what is meant by "S can do x better than J" since other factors must be taken into consideration, e.g., the amount of time it takes for S to do x as compared with J, the effort involved, etc.

Objection 3. If someone never wills to do x, then we can never know if he would have done it a reasonable number of times. And hence, according to the analysis we can only know that a person has an ability if he wills to exercise it. But, surely we do know that, e.g., most people have the ability to touch their right knee with their left elbow though they may never have willed to do so.

Reply 3. Our analysis includes the conditional form—if A and B, then C, thus when one or both of the antecedents are false, the result is a counterfactual conditional. The objection presupposes that whereas we might know that someone has an ability which he has never exercised, the corresponding counterfactual yielded by our analysis could not be known to be true. But it is simply false that we can never know the truth of counterfactuals. For example, there is no doubt that statements such as "if the vase had been dropped it would have shattered" are sometimes true, and known to be true. For every case in which a statement attributing an unexercised ability to a person is true and known to be true, the corresponding counterfactual statement yielded by our analysis will be true and known to be true. In trivial cases where there is no doubt about the ability, there will be no doubt about the corresponding counterfactual. In those cases in which the counterfactual is doubtful there will be a similar uncertainty about the ability.[5]

Objection 4. The proposed analysis is intended to account for the "can" of physical ability. But if we apply it to the case of a physically fit person suffering from extreme claustrophobia, we might be forced to say that he can walk into a closet and shut the door even though it is obvious that he cannot do so.

Reply 4. This objection is the result of confusing the "can" of physical ability and what we call the "can" of voluntary ability. Simply because a person has the physical ability to do a kind of action, it doesn't follow that he has the voluntary ability to do that kind of action. For in addition to the physical ability to do a kind of action, one must also have the ability to will to do it in order to have the voluntary ability to do it.

II

A voluntary ability consists of both a physical ability and the ability to will. Our concern up to now has been with the "can" of physical ability. But, to provide an analysis of "S can do x" where this expression refers to a voluntary ability, we must now provide an analysis of the ability to will. To say that S can will to do x

[5] A parallel objection and reply could be made in the case where there is never a reasonable opportunity.

(a kind of action) is to say that it is possible to describe some state of affairs such that S would believe there were reasonable incentives for doing x and believing this, would will to do x; and it is possible to describe some state of affairs such that S would believe there were reasonable incentives for not doing x and believing this, would will not to do x.[6]

One might be tempted to substitute for our analysis of the ability to will the following less complex formula: It is possible to describe some reasonable incentives for doing x such that *if* S believed they were present he would will to do x, etc. However, this would be an inadequate substitute because it would allow that one might have the ability to will even though he lacks an essential element, viz., it might be that S cannot believe that there are any reasonable incentives for doing x. Thus one would have to add to the above, "S *can* believe that there are reasonable incentives for doing x." It would then be necessary to analyze this in the following way: It is possible to describe some state of affairs such that S would believe there were reasonable incentives for doing x, etc. We believe that this temptation should be resisted because in addition to our view that one should not multiply analyses beyond necessity, separating the analysis of "can believe . . ." from the analysis as a whole might suggest that a person could have the ability to will even though he could not have the necessary beliefs about reasonable incentives.

Incentives for willing to do x are a subclass of the envisaged consequences of doing x, where (1) x is a kind of action that one might have the physical ability to do and (2) the description of x contains no incentive either for doing or refraining from doing the action. They are that subclass which a rational man would regard as reasons for willing to do x.[7] An unreasonable incentive for willing to do x is one which it would be unreasonable to expect any rational man to resist. A reasonable incentive for willing to do x is an incentive for willing to do x which is not unreasonable. Of course, what counts as an unreasonable incentive will depend on the kind of action in question and the situation of the agent.

From the analysis it is clear that it will be much easier to show that one *has* the ability to will than to show that one *lacks* it. Since to show that one has the ability, one need only will to do x when one believes that there are reasonable incentives for doing it, and will not to do x when one believes that there are reasonable incentives for not doing it.[8] However, to show that one lacks the ability to will to do x we would have to establish either that it is impossible to describe any state of affairs such that S would believe there were reasonable incentives for doing x and believing this would will to do x, or that it is impossible to describe any state of affairs such that S would believe there were reasonable incentives for not doing x and believing this would will not to do x.

Obviously, it is extremely difficult to establish either of these alternatives. Nonetheless, we can have evidence, sometimes overwhelming evidence, that one lacks

---

[6] Note that we say "S would will not to do x" rather than "S would not will to do x" (which does not seem to be strong enough) or "S would will to do not—x" (which seems unintelligible unless it simply means "S would will to refrain from doing x" which is equivalent to what we say).

[7] For a more detailed account of a rational man and reasons, see Chapter II of *The Moral Rules* by Bernard Gert.

[8] One need not even will to do x every time one believes that the same reasonable incentive is present. All that is required to prove the ability to will to do x is that it be possible to describe some reasonable incentive that at least sometimes leads one to will to do x, etc.

the ability to will to do x. We can have this evidence because we can present S with numerous and varied reasonable incentives for willing to do x. When trying to determine whether or not S has the ability to will, it is not necessary that the incentives actually be present, but only that the person believe that they are. Thus, though there are often a limited number and variety of reasonable incentives that can actually be presented, there is virtually no limit on the number and variety of reasonable incentives that S can be induced to believe are present, by hypnosis or deceit.

In determining whether one has or lacks the ability to will to do x, it is important to present a number of different *kinds* of incentive. That no amount of money would induce S to will to do x does not show that he lacks the ability to will to do it. For he may will to do it quite readily when presented with a different kind of reasonable incentive, e.g., the avoidance of pain or shame for himself or others. We do not hold that a man who has the ability to will to do x will will to do x whenever he believes that a reasonable incentive for willing to do x is present. Thus, a man may have the ability to will to do x, believe that reasonable incentives for willing to do x are present, and yet not will to do x. But, if he fails to will to do x, no matter what reasonable incentives he believes to be present, then he would conclude that he lacks the ability to will to do x.

This can be seen from the following case. Imagine that S has been hypnotized so that he believes everything that he is told by the hypnotist. Thus, he believes that such and such will be a consequence of his willing to do x, when told this by the hypnotist. Let us suppose that he is told that he will receive a certain sum of money for willing to do x, and yet fails to will to do so. Then he is told that he will avoid pain if he wills to do x, and still fails to do so. Next he is told that others will avoid suffering if he wills to do x, and still fails to do so. If after having been presented with numerous and varied reasonable incentives S still does not will to do x, then we have conclusive evidence that he does not have the ability to will to do x. We do not suggest the use of hypnosis to establish the *presence* of an ability, but only the *absence* of an ability. We use this example simply because hypnosis is such a simple and effective way to deceive someone.

Further, even if a man insists that he would will to do x if there were reasonable incentives for doing it and yet it is impossible to describe *any* state of affairs which he would regard as providing reasonable incentives for doing x, then he lacks the ability to will to do x. Imagine the following case: A lukewarm pacifist claims that *if* there were reasonable incentives for taking a human life then he would be prepared to do so, but that it is impossible to describe states of affairs which he would regard as providing adequate grounds for killing a human being. That is, he does not regard the preservation of society, the preservation of numerous innocent lives, much less the acquisition of wealth and power for himself, etc., as adequate grounds for killing. Such a person, we conclude, lacks the ability to will to take a human life.

When discussing the ability to will our basic analysis of *same kind of action* is in terms of the *lack* of the ability to will. For, normally when people are concerned with the ability to will, they are concerned with the kinds of action that one lacks the ability to will. That is, they group together the abnormal cases not the normal ones. People who suffer from compulsions as well as those who suffer from phobias lack the ability to will to do certain kinds of actions. The compulsive hand washer *lacks* the ability to will to wash his hands precisely because there are no reasonable incentives for which he would refrain from doing so. Here our analysis of same kind of action is: A and A' are the same kind of action for S if they share a feature such that S *lacks* the ability to will to do any action having that feature. What will be the same kind of action for one person may not be the same kind of action for another. However, frequently the same kind of action for one person will be the same kind of action for many other persons, e.g., for all extreme claustrophobiacs, A and A' will be the same kind of action provided that they share the feature of entering a small confined place.

Even though we naturally talk about kinds of action that one *lacks* the ability to will, it will prove useful to offer an analysis of what counts as the same kind of action that one *has* the ability to will. Thus, we say: A and A' are the same kind of action that S has the ability to will, if and only if A and A' are the same kind of action with regard to physical abilities (see above) *and* neither A nor A' are a kind of action that S lacks the ability to will. Admittedly a consequence of this analysis is grouping together as the same kind of action, actions which are radically different; e.g., for someone with the ability to will to strangle his wife, strangling his wife will be the same kind of action (with respect to his having the ability to will) as tightening his fingers with a certain amount of force around an object having a certain diameter, resiliency, etc. However, we think that the usefulness of being able to talk about kinds of actions one *has* the ability to will should be apparent from the following: every kind of action that one has the ability to will to do involves a kind of action completely describable as a kind of action that one has the physical ability to do. That is, the ability to will to strangle one's wife involves the ability to will to tighten one's fingers with a certain amount of force around a physical object of a certain diameter and resiliency. Some of the kinds of actions that one has (or lacks) the ability to will to do are completely describable as kinds of actions one has the physical ability to do, e.g., lift a 10-pound bag of sugar. Of course, having the ability to will to do a kind of action does not entail having the physical ability to do it.

As we use the term "physical ability," the kinds of actions that one has or lacks the physical ability to do are describable in such a way that the description, taken by itself, provides no incentives for or against doing the action. If the description of those kinds of actions which one has the ability to will is the same as a description of kinds of actions one has the physical ability to do, then taken by themselves, these descriptions also will provide no incentives for or against willing to do that kind of action. On the other hand, descriptions of those kinds of actions that one may have the ability to will which are *not* identical with some description of a kind of action that one may have the physical ability to do, taken by themselves, may provide incentives either for or against willing to do that action. For example, the description "strangling one's wife" does provide a *prima facie* incentive for willing not to do that action. Descriptions of these kinds of actions can be replaced by descriptions of kinds of actions which one might have the physical ability to perform plus a description of the envisaged consequences of this exercise of one's physical ability. Therefore, by "subtracting" from the description of a kind of action that one might have the ability to will that part which describes a kind of action that one might have the physical ability to do we may be left with a description of an incentive for willing to do or willing to refrain from doing that action.

What we have in mind is illustrated by the following: "strangling one's wife" may be regarded as a description of a kind of action that one may have the ability to will to do. Let us replace this description with the following: "tightening one's fingers with a certain amount of force around an object of a certain diameter and resiliency, etc., consequently doing serious physical harm to one's wife." Now, if we subtract from the above that part dealing with physical abilities only, we have as a remainder a *prima facie* incentive for refraining from the action. We do not say that the latter description is equivalent to the former, but only that it may be a description of a kind of action which is described by the former.

For similar persons in similar situations, incentives which would be unreasonable for willing to do an action completely describable as a kind of action one may have the physical ability to do may be reasonable incentives for willing to do those actions the description of which includes a *prima facie* incentive. That is, if the description of an action includes a reasonable incentive for willing to do the action, it will be reasonable to offer much greater incentives for willing to refrain from doing the action, and conversely. It might be said that the less incentive required for differing choices, the greater is the ability to will to do that action. This sounds very plausible, in that it makes trivial kinds of actions those most subject to the will and momentous ones less so.

Just as from the fact that a person does x it does not follow that he has the physical ability to do x, so too from the fact that a person *wills* to do x it does not follow that he has the ability to will to do x. The example of the compulsive hand washer mentioned earlier is a clear case of a person who although he frequently wills to wash his hands lacks the ability to will to do so. The person suffering from extreme claustrophobia may provide another case. For such a person there are no *reasonable* incentives for which he would will to go into a small closet and shut the door. That is, he would not will to do so for a reasonable sum of money, or to develop some film, etc. We want to say that our claustrophobiac lacks the ability to will to go into the closet. And yet there might be unreasonable incentives given which he would will to do so, e.g., at the point of a sword, or if this was the only way to escape from a horde of poisonous spiders.[9] Our claustrophobiac does not have the voluntary ability to walk into a closet and shut the door even though he has the physical ability to do so, i.e., *if* he *wills* to do so then, given a reasonable opportunity he will do so a reasonable number of times. It's just that he lacks the ability to will to do so.

III

As we have described them, voluntary abilities are a combination of physical or intellectual abilities and the ability to will. One must have both of these in order to have a voluntary ability. Voluntary abilities just like physical abilities and the ability to will are concerned with kinds of actions rather than particular acts. Since

---

[9] Just as with capacities, capabilities, and physical abilities, the ability to will to do a kind of action may be gained or lost, e.g., when a person is changed by undergoing psychoanalytic treatment, or conversely, when he develops a phobia.

we have, so far, been concerned only with the ability to do kinds of actions rather than particular acts, we have said nothing which *prima facie* is relevant to the problems of free will and of the nature of voluntary action. However, we do think that our analysis of voluntary ability can contribute something to the resolution of these issues, and in this section, we hope to make this evident.

We are now in a position to answer four questions, viz., what does it mean to say, (1) S can do a particular act? (2) S did a particular act voluntarily? (3) S is free to do a particular act? (4) S did a particular act freely? In answering some of these questions it is necessary to use the notion of voluntary ability so that it would be useful to present the complete analysis of voluntary ability here. "S can do x," i.e., "S has the voluntary ability to do x" means: If S wills to do x, then simply given reasonable opportunity, S will do x a reasonable number of times. But willing to do x is not a necessary condition for doing x. And S can will to do x, i.e., it is possible to describe some state of affairs such that S would believe there were reasonable incentives for doing x and believing this, would will to do x; and it is possible to describe some state of affairs such that S would believe there were reasonable incentives for not doing x and believing this, would will not to do x.

"S can do a particular act" means S has the voluntary ability to do that *kind* of action, and a reasonable opportunity to do it. "S did a particular act voluntarily" means S had the ability to will to do that kind of action, willed to do it, and did it. Thus, the answers to the first two questions can be given very simply on e the concept of a voluntary ability and related concepts have been worked out. But, while these answers are easily arrived at, they are not so easily understood.

Suppose we are wondering, if here and now, S can do x. According to the answer that we have given, only two factors are relevant: (a) Does he have the voluntary ability to do that kind of action, and (b) Does he have a reasonable opportunity to exercise that ability here and now? If we answer both of those questions in the affirmative, then, according to our analysis, he can do the particular act under consideration.

This, so far, is not surprising, or troublesome; it seems consistent with what we ordinarily think about the matter. But it does become somewhat puzzling in those cases in which the person who has the voluntary ability and a reasonable opportunity does in fact will to do the action in question and yet fails to do it. It may be objected that according to our analysis it is possible that all the conditions for a particular act being done are satisfied and yet the agent fails to perform as expected. This objection, however, assumes that failure to do an act under the conditions envisaged entails that one could not have done that particular act. It seems to us that this is false. We do allow that it is possible that a person can do a particular act, and yet not do it even though he has a reasonable opportunity and he wills to do it. And our analysis allows for this; for in establishing a voluntary ability we do not demand consistent success, only reasonable success. Thus, it is perfectly consistent, according to our analysis to conclude that a man can do a particular act, and to stick to this even when he has a reasonable opportunity, wills to do it and fails.

Though there may be some sense of "He can do this," when "this" refers to a particular act, in which all that is involved is his doing it here and now, this seems to us at best a colloquialism with little or no philosophical interest. Perhaps this may be seen from the following: Suppose someone says he can sink a very tricky putt, does so, and says with glee "You see I told you so," and his partner replies "Just a matter of luck." There is a genuine dispute here, one that could be settled by further facts, not merely by one person repeating that he had done it. But if one takes "He can do this" merely to be a prediction that he will do this, then there could be no dispute, and one is not talking about abilities at all.

The answer to the second question—"What does it mean to say that S did a particular act voluntarily?"—also raises some interesting issues. There is certainly a difference between a man doing something intentionally and his doing it voluntarily, and yet it is not that doing something intentionally and doing it voluntarily are *doing* different kinds of things. To do something voluntarily it is necessary that one does it intentionally, but this is not sufficient. A person may intentionally do a number of things while under the influence of drugs or suffering from some neurosis or psychosis. Yet we do not want to say that these things are done voluntarily. According to our analysis, the difference between an intentional act and a voluntary one lies not in what is done on that particular occasion, but on whether the person in question had the ability to will to do that kind of action. Thus, an act is done voluntarily if the agent has the ability to will to do that kind of action and does in fact intentionally do it on a particular occasion.

Since having the ability to will to do a kind of action includes the ability to will *not* to do that kind of action, this analysis distinguishes clearly between intentional and voluntary acts. For an intentional act done by one who lacks the ability to will to do that kind of action (a paradoxical sounding, but perfectly intelligible case) is not a voluntary act, but a compulsive one or something like that. Our distinction between a voluntary act and an intentional one does not depend upon a fictitious mental occurrence, but on the state of the agent. We may know that a person did something intentionally and yet not know whether it was done voluntarily simply because we do not know enough about the mental state of the person in question, i.e., we do not know if he had the ability to will to do the kind of action involved (in spite of the fact that he did indeed will to do it).

From what we have said so far, it is possible that one does not have the voluntary ability to do a particular act and yet do it voluntarily. This seeming paradox arises from the fact that for S to have the voluntary ability to do a particular act he must have both a physical or intellectual ability and the ability to will, whereas for S to have done the act voluntarily all that is required is that S had the ability to will to do that kind of action and intentionally did it. Consequently, one may lack the physical ability to do a kind of action, but have the ability to will to do it, and in fact, will to do it and do it on a particular occasion. The agent would have done the act voluntarily even though he did not have the voluntary ability to do it. What we have in mind is that people exceed their abilities on occasion. In a moment of great stress it is perfectly possible for a person voluntarily to do something while it would also be correct to say he lacks the voluntary ability to do that kind of thing, e.g., a woman lifts an automobile thus freeing her child trapped beneath.

Our answer to the question, "What does it mean to say that S is free to do a particular act?" makes use of the account given of "S can do a particular act." A person may have the voluntary ability to do a kind of action and a reasonable opportunity but at the same time be under duress such that his will is unduly influenced. We say, therefore, that a person is free to do a particular act if, and only if, he has the voluntary ability to do that kind of action, a reasonable opportunity, and there are no unreasonable incentives influencing his will either to do or to refrain from doing that act.

A question which we have not yet answered is: What does it mean to say that S did a particular act freely? Here we make use of our answer to the second question: "What does it mean to say that S did a particular act voluntarily?" For an act to be done freely it must be done voluntarily, but this is not enough. According to our analysis an act done voluntarily must be one of a kind that a person has the ability to will to do and that he does will to do. But, although he has the ability to will to do that kind of action, and does in fact will to do it on this particular occasion, thus doing it voluntarily, it may be that on this particular occasion he willed to do it because he was subjected to unreasonable incentives. Here we should not want to say that his act was done freely. Thus our analysis of a free act, or an act freely done, is one which a person does voluntarily, i.e., he does it intentionally and has the ability to will to do it, and there were no unreasonable incentives successful in leading him to do it.

Consequently, we make a sharp distinction between those cases in which one is subjected to unreasonable pressures or incentives which force him to will to do an act which he has the ability to will to do, and those cases in which he does not have the ability to will at all. The latter we do not even call voluntary acts, the former we call voluntary but not free. Thus, we make a distinction between normal people caught in extraordinary circumstances who will to do an act because they were subjected to unreasonable incentives and the mentally ill who intentionally do an act because they do not have the ability to will otherwise. Of course, this distinction is not absolutely sharp. There are cases in which we may not be sure whether one has been subjected to unreasonable incentives or whether one's ability to will has been taken away, e.g., brainwashing.

The importance of distinguishing between voluntary acts and free ones lies primarily in questions of assigning responsibility. An act which is not a voluntary one is not one for which the agent is responsible. But an act which is not free because of the presence of successful unreasonable incentives may still be one for which we might assign responsibility. As long as we think someone's ability to will is intact, which it is in a voluntary but unfree act, we think it may be appropriate to assign responsibility. We may hold that no matter how unreasonable the incentives, some acts should not be done. We do in fact distinguish between those who were unable to do other than they did, and those who though they had the ability to do otherwise were subjected to unreasonable incentives. The latter is a matter of degree, the former an absolute. In the latter case when the person under consideration is at the time of his action thought to have the ability to will, then no matter what the circumstances were, he *may* be held responsible to some degree for his voluntarily doing the act. Voluntary acts are always susceptible to praise or condemnation, though to say that they were *not* freely done is to admit that the praise or the condemnation is to be softened, perhaps even completely withheld.

There are, of course, problems in deciding what are reasonable and what unreasonable incentives, but these problems cannot be solved in the abstract, rather they must be related to individual cases. This notion of reasonable incentives is important, for not only does the presence of successful unreasonable incentives make an act not free, or perhaps better, less free, but also the notion of reasonable incentives is important in establishing whether someone has the ability to will to do a kind of action or not.

In ordinary discourse the term "voluntary" as applied to actions has a number of senses which though related are, nonetheless, distinct. Of these, three are central: (1) a voluntary act is simply an intentional (as opposed to an accidental) act; (2) a voluntary act is a free (as opposed to a constrained) act; (3) a voluntary act is one which proceeds from the will of an agent who has what we have described as the ability to will to do that kind of action.

The terms "intentional act" and "free act" seem to be appropriate for the first and second categories. We reserve the term "voluntary act" for the third category. We do not claim that these distinctions accurately reflect any consistent pattern of ordinary usage. We simply claim that the conceptual distinctions developed in this paper will prove useful in philosophical discussion of the problem of free will and the nature of voluntary action.

section III

ACTION AND LOGICAL SYSTEMS:

SYSTEMIC DEFINITIONS OF

"A PERSON PERFORMS AN ACTION" AND

"A PERSON CAN PERFORM AN ACTION"

INTRODUCTION

THE LOGIC OF ACTION

1. THE PROBLEMS

The Introductions to sections I and II investigated the tenability of *extra*-systemic analyses of the fundamental action-locutions "A person performs an action" and "A person *can* perform an action." That is, we investigated the possibility of translating these locutions into nonaction language, in particular the languages of behavior, physics, and ethics. After considering the reasonable proposals, we concluded that "A person performs an action" cannot be translated, without loss of meaning, into nonaction talk. A similar conclusion was reached for "A person *can* perform an action," except where "can" means "has the opportunity to." These conclusions were stated metaphorically by saying that action-locutions form a linguistically closed system; or in Melden's words, there is a fallacy in action theory strictly analogous to the Naturalistic Fallacy in moral theory. If these conclusions are in fact justified, then the next step is to investigate the nature of the action-locution system.

In this section, three attempts to understand the nature of this system are presented. First, Arthur Danto suggests that one can construct an action logic by modeling it on an epistemic logic. The assumption that permits this method of construction is that an isomorphism (that is, a one-to-one correspondence) exists between action-locutions and epistemic-locutions, in particular between "basic action" and "basic sentence (or proposition)." Second, many philosophers argue that reference to purposiveness, or goal-directedness, is the characteristic common to all action-locutions and what distinguishes them from the locutions of, say, physics and biology. Accepting this starting point, Roderick Chisholm develops the foundation for a locution system that, presumably, is adequate to express all meaningful claims about human action. The third viewpoint is that although action talk is fundamentally different from physical talk, action talk somehow "rests on" physical talk. In the selection from *Norm and Action* reprinted below, Georg Henrik von Wright constructs a formal calculus of human action that is an extension of a calculus of physical events.

Before undertaking a more detailed discussion of these three systemic proposals, let us consider two preliminaries. In sections I and II, we presented counter-examples to extra-systemic proposals, that is, cases where the proposed analyses conflict with the preanalytic data, and arguments showing that the proposed analyses are circular. These methods are essentially negative. As the first preliminary, we will review the positive reasons of Thomas Reid, the eighteenth-century Scottish common sense philosopher, for taking action talk to be system bound. Further, Danto, Chisholm, and Von Wright assume in their systemic accounts that adequate descriptions of actions can be supplied upon demand. As the second preliminary, we will review Nicholas Rescher's theory about adequate action description in his paper "On the Characterization of Actions."

2. THOMAS REID, A FORERUNNER

Agents are distinguished from other things in the world, according to Reid, by the fact that they have the power to act. Only agents, that is, have it within their power to perform actions. "The exertion of active power," Reid says, "we call *action* . . . ." [1]

What is active power? Reid claims that a "logical definition" cannot be given for it. [2] In this respect, "active power" is like "thought," "number," "motion," and "duration." "When men attempt to define such things," Reid says, "they give no light. They may give a synonymous word or phrase, but it will probably be a worse for a better. If they will define, the definition will either be grounded upon a hypothesis, or it will darken the subject rather than throw light upon it." [3] Nonlinguistically, he is saying that the concepts of active power, number, and so on, are unanalyzable; that is, we cannot reduce these concepts to simpler concepts, though we can certainly make useful explanatory remarks about them. Most contemporary philosophers do not accept Reid's view that there are unanalyzable or simple notions; they feel that it is a small step away from obscurantism. Reid, perhaps, can be sympathetically reinterpreted as claiming that certain locutions are system bound; these locutions are analyzable only in the context of locutions of the same logical type. Though history has not confirmed Reid's intuitions about, for example, "number," it appears that he is correct about "active power" (or more exactly, "It is within a person's power that . . .").

An opponent to Reid might object that the concept of active power is merely a figment of the philosopher's imagination. "Active power" does not refer to anything that exists: there are only observable behavioral patterns. An adequate explanation of human activity, therefore, cannot be in terms of "active power." Reid's

---

[1] *Essays on the Active Powers of Man*, p. 14. Page numbers refer to the 1768 edition and appear in square brackets in the reprinted text. (See p. 239 below.)

[2] See for example, *ibid.*, pp. 5, 6, and 12. (See pp. 236–238 below.)

[3] *Ibid.*, p. 6. (See p. 236 below.)

immediate response is that he himself is conscious of having and exerting this power. However, since introspective evidence is notoriously suspect, Reid adduces several arguments to show that persons in fact have the power to act.

He first argues that "every distinction which we find in the structure of all languages, must have been familiar to those who formed the languages at first, and to all who speak them with understanding." Further, ". . . there is no language so imperfect but that it has active and passive verbs and participles; the one signifying some kind of action; the other being acted upon." [4] Disregarding anthropological criticism, use of the active mood does not guarantee that reference is being made to active power. "The wind whistled loudly" and "The alarm clock awakened John," for example, do not assert that the wind or the alarm clock has the power to perform actions. Reid's counter that cases of this sort are exceptions to the rule, resulting primarily from the manifold uses of language, is unsatisfactory.[5] Unless we are supplied with criteria for determining which sentences are exceptions to the rule, we cannot appeal to the grammatical distinctions between active and passive modes of expression in order to justify the claim that persons have the power to act. There is, moreover, good reason to believe that no criteria for *the* correct mode of expression can be supplied: for it has been persuasively argued that each expression stated actively is synonymous with some expression stated passively, and conversely.[6]

Reid's second main argument is that since "there are many things we can affirm or deny concerning power, with understanding," persons in fact have the power to act.[7] This argument, however, is invalid. From the fact that one can distinguish between true and false sentences that attribute a property to a subject, it does not follow that there is something that has this property. "Robert is not his own brother" is true and known to be true, and "Robert is his own brother" is false and known to be false, even though there is nothing that is its own brother. Hence, it cannot be inferred from the fact that one can distinguish between true and false sentences that attribute active power to a subject that there is something that has the power to act.

Third, Reid argues that "there are many operations of mind common to all men who have reason, and necessary in the ordinary conduct of life, which imply *a belief* of active power in ourselves and in others." [8] Reid's examples of these operations of the mind include: "volitions and efforts to act," deliberations, commands, solving problems, making promises, guiding and persuading others. Reid should draw a different conclusion from his premises. Deliberations, and others on Reid's list, are inconsistent with our not having the power to act, rather than inconsistent with not *believing* that we have the power to act. To deliberate is to choose between alternative goals, or if the goal is already chosen, to choose between alternative means of achieving it. Something has a goal or purpose, further, only if it has the power to act. And since persons in fact deliberate, it follows that they

---

[4] *Ibid.*, p. 14. (See p. 239 below.)
[5] Cf. *ibid.*, pp. 15 and 16. (See pp. 239–240 below.)
[6] Cf. J. J. Katz and P. M. Postal, *An Integrated Theory of Linguistic Descriptions* (Cambridge, Massachusetts: The M.I.T. Press, 1964), 72 ff; and J. J. Katz and E. Martin, "The Synonymy of Actives and Passives," *The Philosophical Review*, LXXVI (1967), 476–491.
[7] *Ibid.*, p. 22; cf. p. 19. (See pp. 241–243 below.)
[8] *Ibid.*, p. 19; italics added. (See p. 242 below.)

have the power to act. The controversial premise in this defense of Reid is that something has a goal only if it has the power to act. This premise, however, appears justified. Dead men and natural processes have no goals. Natural processes have terminating points, but they do not occur *for the purpose of* bringing about their end-states. Sometimes we speak as if a natural process has a goal; for example, "The floods came in order to punish the wicked." In these cases, we are saying what the goal of the natural occurrence would be if it were an agent.

After satisfying himself that persons have the power to act, Reid claims that the exertion of this power is brought about by the will. "Human power . . . ," he says, "can only be exerted by will, and we are unable to conceive any active power to be exerted without will." [9] It can be consistently and reasonably maintained, however, that persons have the power to perform actions, but there is nothing called "the will" that one exerts in acting. In short, Reid's significant contribution to action theory is not his detailed explanation of human activity, which involved reference to the will and often resembled a reconstruction of common sense psychology, but rather his foresight in maintaining that the power to act is genuinely attributable to persons and cannot be reduced to, say, mere patterns of behavior.

3. ADEQUATE ACTION DESCRIPTION

In order to construct a satisfactory action language, whether formalized or not, one must have a criterion for specifying in an accurate and uniform manner the *form* of an adequate action description. Suppose that a man signaled for the chairman's attention by raising his left hand. A satisfactory action language could not permit "He signaled" to count as an adequate description of what this man did; for "He signaled" does not reflect the fact that he signaled with his left hand, that he signaled in order to attract someone's attention, and so on. In "On the Characterization of Action," Nicholas Rescher develops a criterion for an adequate action description. [10]

It is important to be clear about the nature of Rescher's enterprise. An adequate action description is to be differentiated from an individuating action description on the one hand and from a complete action description on the other hand. An action description individuates just in case it differentiates the action in question from all other actions. Specification of the agent, act-type, and occasion, or spatio-temporal indicators, such as pointing, are sufficient to identify a particular action. But individuating descriptions are often descriptively vague. Pointing and saying "That shooting" identifies the action but leaves essential descriptive features unspecified. On the other hand, one can adequately describe an action without giving a complete description. Complete descriptions of actions, or anything else, involve specification of all details, including relational details. Perhaps, to describe an action completely it is necessary to relate the action to the entire detailed history of the world. [11] We need, however, only to indicate the primary aspects of the action to describe it adequately.

[9] *Ibid.*, p. 38. (See p. 244 below.)

[10] Cf. Donald Davidson, "The Logical Form of Action Sentences" and the comments on this paper by E. J. Lemmon, H. N. Castaneda, and R. M. Chisholm in *The Logic of Decision and Action*, ed. Nicholas Rescher (Pittsburgh: The University of Pittsburgh Press, 1967).

[11] Nicholas Rescher, "On the Characterization of Actions," pp. 247 ff. below. Cf. Anthony Kenny, *Action, Emotion and Will* (London: Routledge & Kegan Paul Ltd., 1963), Chapter 7, "Actions and Relations," especially pp. 159 ff.

Rescher begins by delineating the extension of the class of human actions. Human actions, as assumed throughout our discussion, are to be differentiated from natural processes, from purely passive behavior, and from mere nondoings. Actions are not in general achievements or terminations of activities: getting a joke is something that happens to a person, not something he *does*. Rescher also claims that something is an action only if it includes some physical component. "Every action," he says, "must have an overt physical component and involves bodily activity of some sort. . . . purely mental acts done solely *in foro interno* cannot qualify as actions." [12] This last claim about action, however, is controversial. Mentally solving a simple mathematical puzzle, using the mnemonic device of mentally reciting the alphabet in order to recall the restaurant, and deciding on a name for my pet cat do not involve physical activity, but appear to be actions I perform.[13]

Rescher's specification of the class of human actions, in any case, is sufficiently accurate not to affect his list of the primary aspects of an action. An adequate action description, or as Rescher prefers to call it, a canonical action description, involves: (1) specification of the *agent;* (2) specification of the *act-type;* (3) specification of the *modality* of action, that is, the *means* and *manner* of performing it; (4) specification of the *setting,* including temporal, spatial, and circumstantial aspects; and (5) specification of the *rationale* of the action, including the causal, motivational, and intentional aspects.

The fifth factor needs some clarification. Rescher correctly points out that an adequate action description includes reference to the agent's intentions, motives, goals, or so on. Rescher agrees with the conclusion of the introduction to section I that mere behavioral language is inadequate to describe human action. "Like the concept of a *person* in general, in which physical and mental aspects are inseparably united," he says, "the concept of action has both *overt,* physical, and observable, and *covert,* mental, and unobservable involvements. . . . The covert side relates to certain considerations as to his *state of mind* (thoughts, intentions, motives, awareness, etc.) at the time of action." [14] The claim that there is a "covert" element in the *description* of action should be differentiated from the related but different claim that causal or behavioristic *explanation* is not adequate to account for human action. *Prima facie,* at least, there is a difference between saying that there is an intentional, motivational, or purposive element in action and saying that human action can be appropriately explained teleologically. Rescher claims that an adequate description of human action includes a reference to the purposive or intentional element in action; he does not claim here, though he could consistently claim, that teleological explanation is appropriate (or essential) for accounting for human action.

4. KNOWLEDGE AND ACTION

One extremely interesting way to develop an action language is to assume that it is strictly analogous to the language of empirical knowledge. Or as Arthur Danto puts it, a language of action can be constructed on the assumption that the theory

---

[12] Rescher, p. 248 below.

[13] The problem of the existence of "mental actions" is discussed in some detail by Richard Taylor in "Thought and Purpose," reprinted below, pp. 267–283, and in "The Stream of Thoughts vs Mental Acts," *The Philosophical Quarterly,* XIII (1963), 311–321.

[14] P. 251 below.

of empirical knowledge and the theory of action are isomorphic models for the same uninterpreted calculus.[15]

It has often been maintained that empirical knowledge is founded on *basic sentences* (or *basic propositions*), that is sentences that are empirically justified but not justified by other empirical sentences. Many epistemologists take reports of perceptual experiences, for example, "I see a red color patch in front of me now," to be paradigmatic cases of basic sentences. Without such a stopping point for justification, it is argued, we could not know that an empirical sentence is completely justified; and since a sentence is known to be true only if it is completely justified, we could not, then, know any empirical sentence to be true. Commenting on the nature of basic sentences, Bertrand Russell says ". . . a basic proposition . . . must be known independently of inference from other propositions [and] . . . it should be possible so to analyze our empirical knowledge that its primitive propositions (apart from logic and generalities) should all have been . . . basic propositions." [16] Similarly, Danto claims that there are *basic actions* which form the basis for a theory of action. On the action model, "is caused by" replaces "is inferred from" or "is justified by." Hence, basic actions are actions that are not caused by any other actions of the agent. Or alternatively, a basic action is one that is not performed *by* first performing other actions. For most persons, examples of basic actions would be raising one's arm, winking, and thinking of a one-digit number. What is to count as a basic action, however, depends on the normality of the agent—some persons can wiggle their ears as basic actions, though most cannot— and on the *way* in which the action is performed. What is a basic action in one instance can be performed as a nonbasic action in another: I can simply raise my hand or I can cause it to rise by lifting it with my other hand.[17]

Rather than attempt to develop and extend the analogy between action theory and epistemology, let us examine the primary basis for the analogy, namely, the nature of basic and nonbasic action. Danto's definitions of "basic action" and "nonbasic action" can be reformulated in the following manner:

(D1) For every person S and every *a*, *a* is a basic action performed by S if and only if (i) *a* is an action performed by S and (ii) there is no other action *b* such that S performed *b* and *b* caused *a*.

[15] See Arthur Danto, "Basic Actions," p. 262, n. 2 below. Cf. Danto's "What We Can Do," *The Journal of Philosophy*, LX (1963), 436, and "Freedom and Forbearance" in *Freedom and Determinism*, ed. Keith Lehrer (New York: Random House, Inc., 1966), pp. 47 ff.

[16] *An Inquiry into Meaning and Truth* (Baltimore, Maryland: Pelican Books, 1962; first published 1940), p. 131. The precise form and function of basic sentences are points of controversy. A perspective on the issues and positions can be obtained by considering, in addition to Russell's *Inquiry*, the following: Wittgenstein's view of atomic propositions in his *Tractatus* (London: Routledge & Kegan Paul Ltd., 1961; first English edition 1922); Moritz Schlick, "Über das Fundament der Erkenntnis" in *Erkenntnis*, 1934, translated by David Rynin in *Logical Positivism*, ed. A. J. Ayer (Glencoe, Illinois: Free Press, 1959); R. Carnap, *Logische Syntax der Sprache* (Vienna, 1934), translated by Amethe Smeaton as *The Logical Syntax of Language* (London: Kegan Paul, Trench, Trubner & Co. Ltd., 1937); C. Hempel, "On the Logical Positivist's Theory of Truth," *Analysis*, II (1934–1935), 49–59; A. J. Ayer, "Basic Propositions," in *Philosophical Analysis*, ed. M. Black (Ithaca, New York: Cornell University Press, 1950), reprinted in Ayer's *Philosophical Essays* (London: Macmillan & Co. Ltd., 1954); Karl Popper, *The Logic of Scientific Discovery* (New York: Basic Books, Inc., 1959), Chapter 5; and R. M. Chisholm, *The Theory of Knowledge* (Englewood Cliffs, New Jersey: Prentice-Hall, Inc., 1966), Chapter 2.

[17] See Danto below, pp. 256 ff., especially pp. 261–262.

(D2)   For every person S and every *a, a* is a nonbasic action performed by S if and only if (i) *a* is an action performed by S and (ii) it is not the case that *a* is a basic action performed by S.

It is important to note that Danto does not analyze the notion of action, but rather attempts to construct a theory of action using this concept. In this respect, Danto's enterprise is entirely systemic.

Definitions (D1) and (D2), however, are problematical for at least two reasons. First, some actions that would intuitively be classified as nonbasic are designated as basic on definitions (D1) and (D2). The actions of a normal man, say Jones, knotting his tie, typing, or playing the piano are nonbasic. A man knots his tie *by* grasping the short end, *by* lifting the short end up, and so on. Similarly, a person types *by* moving his left index finger, *by* moving his right forefinger, and so on. Knotting one's tie and typing are dependent on other things one does. But what action of Jones causes him to, for example, knot his tie? Contrary to what Danto supposes, no action performed by Jones causes him to knot his tie. Knotting one's tie *is* the set of basic actions of grasping the short end, raising one's hand, and so on. Hence, knotting one's tie is not caused by this set of basic actions. For an event A causes an event B to occur only if A and B are distinct. If A and B are not distinct and A causes B, then event A causes itself or event B is the effect of itself; but these consequences are contrary to our ordinary understanding of "cause" and "effect." [18] Since Jones knotting his tie is not caused by his grasping the short end, and so on, and since presumably these basic actions are the only candidates among his actions for the cause of his knotting his tie, there are no actions performed by Jones that cause him to knot his tie. Thus, by definitions (D1) and (D2), we obtain the highly counterintuitive result that Jones' knotting his tie is a basic action. What is required to rectify this situation is a tripartite distinction between basic actions, actions that are sets of basic actions, and purely nonbasic actions. We will return to this point shortly.

The second and more important criticism is that Danto's definitions (D1) and (D2) make the false claim that when a person is acting nonbasically, his actions are caused by other *actions* of his. There is, rather, a causal connection between the *events* a person brings about in performing actions. Consider the case in which a normal person, say Jones again, performs the obviously nonbasic action of moving a stone by pushing it with a staff. What *action* does Jones perform that causes him to perform another *action?* In moving the stone by pushing it with the staff Jones performs certain basic or simple actions—however "basic action" or "simple action" are to be defined: these actions include his grasping the staff, his moving his arm, and so on. But his actions of grasping the staff, and so on, do not cause him to perform other actions. Rather, these actions cause the staff to move, the stone to move, and so on. However, the staff's moving and the stone's moving are not Jones' actions: they are events he brings about. That the stone's moving, for example, is not an action is clear from the fact that this happening is adequately described without referring to some person as an agent, as a performer

---

[18] *Ibid.,* p. 261 below. In "What We Can Do" (p. 436), Danto says ". . . whatever further may be said in the analysis of '*m* causes *n,*' *m* causes *n* only if *m* and *n* are distinct events. There may be other senses of '. . . causes—' but this is the only sense I am interested in here."

of actions. Further, Jones' basic actions do not cause the entire state of affairs of Jones moving the stone by pushing it with the staff; for the actions of grasping the staff, and so on, are not distinct from this total state of affairs. Danto, in short, has confounded the events one brings about in performing an action with the action one performs. What is needed to rectify this situation is a redefinition of "nonbasic action" in which the causal relationship is presumed to obtain between the events brought about in performing the action.[19]

Let us now put Danto's analogy between action theory and epistemology on a sturdier foundation. Some events a person brings about are essential to the performance of the action, whereas others are accidental by-products. In raising one's hand, for example, a person brings about the event of his hand rising. Dust motes being moved, shadows being cast, and so on, are nonessential events resulting from a person raising his arm. A person could raise his arm without moving dust motes, but he could not raise his arm without his arm rising. Let us call an event that is essential to the performance of an action an *event-component* of that action. Now some actions have more than one event-component. My pushing a stone with a staff includes the event-components of my body moving from one position to another, the staff moving from one position to another, and the stone moving from one position to another. If a blade of grass were flattened by the moving stone, the flattening of the blade would not be an event-component of my action of moving the stone by pushing it with the staff, though it would be an event-component of a different action that I might instead have performed, for example, flattening the grass by moving a stone pushed with a staff over it. These examples suggest that an event-component is an event referred to by an event-description that is entailed by an adequate action description. For example, my hand's rising is an event-component of my raising my hand, since "my raising my hand" entails "my hand rises." [20]

This explication of "event-component," however, is not quite correct. "My raising my hand" not only entails "my arm rises," but it also entails "my arm rises halfway," "my arm rises quarter-way," and so on *ad infinitum*. That is, if the only requirement for being an event-component description were entailment by an adequate action description, then for each action there would be an infinite number of event-components. In order to forestall this Zenonian criticism, an event-component should be taken to be a "maximal event." More exactly, utilizing Rescher's criterion for an adequate action description, an event-component of a person's action is definable in the following manner:

(D3) For every person S, every individual action a, and every e, e is an event-component of S's having performed a if and only if:
   (i) e is a single event;
   (ii) an adequate description of S's having performed a entails a statement expressing that e occurred; and
   (iii) there is no e' such that: (a) e' is a single event; (b) e' is not identical to e; (c) an adequate description of S's having performed a entails a statement expressing

---

[19] I have previously made these two criticisms of Danto's views in "Danto on Basic Actions," *Nous*, II (1968), pp. 187–190. Cf. Frederick Stoutland, "Basic Actions and Causality," *The Journal of Philosophy*, LXV (1968), 467–475.

[20] Cf. Von Wright's notion of an intrinsic result of an action, pp. 309 f. below.

that e′ occurred and (d) a statement expressing that e′ occurred entails a statement expressing that e occurred.

Suppose that Jones lifted his glass. Unlike his glass rising, his glass rising halfway is not an event-component of his action. Although "his glass rose halfway" is entailed by "he lifted his glass" and refers to an event, there is another event, for example, his glass rising all the way, such that a statement expressing that it occurred is entailed by "he lifted his glass" and entails "his glass rose halfway." [21]

We are now in a position to offer definitions of "simple (basic) action" and "nonsimple (nonbasic) action" that are not subject to the criticisms made against Danto's proposals.

(D4) For every person S and every a, a is a simple action performed by S if and only if (i) a is an individual action performed by S and (ii) there is an e such that e is the one and only event-component of S's performing a.

There are two kinds of nonsimple actions, namely, complicated actions and complex actions.

(D5) For every person S and every a, a is a complicated action performed by S if and only if (i) a is an individual action performed by S and (ii) there is an e_1 and an e_2 such that e_1 and e_2 are each event-components of S's performing a and e_2 is caused by e_1.

(D6) For every person S and every a, a is a complex action performed by S if and only if (i) a is an individual action performed by S, (ii) there are at least two event-components of S's performing a, and (iii) there is no e_1 and e_2 such that e_1 and e_2 are each event-components of S's performing a and e_2 is caused by e_1.

My having raised my hand is an example of a simple action. For my having raised my hand is an action that has one and only one event-component, namely, my hand's having risen. Most bodily actions are complicated, though some purely mental actions are also complicated. Suppose that Jones uses the mnemonic device of thinking of phonetic symbols in order to recall an acquaintance's name. This individual action of Jones satisfies definition (D5): there is an event-component, the remembering of the acquaintance's name, that is caused by another event-component of his action, namely, the imagining of a specific phonetic symbol. In addition to simple and complicated actions, persons also perform complex actions. A normal man knotting his tie is a complex action. There is a set of his actions— lifting the long end up, and so on—such that no two event-components of these actions stand in the relation of cause and effect. Or to say it another way, there is a set of his actions—lifting the long end up, and so on—such that this set is identical with Jones' action of knotting his tie, has at least two members, and each member is a simple action of Jones. A person's action, further, can be a combination of simple, complicated, and complex actions and involve both mental and

---

[21] It is worthwhile noting that the locution "A person brings about an event" is definable by means of the notion of an event-component. In particular, for every person S and every event e, S brings about e if, and only if, there is an individual action a such that S performs a and e is an event-component of S's performing a.

bodily components. In building a table, for example, Jones devises a working plan, adds some numbers, grasps the saw, hammers some nails into the boards, and paints the assembly.

Definitions (D3) to (D6), then, provide a basis for the development of action theory in much the same way that the notion of a basic sentence or proposition provides a basis for the development of the theory of empirical knowledge. As all genuine empirical knowledge claims, except basic sentences, are justified by or inferred from basic sentences, so all genuine human actions, except simple actions, are causally related to simple actions. However, a more complete investigation into the isomorphism between action theory and the theory of empirical knowledge, though a promising enterprise, cannot be undertaken here.

5. PURPOSE AND ACTION

According to one well-founded view, human action cannot be analyzed extra-systemically because, unlike mere bodily and mental happenings, actions are *purposive*. When performing an action, an agent alters the environment in an attempt to satisfy his goals. More exactly, the following theses might be maintained:

(A) All human actions are purposive;
(B) Only human actions are purposive.

It is worth emphasizing that (A) and (B) are *descriptive* theses. They are to be differentiated from the closely related but different claims that purposive or teleological *explanation* is appropriate to account for human action, and that only purposive or teleological explanation can account for human action. The kind of explanation that can be appropriately given to a class of phenomena may well determine the nature, and hence, description, of the phenomena; but until that issue is satisfactorily settled, it is best to distinguish between the description and explanation of human action.

Thesis (B) has been attacked, on the one side, by claiming that bodily happenings are goal-directed. The goal of a nervous twitch can be thought of as the adjustment of a chemical imbalance resulting from the internal functioning of the organism. On the other side, it has been attacked on the ground that machines are goal-directed. A heat-seeking torpedo, for example, will adjust its course according to external stimuli provided by the target. In defense of (B), it has been argued that homeostatic processes within an agent's body are not goal-directed in the relevant sense. We are directly aware of and can directly change and control our purposes; but ordinarily we are not directly aware of and cannot directly change and control our bodily processes. And with respect to heat-seeking torpedos, computers, and automatic alarm clocks, these machines are goal-directed only in a derivative sense, only in the sense that human agents program their own purposes and goals into the machines. Detailed consideration of the important thesis (B), however, is better left for works on the philosophical foundations of biology and on the problems of other minds.[22] Here we will first examine Richard Taylor's criticism of thesis (A) in his most recent work in this area, "Thought and Pur-

---

[22] The literature on this subject is voluminous; a reasonable starting point is *Purpose in Nature*, ed. J. V. Canfield (Englewood Cliffs, New Jersey: Prentice-Hall, Inc., 1966).

pose"; and second, review Roderick Chisholm's proposed reconstructive language of action, which presupposes the truth of thesis (A).

Prima facie the claim that some actions are nonpurposive is false. As Charles Taylor puts it, ". . . the notion of action normally involves that of behavior directed towards a goal. For action terms generally cannot be applied at all unless behavior is directed to some goal, and specific action terms cannot be applied in an unqualified manner unless behavior is directed towards the specific goal concerned."[23] The distinguishing feature between blinkings, nervous spasms, coughs, etc., and winkings, arm-raisings, singings, etc., is that in the latter cases the agent brings about the behavior *intentionally,* or *on purpose.* It is essential to emphasize that doing something intentionally, or on purpose, is not doing something in the presence of a special kind of mental event, called perhaps "an intention."[24] If intentional doings were bodily happenings accompanied or caused by mental events, we would, at best, be advocating a volitional theory. Rather, doing something intentionally or on purpose appears to be a way or manner of doing it.

Taylor argues against thesis (A) in the following way. As we have seen, actions are either simple or nonsimple. Nonsimple actions are actions in which we do one thing *by* doing another. When I move a stone by moving my hand, or when I think of an acquaintance's name, "Shilling," by thinking of shillings, I perform one action *for the purpose of* something else, or alternatively, I do something *by means of* doing something else. In the case of simple actions, however, I do not do one thing *in order to do* something else. This disparity between simple and nonsimple actions becomes clear when we compare statements of the form

(1) I do X, causing (event) E to occur

with statements of the form

(2) I make E occur *by* doing X.

Statements that have the form of (2) entail, but are not entailed by, statements that have the form of (1). For example,

(1') I move my hand, causing the stone to move

is entailed by, but does not entail,

(2') I move the stone by moving my hand.

The disparity between simple and nonsimple actions, between actions described by statements that have the form of (1) and statements that have the form of

[23] C. Taylor, *The Explanation of Behavior* (London: Routledge & Kegan Paul Ltd., 1964), p. 32. Some other recent defenders of (A) are: Richard Taylor in his earlier work *Action and Purpose* (Englewood Cliffs, New Jersey: Prentice-Hall, Inc., 1966); Wilfrid Sellars in, for example, *Science and Metaphysics* (London: Routledge & Kegan Paul Ltd., 1967), pp. 175 ff., and in "Thought and Action" in *Freedom and Determinism,* ed. Keith Lehrer; and Kurt Baier, pp. 112 ff. above and "Action and Agent" in *The Monist,* XLIX (1965), 183–195.

[24] Cf. Taylor, "Thought and Purpose," p. 282 below.

(2), Taylor concludes, is that the element of purposiveness is absent in the case of simple actions. And since simple actions are nonpurposive, thesis (A), which states that every action is purposive, is false.

This argument, however, is not adequate to show that some actions are non-purposive. The reason why (1') does not entail (2') is not that there is an element of purposiveness present in (2') and absent in (1'), but rather that (2') is, simply, a more complicated action of the same general type as (1'). The same relationship that obtains between (1') and (2')—and, in general, between (1) and (2)—also obtains between the following statements:

(3) I move the stone by moving my hand;
(4) I flatten the grass by moving the stone, which I moved by moving my hand.

Statement (4) entails (3), but not conversely. The relevant difference between (3) and (4) is not the element of purposiveness—even Taylor would agree that they both describe purposive actions—but rather (4) is a more complicated action of the same general type as (3). Since the relationship between (1') and (2') is the same as that between (3) and (4), no justification has been given for drawing Taylor's conclusion that (1') and (2') (and, in general (1) and (2)) differ with respect to the purposiveness of the actions described. Taylor's mistaken assumption seems to be that purposive actions can only be adequately described by statements that have the form "S X's by Y-ing," or "S X's in order to Y," where X and Y are not identical. But sometimes, at least, I (just) raise my arm intentionally, or I (just) wink on purpose. The mistaken rationale of Taylor's entire argument results, perhaps, from his fundamental error of taking the relationship between the categories of purpose and agency to be exactly the same as that between the categories of agency and causation, causation and change, and change and being.

Taylor also believes that the element of purposiveness in action is adequate to distinguish between what one does in acting and what happens as a consequence of what one does. My flattening the grass by pushing the stone over it and my pushing the stone, which has as one of its causal consequences the flattening of the grass, are photographically the same: but in the former case the grass being flattened was "part of" my action because I intentionally flattened it. That is, Taylor suggests that acts are differentiated from their consequences in that acts are intentionally or purposively done.[25]

While I have sympathy with this criterion for distinguishing between acts and consequences, Taylor's adoption of it is puzzling. If he were correct in claiming that simple actions are nonpurposive, then in the case of simple actions, there would be no distinction between an act and its consequence—for both would be nonpurposive. But surely we have to distinguish between a person raising his hand and the unknown and incidental causal consequences that happen, such as dust motes being moved. Taylor, in short, cannot consistently maintain that the criterion for differentiating acts from consequences is that there is an element of purposiveness or intentionality in the action but not in its consequence and that some actions are nonpurposive, nonintentional.

[25] See ibid., pp. 277 ff.

To sum up, then, though much of what Taylor says in his admirably clear essay "Thought and Purpose" is correct, especially the claim that mental actions are exactly analogous to physical actions, he has not justified his contention that some actions are not purposive. Hence, the *prima facie* claim that thesis (A) is true, that is, that all human action is purposive, remains acceptable.

Presupposing the truth of (A), Roderick Chisholm carefully reconstructs a language of human action. The primitive, or undefined, locution in his language is ". . . at time *t*, . . . [a person] makes *B* happen in the endeavor to make *A* happen," where *A* and *B* are states of affairs that are not necessarily distinct.[26] "In the endeavor to" expresses the purposive or goal-directed element in Chisholm's primitive. Typical of locutions that express goal-directedness or purposiveness, "in the endeavor to" is not a success phrase: if I make something happen, say the stone rolling, in the endeavor to make something else happen, say the grass being flattened, it does not follow that this second state of affairs, the grass being flattened, will in fact be realized. Another relevant feature of Chisholm's primitive is its appeal to the concept of a person or agent making something happen (what Chisholm calls "immanent causation"). A person making something happen is different from one event or state of affairs making, or causing, another to happen (what Chisholm calls "transeuent causation"). Agent causation involves an ontological commitment to the existence of substantival, transempirical selfs.[27]

In claiming that there are agents that are not mere conglomerations of experiences and behavioral tendencies, Chisholm is in the company of Berkeley and Thomas Reid and, on the contemporary side, C. A. Campbell and Richard Taylor.[28] Many Anglo-American philosophers, taking their cue from Hume, however, have been unwilling to accept the view that the self is transempirical. Rejection of agent causation probably results from the metaphysical presupposition that causation is really a kind of push or pull or from the phenomenalistic assumption that only those things available to our senses exist. In any case, the claim that there are transempirical agents can be reinterpreted in a way not offensive to those with nominalistic inclinations. Some philosophers of science, often called "instrumentalists," argue that scientific theories are sets of rules for analyzing and describing certain classes of phenomena. Theories, they claim, are more than summary statements of observed data. In order to carry out the analysis of certain kinds of phenomena, moreover, it is expedient to assume or hypothesize the existence of nonobservable ("theoretical") entities. For example, in order to account for certain surface phenomena of solids, it is advantageous to assume that extremely small charged particles, called "electrons," are escaping.[29] Similarly, it

---

[26] See R. Chisholm, "Freedom and Action," pp. 284–285 below.

[27] See "Freedom and Action" in *Freedom and Determinism*, ed. Lehrer, pp. 17 ff.

[28] See C. A. Campbell's *On Selfhood and Godhood* (New York: Humanities Press, Inc., 1957), Lecture IX and Taylor's *Metaphysics* (Englewood Cliffs, New Jersey: Prentice-Hall, Inc., 1963), Chapters 4 and 5.

[29] Clearly, much remains to be said about the difficult questions of criteria for elimination and acceptance of theoretical terms within a theory. For an introduction to the issues involved, see E. Nagel, *The Structure of Science* (New York: Harcourt, Brace & World, Inc., 1961), pp. 129 ff., and I. Scheffler, *The Anatomy of Inquiry* (New York: Alfred A. Knopf, Inc., 1963), Part II, "Significance." Also see R. Carnap, "The Methodological Character of Theoretical Concepts" and C. Hempel, "The Theoretician's Dilemma: A Study in the Logic of Theory Construction" in *Minnesota Studies in the Philosophy of Science* (Minneapolis: University of Minnesota Press, 1956–1958), vol. I, 38–76, and vol. II, 37–98, respectively.

might be argued that "agent" is a theoretical term within a theory that accounts for, in an economical and enlightening way, certain phenomena of ordinary experience. Though this method of reconciliation might be rejected by an agency theorist, it does justify adopting an action language that makes reference to agent causation.[30]

There is little reason to summarize the details of Chisholm's action language, since it is clearly and systematically presented. In the selection from "Freedom and Action," he defines by means of his primitive the key action-locutions "A person undertakes (tries) to make something happen," "A person tries to make one thing happen for the purpose of making another happen," and "A person makes something happen in the way in which he intended." In " 'He Could Have Done Otherwise,' " Chisholm extends his language to include the modal notions "directly within one's power" and "indirectly within one's power." Something is indirectly within one's power provided that, roughly, the agent is free to undertake the preliminary steps necessary to put the act directly within his power. It is important to note that Chisholm's notion of something being within one's power is indeterministic, in the sense that something is within one's power only if he is free to undertake it. (The notion of something being within one's power developed in the Introduction to section II was neutral with respect to whether one is free to undertake the action in question.) Finally, one should be aware of the limited scope of Chisholm's enterprise. A fully adequate action language must be able to formulate statements about a person's choosing, deciding, deliberating, statements about one's hopes, wishes, wants, desires, motives, and so on. Chisholm's recent work is a prolegomena to a complete systemic action language.

6. EVENTS AND ACTIONS

The underlying rationale of Von Wright's formal, systemic action language is that the logic of action is an extension of the logic of events, which in turn is an extension of ordinary propositional logic. For actions are performed only if events occur, and events are transitions between states of affairs that are described by propositions. Von Wright's aim in constructing an action logic, though one we shall not pursue, is to develop a deontic logic, that is, a logic of norms.

Let us begin with Von Wright's semantics for propositional logic. He distinguishes between individual and generic propositions. An individual proposition (for example, that Brutus killed Caesar) is either true or false, whereas a generic proposition (for example, that Brutus kissed Caesar) by itself has no truth-value. A generic proposition gains a truth-value when it is instantiated to a particular *occasion*. "Occasions are the 'individualizers' of generic propositions." [31] Unfortunately, Von Wright is of little help in explicating this important notion of an occasion; at his most informative, he says:

> [The notion of an occasion] is related to the notions of space and time. It would not be right, however, to identify occasions with "instants" or "points" in space and time. They should rather be called spatio-temporal *locations*.[32]

[30] It is interesting to note that Berkeley, a steadfast agency theorist, was also a founding father of instrumentalism (see, for example, his *De Motu*).

[31] Von Wright, *Norm and Action* (New York: Humanities Press, Inc., 1963), p. 23.

[32] *Ibid.*

Generic propositions, further, are different from general propositions. General propositions (for example, that all ravens are black) have truth-value but are not instantiations of generic propositions.[33]

In addition to the connectives $\sim$, &, v, $\rightarrow$, and $\rightleftarrows$, which have their ordinary meanings, Von Wright introduces the variables p, q, r, . . . , which are schematic representations of sentences that express *generic* propositions.[34] These sentences, further, describe a certain kind of fact, namely, generic states of affairs. Thus, for example, the sentence "It is raining" expresses the generic proposition that it is raining and describes a generic state of affairs, the falling of rain.

By claiming that generic sentences describe generic states of affairs, Von Wright proposes a very rich ontology. Since there are increasing degrees of generic-ness for propositions, there would be an indefinite number of states of affairs for each sentence-type. For example, there would be distinct generic states of affairs described by each of the following: "It is raining," "It is raining in the United States," "It is raining in New York," and so on. Some philosophers might maintain, contrary to Von Wright, that generic sentences do not correspond to anything that exists. Only individual states of affairs exist; and if generic sentences name, they name individual states of affairs. One way for Von Wright to conform to this criticism is to have p, q, r, . . . , range over individual sentences. This change would alter the interpretation of the resulting calculus, but, so far as I can see, in no detrimental way. For example, the relevant "can" for the logic would no longer be the ability sense, which pertains to generic actions, but rather the within-one's-power sense, which pertains to individual actions.[35]

Retaining Von Wright's interpretation of the sentential variables, however, an event is to be taken as a pair of (generic) states of affairs ordered by the relation of being successive in time. An event, that is, is a transition from one state of affairs—the initial-state—to another state of affairs—the end-state. It is possible that the initial- and end-states are qualitatively the same; in that case, the event is an "unchange" rather than a change. For example, in Von Wright's extended sense, the door remaining closed from time t_1 to time t_2 is an event: it is an event in which the rate of transition is zero. To symbolize the occurrence of an event, Von Wright introduces the predicate . . . T——, where . . . and —— are filled by well-formed propositional formulae and which is read ". . . is a transformation (transition) to——." Thus, for example, if p means that the window is closed, $pT\sim p$ means that the world goes from a state in which the window is closed to one in which it is open, that is, idiomatically, the window is opened. Now for each state of affairs, one of the following elementary change descriptions applies: pTp, $pT\sim p$, $\sim pTp$, $\sim pT\sim p$. A change description of the world is a conjunction of exactly one elementary change description for each generic feature of the world. Change descriptions, in short, are the event counterparts to Carnap's state descriptions.[36]

---

33 "There are no 'occasions' for the truth or falsehood of general propositions" (*Ibid.*, p. 25).

34 Following Von Wright, symbolic expressions are used autonomously; that is, they are used to mention themselves.

35 Cf. the introduction to section II.

36 In "The Logic of Action—A Sketch" (in *The Logic of Decision and Action*, ed. N. Rescher (Pittsburgh: University of Pittsburgh Press, 1967), p. 123, Von Wright states an axiomatic version of the logic of change. In addition to the axioms of classical propositional logic, Von Wright adopts:

An elementary act is an act the *result* of which is an elementary change. (In Von Wright's terminology, the causal effects of the result of an action are the action's *consequences*.) Act descriptions are symbolized by prefixing a d to a change description. Thus, for example, if p represents the sentence "The door is open," $d(pT{\sim}p)$ represents the sentence "The door is being closed," or as Von Wright prefers to express it, "The doing so that the door is closed." [37] It should be emphasized that since pTp, and so on, are schematic representations of sentences that describe *generic events*, $d(pTp)$, and so on, are schematic representations of sentences that describe *generic acts*.

Two problems with Von Wright's symbolic representation of action sentences are that it neither explicitly specifies the agent who performed the action nor that the agent brought the event about intentionally. Modification of the symbolism to include explicit specification of the agent is needed not only for reasons of perspicacity but also for the eventual extension of the logic to interpersonal action, which is the main area of interest for sociology and the other social sciences. And explicit specification of the intentional aspect of acting is needed in order to indicate clearly that the system concerns action and not mere bodily change.[38]

Now in addition to acts, there are forbearances. "Forbearing," Von Wright claims, is not definable in terms of "change" and "act." Forbearing is different from preventing a state from coming into existence: to keep the door open is to act, not to forbear from acting. He defines his basic notion of forbearing in the following way:

> An agent, on a given occasion, forbears the doing of a certain thing if, and only if, he *can do* this thing, but *does* in fact *not do* it.[39]

This manner of explicating "forbearing," however, leads to serious difficulty: namely, it transforms Von Wright's logic of action into a logic of *free* action. A logic of action should be neutral with respect to the free will issue; to incorporate an answer to that yet unsolved controversy is to beg the philosophical question.[40]

Letting "S" stand for an agent and "*a*" for an action, the definiens of Von Wright's definition of "forbearing" is ambiguous between the following two expressions:

  (i) S performs not-*a* and S is able to (can) perform *a*;
  (ii) It is not the case that S performs *a* and S is able to (can) perform *a*.

(A1) $(p \vee qTr \vee s) \rightleftarrows [(pTr) \vee (pTs) \vee (qTr) \vee (qTs)]$;
(A2) $[(pTq) \& (pTs)] \rightarrow (pTq \& s)$;
(A3) $p \rightleftarrows (pTq \vee {\sim}q)$;
(A4) ${\sim}(pTq \& {\sim}q)$.

The rules of inference are substitution, detachment, and replacement of expressions by provably equivalent expressions. Also see Von Wright's "And Next" in *Acta Philosophica Fennica*, Fasc. XVIII (1965), pp. 293–304, for a fuller development of the logic of change.

[37] Von Wright, *Norm and Action*, p. 312 below.

[38] On this second criticism of Von Wright's symbolism, compare Chisholm's comments to Von Wright's "The Logic of Action—A Sketch" and Von Wright's reply in *The Logic of Decision and Action*, ed. Rescher, pp. 138–139, 145. Also cf. *Norm and Action*, pp. 310–311 below.

[39] Von Wright, *Norm and Action*, p. 314 below; italics in text. Terminologically, Von Wright uses "action" as a general term for acting and forbearing.

[40] I have developed this criticism of Von Wright's action language in "On Von Wright's Logic of Action," forthcoming in *Philosophical Studies*.

It seems that (ii) is not a satisfactory interpretation of the definiens. For if it were, the number of actions a person normally forbears from performing at a given time is absurdly large. A normal person has the ability to (can), for example, point to an infinite number of points in space; however, it is false (or prohibitively strange) to say that a person is then forbearing from performing an infinite number of actions. Rather, it seems that Von Wright should be interpreted as claiming that an agent forbears from performing *a* just in case the situation expressed by (i) obtains.[41]

Now for every action, if an agent performs it, then he *can* perform it; that is, it is impossible for an agent to perform an action that he cannot perform. Since not-*a* is an an action, it follows that a person performs not-*a* only if he *can* perform not-*a*. Moreover, to say that a person performs not-*a* is to say that he refrains from performing *a*. The patrolman who keeps his arm at his side and refrains from shooting the fleeing youth performed an action; he performed the action of not shooting the youth.[42] It follows on interpretation (i) of the definiens, then, that a person forbears from performing *a* only if he can perform *a* and he can refrain from performing *a*. And since a person is free with respect to performing an action just in case he can perform and can refrain from performing it, an agent forbears from performing an action for Von Wright only if he is free to perform it. Hence, Von Wright's logic is a logic of free action: we are free with respect to a large proportion of our actions, namely, *all* our forbearances. Whether we are free with respect to *any* actions, let alone every forbearance, however, should not be decided by building it into the action logic. The source of this difficulty is construing "forbearance" as a modal term, that is, one that can be adequately explicated only in terms of "can." "Forbearance," rather, is nonmodal.

[41] Professor von Wright, however, disagrees with this reading of the text. In private correspondence dated April 11, 1968, he says "I think it is the *second* [interpretation of the definiens, that is, (ii)] which corresponds to my notion of forbearing (in *Norm and Action*, and also in the Pittsburgh paper [that is, "The Logic of Action—A Sketch" in *The Logic of Decision and Action*, ed. Rescher])."
[42] Arthur Danto, "Freedom and Forbearance" in *Freedom and Determinism*, ed. Lehrer, pp. 51 ff., makes a similar suggestion about refraining.

HISTORICAL BACKGROUND

from ESSAYS ON THE ACTIVE POWERS OF MAN:

ESSAY I. OF ACTIVE POWER IN GENERAL

Thomas Reid

CHAPTER I. OF THE NOTION OF ACTIVE POWER

To consider gravely what is meant by *Active Power*, may seem altogether unnecessary, and to be mere trifling. It is not a term of art, but a common word in our language, used every day in discourse, even by the vulgar. We find words of the same meaning in all other languages; and there is no reason to think that it is not perfectly understood by all men who understand the English language.

I believe all this is true, and that an attempt to explain a word so well understood, and to show that it has a meaning, requires an apology.

The apology is, that this term, so well understood by the vulgar, has been darkened by philosophers, who, in this as in many other instances, have found great difficulties about a thing which, to the rest of mankind, seems perfectly clear.

This has been the more easily effected, because Power is a thing so much of its own kind, and so simple in its nature, as not to admit of a logical definition. [6]

It is well known that there are many things perfectly understood, and of which we have clear and distinct conceptions, which cannot be logically defined. No man ever attempted to define magnitude; yet there is no word whose meaning is more distinctly or more generally understood. We cannot give a logical definition of thought, of duration, of number, or of motion.

When men attempt to define such things, they give no light. They may give a synonymous word or phrase, but it will probably be a worse for a better. If they

Reprinted from Sir William Hamilton's edition of Thomas Reid's *Works* (8th ed., Edinburgh, 1895, 2 vols.). Hamilton's notes have been excluded. The numbers in brackets refer to the pagination of the 1768 edition.

will define, the definition will either be grounded upon a hypothesis, or it will darken the subject rather than throw light upon it.

The Aristotelian definition of motion—that it is *"Actus entis in potentia, quatenus in potentia,"* has been justly censured by modern philosophers; yet I think it is matched by what a celebrated modern philosopher has given us, as the most accurate definition of belief—to wit, "That it is a lively idea related to or associated with a present impression." ("Treatise of Human Nature," vol. i, p. 172.) "Memory," according to the same philosopher, "is the faculty by which we repeat our impressions, so as that they retain a considerable degree of their first vivacity, and are somewhat intermediate betwixt an idea and an impression."

Euclid, if his editors have not done him injustice, has attempted to define a right line, to define unity, ratio, and number. But these definitions are good for nothing. We may indeed suspect them not to be Euclid's; because they are never once quoted in the *Elements,* and are of no use.

I shall not therefore attempt to define Active Power, that I may not be liable to the same censure; but shall offer some observations that may lead us to attend to the conception we have of it in our own minds.

1. Power is not an object of any of our external senses, nor even an object of consciousness. [7]

That it is not seen, nor heard, nor touched, nor tasted, nor smelled, needs no proof. That we are not conscious of it, in the proper sense of that word, will be no less evident, if we reflect, that consciousness is that power of the mind by which it has an immediate knowledge of its own operations. Power is not an operation of the mind, and therefore no object of consciousness. Indeed, every operation of the mind is the exertion of some power of the mind; but we are conscious of the operation only—the power lies behind the scene; and, though we may justly infer the power from the operation, it must be remembered, that inferring is not the province of consciousness, but of reason.

I acknowledge, therefore, that our having any conception or idea of power is repugnant to Mr. Locke's theory, that all our simple ideas are got either by the external senses, or by consciousness. Both cannot be true. Mr. Hume perceived this repugnancy, and consistently maintained, that we have no idea of power. Mr. Locke did not perceive it. If he had, it might have led him to suspect his theory; for when theory is repugnant to fact, it is easy to see which ought to yield. I am conscious that I have a *conception* or *idea* of power; but, strictly speaking, I am not conscious that I have *power.*

I shall have occasion to show, that we have very early, from our constitution, a conviction or belief of some degree of active power in ourselves. This belief, however, is not consciousness—for we may be deceived in it; but the testimony of consciousness can never deceive. Thus, a man who is struck with a palsy in the night, commonly knows not that he has lost the power of speech till he attempts to speak: he knows not whether he can move his hands and arms till he makes the trial; and if, without making trial, he consults his consciousness ever so attentively, it will give him no information whether he has lost these powers, or still retains them. [8]

From this we must conclude, that the powers we have are not an object of consciousness, though it would be foolish to censure this way of speaking in popular discourse, which requires not accurate attention to the different provinces of our various faculties. The testimony of consciousness is always unerring, nor was it ever called in question by the greatest skeptics, ancient or modern.

2. A *second* observation is—that, as there are some things of which we have a *direct,* and others of which we have only a *relative,* conception; Power belongs to the latter class. . . .

Our conception of power is relative to its exertions or effects. Power is one thing; its exertion is another thing. It is true, there can be no exertion without power; but there may be power that is not exerted. Thus, a man may have power to rise and walk when he sits still. [11]

But, though it be one thing to speak, and another to have the power of speaking, I apprehend we conceive of the power as something which has a certain relation to the effect. And of every power we form our notion by the effect which it is able to produce.

3. It is evident that Power is a *quality,* and cannot exist without a subject to which it belongs.

That power may exist without any being or subject to which that power may be attributed, is an absurdity, shocking to every man of common understanding.

It is a quality which may be varied, not only in degree, but also in kind; and we distinguish both the kinds and degrees by the effects which they are able to produce.

Thus a power to fly, and a power to reason, are different kinds of power, their effects being different in kind. But a power to carry one hundred weight, and a power to carry two hundred, are different degrees of the same kind.

4. We cannot conclude the want of power from its not being exerted; nor from the exertion of a less degree of power, can we conclude that there is no greater degree in the subject. Thus, though a man on a particular occasion said nothing, we cannot conclude from that circumstance, that he had not the power of speech; nor from a man's carrying ten pound weight, can we conclude that he had not power to carry twenty.

5. There are some qualities that have a *contrary,* others that have not: Power is a quality of the latter kind.

Vice is contrary to virtue, misery to happiness, hatred to love, negation to affirmation; but there is no contrary to power. Weakness or impotence are defects or privations of power, but not contraries to it. [12]

If what has been said of power be easily understood, and readily assented to, by all who understand our language, as I believe it is, we may from this justly conclude, that we have a distinct notion of power, and may reason about it with understanding, though we can give no logical definition of it.

If power were a thing of which we have no idea, as some philosophers have taken much pains to prove—that is, if power were a word without any meaning—we could neither affirm nor deny anything concerning it with understanding. We should have equal reason to say that it is a substance, as that it is a quality; that it does not admit of degrees as that it does. If the understanding immediately assents to one of these assertions, and revolts from the contrary, we may conclude with certainty, that we put some meaning upon the word *power*—that is, that we have some idea of it. And it is chiefly for the sake of this conclusion, that I have enumerated so many obvious things concerning it.

The term *active power* is used, I conceive, to distinguish it from *speculative powers*. As all languages distinguish action from speculation, the same distinction is applied to the powers by which they are produced. The powers of seeing, hearing, remembering, distinguishing, judging, reasoning, are speculative powers; the power of executing any work of art or labor is active power.

There are many things related to power, in such a manner that we can have no notion of them if we have none of power. [13]

The exertion of active power we call *action;* and, as every action produces some change, so every change must be caused by some exertion, or by the cessation of some exertion of power. That which produces a change by the exertion of its power we call the *cause* of that change; and the change produced, the *effect* of that cause.

When one being, by its active power, produces any change upon another, the last is said to be *passive,* or to be acted upon. Thus we see that action and passion, cause and effect, exertion and operation, have such a relation to active power, that, if it be understood, they are understood of consequence; but if power be a word without any meaning, all those words which are related to it, must be words without any meaning. They are, however, common words in our language; and equivalent words have always been common in all languages.

It would be very strange indeed, if mankind had always used these words so familiarly, without perceiving that they had no meaning; and that this discovery should have been first made by a philosopher of the present age.

With equal reason it might be maintained, that though there are words in all languages to express sight, and words to signify the various colors which are objects of sight; yet that all mankind, from the beginning of the world, had been blind, and never had an idea of sight or of color. But there are no absurdities so gross as those which philosophers have advanced concerning ideas.

CHAPTER II. THE SAME SUBJECT

There are, I believe, no abstract notions, that are to be found more early, or more universally, in the minds of men, than those of *acting* and *being acted upon.* Every child that understands the distinction between striking and being struck, must have the conception of action and passion. [14]

We find accordingly, that there is no language so imperfect but that it has active and passive verbs and participles; the one signifying some kind of action; the other being acted upon. This distinction enters into the original contexture of all languages.

Active verbs have a form and construction proper to themselves; passive verbs a different form and a different construction. In all languages, the nominative to an active verb is the agent; the thing acted upon is put in an oblique case. In passive verbs, the thing acted upon is the nominative, and the agent, if expressed, must be in an oblique case; as in this example—*Raphael drew the Cartoons; the Cartoons were drawn by Raphael.*

Every distinction which we find in the structure of all languages, must have been familiar to those who framed the languages at first, and to all who speak them with understanding.

It may be objected to this argument, taken from the structure of language, in the use of active and passive verbs, that active verbs are not always used to denote an action, nor is the nominative before an active verb, conceived in all cases to be an agent, in the strict sense of that word; that there are many passive verbs which have an active signification, and active verbs which have a passive. From these facts, it may be thought a just conclusion, that, in contriving the different forms of active and passive verbs, and their different construction, men have not been governed by a regard to any distinction between action and passion, but by chance, or some accidental cause. [15]

In answer to this objection, the fact on which it is founded must be admitted; but I think the conclusion not justly drawn from it, for the following reasons:—

1. It seems contrary to reason to attribute to chance or accident what is subject to rules, even though there may be exceptions to the rule. The exceptions may, in such a case, be attributed to accident, but the rule cannot. There is perhaps hardly anything in language so general as not to admit of exceptions. It cannot be denied to be a general rule, that verbs and participles have an active and a passive voice; and, as this is a general rule, not in one language only, but in all the languages we are acquainted with, it shows evidently that men, in the earliest stages, and in all periods of society, have distinguished action from passion.

2. It is to be observed, that the forms of language are often applied to purposes different from those for which they were originally intended. The varieties of a language, even the most perfect, can never be made equal to all the variety of human conceptions. The forms and modifications of language must be confined within certain limits, that they may not exceed the capacity of human memory. Therefore, in all languages, there must be a kind of frugality used, to make one form of expression serve many different purposes, like Sir Hudibras' dagger, which, though made to stab or break a head, was put to many other uses. Many examples might be produced of this frugality in language. Thus, the Latins and Greeks had five or six cases of nouns, to express the various relations that one thing could bear to another. The genitive case must have been at first intended to express some one capital relation, such as that of possession or of property; but it would be very difficult to enumerate all the relations which, in the progress of language, it was used to express. The same observation may be applied to other cases of nouns. [16]

The slightest similitude or analogy is thought sufficient to justify the extension of a form of speech beyond its proper meaning, whenever the language does not afford a more proper form. In the moods of verbs, a few of those which occur most frequently are distinguished by different forms, and these are made to supply all the forms that are wanting. The same observation may be applied to what is called the *voices* of verbs. An active and a passive are the capital ones; some languages have more, but no language so many as to answer to all the variations of human thought. We cannot always coin new ones, and therefore must use some one or other of those that are to be found in the language, though at first intended for another purpose.

3. A third observation in answer to the objection is, that we can point out a cause of the frequent misapplication of active verbs, to things which have no proper activity—a cause which extends to the greater part of such misapplications,

and which confirms the account I have given of the proper intention of active and passive verbs.

As there is no principle that appears to be more universally acknowledged by mankind, from the first dawn of reason, than that every change we observe in nature must have a cause; so this is no sooner perceived, than there arises in the human mind a strong desire to know the causes of those changes that fall within our observation. *Felix qui potuit rerum cognoscere causas,* is the voice of nature in all men. Nor is there anything that more early distinguishes the rational from the brute creation, than this avidity to know the causes of things, of which I see no sign in brute-animals. [17]

It must surely be admitted, that, in those periods wherein languages are formed, men are but poorly furnished for carrying on this investigation with success. We see that the experience of thousands of years is necessary to bring men into the right track in this investigation, if indeed they can yet be said to be brought into it. What innumerable errors rude ages must fall into with regard to causes, from impatience to judge, and inability to judge right, we may conjecture from reason, and may see from experience; from which I think it is evident, that, supposing active verbs to have been originally intended to express what is properly called action, and their nominatives to express the agent; yet, in the rude and barbarous state wherein languages are formed, there must be innumerable misapplications of such verbs and nominatives, and many things spoken of as active which have no real activity.

To this we may add, that it is a general prejudice of our early years, and of rude nations, when we perceive anything to be changed, and do not perceive any other thing which we can believe to be the cause of that change, to impute it to the thing itself, and conceive it to be active and animated, so far as to have the power of producing that change in itself. Hence, to a child, or to a savage, all nature seems to be animated; the sea, the earth, the air, the sun, moon, and stars, rivers, fountains and groves, are conceived to be active and animated beings. As this is a sentiment natural to man in his rude state, it has, on that account, even in polished nations, the verisimilitude that is required in poetical fiction and fable, and makes personification one of the most agreeable figures in poetry and elo-quence.

The origin of this prejudice probably is, that we judge of other things by our-selves, and therefore are disposed to ascribe to them that life and activity which we know to be in ourselves.

A little girl ascribes to her doll the passions and sentiments she feels in herself. Even brutes seem to have something of this nature. A young cat, when she sees any brisk motion in a feather or a straw, is prompted, by natural instinct, to hunt it as she would hunt a mouse. [18]

Whatever be the origin of this prejudice in mankind, it has a powerful influence upon language, and leads men, in the structure of language, to ascribe action to many things that are merely passive; because, when such forms of speech were invented, those things were really believed to be active. Thus we say, the wind blows, the sea rages, the sun rises and sets, bodies gravitate and move.

When experience discovers that these things are altogether inactive, it is easy to correct our opinion about them; but it is not so easy to alter the established forms of language. The most perfect and the most polished languages are like old furniture, which is never perfectly suited to the present taste, but retains something of the fashion of the times when it was made.

Thus, though all men of knowledge believe that the succession of day and night is owing to the rotation of the earth round its axis, and not to any diurnal motion of the heavens, yet we find ourselves under a necessity of speaking in the old style, of the sun's rising and going down, and coming to the meridian. And this style is used, not only in conversing with the vulgar, but when men of knowledge converse with one another. And if we should suppose the vulgar to be at last so far enlightened as to have the same belief with the learned, of the cause of day and night, the same style would still be used.

From this instance we may learn, that the language of mankind may furnish good evidence of opinions which have been early and universally entertained, and that the forms contrived for expressing such opinions, may remain in use after the opinions which gave rise to them have been greatly changed. [19]

Active verbs appear plainly to have been first contrived to express action. They are still in general applied to this purpose. And though we find many instances of the application of active verbs to things which we now believe not be active, this ought to be ascribed to men's having once had the belief that those things are active, and perhaps, in some cases, to this, that forms of expression are commonly extended, in course of time, beyond their original intention, either from analogy, or because more proper forms for the purpose are not found in language.

Even the misapplication of this notion of action and active power shows that there is such a notion in the human mind, and shows the necessity there is in philosophy of distinguishing the proper application of these words, from the vague and improper application of them, founded on common language or on popular prejudice.

Another argument to show that all men have a notion or idea of active power is, that there are many operations of mind common to all men who have reason, and necessary in the ordinary conduct of life, which imply a belief of active power in ourselves and in others.

All our volitions and efforts to act, all our deliberations, our purposes and promises, imply a belief of active power in ourselves; our counsels, exhortations, and commands, imply a belief of active power in those to whom they are addressed.

If a man should make an effort to fly to the moon—if he should even deliberate about it, or resolve to do it—we should conclude him to be a lunatic; and even lunacy would not account for his conduct, unless it made him believe the thing to be in his power.

If a man promises to pay me a sum of money tomorrow, without believing that it will then be in his power, he is not an honest man; and, if I did not believe that it will then be in his power, I should have no dependence on his promise. [20] . . .

It might further be observed, that power is the proper and immediate object of ambition, one of the most universal passions of the human mind, and that which makes the greatest figure in the history of all ages. Whether Mr. Hume, in defense of his system, would maintain that there is no such passion in mankind as ambition, or that ambition is not a vehement desire of power, or that men may have a vehement desire of power, without having any idea of power, I will not pretend to divine. [21] . . .

What convinces myself that I have an idea of power is, that I am conscious that I know what I mean by that word, and, while I have this consciousness, I disdain equally to hear arguments for or against my having such an idea. But, if we would convince those, who, being led away by prejudice or by authority, deny that they have any such idea, we must condescend to use such arguments as the subject will afford, and such as we should use with a man who should deny that mankind have any idea of magnitude or of equality. [22]

The arguments I have adduced are taken from these five topics:—1. That there are many things that we can affirm or deny concerning power, with understanding. 2. That there are, in all languages, words signifying, not only power, but signifying many other things that imply power, such as action and passion, cause and effect, energy, operation, and others. 3. That, in the structure of all languages, there is an active and passive form in verbs and participles, and a different construction adapted to these forms, of which diversity no account can be given, but that it has been intended to distinguish action from passion. 4. That there are many operations of the human mind familiar to every man come to the use of reason, and necessary in the ordinary conduct of life, which imply a conviction of some degree of power in ourselves and in others. 5. That the desire of power is one of the strongest passions of human nature. . . .

CHAPTER V. WHETHER BEINGS THAT HAVE NO WILL NOR UNDERSTANDING MAY HAVE ACTIVE POWER

That active power is an attribute, which cannot exist but in some being possessed of that power, and the subject of that attribute, I take for granted as a self-evident truth. Whether there can be active power in a subject which has no thought, no understanding, no will, is not so evident. . . .

Mr. Locke observes very justly, "That, from the observation of the operation of bodies by our senses, we have but a very imperfect obscure idea of active power, since they afford us not any idea in themselves of the power to begin any action, either of motion or thought." He adds, "That we find in ourselves a power to begin or forbear, continue or end, several actions of our minds and motions of our bodies, barely by a thought or a preference of the mind, ordering, or, as it were, commanding the doing or not doing such a particular action. This power which the mind has thus to order the consideration of any idea, or the forbearing to consider it, or to prefer the motion of any part of the body to its rest, and vice versa, in any particular instance, is that which we call the will. The actual exercise of that power, by directing any particular action, or its forbearance, is that which we call volition or willing." [35]

According to Mr. Locke, therefore, the only clear notion or idea we have of active power, is taken from the power which we find in ourselves to give certain direction to our thoughts; and this power in ourselves can be brought into action only by willing or volition.

From this, I think, it follows, that, if we had not will, and that degree of understanding which will necessarily implies, we could exert no active power, and, consequently, could have none; for power that cannot be exerted is no power. It follows, also, that the active power, of which only we can have any distinct conception, can be only in beings that have understanding and will.

Power to produce any effect, implies power not to produce it. We can conceive no way in which power may be determined to one of these rather than the other, in a being that has no will. . . .

In certain motions of my body and directions of my thought, I know not only that there must be a cause that has power to produce these effects, but that I am that cause; and I am conscious of what I do in order to the production of them.

From the consciousness of our own activity, seems to be derived not only the clearest, but the only conception we can form of activity, or the exertion of active power.

As I am unable to form a notion of any intellectual power different in kind from those I possess, the same holds with respect to active power. If all men had been blind, we should have had no conception of the power of seeing, nor any name for it in language. If man had not the powers of abstraction and reasoning, we could not have had any conception of these operations. In like manner, if he had not some degree of active power, and if he were not conscious of the exertion of it in his voluntary actions, it is probable he could have no conception of activity, or of active power. [37] . . .

Human power, therefore, can only be exerted by will, and we are unable to conceive any active power to be exerted without will. Every man knows infallibly that what is done by his conscious will and intention, is to be imputed to him, as the agent or cause; and that whatever is done without his will and intention, cannot be imputed to him with truth.

We judge of the actions and conduct of other men by the same rule as we judge of our own. In morals, it is self-evident that no man can be the object either of approbation or of blame for what he did not. But how shall we know whether it is his doing or not? If the action depended upon his will, and if he intended and willed it, it is his action in the judgment of all mankind. But if it was done without his knowledge, or without his will and intention, it is as certain that he did it not, and that it ought not to be imputed to him as the agent.

When there is any doubt to whom a particular action ought to be imputed, the doubt arises only from our ignorance of facts; when the facts relating to it are known, no man of understanding has any doubt to whom the action ought to be imputed.

The general rules of imputation are self-evident. They have been the same in all ages, and among all civilized nations. No man blames another for being black or fair, for having a fever or the falling sickness; because these things are believed not to be in his power; and they are believed not to be in his power, because they depend not upon his will. We can never conceive that a man's duty goes beyond his power, or that his power goes beyond what depends upon his will. [39] . . .

CHAPTER VII. OF THE EXTENT OF HUMAN POWER

. . . We can only speak of the power of man in general; and as our notion of power is relative to its effects, we can estimate its extent only by the effects which it is able to produce.

It would be wrong to estimate the extent of human power by the effects which it has actually produced. For every man had power to do many things which he did not, and not to do many things which he did; otherwise he could not be an object either of approbation or of disapprobation to any rational being. [49]

The effects of human power are either immediate, or they are more remote.

The immediate effects, I think, are reducible to two heads. We can give certain motions to our own bodies; and we can give a certain direction to our own thoughts.

Whatever we can do beyond this, must be done by one of these means, or both.

We can produce no motion in any body in the universe, but by moving first our own body as an instrument. Nor can we produce thought in any other person, but by thought and motion in ourselves.

Our power to move our own body, is not only limited in its extent, but in its nature is subject to mechanical laws. It may be compared to a spring endowed with the power of contracting or expanding itself, but which cannot contract without drawing equally at both ends, nor expand without pushing equally at both ends; so that every action of the spring is always accompanied with an equal re-action in a contrary direction.

We can conceive a man to have power to move his whole body in any direction, without the aid of any other body, or a power to move one part of his body without the aid of any other part. But philosophy teaches us that man has no such power.

If he carries his whole body in any direction with a certain quantity of motion, this he can do only by pushing the earth, or some other body, with an equal quantity of motion in the contrary direction. If he but stretch out his arm in one direction, the rest of his body is pushed with an equal quantity of motion in the contrary direction. [50]

This is the case with regard to all animal and voluntary motions, which come within the reach of our senses. They are performed by the contraction of certain muscles; and a muscle, when it is contracted, draws equally at both ends. As to the motions antecedent to the contraction of the muscle, and consequent upon the volition of the animal, we know nothing, and can say nothing about them.

We know not even how those immediate effects of our power are produced by our willing them. We perceive not any necessary connection between the volition and exertion on our part, and the motion of our body that follows them.

Anatomists inform us, that every voluntary motion of the body is performed by the contraction of certain muscles, and that the muscles are contracted by some influence derived from the nerves. But, without thinking in the least, either of muscles or nerves, we will only the external effect, and the internal machinery, without our call immediately produces that effect.

This is one of the wonders of our frame, which we have reason to admire; but to account for it, is beyond the reach of our understanding.

That there is an established harmony between our willing certain motions of our bodies, and the operation of the nerves and muscles which produces those motions, is a fact known by experience. This volition is an act of the mind. But whether this act of the mind have any physical effect upon the nerves and muscles; or whether it be only an occasion of their being acted upon by some other efficient, according to the established laws of nature, is hid from us. So dark is our conception of our own power when we trace it to its origin. [51]

We have good reason to believe, that matter had its origin from mind, as well as all its motions; but how, or in what manner it is moved by mind, we know as little as how it was created.

It is possible, therefore, for anything we know, that what we call the immediate effects of our power, may not be so in the strictest sense. Between the will to produce the effect, and the production of it, there may be agents or instruments of which we are ignorant.

This may leave some doubt, whether we be, in the strictest sense, the efficient cause of the voluntary motions of our own body. But it can produce no doubt with regard to the moral estimation of our actions.

The man who knows that such an event depends upon his will, and who deliberately wills to produce it, is, in the strictest moral sense, the cause of the event; and it is justly imputed to him, whatever physical causes may have concurred in its production.

Thus, he who maliciously intends to shoot his neighbor dead, and voluntarily does it, is undoubtedly the cause of his death, though he did no more to occasion it than draw the trigger of the gun. He neither gave to the ball its velocity, nor to the powder its expansive force, nor to the flint and steel the power to strike fire; but he knew that what he did must be followed by the man's death, and did it with that intention; and therefore he is justly chargeable with the murder. [52]

Philosophers may therefore dispute innocently, whether we be the proper efficient causes of the voluntary motions of our own body; or whether we be only, as Malebranche thinks, the occasional causes. The determination of this question, if it can be determined, can have no effect on human conduct.

The other branch of what is immediately in our power, is to give a certain direction to our own thoughts. This, as well as the first branch, is limited in various ways. It is greater in some persons than in others, and in the same person is very different, according to the health of his body and the state of his mind. But that men, when free from disease of body and of mind, have a considerable degree of power of this kind, and that it may be greatly increased by practice and habit, is sufficiently evident from experience, and from the natural conviction of all mankind.

Were we to examine minutely into the connection between our volitions, and the direction of our thoughts which obeys these volitions—were we to consider how we are able to give attention to an object for a certain time, and turn our attention to another when we choose, we might perhaps find it difficult to determine whether the mind itself be the sole efficient cause of the voluntary changes in the direction of our thoughts, or whether it requires the aid of other efficient causes.

I see no good reason why the dispute about efficient and occasional causes, may not be applied to the power of directing our thoughts, as well as to the power of moving our bodies. In both cases, I apprehend, the dispute is endless, and if it could be brought to an issue, would be fruitless.

Nothing appears more evident to our reason, than that there must be an efficient cause of every change that happens in nature. But when I attempt to comprehend the manner in which an efficient cause operates, either upon body or upon mind, there is a darkness which my faculties are not able to penetrate [53]. . . .

ACTION DESCRIPTION

ON THE CHARACTERIZATION OF ACTIONS

Nicholas Rescher

I. INTRODUCTION

1. The Problem of Act Description.   Clearly, the fundamental question of the theory of action is that at issue in such formulations as:

What is the nature of action?
What is an action?
What sorts of things are actions?

However, virtually all of the extensive literature on action has concerned itself with points of detail, and the generic concept of "an action" as such, in its full and ramified generality, has not been explored as fully as one might wish. The present discussion will approach this key question of *What is an action?* obliquely, from the angle of the question *How is an action to be described?* It is hoped that by shedding light upon the descriptive characterization of action it will prove possible to clarify the nature of action itself.[1]

2. Some Fundamental Contrasts.   It is a useful preliminary to delineate somewhat more sharply the class of phenomena with whose description we shall be concerned. The following fundamental contrasts must be borne in mind.

Reprinted by permission of the author.
[1] It deserves remark that the *identification* of an action is a matter infinitely simpler than its *description* because of the individuating role of spatiotemporal indicators. Both "That stroking of a beard" (pointing) and "Winterson's beard stroking just now" suffice fully to *identify* an action but do very little towards *describing* it. Identifications can be virtually barren of descriptive detail.

Actions vs. processes.   An action must always be something *done* by an agent. The locution "He (the agent) did *X*" must always be applicable. This differentiates *actions* (e.g., Smith's shaking of the glass) from the *processes* of inert nature (e.g., the evaporation of the spilled drops).

Actions vs. passions.   In saying an action is something an agent *does,* we insist on its being an instance of his agency. This sets his actions apart from those things that merely "happen to" him—for example his *sitting down* (because he feels weak) from his *falling down* (because he slipped on a banana peel).

But many sorts of things other than their actions can also be said to be *done* by agents. The remaining distinctions will exhibit some of these.

Actions vs. mere behavior.   An agent can be said to "do" various things (gasp or hiccough, tremble for fear or beam for joy) with respect to which the exercise of agency does not come into play. Such doings are not to be classed as actions: an action—in contrast with something that "happens to" one or that one "just happens to do"—is an item of behavior over whose occurrence one exercises *control.*

Actions vs. terminations.   The distinction between activity verbs (e.g., listening for, looking at, searching for) and achievement verbs (hearing, seeing, finding) is familiar from other contexts. The former category will represent actions but the latter—in which only the result of the activity is at issue—will not. Going through the crowning ceremony is an action, but entering upon one's reign is not.

Refraining vs. nonaction.   Inaction has two importantly different modes. The one is *refraining:* When sitting at my desk writing I may refrain from scratching an itching mosquito bite—that is I "hold myself back" or "keep myself from" doing a certain action. This sort of keeping oneself from doing something that is at issue in refraining is importantly different from a second type of inaction which may be illustrated as follows. When sitting at my desk writing there is an endless number of things I am not doing: reading the newspaper, chatting with a friend, driving a car, etc. But these *nonactions* are not doings of any sort, I am not somehow active in keeping myself from doing them. And thus, unlike refrainings, they are not actions at all. There is a critical difference between doing not-*X*, which is an action, and not-doing *X*, which need not be.

Actions vs. mental acts.   An action must have the aspect of physical activity, either positively by way of doing or negatively by way of refraining. Thus purely mental acts done solely *in foro interno* cannot qualify as actions. Giving overt verbal agreement is an action, giving tacit assent is not; being worried is not of itself an action, though pacing worriedly is. Every action must have an overt physical component and involves bodily activity of some sort. It is thus no accident that paradigm actions are done by *persons*—i.e., agents with corporeal bodies.

So much for the preliminary delineation of the sphere of "actions." We shall now turn to our main task: an examination of the descriptive aspects of action.

II. THE DESCRIPTIVE ASPECTS OF ACTION

We shall attempt to develop the tools for what might be called the *canonical description* of an action. The object here is to give an essentially exhaustive *catalogue of the key generic elements of actions,* so as to provide a classificatory matrix of rubrics under which the essential features of actions can be classed. The following tabulation represents an attempt at the compilation of such a catalogue:

The Descriptive Elements of an Action

(1) *Agent* (WHO did it?)

(2) *Act-type* (WHAT did he do?) [2]

(3) *Modality of Action* (HOW did he do it?)
    a. Modality of manner (IN WHAT MANNER did he do it?)
    b. Modality of means (BY WHAT MEANS did he do it?)

(4) *Setting of Action* (IN WHAT CONTEXT did he do it?)
    a. Temporal aspect (WHEN did he do it?) [3]
    b. Spatial aspect (WHERE did he do it?)
    c. Circumstantial aspect (UNDER WHAT CIRCUMSTANCES did he do it?)

(5) *Rationale of Action* (WHY did he do it?)
    a. Causality (WHAT CAUSED him to do it?)
    b. Finality (WITH WHAT AIM did he do it?)
    c. Intentionality (FROM WHAT MOTIVES did he do it?)

Each of these elements of the canonical description of an action must be discussed briefly.[4]

(1) *The Agent:* The agent of an action may be an individual or a group (crowds, boards of directors, parliaments, etc.) that is capable of action. Groups can act distributively, as single individuals (as when the audience applauds), or collectively as a corporate whole (as when the Congress votes to override a presidential veto).

(2) *The Act-Type:* An act-type can be specified at varying levels of concreteness. It can be a *fully generic act-type* (e.g., "the opening of a window," "the sharpening of a pencil"). Such a generic act-type characterization can be rendered more specific ("the opening of this window," "the sharpening of that pencil") whenever a concrete object involved in the action is indicated (*this* window, *that* pencil). Such a *specific act-type* is one which, though still a general type, involves a concrete particular. And it goes without saying that any particular action can be described (i.e., placed within types) at varying levels of generality. In a particular case we might say "He raised *a* hand" or "He raised *his right* hand." Those items that correspond to the question "Upon what did the agent act?"—i.e., that deal with the recipients or the grammarian's *objects* of an action—are to be viewed as definite parts of what we call the "act-type." Thus if Bob hands a book to Jim, the act-type is not a *handing*, but either the specific "handing a book to Jim" or the generic "handing a book to someone."

(3) *The Modality of Action:* Modality of manner is a straightforward conception. Suppose an action to be done—say that Jones shook hands with Smith. Did he do

---

[2] Note that this is the fundamental item in the specification of an action, and that the "it" that occurs in the wording of all the other questions refers to *the relevant instance of the act-type in question.*

[3] To individuate a (concrete) action it is sufficient to specify the agent, the act-type, and the occasion (time) of acting. But to say this is not, of course, to say that the adequate *description* of an action does not require a good deal more.

[4] I am not unmindful of the similarities between the questions presented in the tabulation and those inherent in Aristotle's *Categories.* But the relationships, though real, are too intricate to warrant setting out here.

it firmly or weakly, rapidly or slowly, clumsily or deftly, gently or roughly? All of these—endlessly variant—characterizations of the *way* in which the action was accomplished relate to the modality of manner.

Some action-qualifications seem *prima facie* to indicate the agent's state of mind, but are in fact descriptive of his manner of acting. Thus "he sighed contentedly" or "he said good-bye sadly" in fact describe the manner of his sigh or farewell. "He was sad and he said farewell" does not convey the same information at all—he may have "put up a bold front" and said farewell cheerfully. He may well "have been sad and tied his shoelace" and so we may well say "he tied his shoelace sadly" —but now we have a mere indication of his state of mind, rather than an act-description. There is no special way of tying a shoelace that counts as "tying one's shoelace sadly."

White opened the curtains. Did he do so with the pull-rope, or with his hands, or with a stick? Such characterizations of the means (instruments) by which the action was done relate to the modality of means. The means can be generic ("He killed the man with *a* revolver") or specific ("He killed the man with *this* 35 caliber, Smith and Wesson, series 1935c, serial no. 1056773 revolver").

Of course if Robinson breathed or twiddled his thumbs, it makes little sense to ask about the means by which he did so (though we could, of course, inquire about the manner). Normal bodily movements are accomplished without overt means. And many other types of actions are such that—barring exotic cases—the means of action is implicitly specified within the action-type itself.

(4) *The Setting of Action:* Suppose an act of a certain type to be done by a certain agent in a certain manner with a certain means ("He opened the can of soup smoothly with a can opener"). The question still remains as to the specific setting of the action that fixes its position in time, and space, and in the course of events (his doing so in the kitchen yesterday afternoon while the radio was playing). Every action must have a chronological occasion in occurring at a certain time or times, a positional location in occurring at a certain place or places, and a circumstantial setting fitting it among other things going on within its relevant environment. The ensemble of these three elements constitutes what we have termed the *setting* of the action.

(5) *The Rationale of Action:* Suppose an action to be performed—say that Smith strikes his fist upon the table. An explanation of this fact may well proceed in causal terms: he acted "out of rage," or "out of drunkenness," or "by an irrepressible urge," or even "due to posthypnotic suggestion." Such act-characterizations represent answers (i.e., partial answers) to the question *Why did he do it?* and they all answer this question in the mode of *causality*. Bypassing—or, in effect, declaring irrelevant the entire issue of Smith's wishes and desires, these act-explanations proceed, not in terms of the agent's choices, but in terms of the impersonal "forces" that are at work. Denying—or ignoring—that the act was a matter of the agent's deliberate choices, they address themselves to the purely *causal* aspect of the question of what led him to do it.[5] And correspondingly: Such ex-

---

[5] In common parlance "to cause" and "to motivate" do not contrast neatly in the way philosophers would wish to draw the contrast. Compare the locutions: "Her hesitancy caused him to persevere" or "My importunity caused him to reconsider the decision."

planations can be fully satisfactory by themselves only in those cases where the denials are appropriate.[6]

When an agent's action was a matter of choice—i.e., was something he "chose" rather than something he "was caused" to do—the aspect of finality comes upon the scene, and we can ask "*With what aim* did he do it?" Although both causes and motives provide answers to the question "What led him to do it?" the latter alone answers the question "What *considerations* led him to do it?" (Both causal and motivational explanations can in many cases be given of one and the same action—e.g., Smith's sitting down when he feels his knees giving way because of dizziness.) We can, in short, inquire into the agent's purposes, wishes, goals, and objectives: his reasons, objectives, and intentions. Now we may say such things as that he did it "out of ambition," or "out of concern for her feelings," or "out of avarice" (i.e., for reasons of prestige, advancement, gain, etc.). Such act-characterizations tell us in the case of an act that was a matter of the agent's voluntary choice,[7] what objectives were operative in his doing it; they related to the finalistic aspect of the action.

Consider the following group of contrasts: voluntarily/involuntarily; deliberately/inadvertently (or accidentally); intentionally/unintentionally (or by mistake); consciously/out of habit (or automatically); knowingly/unwittingly (or unthinkingly); willingly/unwillingly (or reluctantly). All these [8] relate to what may in the aggregate be called the motivational aspect of action—the considerations having to do with generic features of the agent's state of mind and train of thought with respect to the action, in particular, his intentions and motives. They set a general frame of reference within which the specific issue of causal vs. motivational explanations can be posed. Clearly if X did A unwittingly and involuntarily, out of habit, an explanation along causal lines is called for,[9] while if he did it consciously and deliberately we would require a motivational explanation. But A would not even qualify as an action if it were not the sort of thing standardly done for motives or out of motivated but automatized habits. In action—unlike mere behavior—the motivational aspect must always play a role.

The dichotomy of the *rationale* of action on the one hand and its *type-modality-setting* upon the other reflects the amphibious nature of the concept of action. Like the concept of a *person* in general, in which physical and mental aspects are inseparably united, the concept of action has both *overt*, physical, and observable, and *covert*, mental, and unobservable involvements. The overt side relates to the issue of *what* he did and its ramifications into *how-and-in what context* he did it. The covert side relates to certain considerations as to his *state of mind* (thoughts, intentions, motives, awareness, etc.) at the time of action. All this latter aspect of action is comprehended under our rubric of the *rationale* of action.

---

[6] Think here of Socrates' objection in Plato's *Phaedo* to the purely biomedical explanation of human actions. (*Phaedo,* 98C–99B.)

[7] Or rather, simply "choice": voluntary choice is a pleonasm.

[8] And there are of course a great many others, e.g., gladly/reluctantly and confidently/hesitantly.

[9] As with items of behavior best not called actions, though in many ways related to them, such as reflex *reactions*, or such "automatic" behavior as sneezing. In the interests of clarity such items, with respect to which the issues of finality and intentionality do not arise at all, should be excluded from the rubric of *actions*.

It might be said that one ought to separate these issues of explicability from the other perhaps more strictly descriptive aspects of the characterization of an action. "Keep" (so the advice might run) *"what* the agent did sharply apart from the issue of *why* he did it." This course is infeasible. The language of human action is everywhere permeated by the coloration of intentionality and purposiveness. Even in such simple locutions as "He gave her the book," "He turned on the light," or "He flourished his cane," we find not simply behavioristically overt descriptions of matter in motion but fertile clues and suggestions as to the intentional aspects of the transaction ("gave" vs. "handed," "turned on" vs. "caused to go on," "flourished" vs. "moved about").

It is, however, in principle feasible and in practice desirable to maintain a line of separation between the *description* of action and its *evaluation*. There are a vast host of act-characterizing terms bearing upon the evaluative assessment of actions: Was the act prudent or rash, considerate or thoughtless, courteous or rude, appropriate or inappropriate, etc.? Such issues relate to the evaluation of the action, not to its actual depiction. They are thus not a proper part of our survey of the descriptive elements of an action.

Certain act-characterizations are descriptive not so much of the action itself as of the relationship it bears to other actions of the agent himself or of people in general. Was the act typical or atypical, characteristic or unusual, expected or unexpected, etc. Such considerations, while indeed descriptive rather than evaluative in nature, have their primary orientation directed away from the action itself.

Something similar obtains with respect to adverbs that describe not an action itself but its antecedents or results. If X did A "for the first time in history" or "in vain" or "prematurely," these qualifiers do not describe the action, but indicate its relationships to extraneous occurrences. Here too we orient the direction of consideration away from the action itself.[10]

III. THE PROBLEM OF INFINITE DIVISIBILITY

The common-language distinction between individual actions (e.g., the turning of a key in a lock) and complex courses of action (e.g., the successive placement of the dial of a combination lock into a sequential series of appropriate settings) is well known. But is this distinction viable? Is not every action actually a course of actions? Cannot all actions be divided into further components? To write the word "and" must one not first write the letter A? In fact, the multiplicity of components is endless—just as in the paradox of Zeno of Elea. In "moving his right foot forward one step" does Smith not first "move his right foot forward one-half step" and in doing this does he not first "move his right foot forward one-quarter step," *ad infinitum?*

This question of the infinite divisibility of action must, however, be answered negatively. Moving one's foot forward half a step, etc.,[11] are all *potential* actions: they are indeed things one *could* do if the doing of them were "on one's mind" and one *wanted* to do them. But actions are done either intentionally or by habit resulting from intentional actions. And in learning to walk we learn to *take steps*

---

[10] There can be borderline cases. When one says of the Japanese general whose campaign was disastrous that he killed himself *in the traditional way* one seemingly merely relates his action to others, but in fact does so in a manner laden with descriptive implications.

[11] At any rate up to a point.

—not first to *take quarter steps* and then expand them into half steps and then into full steps. Thus the man who "takes a step forward" in the sorts of circumstances in which the locution would ordinarily be applicable, does not perform composite action at all. When one lifts a spoonful of sugar out of the sugar bowl one does in fact lift out its component grains; but the *action* of taking the sugar is not composed of the *action* of taking the grains. Action has its intentional aspect: if it is the spoonful that is "on my mind" (consciously or implicitly) and not at all the grains, then my action in taking the spoonful cannot be subdivided into further actions specified with reference to the grains.

Some "actions" are in fact courses of action: they can be partitioned into component actions, as with the opening of a combination lock. But other actions are *simple* and indivisible. And precisely because of the mentalistic finitude of human beings who cannot have in mind an infinity of diverse items, every compound course of action will be divisible into some terminating—and so finite—list of component simple actions.

IV. THE PROBLEM OF INFINITE POLYADICITY

In his book *Action, Emotion and Will,*[12] Anthony Kenny poses the issue of what he calls the "variable polyadicity" of action. This arises from the thesis that any action-performance statement is incomplete and capable of further elaboration. Given that "Jones buttered a slice of toast at 3 P.M. yesterday" we can go on to elaborate this endlessly, by specifying more and more detail as to when, where, how, etc. Kenny thus suggests that any characterization of an action is *inherently incomplete,* and capable of fuller and fuller elaboration. "If we cast our net widely enough, we can make 'Brutus killed Caesar' into a sentence which describes, with a certain lack of specification, the whole history of the world."[13] If this view of the matter is accepted, we have the result that every action-presenting statement inevitably is fundamentally incomplete in omitting features essential to the characterization of the action under discussion (though it may well be fully adequate to all the purposes at issue).

To begin with, it should be remarked that this limitless polyadicity does not pertain in any specifically characteristic way to actions as such, but rather to *descriptions* in general. In describing anything whatever, we can always provide endlessly greater detail about its specific features and its relations to other things. Completeness in description is never possible. This inherent incompleteness of descriptions in general will also pertain to the descriptions of actions in particular. But this does not reveal any inevitable incompleteness specific to act characterization as such. Nor does it militate against the principal finding of our present discussion—that action descriptions can be analyzed into specifications at varying levels of detail of answers to a manageably small number of questions about different aspects of action.

If our survey of the descriptive aspects of an action is at all adequate, it provides a resolution of this problem. For our discussion indicates that, while the description of an action can indeed be elaborated more and more (perhaps indefinitely so), this can be viewed as the increasingly detailed specification of a limited and

---

[12] London: Routledge & Kegan Paul Ltd., 1963.
[13] *Ibid.,* p. 160.

manageable number of distinctive characteristic aspects of action. Indeed, actions appear to have only a rather small number of basic *dimensions,* representing the diverse avenues along which the various fundamental aspects of action can be explored. No doubt, greater detail can always (endlessly) be developed with respect to each of these: but this does not contravene the inherent finitude of the variety of such aspects themselves.[14]

[14] This essay is an expanded version of my note on "Aspects of Action" in *The Logic of Decision and Action,* ed. N. Rescher (Pittsburgh: University of Pittsburgh Press, 1967), pp. 215–219.

THE EPISTEMIC-MODEL APPROACH

BASIC ACTIONS

Arthur C. Danto

"Well, why should we want to know?" said Verity, giving a yawn or causing herself to give one.

I. Compton-Burnett, Two Worlds and Their Ways

I

"The man *M* causes the stone *S* to move." This is a very general description of a very familiar sort of episode. It is so general, indeed, that it does not tell us whether or not *M* has performed an action. The description holds in either case; so it *could* have been an action. Without pausing to inquire what further features are required for it definitely to have been an action, let us merely note that *there are* actions that fall under the general description of "causing something to happen." Yet, since this description leaves it unclear whether or not an action has been performed, performing an action cannot be one of the truth conditions for "causing something to happen." And since this description cuts across those two cases, we may assume we are employing the same sense of the expression "causes something to happen" in both. Presumably, we are using "causes" in just the same sense whether we say that the man *M* causes the stone *S* to move *or* we say that the stone *S* causes the pebble *P* to move. If it *is* clear from the latter sentence that an action has *not* been performed, this clarity will be due to certain facts about stones rather than to any difference in the concept of causality. It is commonly

From *American Philosophical Quarterly*, II (April 1965), 141–148. Reprinted by permission of the author and the *American Philosophical Quarterly*.

assumed that stones never perform actions, although men sometimes do. Hence the indefiniteness of our original sentence is not due to any ambiguity in the concept of causality, but rather to certain facts about men, or to certain assumed facts. The concept of causality allows us to ignore differences between men and stones, as well as differences between performing an action and not.

I shall persist in speaking of *individuals* (the man M, the stone S) causing things to happen, even though our concept of causality has been classically analyzed as a relationship between pairs of *events*. According to the classical analysis, the movement of the pebble P is one event, the effect of another event, which I shall, with studied ambiguity, simply designate an S-event, in this case its cause. Comparably, the movement of S in my other example is one event, the effect of another event, similarly and no less ambiguously to be designated an M-event, which is its cause. And this M-event, whether or not it is an action performed by M, is correctly (if rather generally) to be described as *causing something to happen*—namely, the movement of S.

I shall now suppose that my original sentence in fact describes an action performed by M (moving the stone S). Of this particular spatial translation of S we may say three distinct and relevant things: that it is (a) an action, performed by M; that it is (b) something that was *caused* to happen (in this case by M); and that it is (c) the effect of an event distinct from itself (in this case the M-event). That this event can be both (a) and (b) follows from the remarks in the first paragraph. That—disregarding the special information in parentheses—(c) must hold if (b) does—follows from the analysis of causality referred to in the second paragraph. That it is (b) follows, I suppose, from the fact that S is a stone: stones don't *just* start to move without something causing them to move.

We must now look into the M-event itself. Do all three characterizations apply to *it*? This, I fear, cannot be decided without investigation. Let us suppose, however, that the M-event is both (a) and (b), for it might well be. Then it must also be (c), and there must then be yet another event, distinct from it, which is its cause. This may be yet a further M-event, and about it we may raise the same question. It would be rash to claim that we have slid into an infinite regress, damaging or otherwise. But if a given M-event is both (a) and (b) and, hence, (c), then ultimately its being (c) must lead us to a further M-event, which is (a) and *not* (b). And unless some M-events are (a) and not (b), *no* M-events are ever (a). That is, if there are any actions at all, there must be two distinct *kinds* of actions: those performed by an individual M, which he may be said to have *caused* to happen; and those actions, also performed by M, which he cannot be said to have caused to happen. The latter I shall designate as *basic actions*.

In this paper, I shall defend (and explore the consequences of) four theses which I regard as fundamental to the theory of action:

(1) If there are any actions at all, there are basic actions.
(2) There are basic actions.
(3) Not every action is a basic action.[1]

[1] Thesis (3) is explored in detail in my paper, "What We Can Do," *The Journal of Philosophy,* vol. 60 (July, 1963), pp. 435–445.

(4) If *a* is an action performed by *M*, then either *a* is a basic action of *M*, or else it is the effect of a chain of causes the originating member of which is a basic action of *M*.

I wish first to make quite clear the sense in which an individual does not cause his basic actions to happen. When an individual *M* performs a basic action *a*, there is no event distinct from *a* that both stands to *a* as cause to effect *and* is an action performed by *M*. So when *M* performs a basic action, he does nothing first that causes it to happen. It will be convenient to consider two possible objections to this.

It may be objected, first, that there are or may be other senses of "causes" than the sense mentioned above, in accordance with which it would be proper to say that *M* causes his basic actions to happen. Thus, *if* raising an arm were an instance of a basic action, an individual who does this might still be said to cause it to happen in some sense of "cause" other than the sense that I reject in application to basic actions. I accept this objection: there *may be* such other senses of "cause." But (i) we should still require exactly the same distinction that I am urging within the class of actions, and I should therefore be defending the *verbally* distinct thesis that unless there were actions an individual causes to happen in this *new* sense, there would be no actions he caused to happen in the original sense, either. So, unless there were actions of the former sort, causing a stone to move would, for example, never be an *action* that anyone performed (although men might still cause stones to move, since performing an action is not a truth-condition for "causing something to happen"). And (ii) this new sense of "cause" would *not* apply *whether or not* an action had been performed. It should, indeed, be absolutely clear from the sentence "*M* caused *a* to happen"—using this special sense of "cause"—that *M* had performed an action. Those who find it convenient to maintain that the concept of causality is invariant to the distinction between performing an action and not, would have as little use for this new sense of "cause" as I do. Neither they nor I would want to say that *stones* cause *anything* to happen in this new sense of "cause." Not that I wish to restrict the performance of basic actions to men alone. Other individuals may, for all I know, perform them as well. Some theologians have spoken as though everything done by God were a basic action. This would prohibit us, of course, from saying that God caused anything to happen (the making of the Universe would be a basic action). And, for reasons which will soon emerge, this would make the ways of God inscrutable indeed.

It may be objected, second, that if we take the absence of a cause to be the distinguishing mark of a basic action, then we must class as basic actions a great many events that we should be disinclined, on other grounds, to accept as actions at all, e.g., the uniform rectilinear motion of an isolated particle, or perhaps any instance of radioactive decay. This objection is readily deflected. I have not claimed that basic actions are not caused, but only that a man performing one does not cause it by performing some other action that stands to it as cause to effect. Moreover, the absence of a cause would not be a sufficient criterion for a basic action, even if basic actions *were* uncaused. It would serve only to mark off a special class of actions from the rest. Of course, only what is already an action can be a *basic* action. And I have not so much as tried to say what are the general criteria for actions.

II

I have avoided citing unconditional instances of basic actions, in part because any expression I might use, e.g., "moving a limb," could also be used to designate something that was caused to happen, or something that was not an action, much less a basic one. I think there is nothing that is always and in each of its instances an unmistakably basic action. This is reflected by language in the fact that from the bare description "*M*'s limb moved," for example, one could not tell whether *M* had performed a basic action or even an action. Nor could one tell this by observing only the motion of the limb without bringing in differentiating contextual features. I have accordingly contented myself with the neutral expression "*M*-event," declaring it to be a basic action when I required an instance.

Now I wish to specify some of the differentiating contextual features, and I shall consider four distinct cases, all of which might indifferently be covered by the same description, so that the description alone leaves it unclear whether an action has been performed or not. Of the four cases, three *(C-1, C-2, C-4)* will indeed be actions, and of these one *(C-4)* will be a basic action. The four cases together might be termed a *declension* of the description. Not every such description admits of the full declension, for some appear never to be exemplified as basic actions at all. "Moving a stone," I should think, never, or not ordinarily, is exemplified as a basic action, though we have seen that it may be exemplified by an action. I want to begin with a deliberately controversial example and shall decline the expression "*M* laughs."

C-1. *M* causes himself to laugh. I am thinking here of cases where someone does something to make himself laugh, and does not simply laugh because of something he happens to do. Thus I may do something ridiculous and laugh because I find it so, but I did not do this ridiculous thing in order to make myself laugh. Again, I sniff a cartridge of nitrous oxide, not knowing it to be nitrous oxide, but just to find out what it is. But, since it is nitrous oxide, I laugh, though I did not sniff to make myself laugh. I wish to include only cases where I do something ridiculous or sniff from a private cartridge of nitrous oxide *in order to* laugh, perhaps because I think laughter good for the liver or because I just enjoy laughing and cannot always wait for someone or something to come along and cause me to laugh. I definitely want to exclude a comedian who laughs at some reruns of his antic films (unless he had them rerun for this special purpose), and definitely want to include someone who deliberately engages in auto-titillation to excite spasmodic laughter. Doubtless, episodes falling under *C-1* are rare in normal adults in our culture, but this is irrelevant. Also irrelevant is the fact that people don't laugh *at* the nitrous oxide they sniff, though they do laugh at the silly faces they pull, for their own delectation, in mirrors.

C-2. Someone or something other than *M* causes *M* to laugh. This is the typical case for adults and children in our culture. It is for my purposes again irrelevant whether the cause of *M*'s laughter is also its object, or whether it has an object at all (as it does not if he is tickled or submitted to nitrous oxide). Similarly, it is irrelevant whether, in case someone causes *M* to laugh, the former has performed an action or not, whether, that is, he did what he did in order to make M laugh. For it is what M does that uniquely concerns us here.

C-3. M **suffers a nervous disorder symptomized by spasmodic laughter.** This is comparable, say, to a tic: M laughs unpredictably, and for "no reason." Such laughter is mirthless, of course, but so are some instances falling under the two first cases. It may be argued that the entire case falls under *C-2*, and that in identifying it as the symptom of a nervous disorder, I have marked off a class of causes for M's laughter. Still, the case requires special consideration, in that M's laughing here is never an action, whereas his laughter under *C-2* sometimes *is*.

C-4. M **has the true power of laughing.** By this I mean that M laughs when he wants to without (in contrast with *C-1*) having to cause himself to laugh; without (in contrast with *C-2*) someone or something having to cause him to laugh; without, finally, as in *C-3*, suffering from the relevant nervous disorder. This does not mean that M is normal, but only that his abnormality is of a benign sort; i.e., it is by way of a gift. His laughing may have an object: he may, when he wishes, direct a stream of laughter at whom or what he chooses, without the chosen object ever being a *cause* of his laughing.

Instances falling under *C-4* are perhaps rare, but these alone would qualify as basic actions performed by M when "M laughs" is true. I have identified the case not so much by specifying what differentiating contextual features must be present, but by specifying what differentiating contextual features must be *absent*. Notice that M's laughing here differs markedly from the ability most of us have of making laugh-like noises, e.g., for the sake of politeness, or to save our reputation for seeing a joke when we don't see it, or to play a mocker's role in an amateur theatrical. Most of us can pretend so to laugh: but I speak here of laughing, not of "laughing."

I want now to comment on these four cases.

When M laughs under *C-1*, we may say of his laughing three distinct things: that it is (a) an action of M's; that it is (b) something that M causes to happen; and that it is (c) the effect of some event, distinct from itself (an M-event) which is its cause. M's laughing here is an action in just the same sense in which his causing a stone to move is an action. Causing himself to laugh is the action he performed, though of course the description "M caused himself to laugh" leaves it unclear, as in the case of the stone, whether he performed an action at all. One could mark that difference only by bringing in the general differentiating features of action.

In *C-2*, M does not cause himself to laugh, and one may find reasons for balking at the claim that his laughing, in such a case, is an action of his at all. For consider this argument. When M causes a stone S to move, we may agree that the action is M's. But we reject the claim that it is an action of S's. So parity suggests that when someone moves M to laughter, this may be an action performed by the former, but not an action of M's.

What I must do is to show that parity is inoperative, and so justify my claim that instances of *C-2* are actions in contrast with instances of *C-3*. Well, I shall somewhat artificially suggest that M's action here requires this description: what he does is to *not not laugh*. The double negative is not, in the language of action, a triviality. Logically, of course, the double negative of a proposition is just that proposition, and from a strictly logical point of view, we could say the same thing, albeit more awkwardly, with "The man M causes the stone S to not not move" as we straightforwardly say with "The man M caused the stone S to move." I wish, in fact, to retain that regular inferential feature of double negation which allows us to proceed from not not A to A, but for the case of action I wish to exclude the reverse inference. For my double negative marks the case of *negligence,* and whether a negligence is to be ascribed to someone is a case for independent investigation. So, pending such investigation, we cannot say, on the basis of knowing that a man laughs, that he is to be charged with negligence. And for this reason we cannot automatically go from "laughs" to "not not laughs." Indeed, since we don't ascribe negligence to stones, it would be invalid, given my convention, to proceed from "the stone moves" to "the stone not not moves."

Do we quite want to say, then, that C-2 is to be restated thus: *Someone or something other than M causes M to not not laugh?* Perhaps we would, in spite of flaunting usage. What we would be saying, however, is only this: that M was excited to laugh and did nothing to inhibit his laughter. And it is our common assumption that men are normally capable of doing something which, in effect, stops the flow of laughter from issuing forth in, say, public guffaws. Whether men are called upon to exercise these inhibitory practices varies from context to context: in the music hall there is license to suspend them, to "let oneself go," but at High Mass there is not. It is in such contexts only that laughter is *pronounced* a negligence, but blaming, surely, does not make of something an action when it would not otherwise have been so. It is only insofar as something is an action already that blaming it, or blaming someone for doing it, is appropriate.

With regard to C-3, however, the laugher stands liable to no special charge of negligence: his laughing fails to be a case of not not laughing, for identification of it as a nervous disorder, or in the syndrome of one, locates it beyond the control of the man who is so afflicted. It is, indeed, almost a paradigm case of this: like a hiccough. One *might* blame the man for being in a place where his symptom, easily mistakable as a negligence, might break out unpredictably. Or we might blame him again for a kind of negligence in "not doing something about it," viz., going to a nerve specialist, assuming there is a known cure. At all events, it is plain enough why C-3 differs from C-2. The critical issue, of course, is the matter of *control,* and this brings us to C-4. And the rest of this paper is by way of a comment on C-4.

Most readers, I think, will resist the suggestion that C-4 is a case of action. There is good reason for this. For most of us, laughing as a *basic action* is unintelligible. I shall hope to show why this is so, and showing it will involve a demonstration of thesis (2). Meanwhile, the reader might ponder the precise analogue to this in the case of *moving an arm,* which admits of a full declension. Thus C-1: M causes his arm to move, i.e., by striking it with his other arm; C-2: someone or something other than M causes M's arm to move, e.g., by striking it; C-3: M suffers from a nervous disorder, so his arm moves spasmodically and unpredictably, as a kind of tic; and C-4: M moves his arm without suffering from a nervous disorder, without someone or something causing it to move, without having to do anything to cause it to move. Here, I am certain, C-4 is the *typical* case. Moving an arm is one of the standard basic actions. If we now seek to determine in what way this behavior *is* intelligible, we should have no great difficulty in seeing why laughing under C-4 is *not.*

III

Suppose now that moving a stone is an action performed by M. It is difficult to suppose that *moving a stone* admits of a full declension, largely because it seems to lack cases for C-3 and C-4. In fact there are difficulties in finding instances for C-1 and C-2 unless we change the sense of possession (M's arm, M's stone) from philosophical to legal ownership. But for the moment I shall be concerned only with the fact that we move stones only by causing them to move. This then means that, in order to cause the motion of the stone, something else must be done, or must happen, which is an event distinct from the motion of the stone, and which stands to it as cause to effect. Now this other event may or may not be a basic action of M's. But if it is not, and if it remains nevertheless true that moving the stone *is* an action of his, then there must be something else that M does, which causes something to happen which in turn causes the motion of the stone. And *this* may be a basic action or it may not. But now this goes on forever unless, at some point, a basic action is performed by M. For suppose every action were a case of the agent causing something to happen. This means, each time he does a, he must independently do b, which causes a to happen. But then, in order to do b, he must first independently do c, which causes b to happen. . . . This quickly entails that the agent could perform no action at all. If, accordingly, there are any actions at all of the sort described by "causing something to happen," there must be actions which are *not* caused to happen by the man who performs them. And these are basic actions.

But this argument is perfectly general. If there are any actions at all, there are basic actions. This is a proof of thesis (1). Moreover, if M performs an action describable by "causing something to happen," he must also, as part of what he does, perform an action that he does not cause to happen. And this is a proof of thesis (4). It would be a proof of thesis (2) if in fact there were actions described as "causing something to happen." This would then require us to accept thesis (3) as true: for such an action would not be a basic action, and so not every action is basic.

I do not wish to suggest, however, that the only proof we are entitled to, for the existence of basic actions, is by way of a transcendental deduction, for I believe we all know, in a direct and intuitive way, that there are basic actions, and which actions are basic ones. To show that we do know this will clarify one of the ways in which laughing is a controversial instance of a basic action.

I must make a few preliminary remarks. First, every *normal person* has just the same *repertoire R* of basic actions, and having R is what defines a normal person for the theory of action. Second, persons may be *positively abnormal* when their repertoire of basic actions includes actions not included in R, and may be *negatively abnormal* when actions included in R are not included in their repertoire. Some persons may be both positively and negatively abnormal, e.g., someone who laughs as a basic action but who is paralyzed in one arm. If someone's repertoire is empty, he is capable of no basic actions, and hence of no actions. Such a deprived entity is a *pure patient*, e.g., like a stone. Plainly, our repertoire of actions is greater than our repertoire of basic actions, though a being who performed every possible action and all of whose actions were basic actions may be conceived of: such a being would be a *pure agent*. For the present, however, I am concerned with beings intermediate between pure patients and pure agents, and I want now to say that basic actions are *given* to such beings in two distinct senses, each of which bears a definite analogy to a sense that the term has in the theory of knowledge.[2]

(i) In the theory of knowledge, to say that p is *given* is in part to point a contrast: one is saying that p is not inferred from some other proposition. Analogously, when I speak of an action as given, I shall mean to say, in effect, that it is a basic action, and point a contrast with actions we *cause* to happen. The notion of givenness is understood this way: p is a starting point for an inference to another and (commonly) different proposition q for which p provides at least part of the evidence. Analogously, an action a, if a basic action, is a starting point for the performance of another action b, of which it is at least part of the cause. "Is caused by" and "is inferred from" are analogous relations in the theories of knowledge and of action, respectively.

(ii) It has been argued that the distinction between *basic sentences* and sentences of other kinds is not ultimate, that a sentence which, in one context, is indeed a starting point for an inference to another, may, in a different context, itself be inferred to, and hence an end point in an inference.[3] Analogously, an action a may, in one context, be a starting point and basic, while it may be caused to happen in a different one. There is some justice in this latter claim: as we have seen, one cannot tell from the bare description "moving an arm" whether a basic action is referred to, or even an action. But, thinking now of sentences, perhaps some restriction can be put on the *kind* of sentence which can be given in sense (i). If p is given in one context and inferred in another, there might nevertheless be sentences which are never basic and always are inferred. And a corresponding restriction might hold in the theory of action: even if any action that is ever basic might, under a sufficiently general description, be caused to happen in another context, there might be actions that never are basic under any description. In the theory of knowledge, one such restriction is often defended, namely that basic sentences are those and only those which can be conclusively verified by sense experience, and that no other kind of sentence ever can be given. But within the class of potentially given sentences, a division might be made along the customary lines of sense-modality, i.e., those verified by seeing, or by audition, or by touch, etc. We might then define an *epistemically* normal person as one who experiences in all modes. A negatively abnormal person would then be deficient in at least one such mode, e.g., is blind; and a positively abnormal person then experiences in

---

[2] The analogy between theory of knowledge and theory of action runs very deep indeed, almost as though they were isomorphic models for some calculus. Obviously, there are things we can say about actions that do not hold for cognitions, etc., but this means very little. Suppose we have two models M-*i* and M-*j* for a calculus C, and suppose that "star" plays in the same role in M-*i* that "book" plays in M-*j*. It is hardly an argument against their both being models for C that we don't print stars or that books are not centers of solar systems. I shall use theory-of-knowledge features as a guide for structuring the theory of action. When the analogy gives way, it will be interesting to see why it does.

[3] Though not always without some awkwardness. Suppose it were held that only sentences can be given which have the form of first-person reports of sense-experience, e.g., "I now see a reddish x . . ." Such a sentence is not easily rendered as the conclusion of an inference, though it can be so rendered, I suppose, if I both knew that something x had an unmistakable taste and that whatever has this taste is red. Then, by tasting x and seeing only its silhouette, I might feel secure in inferring that I was seeing a reddish x. Of course there are philosophically crucial senses of "see" which would rule this out, and make it, indeed, self-contradictory to say both "I see a reddish x" and "I see the black silhouette of x."

some mode outside the normal repertoire, e.g., has some "sixth sense." The analogy to the theory of action is obvious. But by means of it we may introduce our second sense of given: the normal modes of experience are "given" in the sense that they constitute the standard cognitive equipment. The normal person has various classes of starting points for inferences as he has various classes of starting points for actions. These are given in the sense that they are not for the most part *acquired*. Thus we speak of the "gift of sight," etc. This does not mean that there need be any sentences in the superstructure to which a negatively abnormal person might not infer: he is deficient only at the base: and then not *totally* deficient (or if he is, then he cannot have any empirical knowledge, is *cognitively impotent*). And similarly, *toutes proportions gardées*, with the negatively abnormal person as defined in the theory of action.

Now when a blind man says that he can know whether a certain object is red or not, there are two senses or uses of "can" that are compatible with his abnormality. He must mean either that he can *infer* to "x is red" from other sentences or that his case is not medically hopeless, that by means of a cure he may be restored to that state of normality in which such sentences may be known by him directly and not, as it were, *merely* by means of inference. Yet there is a true and in fact an *analytic* sense in which a blind man cannot know whether a certain object is red, nor, on certain accounts of meaning, so much as know what such a sentence *means* (the non-analytic senses are usually false). The situation of a *paralyzed* man is perfectly analogous. When he sincerely says that he can move his arm, he must mean either that he can *cause* it to move, or that his situation is not medically hopeless. But, in again a true and an analytical sense, he cannot move his arm and does not know, does not so much as understand, what it means to move his arm in the way in which a normal person understands this. For this is the kind of understanding that is alone given to those who have the power to move their arms in the normal, basic way. This kind of understanding cannot so much as be conveyed to a negatively abnormal person while he is so.

Some of the chief difficulties philosophers have encountered in the theory of action are due to their having approached it from the point of view of the negatively abnormal. From *that* point of view, basic action is hopelessly mysterious. There is, however, perhaps no better way of eliciting the quality of our knowledge of these things than to think of endeavoring to remove the mysteriousness surrounding these actions in the thwarted comprehension of the negatively abnormal person. We may achieve some sympathy for his plight by imagining *ourselves* similarly confronting someone who is *positively* abnormal, who can perform, as a basic action, what we at best can cause to happen, and then asking *him* to give us an understanding of his gift. The fact is that we cannot explain to the negatively abnormal, nor can the positively abnormal person explain to us, the way in which the basic action is performed (and this must be appreciated in the same way as the impossibility of explaining to a blind man what red literally looks like, or, if you wish, of our understanding what ultra-violet literally looks like). Suppose—just to take one case—a paralytic asks us what we do *first* when we raise an arm. We should be obliged to say we cannot answer, not because we do not know or understand what we do, but because we know and understand that there is *nothing* we do first. There is no series of steps we must run through, and since the request is implicitly for a *recipe*, we cannot say how we move our arm. A basic action is perfectly simple in the same sense in which the old "simple ideas" were said to be: they were not compounded out of anything more elementary than themselves, but were instead the ultimately simple elements out of which other ideas were compounded.

In one sense, then, we do, and in another we do not, know how we move an arm. But the sense in which we do not know is inappropriate. It is that sense which requires an *account,* and our incapacity for giving any such account is what has induced puzzlement, among philosophers and others, concerning the moving of an arm (and other basic acts generally). But this puzzlement should be dissipated upon the recognition that we have made a grammatical mistake in the inflected language of action. We have taken "moving an arm" as always a case of *C-1,* when *in fact C-4* is the standard case for normal persons moving normal arms normally. But having once committed this mistake, we look for a cause that is not there. And failing to find what we ought never to have expected to find, we complain that we do not know how we do move our arms. But of course we know. It is only that we cannot explain the manner of its doing. For there is no action, distinct from the action itself, to be put into the *explanans.* This is due to what I am terming the *givenness* of basic actions. Reference to basic actions belongs in the explanantia for explaining how things are done. So the paralytic, as long as he remains one, cannot understand: *Just raising the arm is what we do first.*

IV

A paralytic might think there is some *effort* he is not putting forth, by which, if he did or could put it forth, he might as a consequence move his arm. But I want to say that he cannot try to move his arm if moving his arm is not already in his repertoire of basic actions. So in a sense he is right. If he could make the required effort, he could move his arm. But he cannot make that effort, cannot try, for he cannot in the only appropriate sense move his arm.

Consider the analogous situation with someone epistemically abnormal, say a deaf man. To ask a deaf man to try to hear a certain sound is rendered inappropriate by the fact that he is deaf. To try to hear, say, faint and distant music is to make an effortful listening. Only those who can already hear can make this effort. And what would count as trying (listening) in the deaf man's case? He could cup his ear, could place his ear to the ground, could contort his face and close his eyes. All this, however, is the pantomime of listening. Had he grinned or wagged a finger, it would have been as helpful. For there is no one thing that is better than any other in his situation. It is exactly this way with trying to move an arm. It is appropriate only to ask someone to try to move his arm when something externally inhibits normal movement, e.g., the arms are pinioned, and cannot be moved *freely* and *without effort.* But the paralytic cannot move his arm at all.

Consider these cases:

(*a*) I am a normal person who has swallowed a drug which gradually takes away the power to move an arm, rendering me, so long as it is in full effect, negatively abnormal. I make tests at five-minute intervals. It gets harder and harder to move my arm. And then I reach a point where I cannot move my arm and cannot *try* to. I have lost the power of trying, together with the power for doing.

(*b*) Someone thinks it would be spectacular to be able to extend and retract his fingernails, the way a cat does with its claws. We tell him it cannot be done, and he retorts that no one has ever tried, and he means to try. But in what should his trying consist? He could shake his fingers hard, could order them to extend, could pray, or could draw his soul up into a vast single wish. There is no rational way, for there is no way at all for a normal person. I don't mean that no one is or ever will be able to move his nails and to try to move them (e.g., with tight gloves on). If a man were prepared to suffer some sort of surgery, he might be able to cause his nails to go in and out, but we had not understood that he meant this by "trying." It is after all not the way cats do it. It is more the way we move a loose tooth.

(c) I am a normal person, challenged to move a normal stone. I take the challenge to imply the stone is not normal—perhaps it has some incredible density, or is fixed to a shaft driven deeply into the earth. But I decide to try, and the stone moves quite easily, having been a normal stone all along. So I conclude that the challenge was not normal. It turns out I was being asked to move the stone "the way I move my arm." But this is not something I even can try to do. I can, with ridiculous ease, cause the stone to move. So I can try to cause it to move as well. But I cannot try to move it as a basic action—that would be a proper encounter with nothingness.

One can do with effort only what one can do effortlessly; and "trying," the effort of will, is not something apart from the action that stands to it as cause to effect. It is the required action already being performed in untoward circumstances. Doing something with effort is not doing two things, any more than doing something gracefully is doing two things. Moving an arm is not then the result of an act of will: it *is* an act of will. But to speak of an act of will when the going is smooth is to behave a little like the dypsomaniac who wants to know what sorts of pink rats ordinary people see.[4]

It should be plain now why laughing, if performed as a basic action, is controversial. It is because whoever could so laugh would be positively abnormal, and we cannot understand what he does. In relation to him, we are in just the same position as the paralytic in relation to us. We lack a kind of gift.

V

It is easy enough to sympathize with those who feel an action is not intelligible unless we can find a causal picture for it. But this is only because they have taken intelligibility to consist in having a causal picture. Dominated by this requirement, they may tend to invent some such picture, populating their inner selves with entities whose job it is to serve the automotive functions demanded by the causal model of intelligibility. But I am asking that we do not strain, and that we use the causal model only where it is natural to use it.

That there are actions, like moving an arm, which do not really require any other action as cause (and so no "inner" action as a cause) entails, I believe, no refutation of dualism. For all the distinctions I am thinking of are reproduced within the mental world, and cut across the distinction between body and mind.

[4] It is not difficult to see why it should be thought that there are two distinct things in the case of trying. It is because we often speak of trying and failing. So, if we can try and also succeed, trying is one thing and succeeding is another. And if succeeding consists in raising an arm, *trying* here must be something different, since failing consists in *not*-raising one's arm, and trying then could hardly consist in raising it. But this is not the important sense of the word for the theory of action.

If, for instance, we take the description "*M* images *I*" where *I* is a mental image, then it is unclear, as it was in the case of "laughing" or "moves an arm," whether *M* has performed an action or not, or, if an action, then a basic action or not. The whole declension works for, *C-1*: *M* may cause an image to appear in his mind, perhaps by taking a drug; *C-2*: Someone or something other than *M* may cause an image to appear in *M*'s mind; *C-3*: *M* is haunted by an image which appears spontaneously, recurrently, and unpredictably—a symptom, of perhaps a psychic disorder; and *C-4*: *M* simply produces an image, as I and all those with the requisite alpha rhythms are able to do, i.e., as a basic action.[5]

I shall not press for a full parity, though I *am* prepared to defend the view that there is a problem of Other Bodies precisely analogous to the problem of Other Minds. All I wish to emphasize is that, whatever disparities there may be between the concept of mind and the concept of body, men may be said to act mentally in much the same way that they may be said to act physically. Among the things I take Descartes to have meant when he said that we are not in our bodies the way a pilot is in a ship, is that we do not always do things, as pilots must with ships, by causing them to happen. We do not turn, as it were, an inner wheel in order, through some elaborate transmission of impulse, to cause an external rudder to shift and, by so doing, get our boat to turn. We act directly. But then neither am I in my *mind* the way a pilot is in a ship. Or rather, I sometimes cause things to happen with my body and with my mind, and I sometimes just act with them directly, as when I perform basic actions. It is best, however, to avoid similes. Any philosophical problems we have with ourselves would only reappear in connection with anything sufficiently similar to us to be a suitable analogue. But if we find ourselves unintelligible, nothing sufficiently similar to us to be helpful is likely to be more clear.

[5] But I am not sure whether we are positively abnormal, or those who have no images are negatively abnormal.

THE TELEOLOGICAL APPROACH

THOUGHT AND PURPOSE

Richard Taylor

It was once fairly common for philosophers to set forth what were somewhat grandly referred to as "the categories," sometimes arranged in neat tables. One finds them in Aristotle and Kant, for example, and it has always puzzled me just what they were supposed to be, or what they were supposed to show.

I am going to begin by proposing a small table of categories of my own, however, for it seems to me such a table can be constructed which does indeed show something. These are not exactly categories in the traditional sense, to be sure, for they are not mutually exclusive. Indeed, it is the manner in which they overlap each other that gives them their significance. They do seem to be categories in the sense employed by Aristotle, however, for they seem to be very basic concepts that are presupposed in our understanding of nature. They are basic, in the sense that they are not reducible to anything more simple, nor to each other. My table of them is as follows:

     I. Existence and nonexistence (being).
    II. Motion and rest (change).
   III. Cause and effect (causation).
   IV. Action and passion (agency).
    V. Means and ends (purpose).

From "Thought and Purpose" by Richard Taylor, also published in *Inquiry*, II, no. 2 (1969), Universitetsforlaget, Oslo, Norway.

Now each of these is, I believe, presupposed in our understanding of nature, including, of course, human nature. This is obvious in the case of the first two, a little less obvious in the case of the third, and much less obvious in the case of the remaining two. But, I shall maintain—and this is the first point of what follows—that none of the concepts in this list can be reduced to any appearing above it. Hence, while the table may not be complete—and no claim is made that it is—it would be demonstrably incomplete if any item on it were omitted. All of these concepts are presupposed in our understanding of nature.

Putting the matter more generally, it is obvious that men do interpret certain things—certain items of human behavior, for example—as exemplifying the concept of means and ends, or purpose, or goal-directedness. Now in case such things can be construed as merely exemplifying the concept of cause and effect, as has often been tried, or of action and passion, which has also often been tried, then the fifth of my categories would be clearly superfluous, since these other concepts appear above it on my list. If, on the other hand, there are items of nature which cannot be understood except in terms of means and ends, and such interpretations cannot then be reformulated in terms of the other categories on my list, then we shall have to regard the concept of means and ends as a basic category, along with the others. And I mean to show that just this is the case; that is, that the concept of means and ends is a category, in the sense explained.

The second and not really subordinate point of my discussion will be to show that all five categories apply in the realm of thought as well as in the realm of behavior. This is fairly obvious in the cases of the first three, provided we interpret "motion" in the Aristotelian way, as meaning simply *change*, rather than as meaning the more specific sort of change which he called *local* motion (locomotion), or change of place (locus). That is, it is never questioned that change occurs in human thinking, or that some of these changes are related as causes and effects. It has been a matter of much dispute, however, whether such changes can ever be truly represented as *actions*—i.e., whether there are such things as *mental acts,* in any sense that cannot be interpreted simply as cause and effect. And it is, of course, even more disputable whether the concept of means and ends is essential to understanding thought. Indeed, in some circles the very suggestion would be dismissed as heresy, and I believe most philosophers would deem it, at best, a curious suggestion. I nevertheless propose to show that the concept of means and ends, as well as that of action and passion, is presupposed in our understanding not only of behavior, but of thought as well, and that neither of these concepts is reducible to anything else on my list.

If I am right in all this, then the consequences are fairly significant. Over vast areas of inquiry, usually denominated "scientific," it is deemed bad enough to have to speak of causation, which is, I think rightly, thought to be a metaphysical notion. But I think it would not be unfair to say that throughout virtually the whole realm of empirical psychology and, indeed, throughout most of the anthropological sciences, the notions of agency and purpose, considered as basic categories of understanding, irreducible to any others, are considered to be not only foreign to scientific understanding, but positively opposed to it. I do not know why this attitude should prevail, but it does. If, however, what I am maintaining is correct—namely, that all five of these concepts *are* categories—then it of course would follow that any attempt to understand human nature without all of them is certain to fail, in the sense that it will inevitably leave something out. For to say they are categories is to say that they are essential to our understanding of nature, and in particular, human nature, and that none is reducible to any of the others.

Being.   Parmenides and his disciples are perhaps the only philosophers who ever attempted to abolish all of these categories except the first, refusing to admit even the reality of change. Change, Parmenides seems to have thought, is but an illusion, nonexistent in nature, and he considered the true conception of nature to be simply *being,* understood as a vast, eternal and changeless plenum.

We need not, I think, consider any counterarguments to this. I mention Parmenides here only to illustrate the eagerness philosophers have always felt to reduce the concepts on my list to simpler ones appearing above them, and this philosopher seems to have thought that all could be dispensed with except the first. Gorgias, I believe, went even one step farther, maintaining that nothing exists, or that even my first category is not needed for an understanding of nature; but he was doubtless facetious in this, and it is in any case not worthy of consideration.

Causation.   It is a simplification but not, I think, a gross one to say that Hume tried to reduce the third of my categories (causation) to the second (change). The attempt has been made many times by those who are inspired by Hume's approach to things. What we take to be a relation of causation between changes, involving, as Hume never doubted, the element of necessity, compulsion, or making something happen, is, it is often claimed, really only an invariance or constancy in the joint occurrence of certain kinds of changes. It involves nothing metaphysical.

I shall not attempt to refute this familiar philosophical view, or even to set it forth beyond the bare adumbration just given. I have done this elsewhere, and so have many others. Here we need only to note the nature of the difficulty involved in it, and what it suggests. The difficulty is, that whenever causation is analyzed in terms of relationships involving no element of compulsion or unavoidability, then it seems always possible to *arrange* that certain changes should be related in the manner suggested—for example, that they should be invariably conjoined, and so on—even though they are manifestly not causally related. This of course suggests that causation is a category not reducible to anything more simple, or in other words, that in describing certain changes as causally related, one is asserting *more* than a constancy or invariance of changes of that kind. Of course the "more" that one is asserting is that causes render their effects unavoidable, or in some sense "make" them occur. And this amounts to saying that some changes are sometimes the causes of others, in a sense according to which causation is a category, as I am using the term.

Agency.   Much of modern thought, more or less beginning with Descartes and Spinoza, has involved the attempt to reduce agency to causation, that is, to reduce the fourth of my categories to the third, and thus eliminate it as a category. Indeed, it is today still widely taken for granted that this has been done, that to describe an event as a man's *action* is merely to assert that the event was *caused* in a certain way—say, by the man's "volition" or whatnot. Descartes himself maintained that whether something is regarded as an action or a passion merely depends on how we look at it. All that is actually present, in any alleged action, is cause and effect.

The original notions of action (or activity) and passion (or passivity) are quite readily understood in terms of examples. Thus, if one man lifts another off his feet, the first acts, and the second is acted upon. The second man is a passive subject of change, and the change he undergoes is accordingly called a passion. The same idea is expressed by saying that the first man is an agent, the second a patient, or that the first man does something, and the second suffers something. Similarly, if a man speaks, his speaking is an action, whereas another's hearing those spoken sounds is a passion. Of course the word "passion" has now been corrupted, and is often applied to all sorts of feelings, whether they are passively suffered or not, but it is significant to note that these are usually thought of as feelings whose causes lie outside one's own agency and beyond his control.

Now until quite recently in philosophy it was more or less generally assumed that a man's actions are simply instances of his bodily behavior having rather special causes within himself, that is to say, bodily changes caused by his volitions, motives, choices, decisions, and whatnot. Thus, to speak of the upward motion of a man's arm as that man's action was thought to mean only that his arm was caused to rise by his volition, choice, or decision to raise it. Action, accordingly, was thought to be only a special instance of cause and effect.

Any such view amounts, of course, to the reduction of my fourth category to the third, thus eliminating the fourth as a category. I shall not attempt to refute this view, either, or even to state it with any precision or thoroughness, for I have done this elsewhere, and so have many others. I shall instead simply note what appears to be its chief difficulty; namely, that what is alleged to be a cause in such cases cannot be described in any meaningful way. More precisely, the alleged *cause* of any instance of behavior that is called an action cannot, it seems, be described except in terms of that behavior itself which is supposed to be its effect. If, for example, one asserts that a man's arm is caused to rise by his own volition to raise it, then it seems impossible to give any kind of description of that volition other than saying that it is an arm-raising volition. If, however, there actually *is* such a change, serving as the cause of one's arm rising, then there must be some way of describing it which will distinguish it from other volitions, such as the volition to raise one's foot. But there is no such description. And it seems, accordingly, that there was nothing there to describe. The alleged "cause" turns out to be only the invention of philosophy, an invention born of the very effort to reduce agency to simple causation. The same remarks apply, of course, to any other inner changes that are proposed as the causes of bodily behavior, such as decisions, choices, and whatnot. Either such inner changes actually occur, and do cause such behavior (as inner fear causes visible perspiration), and can be at least rudimentarily described independently of their effects, in which case we are dealing, not with action, but with simple cause and effect; or else there is no reason to suppose that any such inner change even occurs, since no description of it can be given independently of its alleged effect. In that case we may indeed be dealing with actions, but not, evidently, with causes and effects.

Purpose. The attempts to reduce the last of my categories to the fourth are legendary. In fact it is quite generally supposed, even in philosophy, that the concept of purpose is no category at all, that it is not a concept, irreducible to any other, necessary for understanding human nature. In the sciences I think it is fair to say that this is simply taken for granted—so much so, indeed, that any attempt to introduce the concept of purpose, even into psychology, is met with hostility. The concept of purpose or, what is the same thing, final causes, is thought to be archaic at best, and at worst, unscientific.

I believe that recent philosophy has fairly well shown that the concept of *agency* is necessary for the understanding of human behavior. And if this is really true, then it of course follows that there can be no far-reaching science of human behavior which refuses to utilize that concept. I further believe, however, that the concept of *purpose* is equally necessary for understanding human behavior, and in case this is true, then we shall get a similar result. But even philosophers are reluctant to take this step. It is bad enough, certainly, that we should need a concept of agency, irreducible to the more familiar idea of causation. But it quite understandably strikes some minds as appalling that we might require, in addition to the concept of agency, a special category of purpose, irreducible to the others in my list. I mean to show, however, that not only is the category of purpose necessary for the understanding of human behavior, but that it is needed for the understanding of thinking as well.

To do this I must go about the thing stepwise. That is, I propose to show, first, that the category of agency applies not only to human behavior, but also to thought; or in other words, that, just as there are overt or observable human actions, so also there are mental acts or, better, that thought is also sometimes an activity, in the same sense that behavior is such. I propose next to show that human behavior is sometimes purposeful, in an irreducible sense. And then, finally, I shall show that, in the very sense that human behavior is sometimes purposeful, so likewise is human thinking.

How the problem of action arises. Consider statements of the following form:

    i. *E* occurs.
    ii. Something makes *E* occur.
    iii. I make *E* occur.
    iv. Something causes me to make *E* occur.

For example, consider these:

    i. My arm rises.
    ii. Something makes my arm rise.
    iii. I raise my arm.
    iv. Something causes me to raise my arm.

Now of course no concept of purpose is involved in any of these statements. That will be introduced later. Here we have only the first four categories on my list.

What is significant about this list of statements is that each entails all those appearing above it, and none entails any of those beneath it. Thus, though it might be true that my arm rises, it does not *follow* (even though we may assume it to be true) that something causes it to rise. It is perfectly possible, though perhaps never true, that this change occurs without any cause whatever. Similarly, though it may be true that something causes my arm to rise, it does not follow that I raise it. It might, for example, be caused to rise by the upward impact of some heavy object, in which case it would be true that something causes it to rise, but not true that I raise it. And finally, though it may be true that I raise my arm, it does not follow (even though some might want to assume it to be true) that anything causes me to raise it. It is perfectly possible, whether in fact it is or is not ever true, that I raise my arm, even though nothing causes me to do so.

If, on the other hand, the fourth statement is true, then it follows that all the others are true, simply because the fourth statement entails all these.

Now certain characteristic philosophical doctrines can be quite aptly illustrated in terms of these entailment relationships. Thus (a) there is a familiar doctrine which amounts to saying that whenever a statement of the first form is true, then the corresponding statement of the second form is true too, even though the first does not entail the second. In other words, in the case of any change, there is a cause of that change. We might call this simply the doctrine of *determinism*, and its denial, *indeterminism*. It is widely thought to be true, but this need not concern us here.

Again, (b) there is a familiar doctrine which amounts to saying that whenever a statement of the second form is true, then the corresponding statement of the third form is true too, even though the second does not entail the third. In other words, if any bodily change occurs in a man, then the man can be properly said to be *doing* the thing in question—raising his arm, digesting his food, perspiring, snoring, falling down, etc. We might appropriately call this doctrine *behaviorism*, and the thing to note is that it *is* a doctrine, and not something that anyone can pretend to have discovered. It is, of course, less widely assumed to be true than the first, particularly in philosophy. The denial of this doctrine is the theory of *agency*.

And finally, (c) there is a doctrine that amounts to saying that whenever any statement of the third form is true, then the corresponding statement of the fourth form is true too, even though the third obviously does not entail the fourth. In other words, whenever a man does anything, then something causes him to do the thing in question. This doctrine is now often called determinism, but it was once more aptly called *fatalism*, construing this as the doctrine that no man can avoid doing whatever he does. And this doctrine (whatever we choose to call it) is of course not generally thought to be true, especially by philosophers. Its denial, often misleadingly called the doctrine of free will, is better called *libertarianism*.

Mental acts.   It is, as noted, the doctrine of human agency that men sometimes perform actions which are not mere items of caused behavior; or, more precisely, that statements of the second form (e.g., "Something makes my arm rise") are sometimes true, when corresponding statements of the third form (e.g., "I raise my arm") are not true. A less precise way of expressing this thesis is to say that statements of the third form, expressive of action, say *more* than the corresponding statements of the second form, which express only causation.

I am not going to set forth any defense of this thesis here, for I have another aim in mind. To me it seems obviously correct, but the defense of it has been abundantly set forth by myself and others elsewhere.

What I shall do instead is assume that this thesis is true, or that there are human actions which are not reducible to behaviors which are not actions, and my purpose now is simply to show that, in case this is true, then the thesis evidently applies to thought as well as to behavior. If agency is a category necessary for the understanding of human behavior, as it seems to be, then it seems also necessary for the understanding of thought. A cruder way to put the point would be to say that if there are human acts, then evidently mental acts should be included among them.

To see this, let us note first some of the various ways a given thought might occur to me. Let us suppose, for example, that the thought in question is some very simple one—say, the name of some person barely known to me whom I am scheduled to lunch with. And let us suppose that the name is "Shilling." Now consider the following:

    i. The thought of the name occurs to me.
    ii. Something causes the thought of the name to occur to me.
    iii. I think the name.
    iv. Something causes me to think the name.

Thus, (i) it might be the case that the name, which I had for days been vainly trying to recall, just comes to mind suddenly, unsought, when I am entirely preoccupied with other things. Or (ii) I might overhear that very name; for example, someone might ask me, "Are you lunching with *Shilling?*" In that case, his utterance of the sound, in my hearing, would simply cause the name to occur to me, even though I was making no effort to recall it. Or (iii) I might think up the name, with considerable effort and no antecedent assurance of success. For example, I might encounter Shilling himself approaching me, and, in the hope of greeting him by name and thus appearing to know him better than I do, try hard to think of his name; and my effort might succeed in the nick of time. Or finally (iv) I might be caused to think up the name, in the sense of being caused to do it, as distinct from having the thought simply inflicted on me as in (ii). A subconscious motivation, for example, might cause me to set myself to trying to remember that name, and I might succeed in the attempt.

Now note that these examples fit exactly the schematism I set forth before; namely,

    i. E occurs.
    ii. Something makes E occur.
    iii. I make E occur.
    iv. Something causes me to make E occur.

Moreover, concerning this array of statement forms, we can say just what was said before. For example, any statement in any of these forms—such as those in my example above—entails all of the corresponding statements above it, and none of those below it. Thus, if anything causes me to try to recall Shilling's name, then, in case I succeed, I do recall it, and something makes it occur to me, and it does occur to me. If, on the other hand, we are given only that the name does occur to me, then it does not follow (though it is doubtless true) that something makes it occur to me. Nor does it follow that I make it occur; it may be that I "think" of it, only in the sense that the thought does somehow occur to me. And finally, even though it may be true that I think of it, as a result, perhaps, of considerable effort of recall, it does not follow that anything causes me to make that effort.

Again, as in the previous case, certain fairly clear philosophical doctrines can be illustrated in terms of these relationships, though the names of such doctrines might be less familiar than the others. Thus, one might affirm that, as a matter of fact, whenever a statement of the first form, using a psychological term such as "thought," is true, then the corresponding statement of the second form is true too, even though the second is not entailed by the first. This doctrine could perhaps be called *mental determinism,* and its denial, the doctrine of *spontaneous thought.* Similarly, one might affirm that, whenever such a statement of the second form is true, then the corresponding statement of the third form is true too, even though the third is not entailed by the second. This could quite aptly be called the doctrine of *association,* and it would amount to saying that all thoughts are caused by other thoughts or by external and internal stimuli. Its denial is, of course, simply the doctrine of *mental acts,* and amounts to asserting that sometimes an agent is the creative source of his own thinking. And finally, one might affirm that, whenever such a statement of the third form is true, the corresponding statement of the fourth form is true too, even without the third entailing the fourth. This would be simply the doctrine of *determinism* or, as I would prefer, *fatalism,* with respect to the realm of thought, for it would amount to saying that no man can avoid thinking about the things that he does think about. Its denial would be quite obvious.

Purpose. Thus far I have been concerned only with the first four categories I listed at the outset. I shall now offer a new schematism in justification of the fifth, that of means and ends, or purpose. I want to show that this is a concept necessary for the understanding of both human behavior and of thought. Whether the concept is also applicable elsewhere—for example, to animal behavior—is a question that need not concern us.

Consider, then, statements of the following form:

    i. E occurs.
    ii. The occurrence of X causes E to occur.
    iii. I do X, causing E to occur.
    iv. I make E occur by doing X.

The foregoing might, for example, be interpreted as follows:

    i. The stone moves.
    ii. The motion of my hand causes the stone to move.
    iii. I move my hand, causing the stone to move.
    iv. I move the stone with my hand (by moving my hand).

Now the first thing to note with respect to such an array of statements is that, as with the previous sets, each entails all those above it, and none beneath it. This can be seen by inspection, and if it is not seen, then the statements are simply not understood.

Thus, from the supposition that I grasp the stone with my hand and move it, everything else in the list follows; but this does not follow from anything else in the list. Though (i) the stone moves, for example, it obviously does not follow that its motion is caused by the motion of my hand—it might be caused to move by some animal, or by an earthquake. Again, (ii) though it is caused to move by the motion of my hand, it does not follow that I move my hand—my hand itself might have been moved by the impact of some object, for example. And again, (iii) though I move my hand, and thereby, as it happens, cause the stone to move, it does not follow that I move the stone with my hand—the moving of the stone might be inadvertent and unintended, a consequence of what I did, but no part of what I was doing. And finally, (iv) I might grasp the stone with my hand, precisely in order to move it, and succeed, thus rendering all four statements in the list true at once.

At this point certain observations will be helpful in clarifying the similarities and differences between the four rather different kinds of fact with which we seem to be dealing, and in eliciting the significance of the entailment relations which I have tried to illustrate.

Agency.   Let us note first, then, that the third and fourth statements, but not the first two, describe actions. This is to say that in the third and fourth, but not in the others, there is an essential reference to an agent. I call this an *essential* reference for this reason only: that if one tries to replace it by reference to some *change* as the cause of my hand's moving, which is in turn the cause of the stone's moving, then both statements are weakened and their meaning altered. They become, in fact, statements of my third category, causation. If, for example, one were to say that some internal change, such as the contraction of certain muscles, causes my hand to move, thereby causing the stone to move, then that would clearly be consistent with *denying* that I move my hand—since the muscles might be caused to contract by spasmodic seizure, by electrical shock, or whatnot. Yet it is *my* moving of my hand that is precisely what is asserted by the third and fourth statements. And we will get the same result if we substitute *any* kind of change, whether it be "mental" or whatever, as the cause of my hand's moving, and for precisely the same reason; namely, that it will always be possible to suppose that such a change, whatever it might be, is itself extraneously caused, and possible to suppose, accordingly, that I do not move my hand. This perhaps suggests why the fourth of my categories, that of agency, cannot be reduced to the third, which is only that of the causation of one change by another.

It is fairly easy to see why the second statement, unlike the third and fourth, does not imply that I have anything to do with moving the stone. The second statement, for example, would be true, but clearly not the third and fourth, in case my hand were severed from my arm and then caused to move by, let us suppose, the impact of some heavy object, its motion then causing the stone to move in a similar way. Under those circumstances we could say that the motion of my hand had caused the motion of the stone, but not that I had moved my hand.

Simple and complex acts.   It is next important to note that while both my third and my fourth statements assert that I do something—move my hand, in the third, and move a stone, in the fourth—these are actions of quite different kinds. Both of these are things that I do, but two rather different senses of doing are here expressed. The third statement describes what is sometimes called a *simple* or *basic* act, and the fourth a *complex* or *nonbasic* act. Their difference is just this: A simple act is one that an agent performs, whose performance does not require the performance of any antecedent act as a means, whereas a complex act is one that is performed by means of some other. Thus, in my fourth statement, it is asserted that I move a stone; however, I accomplish this by means of a prior act of moving my hand. The third statement, on the other hand, does not suggest that I have to do anything else in order to move my hand; I just simply move it. And this is, it should be noted, quite consistent with the observation that my hand is caused to move by the motion of certain muscles, etc. This is simply the relation of cause and effect. It does not mean that I move my muscles as a means of moving my hand. A man who was totally ignorant that he had any muscles would not be at a loss as to how to move his hand. In the situation described by the fourth statement, however, the relation between my hand and the stone is *not* merely that of cause and effect. Here, I *do* move my hand as a means of moving the stone, and if I (somehow) did not know that I had a hand to use in this way, I might indeed be at a loss as to how to move the stone.

The double meaning of "with."   Let us now ask what is meant by saying that I move the stone *with* my hand. Clearly, this is not the "with" of accompaniment, although it includes that meaning. That is, what is asserted in my fourth state-ment is not merely that the motion of the stone is accompanied by the motion of my hand, that the one motion occurs along with the other, even though this is, of course, true. The motion of the stone is accompanied (we may suppose) by the motion of its own shadow; and while it is true that I move the stone (along) with its shadow, it is plainly not true in the same sense that I move the stone with my hand. This latter says *more* than that the two motions occur together, and more than that they are causally connected. And the additional element ex-pressed in the fourth statement is quite obviously this: That I move the stone *by means of* my hand. That is, the fourth statement conveys that it is my (proxi-mate) end or purpose or goal to move the stone, and that the manipulative motion of my hand is my means to that end. This may not, to be sure, be my only pur-pose, or my ultimate one; but the relationship between the motion of the stone and the motion of my hand is, in any case, not merely that of spatial or temporal accompaniment, nor of effect to cause, though it includes those relations. It is, in fact, the relation of end to means, which clearly marks the fourth statement as one expressive of the idea of purpose.

This suggests another way of distinguishing simple from complex acts in a way that has not, I think, hitherto been done. For we can say, I think, that while a simple act, like moving one's hand, need not be purposeful, a complex act, such as moving a stone with one's hand, of necessity is purposeful. My third statement expresses the idea that I in some sense move the stone, but it does not entail that my moving the stone is my action; it might merely be the unintended consequence or effect of my action, which was simply moving my hand. According to my fourth statement, however, my moving the stone *is* my action, for I do this, not inadvertently, but *on purpose.* And every complex act, or every act in which one does something *by doing something else,* seems to be of this character. One's simple acts, in such cases, appear always to be the means to the accomplishment of other things. Indeed, it is hard to see what else the word "by" could mean in such contexts; for to say that one does something *by* doing something else is surely an abbreviated way of saying that he does something *by means of* something else that he does. If this is so, then it would seem to follow that any complex act is of necessity a purposeful action, or one which cannot be understood except in terms of an end or goal.

The basic category of purpose. I believe the foregoing suggestions show that the concept of purpose is a basic category, necessary for the understanding of much voluntary behavior, and not reducible to anything more familiar. For my fourth statement, as we have seen, entails, but is not entailed by, my third, and there appears to be no way of interpreting this fourth statement in such a way as to eliminate the idea of means and end without destroying this entailment relationship.

Thus, to say that I move my hand in order to move the stone does not just mean that I move my hand (agency) and that this causes the stone to move. That idea is expressed by (iii), and (iv), we have seen, expresses more than (iii). Now we can indeed say that, *because* I want the stone to move, I move my hand; but this assuredly does not mean either (a) that my wanting the stone to move causes my hand to move, or (b) that such a wanting causes me to move my hand. The first of these interpretations would be consistent with supposing that there is no agency here at all, but only causation, and the second would presuppose that whenever an agent performs a complex act, something causes him to perform it.

Clearly, to say that I move my hand, because I *want* the stone to move, means that I move my hand *in order* to move the stone, and the word "because" conveys the idea, not of causation, but of means and ends. Another way of expressing the same point would be to say that I have, or can give, a *reason* for moving my hand —viz., that I do it in order to move the stone; but this does not even remotely resemble any cause, either of my hand's moving, or of my moving it. Indeed, from the data given, it cannot even be inferred that any such cause exists, though it would not be possible to deny, from the same data, that there is a reason, a purpose, or an end.

Doing and causing. The irreducibility of the category of purpose to those of agency and causation can be seen in still another way. Let us suppose, for example, that I move the stone in order to clear a path. We can, then, suppose that, in thus clearing a path, I inadvertently produce certain other results as well—for instance, that I disturb the insects under the stone, flatten the grass near the stone, cause the stone's shadow to move, and so on. Now the first thing to note is that, while I in a sense "do" all those things, it is not in the same sense that I do them. And the difference is simply that, while it was my purpose to clear the path, it was not my purpose to flatten the grass, disturb the insects, and so on. These latter occurrences were the *effects* of my action, but not the *ends* of my action. Clearing the path, on the other hand, was an effect of my action, and also, its end or purpose.

Note next, however, that any of these unintended effects *could* have been my ends; reference to any or all of them could have constituted an appropriate answer to the question, "Why did you move the stone?" It could, for example, have been an appropriate answer, though a false one in the case we are imagining, to reply: "In order to disturb the insects beneath it."

Suppose, then, that in moving the stone, I produce all four effects; that is, that I thereby (a) disturb the insects beneath it, (b) flatten the nearby grass, (c) cause the stone's shadow to move, and (d) clear the path. Now it seems fairly obvious that what actually happens in this case—namely, all these things—is exactly the same, no matter which effect is the intended one. Whether my purpose is to clear the path, or to disturb the insects, the effects of my moving the stone are, or certainly might be, exactly the same. My basic act is likewise the same; that is, I might move my hand, thereby moving the stone, in exactly the same way in either case. The difference, therefore, between moving the stone in order to clear the path, on the one hand, and moving it in precisely the same way in order to disturb the insects, is not a difference that can be expressed in any of my categories except the last one. It is not a difference in what happens (change), nor in how I move my hand (agency), nor in the resultant effects (causation). The difference is simply one of intention, or in other words, of my end or purpose.

Thought and purpose.   I want now, finally, to see whether a similar schematism applies to mental activity, as it seems so clearly to apply to observable actions. My first schematism, as we saw, does seem to apply to thinking, with the implication that the concept of agency is as applicable to thought as it is to behavior. If, similarly, my second schematism applies to thought, then this will imply that not only the concept of agency, but that of purpose is likewise applicable to thought; or in other words, that thinking, as well as overtly behaving, is at least sometimes governed by ends or purposes—that is, by final causation.

Consider, then, some very simple psychological feat—for example, my thinking of the name of someone I am to have lunch with. And let us suppose, as before, that the man's name is "Shilling." Now, letting E be the psychological occurrence of my thinking of that name, our question is whether there might be four significantly different ways in which I might do this which fit the following schematism:

     i. E occurs.
    ii. The occurrence of X causes E to occur.
   iii. I do X, causing E to occur.
   iv. I make E occur by doing X.

And it seems clear that there are these four different kinds of fact, though it is important here to get things very clear. For example, (i) it might be that the name simply occurs to me, unsought, when nothing appears to suggest it, and when I am making no effort to recall it. Or (ii) the thought of the British coin having the same name might cause the name to occur to me by association. Or (iii) I might be doing something—say, figuring exchange rates of British and American currency, and in the course of that thinking of shillings—which quite inadvertently causes me to think of the name, again by association. Or finally, (iv)

I might think of British shillings, precisely in order to remind myself of that troublesome name, having hit upon this as an effective mnemonic device.

Thus we can say:

    i. The (thought of) the name occurs to me.
    ii. The thought of shillings causes the name to occur to me.
    iii. I think of shillings, causing the name to occur to me.
    iv. I think of the name by thinking of shillings.

Now we must note with respect to this array of statements that each entails all those above it, and none beneath it—precisely the entailment relations we had in the previous case.

Thus, from the supposition that I think of the name by thinking of shillings—that I use this psychological device for that purpose—everything else in my list follows, as is obvious by simple inspection. This supposition itself, however, does not follow from anything else in the list, nor does anything in the list follow from anything above it. Though (i) the name occurs to me, it does not follow that this is caused by my thinking of shillings—it might be caused by someone simply mentioning it to me, by my seeing it in print, or indeed (logically), by nothing at all. Again, (ii) though my thinking of the name might be caused by my thought of shillings, it does not follow that I think of shillings in any sense implying mental activity—my thoughts of shillings might be caused by my seeing a shilling, or they might simply be inflicted upon me by some cause with which I have nothing to do. (If this is not readily seen, comparison with my previous example will help.) And again, (iii) though I am thinking of shillings, and thereby, as it happens, cause the name to occur to me, it does not follow that I think of the name by thinking of shillings—the thought of the name might be quite unintended, a consequence of what I did, but not part of what I was doing. And finally, (iv) I might think of shillings, precisely in order to remind myself of the name, and succeed, thereby rendering all four statements in my list true at once.

Mental agency.   The connections and overlappings of the four kinds of fact just illustrated give rise, I think, to certain significant philosophical implications, markedly similar to those illustrated by my previous example. There is, for example, a significant difference between (ii) and (iii), and the difference consists precisely of the element of agency present in (iii) but lacking in (ii), though this is far less obvious here than before. That is, there seems to be a difference between thoughts being inflicted upon one—by hearing meaningful discourse, for example—and thinking those thoughts for oneself; and this seems to correspond fairly closely to the difference between having one's hand moved by some inanimate object, for example, and moving it himself. At some points the similarities seem to disappear, but when one reflects on them it is not really clear that they do. For example, I spoke earlier of the possibility that my hand might, even though severed from my body, be caused to move, in which case we could say that my hand had moved, but not that I had moved it. It is hard to see how one could say anything similar to this about one of my thoughts, for one's thoughts seem inseparable from oneself in a way that one's limbs are not. On the other hand, however, it is difficult to see in what sense one can speak of a severed hand as being still *my* hand, as this seems to express no more than a conventional association. And one can, moreover, quite properly describe a man as expressing another man's thoughts, calling attention to their being not his own, in the sense that they are not original with him.

Simple and complex mental acts. The distinction between simple and complex acts that was drawn with respect to my earlier example appears equally applicable to mental activity. Thus, both my third and fourth statements assert that I do something—that I think of shillings, in the third, and that I think of a certain name, in the fourth—but it appears that these are not doings of the same kind. According to (iii), I think of shillings, but I do not do this by first thinking of something else, whereas according to (iv), I think of a name only by first thinking of shillings; and that is precisely the distinction between a simple and a complex act. Or one could express the same point by noting that there would, with respect to (iii), be no answer to the question of *how* I managed to think of shillings—I just did it, without having to do anything else first, and this is precisely the description given before of a simple act. With respect to (iv), on the other hand, there *is* an answer to the question of how I managed to think of the name—I thought of it by first thinking of shillings, thereby recalling the name. And this is exactly the description given of a complex act.

The meaning of "by." My third statement asserts that I am caused to think of a name by first thinking of shillings, but it does not suggest that this is *why* I thought of shillings. My thinking of the name was an effect, but not an intended effect, of my thinking of shillings. According to my fourth statement, on the other hand, my thinking of the name was intended, it was precisely what I was trying to do, and I did it by first thinking of shillings. The fourth statement, accordingly, says more than the third, and the additional element in it is precisely what is conveyed by the word "by."

What then does it mean to say that I think of the name *by* thinking of shillings? Quite clearly, it means "by means of." My aim or purpose is to think of a certain name, and I have learned that I can accomplish this by first thinking of the British coins. I accordingly do this latter, in order to do the former, which is quite clearly the mark of a purposeful act. Now thinking of the name might not, to be sure, be my ultimate purpose, or my only purpose; I may want to think of the name in order to do still something else. For instance, I may want to use it in greeting the man whose name it is, thereby appearing to know him better than I do, and I may have still some further purpose in wanting to do this. Nevertheless, the relationship between my thinking of the coins and thinking of the name is not, in my fourth statement, merely that of cause to effect, since that connection is entirely expressed in my third statement. It is, in addition to this, the relationship of a means to an end.

To this it can be added that, as in the case of bodily acts, every complex mental act would appear to be purposeful in nature, whereas a simple mental act, the mere thinking of something, need not be. For in the case of every complex mental act, I do something by first doing something else—e.g., I think of a name, by first thinking of something else that will cause the name to occur to me—and "by" in such a context can only be an abbreviated way of saying "by means of." A complex mental act, accordingly, like any other complex act, can only be understood in terms of an end or goal.

Purposeful thought.   The foregoing suggestions appear to indicate that the concept of purpose is necessary, not only to understanding human behavior, but to understanding thinking as well. For to say that I think of coins in order to think of a name does not just mean that the former *causes* the latter. That idea is entirely expressed by my third statement, and my fourth, we have seen, expresses more than the third. Clearly, to say that I think of a name by thinking of shillings means that I do the latter *in order* to accomplish the former. Or we could put the same point by noting that if I were asked *why* I thought of shillings, I could give a reason—namely, that I did it, in order to think of a name. Such a *reason* for doing something does not, however, even remotely resemble a cause. Indeed, from the data given, it cannot even be inferred that there was any cause of my thinking of shillings, though it would not be possible to deny, given the same data, that I had a reason for doing so. And that reason is precisely the statement of my purpose.

Mentally doing and causing.   The irreducibility of purposeful thinking to mere associational thought, or the causation of some thoughts by others, can be seen in other ways which are suggested by my earlier remarks on purposeful behavior.

Thus, we are supposing that I think of British coins in order to think of a certain man's name, and that this works; that is, that I am thereby enabled to think of the name. But we can suppose that my thinking of such coins has other effects as well; for instance, that it evokes in me memories of England and accompanying feelings of nostalgia, that it reminds me of some paltry debt I owe, and perhaps other things. Now the first thing to note is that, while in a sense I "do" all these things—that is, I recall a name, remind myself of England, evoke nostalgia, and so on—it is not in the same sense that I do them all. And the difference is that, while it was my purpose to think of the name, it was not my purpose to think of England, feel nostalgic, remember my debt, and so on. These latter things are *effects* of my action, but not ends. Thinking of the name, on the other hand, was not only an effect of my thinking of shillings; it was also its end or purpose.

Now note, however, that any of these other, unintended effects *could* have been my ends; reference to any of them could have constituted an appropriate answer to the question, "Why did I think of shillings?" It could, for example, have been an appropriate answer to reply: "In order to feel nostalgic," in case I had wanted to do that.

Let us suppose, then, that in thinking of British shillings, I produce all these effects; that is, that I thereby (a) think of the name of the man I am to lunch with, (b) think of England, (c) evoke in myself a nostalgia, and (d) remind myself of a small debt. Now it seems fairly obvious that what actually happens in this case—namely, all these things—is exactly the same, no matter which effect was the intended one. Whether my purpose was to think of a certain name, or to feel nostalgic, the effects of my thinking of shillings are, or certainly might be, exactly the same. My basic act of thinking of shillings is likewise the same. The difference, therefore, between thinking of shillings in order to think of a name, on the one hand, and thinking of shillings in exactly the same way in order to evoke in myself a nostalgia, is not a difference that can be expressed in any of my categories except the last one, that of purpose. It is not a difference in what happens (change), nor in my act of thinking (agency), nor in any effects of this act (causation). The difference is only one of intention, or in other words, of my end or purpose.

Postscript.   To look at thinking in this manner—namely, as being sometimes a kind of purposeful activity—is to put it in a rather strange and unfamiliar light, but I believe it raises no special philosophical problems and produces no paradoxes. Certainly it is difficult to see how thinking can be an *act,* but I believe it is no more difficult than seeing how anything else—for example, just raising one's arm—can be an act. The metaphysical peculiarities of agency are not produced by regarding thought as an activity; they are only duplicated there, for they already emerge in regarding behavior as an activity.

Now there is, to be sure, a way of thinking of purposeful activity which would render the foregoing conception of purposeful thought paradoxical. That is, it is sometimes supposed that when one acts purposefully, he must have in mind a *thought* or *idea* of his goal, for otherwise, how could he know what he was aiming at? How then, it might be asked, could it be one's purpose to have a particular thought, such as, the thought of a particular man's name? Would he not first have to get the name in mind, and then take whatever steps seemed appropriate to bringing it to mind? And this, of course, is plainly redundant and absurd. One could hardly be described as taking steps to thinking of a name, if the very first step were to think of that very name.

Such an objection as this, however, is simply contrived, and only invites reconsideration of the presupposition on which it rests; namely, that to aim at something, one must already have in mind whatever he is aiming at. One can be aiming at the solution to a problem without already having that solution before him; he needs only to be able to recognize it as the solution sought, if and when he does get it. And similarly, one can be trying to think of a name, or a number, or indeed anything under the sun, and taking steps appropriate to that end, without already having that name, number, or whatnot already clearly in mind. All that is necessary is that he be able to recognize it, as the thing he was trying to think of, when he does get it, in case he gets it at all.

FREEDOM AND ACTION

Roderick M. Chisholm

. . . .

The concept of an act, or a deed, is both imputative and descriptive. When we say of a man that he *did* something, we may be declaring, by way of imputation, that the man is to be held responsible for making a certain thing happen; that is to say, we may be pronouncing a verdict, notifying our hearers that forthwith we are holding this man responsible. But we are also making a descriptive statement; we are saying that the man was a causal factor in making something happen, or in keeping something from happening. Let us now try to lay bare this descriptive element in the concept of an act, stripping from it all implications of moral and legal responsibility. The point of doing this is to throw light upon the interrelations among several important and perplexing concepts and to contribute toward the solution of certain additional philosophical puzzles.

H. L. A. Hart has suggested that the descriptive facts we presuppose in applying our action concepts might consist simply of facts about the state of the agent's body and what it causes or fails to cause ("His arm went up and knocked over the lamp" as distinguished from "He knocked over the lamp with his arm").[1] But this suggestion, it seems to me, is clearly mistaken. If we ask ourselves, for example, "What facts, in the absence of defeating considerations, would warrant our saying that one man has killed another?" we will find, I think, that these facts cannot be described merely by reference to what is caused by some state of the agent's

From *Freedom and Determinism*, edited by Keith Lehrer, pp. 28–44. © Copyright 1966 by Random House, Inc. Reprinted by permission of Random House, Inc.
[1] H. L. A. Hart, "Ascription of Responsibility and Rights," *Proceedings of the Aristotelian Society*, XLIX (1949), 171–194.

body; similarly for some, at least, of those facts that would defeat the ascription of killing.[2]

What more *is* there, then, to the concept of an act? First, there is the fact that the agent himself, as we have seen, is a causal factor. We must say that at least one of the events that is involved in any act is caused, not by any other event, but by the agent, by the man. Causation is a relation that holds, not only between states or events, but also between agents, as causes, and states or events, as effects. And, secondly, there is the fact that the concept of an act is essentially teleological. Action involves *endeavor* or *purpose,* one thing occurring *in order that* some other thing may occur. And this concept of endeavor, or purpose, must be distinguished from that of *want* or *desire.* A man may endeavor, or undertake, to bring about what he does not desire and what he does not even believe to be a means to anything that he desires; and he may refrain from undertaking to bring about what he does desire.

Some philosophers, however, have attempted to define purpose, or endeavor, in terms of belief, causation, and desire. It has been suggested, for example, that a man might be said to bring about something X *for the purpose of* bringing about something Y, provided that the following three conditions hold: (i) he desires Y; (ii) he believes that, if he brings about X, then he will bring about Y; and (iii) this belief and desire jointly cause him to bring about X.[3] But this type of definition is too broad and does not in fact capture the concept of purpose. Suppose, for example: (i) a certain man desires to inherit a fortune; (ii) he believes that, if he kills his uncle, then he will inherit a fortune; and (iii) this belief and this desire agitate him so severely that he drives excessively fast, with the result that he accidentally runs over and kills a pedestrian who, unknown to the nephew, was none other than the uncle. The proposed definition of purpose would require us to say, incorrectly, that the nephew killed the uncle in order to inherit the fortune.

Let us attempt to set forth the descriptive element in the concept of action by an undefined locution, one indicating both that the agent is a cause and that the action is purposive or teleological. I propose the following:

> There is a state of affairs A and a state of affairs B, such that, at time *t*, he makes B happen in the endeavor to make A happen.

Some readers may find a symbolic notation more perspicuous than ordinary English.[4] For such readers, we may symbolize our undefined locution in the following way:

---

[2] We must not be misled by the fact that our *evidence* for a statement about what the agent caused to happen may consist of statements about what some state of his body caused to happen. It would be a mistake to suppose that "He is a murderer in virtue of the fact that he is A" and "E is our evidence for saying that he is A" together imply "He is a murderer in virtue of the fact that E." My evidence that Jones is married (A) may be the fact that you say he is (E); but (unless your utterance is performative) he cannot be said to be married in virtue of the fact that you say he is.

[3] The classic statement of this point of view is C. J. Ducasse's "Explanation, Mechanism, and Teleology," *Journal of Philosophy,* XXII (1925), 150–155; reprinted in H. Feigl and W. S. Sellars, eds., *Readings in Philosophical Analysis* (New York, 1949). Ducasse's views are developed in further detail in "Life, Telism, and Mechanism," *Philosophy and Phenomenological Research,* XX (1959), 18–24.

[4] The notation employed here is suggested by a similar notation adopted by Henry Leonard in "Authorship and Purpose," *Philosophy of Science,* XXII (1959), 277–294.

$$(\text{Ea}) \quad (\text{Eb}) \quad M^t \quad (\text{b, a}).$$

As an alternative for the English expression "He makes B happen," we might use "He realizes B," "He brings it about that B," or, if "state of affairs" is replaced by "proposition," then "He makes it true that B." The letters may be replaced, in obvious ways, by propositional clauses. The relation of "making happen" is transitive and asymmetrical: if A makes B happen, then B does not make A happen.[5] The states of affairs to which our locution refers may be "unchanges" as well as changes; they may also be complex (e.g., "He makes B happen with an end to making it happen that A and that A makes C happen"). And the subject term of "makes happen" may designate either a state of affairs or a person.

"Make happen" is to be taken in such a way that we may say, of a man who raises his arm, not only that he makes it happen that his arm goes up, but also that he makes it happen, just before, that certain other physiological events occur inside his body, and that he makes it happen, just subsequently, that air particles move in various ways.

The teleological component of our locution (viz., "in the endeavor to make A happen") should be taken as intentional. This means, for example, that a man may make something happen in the endeavor to make A happen without thereby actually making A happen. It also means that, from "He made something happen in the endeavor to make A happen and he did thereby make A happen" and "A is the same concrete event as B," we may not infer "He made something happen in the endeavor to make B happen." And it also means that, if a man makes something B happen in the endeavor to make something A happen, then he can *know*, directly or immediately, that he is making something happen in the endeavor to make A happen, but, as the example from the previous paragraph will indicate, he may not know at all that he is making B happen.

Since we are attempting to describe *action* in terms of *making happen*—or, more accurately, in terms of making things happen *in the endeavor* to make things happen—the "A's" and "B's" of our formulae will not normally be replaceable by expressions which themselves refer to actions. If I am right, the man who raises his arm under ordinary circumstances will make something happen in the endeavor to make it happen, *not* that he raises his arm, but that his arm goes up. (But the paralytic, in the course of his exercises, may make things happen now in the endeavor to make it happen that later he raises his arm.) To act, therefore, is to endeavor to make happen. But from this it does not follow that when a man acts he therefore endeavors to act. What the liar endeavors to do, for example, is not to *lie*, but to make it happen that his hearers are deceived.

And now let us attempt to sketch the rudiments of a purely descriptive action vocabulary. We shall attempt to define three fundamental concepts: first, that of

---

[5] "To make happen," therefore, is to be interpreted somewhat more broadly than "to cause," as the latter term is sometimes interpreted in non-philosophical contexts. In law, for example, the relation of causing may be taken to be nontransitive; cf. H. L. A. Hart and A. M. Honore, *Causation in the Law* (Oxford, 1959), Part I. When "cause" is thus used nontransitively, to say of an agent that he "caused" a certain event is (i) to make a descriptive statement about what he made happen and also (ii) to make an imputative statement implying something about responsibility and liability. Using "cause" in this sense, the owners of the luxury liner, the *Shalom*, according to the *New York Times* (December 28, 1964), asserted that the freighter, *Stolt Dagali*, was "the sole cause" of the collision that occurred on Thanksgiving Day, 1964.

undertaking, or *endeavoring,* to make a certain thing happen; secondly, that of undertaking to make something happen *for the purpose of* making some (other) thing happen; and thirdly, that of a *successful intentional action*—an action that is performed in the way in which the agent intends it.

(1) Our first definition is that of *undertaking,* or *endeavoring,* to make a certain thing happen. We shall say of our agent "He undertakes to make A happen," provided that there is something he makes happen in the endeavor to make A happen.

If we symbolize "He undertakes at t to make A happen" by means of "$U^t a$," then we may formulate our first definition, in the symbolism introduced above, as follows:

Definition 1: $U^t a$ = Df. $(Eb)M^t(b, a)$.

Given what we have said about the interpretation of our undefined locution, the following things will be true if a man undertakes to make something A happen: there will be something that he *is* making happen, but he may not know what this something is; he will know, however, that he is undertaking to make A happen, but he may not know whether he is succeeding in making A happen, and it may be that he is not succeeding in making A happen.

If we use the word "undertaking" for the concept just defined, we must not take it to imply, as it sometimes does, the existence of a commitment; one may *undertake* to make something A happen, in our present sense of the term, without having made a contract or other commitment to make A happen. And if we use "*endeavor,*" we must not take it to imply exertion, effort, or trial and error.

Consider now a pianist who begins to play a sonata; at the moment at which he begins to play (i) he undertakes to play the entire sonata, (ii) he also undertakes to play the first measure or the opening of the first measure, but (iii) he does *not* then undertake to play the last measure, even though the last measure is part of what he is then undertaking to play. How can this be?

The answer is, I think, that undertaking or endeavoring, as an intentional concept, shares the following property with such concepts as approval and desire: it may take a conjunctive state of affairs as object without thereby taking each conjunct of that state of affairs as object. If I wish to be in France when President De Gaulle is there, I may undertake to realize that conjunction, which is my being in France and De Gaulle being in France, without thereby undertaking to make it true that De Gaulle is in France. And so I think we may say this of our pianist: if A, B, C, and . . . N are the consecutive measures of the sonata, then as he starts to play the sonata, (i) he undertakes to play A and B and C and . . . N, (ii) he undertakes to play A, but (iii) he does not then undertake to play N. This fact—that we may undertake a conjunction without undertaking each of its conjuncts—has important implications for moral philosophy. We shall note some of them below.[6]

---

[6] Some of the elements of the object of a conjunctive enterprise may be disjunctions ("Either I shall do this or I shall do that"); some will be conditionals ("If so-and-so occurs I will do this, and if such-and-such occurs I will do that"). And one must distinguish conditional enterprises ("If so-and-so occurs I shall do this") from conditional purposes ("I shall do this in order that, if so-and-so occurs, then such-and-such will occur"). On the nature of plans or enterprises, compare Tadeusz

(2) The second concept that we wish to define is that of undertaking to make something B happen *for the purpose of* making something A happen. This expression differs in a significant way from our undefined "He makes B happen in the endeavor to make A happen." For now we are saying that the agent's purposes are directed upon B as well as upon A. And whereas our undefined expression implies that he does make B happen and does not imply that he makes A happen, the present expression implies neither that he makes A happen nor that he makes B happen.

Let us appeal to the concept of "transeunt causation"—that of one concrete event or occasion *causing* another concrete event or occasion, or, as we shall say for short, that of one event making another event happen. We will take "cause," or "make happen," in a somewhat broad sense, so that any event that contributes causally to the occurrence of another event may be said to cause that other event, or to make it happen.

Shall we say "He undertakes to make B happen for the purpose of making A happen" simply if he undertakes to make B make A happen? No, for a man may undertake to make something B make something A happen, without undertaking to make B happen and without undertaking to make A happen—in which case he will not be undertaking to make B happen for the purpose of making A happen. Consider the following example: the victim is in the water, about to drown; the accomplice is about to shoot the victim; but the leader prevents the shooting and his purpose in so doing is to make the victim's being immersed in water (B) make it happen that the victim dies (A). In such a case, the leader will have undertaken to make B make A happen, but he will not have undertaken to make B happen or to make A happen, and therefore he will not have undertaken to make B happen for the purpose of making A happen.

Let us say, then, that a man undertakes, at *t*, to make B happen for the purpose of making A happen, provided: he undertakes at *t* to make B happen, to make A happen, and to make B make A happen. Thus if the assassin is trying to get to town in order to kill the victim, we could say: "He is undertaking to make it happen that he is in town, that the victim dies, and that his being in town will make it happen that the victim dies."

If we symbolize "He undertakes at *t* to make B happen for the purpose of making A happen" by "P^t (b, a)," and if we symbolize "B makes A happen" by "bCa," then our second definition becomes:

Definition 2: $P^t(b, a) =$ Df. $U^t(a \ \& \ b \ \& \ bCa)$.

Our symbolic notation now enables us to see that there are in fact two rather different interpretations of the English expression "He undertakes to make B happen for the purpose of making A happen." We have defined only one of these, but we also have the means for defining the other. Consider the following example.

Kotarbinski, "The Property of a Good Plan," *Methodos*, XIII (1961), 1–13, and "Practical Error," *Danish Yearbook of Philosophy*, I (1964), 65–71; and on the nature and significance of conditional purposes, compare Roderick M. Chisholm, "What is it to Act upon a Proposition?," *Analysis*, XXII (1961), 1–6.

A certain man, in Providence, dials a Los Angeles telephone number in order to cause a certain prior switching to occur in the telephone offices in Denver. We may say of him that he undertakes to make the Los Angeles number ring for the purpose of causing the Denver switching. But since the Los Angeles ringing, as he realizes, is subsequent to the Denver switching and is caused by it, we cannot say that he undertakes to make the Los Angeles ringing cause the Denver switching. What occurs in such a case is that the man undertakes to make the telephone ring in Los Angeles and to make this *undertaking* itself cause the switching to occur in Denver. Or, in our symbolism, instead of

$$U^t(a \ \& \ b \ \& \ bCa)$$

we have

$$U^t[a \ \& \ b \ \& \ (U^tb) \ Ca].$$

We may assume that the second of these two expressions is true whenever the first is true, but, as the example indicates, the second may be true when the first is false. This distinction, as we shall see, bears directly upon one of the philosophical puzzles pertaining to freedom and action.

(3) Our third and last definition is to be that of an undertaking that is completely successful—an action that is carried out in the way in which the agent intended it. We wish to define a successful undertaking *par excellence*, one which can be said, without reservation, to be intentional.

Our primitive locution enables us to define, without difficulty, a very broad sense of "successful undertaking." We could say, simply, that a man succeeds at t in making A happen, provided that, at t, he makes A happen in the endeavor to make A happen; or, in the terms of our symbolism:

$$M^t(a, a).$$

But this interpretation of "successful undertaking" is too broad and it does not capture the concept of intentional action that we seek. For there are certain types of success, perplexing both to moralists and to jurists, which we hesitate to call "intentional" but which our broad definition would countenance as "successes." For lack of any better terms, I shall call these "inadvertent successes" and "happy failures."

An example of an "inadvertent success" is provided by the prospective assassin who meets up with an accident similar to that of our earlier agitated nephew: *en route* to town to shoot and kill his victim, he accidentally runs over and kills a pedestrian who then turns out to be none other than the intended victim. Should we say that the killing was intentional?

An example of a "happy failure" is provided by the prospective assassin who does everything that he believes to be necessary for the complete execution of his plan and who does indeed succeed despite a crucial failure. In shooting at his victim, he causes him to make an escape and then, in the course of this escape, the intended victim is killed by an unexpected stroke of lightning. Should we say that the killing was intentional?

What we wish to do, then, is to formulate a definition of a successful intentional action and to do so in such a way that we can rule out at least the more extreme cases of inadvertent success and happy failure. I believe we can do this if we make use of the concept defined in our second definition—the definition of "He undertakes at t to make B happen for the purpose of making A happen," or "$P^t(b, a)$." Let us say that our agent makes A happen in the way in which, at t, he intended, provided that this condition holds: he makes happen all of those things which, at t, he undertook for the purpose of making A happen. The "all" here should be taken to imply "some": at t, the man did undertake to make A happen. If we symbolize "He made A happen in the way in which, at t, he intended" by means of "$I^t a$," then we have:

Definition 3: $I^t a = $ Df. $M^t(a, a)$ & (c) $[P^t(c, a) \rightarrow M^t (c, c)]$.

This strict sense of *success* will not apply to the more extreme cases of "inadvertent success" and "happy failure." The author of our inadvertent success—the assassin who inadvertently ran over his intended victim—had undertaken, without success, to bring it about that the victim was subsequently shot (one can undertake today to carry out a project which will bring it about that the victim is shot tomorrow, even if one cannot undertake today to shoot the victim tomorrow). The author of the happy failure—the man whose escaping victim was killed by an unexpected stroke of lightning—had undertaken, without success, to make it happen that the bullet reach its mark.

We tend to think of the author of the happy failure as being the more culpable of the two assassins, for he had reached the point of no return—the point at which, he thought, there was nothing more to undertake.[7] He had undertaken various things with an end to the victim's death and, he then thought, conditions were thereby created in which the death would result without his undertaking anything else. He took what he believed to be the final step. A *preliminary* step toward making something A happen (reaching for the ammunition would be a preliminary step in an assassination) is something the agent undertakes in order that he may undertake something further (shooting the loaded gun) for the purpose of making A happen; a *final step* (pulling the trigger) is one that is not thus taken in preparation for still another step.

If we consider these observations about the "final step" in the light of our previous remarks about the undertaking of conjunctive states of affairs, we may formulate a thesis that is relevant to the morality of intention. Both assassins had undertaken conjunctive enterprises in which the final undertaking was to be the firing of a shot. The first assassin never got to this final undertaking but the second one did. Why do we think of the first assassin as being the less culpable? Both had undertaken a certain conjunction, A and B and C, where C, the shooting, is the most wicked of the conjuncts; but the first man, unlike the second, had not yet undertaken C. The answer to our question, then, may be this: if C is a wicked

---

[7] We also hold an agent culpable for an unfortunate event A if (i) A resulted from one of his undertakings U and (ii) he ought to have known that A was likely to result from U and without his undertaking anything further. Therefore some happy failures (consider the assassin who aims at the heart and hits the stomach) will be indistinguishable, morally, from complete successes.

undertaking, then undertaking A and B and C *and* undertaking C are together more wicked than undertaking A and B and C and not undertaking C.

Our definition of successful undertaking will also apply to those acts that Arthur Danto has called "basic acts": those actions, such as walking, talking, raising our arms, moving our hands, which, as Danto puts it, we perform without performing *other* acts that cause them.[8] In our terms, "A is performed by the agent as a basic act" could be defined as: the agent succeeds in making A happen in the way in which he intended, and there is no B, other than A, which he undertook for the purpose of making A happen. This use of "succeeds," of course, is very broad. Ordinarily we would use the term only in connection with those nonbasic acts which the agent makes happen in the way in which he intended—possibly even confining the term to those acts in which there is (thought to be) some chance of failure or to those which involve some degree of effort. As Danto notes, the issues involved in applying "succeed," "try," and "undertake" to basic acts are very much like those that are involved in applying "know" and "believe" to so-called "basic propositions"—such propositions as are expressed by "Something now looks red" and "I seem to remember having been here before."

We may now outline, briefly and schematically, certain other descriptive action concepts which, though they are closely related to the concept of intentional action (intentional making-happen) which has just been defined, should not be confused with it.

"He makes A happen *voluntarily*," in one important descriptive sense, might now be defined as: there is a state of affairs B such that he undertook to make B happen; in undertaking to make B happen, he believed or knew that, in so doing, he might well make A happen; and his undertaking to make B happen makes A happen. Thus a man who, in his haste, runs through the garden, fully realizing that he will leave his footprints there and thus destroy the garden, may be said to destroy it voluntarily, even though he does nothing for the purpose of destroying the garden. (But "voluntarily" also has an *imputative* use; e.g., we may conclude that he destroyed the garden "voluntarily" if, whatever he himself may have thought, we think he ought to have known that he would destroy the garden.)

"He makes A happen *willingly*" (unlike "He makes A happen voluntarily") may imply something about his desires—perhaps not that he desires A but at least that he does not desire not-A.

"*Involuntarily*," even in its purely descriptive uses, is less clear-cut than "voluntarily." Thus "He made A happen *involuntarily*" could mean: (i) some other agent caused him to make A happen; or (ii) he made A happen but did not do so willingly; or (iii) some state of his body, which he did not make happen (or which he did not make happen voluntarily) made A happen; or (iv) had he known that his act would thus make A happen, he would have undertaken something else instead.

"He made A happen *unintentionally*," in one descriptive use, is likely to mean simply that he made A happen but did not do so voluntarily; but it may also mean the same as (iii), or as (iv), under "involuntarily"—i.e., it may mean either that some state of his body which he did not make happen (or did not make

---

[8] Arthur Danto, "What We Can Do," *Journal of Philosophy*, LX (1963), 435–445.

happen voluntarily) made A happen, or that, had he known that his act would make A happen, he would have undertaken something else instead.[9]

At any given time, as we have noted, there will be many different things, A, B, C, . . . N, that our agent is making happen. Some of these will be intentional and others not, and some will be voluntary and others not. When we come to appraise his action, therefore, we should not ask simply "Is what he is doing voluntary or involuntary, intentional or unintentional?" We should ask instead, of particular things that he is making happen, whether he is making *those* things happen voluntarily or involuntarily, intentionally or unintentionally.

Finally, let us apply the results of our discussion to three additional philosophical puzzles.

(1) Our first puzzle may be put as follows: "Laius, the offensive traveler, was Oedipus' father. It may be that Oedipus intended to kill the offensive traveler, but he certainly did not intend to kill his own father. Yet the killing of the offensive traveler *was* the killing of Oedipus' father. Hence we must say of this event that it *was* intentional and also that it was *not* intentional. How can this be?"

The problem can be solved, I suggest, if we observe G. H. von Wright's distinction between an "act-qualifying" property (e.g., the property of being a killing) and the "act-individuals" that have that property (those particular acts that *are* killings).[10] Thus every act-individual, like every other individual, has many properties; indeed, every act-individual is such that, for every property, either the act-individual has that property or it has the negation of that property. The agent always "knows what he is doing" in that he can know, at any time, what act-qualifying properties he is undertaking to realize at that time, but in every case the act-individual will have properties that he knows nothing about. Since the offensive traveler was Oedipus' father, that act-individual which was the killing of the offensive traveler is the same as that act-individual which was the killing of Oedipus' father; but the act-qualifying property which is the killing of the offensive traveler is different from the act-qualifying property which is the killing of Oedipus' father. If we say that the killing of the offensive traveler was intentional and that the killing of Oedipus' father was not, our statement should not be taken to mean that a certain act-individual both is and is not intentional. It means, rather, that the act-individual which is the killing of the offensive traveler (= the act-individual which is the killing of Oedipus' father) is something that was intended to have the act-qualifying property of being the killing of the offensive traveler, but was not intended to have the act-qualifying property of being the killing of Oedipus' father.

(2) The second of our three puzzles is this: "A responsible act is an act such that, at the time at which the agent undertook to perform it, he had it within his power to perform the act and also within his power not to perform the act. But

---

[9] Compare J. L. Austin's treatment of these concepts in "A Plea for Excuses," *Philosophical Papers* (Oxford, 1961), and in "Three Ways of Spilling Ink," in Carl J. Friedrich, ed., *Responsibility: Nomos III* (New York, 1960). I am indebted to Ann Ferguson for helping me to clarify my views on these and related concepts.

[10] G. H. von Wright, *Logical Studies* (London, 1957), p. 59. Compare C. I. Lewis's distinction between "states of affairs" and "concrete Whiteheadian events," in *An Analysis of Knowledge and Valuation* (La Salle, Ill., 1945), pp. 52–55.

what it is that he thus accomplishes is caused by certain physiological events. (The man raises his arm; yet, as we know from physiology, certain cerebral events cause his arm to go up.) Hence it is false that it is within his power not to perform the act, and therefore he is not responsible."

We have already touched upon this puzzle above. [See Chisholm's "Freedom and Action" in *Freedom and Determinism*, ed. Lehrer, p. 19. Ed.] Let us say, perhaps misusing words, that a man makes something A happen *directly*, provided he makes A happen, and there is no B such that he makes B happen and B's happening makes A happen. Presumably if there is anything that an agent makes happen, then there is something that he makes happen directly. The things he makes happen directly may well be certain cerebral events, and therefore they will be things he is likely to know nothing about.[11] In undertaking to make his arm go up, he made certain such events happen directly, and those events in turn made his arm go up. Hence if raising his arm and not raising it were each within his power, then so, too, was the occurrence and the nonoccurrence of the events that he directly made happen; there is no contradiction, therefore, in saying that these events caused his arm to go up and that he had it within his power not to make the arm go up. A puzzle arises because we tend to suppose that, if a man makes B happen in the endeavor to make A happen, he thereby does something for the purpose of making B happen; but, as we have seen, this supposition is a mistake.

Our solution to the puzzle is consistent with A. I. Melden's observation that "one does not raise one's arm by performing another doing which has the motion of one's arm as effect—one simply raises one's arm."[12] For this observation—that raising one's arm is a "basic action"—is consistent with saying that one makes one's arm go up by making certain cerebral and muscular events happen. Making one's arm go up is an "intentional action," as we have defined this term, but making the cerebral and muscular events happen need not be.

(3) And our final puzzle is this: "If a man has learned what the muscle motions are that cause his arm to go up, and if, in the course of a physical examination, he wishes to move those muscles, then he can do so by raising his arm. But it is the muscle motions that cause the arm to go up. And causation is asymmetrical: if A is the cause of B, then B cannot be the cause of A. The cause, moreover, cannot occur after the effect. How, then, can he move his muscles by raising his arm?"

We will find the answer if we consider, once again, the man who caused the telephone to ring in Los Angeles in order to bring about the prior switching in the telephone offices in Denver. He did not undertake to make the Los Angeles ringing cause the Denver switching; what he did was to undertake to cause the Los Angeles ringing and to make this undertaking cause the Denver switching. And when our present agent makes his arm go up in order to make the muscles move, he does so because he knows that the motion of the muscles will be caused, not by the arm going up, but by his undertaking to make the arm go up.

---

[11] Compare H. A. Prichard, *Moral Obligation* (Oxford, 1949), p. 193. [See pp. 45–46 above. Ed.] This concept of "direct causation" should not be confused with Danto's concept of "basic action," referred to above. Compare the issues involved in the question whether divine intervention in the course of nature always takes place by means of "natural causes." Presumably, if God ever does intervene, there are certain natural events that he makes happen directly, in the sense defined above.

[12] A. I. Melden, *op. cit.*, p. 65. [See p. 26 above. Ed.]

"HE COULD HAVE DONE OTHERWISE"

Roderick M. Chisholm

Suppose we say to a man, "This morning you could have arranged things so that you would be in Boston now but you didn't," meaning thereby that he had it within his power this morning so to arrange things and that he did not exercise this power. How is one to understand this sense of "could" and of "in his power"?

First, I shall note certain things we need *not* be implying when we thus say of a man that he could have done otherwise. Secondly, I shall criticize certain familiar answers to our question. And, thirdly, I shall attempt to sketch what seems to me to be the proper way to answer it.

I

When we say, "This morning you could have arranged things so that you would be in Boston now," we are not implying that the man was able to do this at any other time. Conceivably he will have had only one opportunity in his life to arrange things so that he would be in Boston now, or even to arrange things so that he would ever be in Boston. And so we are not predicating of him a "general ability" to get to Boston, as one might, say, in the case of a lady who lives in Newton.

We are not implying that he *knew how* to exercise this power effectively. For we could consistently add: "What a pity you didn't know you should have traveled toward the east, for had you done so you would be in Boston now." (In this case, he may have known that he had the power without having known how to exercise

From *The Journal of Philosophy*, LXIV, No. 13 (July 6, 1967), 409–417. Reprinted by permission of the author and *The Journal of Philosophy*. Revised by the author.

it. For he may have known that he could travel in any direction and that one of them was such that if he were to travel in that direction then he would be in Boston now; but he may not have known which direction it was.)

Nor are we implying that he *knew that* he had the power. For "He could have" does not imply that he knew that he could have. When we say, "You could have arranged things so that you would be in Boston now," we may add, quite consistently: "And what a pity that you had no idea at the time that you could have." (In this case, although we can say "You could have," we cannot say "You could have if you had chosen." The latter statement, as Kurt Baier points out, would be true only if the agent's success would be due to his "skill, know-how, or practical knowledge, and not to luck." [1] But we can say to the man who didn't realize that getting to Boston had been in his power: "There were things such that, if you had chosen to bring *them* about, then you would be in Boston now.") It would not be entirely wrong to say that *most* of the things that are within our agent's power are things he knows nothing whatever about.

Nor does "He could have," in the present sense of the expression, imply that the act in question was in any sense morally or legally *permissible*. For having said, "You could have arranged things so that you would be in Boston now," we may add, quite consistently: "And it is a very good thing that you didn't, since, as you well knew, that was about the worst thing you could have done this morning." (In this case, one might *also* say, "This morning you *could not* have done it," but taking "could" in its moral or legal sense and not in the sense that now concerns us.)

II

Let us remind ourselves of certain familiar but (so it seems to me) obviously unsuccessful attempts to explicate the present sense of "could" and of "within his power."

Our "could" is not the "could" of logical possibility. If it were, we could say of the man we are now considering, "This morning he could have arranged things so that he would now be on the moon," since what such a statement expresses is something that is logically possible. But the man *we* are considering could not have so arranged things this morning.

Nor is our "could" the "could" of epistemic possibility. To say "You could have arranged things so that you would be in Boston now" is not to say "Your having arranged things so that you would be in Boston now is consistent with everything that is known." [2] For we may truly say that he could so have arranged things even though we know in fact that he did not so arrange them. Nor does "You could so have arranged things this morning" mean the same as "You having arranged them this morning is consistent with everything that was known this morning." Suppose that, unknown to everyone this morning, the man had been locked in his room, sound asleep, and unable to move. In such a case it would be false to say that he could then have arranged things so that he would be in Boston now; but

---

[1] Compare Kurt Baier, "Could and Would," *Analysis*, XXIII (1961), supplement, pp. 20–29.

[2] Hobbes had said that we call propositions contingent "because we do not yet know whether they be true or false"; see *De Corpore*, chapter 10. Compare the criticism of this view, and some of the others noted here, in Richard Taylor, *Action and Purpose* (Englewood Cliffs, N.J.: Prentice-Hall, Inc., 1966), ch. IV.

it might be true to say that his having so arranged them is consistent with everything that was known this morning.

Are we dealing, then, with a "could" that is "constitutionally iffy"? In saying "You could have arranged things this morning so that you would be in Boston now," are we saying: "If you had undertaken (chosen, willed, tried, set out) to bring it about that you are in Boston now, you would have succeeded"? Or, somewhat more plausibly: "There are certain things such that, if this morning you had undertaken (chosen, willed, tried, set out) to bring it about that those things would occur, then you would be in Boston now"? (The second formula is the more plausible because, unlike the first, it is applicable to the man who didn't know this morning that he could then arrange things so that he would be in Boston now.[3])

Whichever of the two types of "if" statement we choose, there would seem to be things consistent with the "if" statement that are not consistent with our "could" statement. If this is true, the "could" statement cannot have the same meaning as the "if" statement. Consider, for example, those things which are such that, if this morning our agent had undertaken (chosen, willed, tried, set out) to bring them about, then he would be in Boston now. And let us suppose (i) that he *could not* have undertaken (chosen, willed, tried, set out) to bring any of those things about and (ii) that he would be in Boston now only if he *had* undertaken (chosen, willed, tried, set out) to bring them about. These suppositions are consistent with saying that he *would* be in Boston now *if* he had undertaken those things, but they are not consistent with saying that he *could* then have arranged things so that he would be in Boston now.[4]

Is our "could" the "could" of physical possibility? In saying "You could have done it" are we saying that your having done it is something that is, or was, physically possible? We must distinguish between two senses of the expression "physically possible."[5]

In saying of a certain state of affairs that it is "physically possible," one of the things we might mean is this: that the state of affairs is one such that the statement that it obtains is, by itself, consistent with the laws of nature. In *this* sense

[3] There are objections to the first formula that do not apply to the second. Some of these were pointed out by J. L. Austin in "Ifs and Cans"; see his *Philosophical Papers* (Oxford: The Clarendon Press, 1961), esp. p. 166. In "J. L. Austin's Philosophical Papers," *Mind*, LXXIII, 289 (January 1964): 1–26, I noted that certain other objections are applicable to the first formula and are not applicable to the second; see esp. pp. 23–24. [See pp. 161–178 and pp. 187–191 above. Ed.]

[4] Presumably it was for reasons such as these that George Washington was said to be unable to tell a lie. The point was, not that he lacked the wit or skill or opportunity to do it, but that he was so good that he couldn't bring himself to deceive. Bayle quotes a seventeenth-century Walloon theologian, one de Wolzogue, who pointed out that, although God would have no difficulty in deceiving if he chose to deceive, nonetheless he *cannot* deceive since he *cannot* choose to deceive. De Wolzogue wrote: "God can deceive if he will . . . but it is impossible for him to have such a will to deceive; it is also impossible for him to endeavor to employ his power for the execution of a deceit, whence I conclude that it is impossible for him to deceive." See Pierre Bayle, *A General Dictionary, Historical and Critical*, article "Rimini (Gregorio de)," note C. According to some Christians, an important point of difference between Mary and Jesus was that, while Mary could sin but never did, Jesus "has not merely actually sinned, but also could not sin," the point being, again, that he could not undertake (choose, will, try, set out) to sin. Compare Ludwig Ott, *Fundamentals of Catholic Dogma* (Cork: Mercier Press, 1952), p. 169. Compare St. Thomas' treatment of the question, "Can God Do What Others Do?" in *On the Power of God*, Question II, Article 4.

[5] The two senses of "physically possible" are clearly distinguished by Bruce Aune in the article, "Can," in *The Encyclopedia of Philosophy* (New York: Macmillan and the Free Press, 1967), ed. Paul Edwards, vol. II, pp. 18–20.

of "physically possible," it is not only physically possible that our man this morning arranged things in such a way that he is in Boston now, but it is also physically possible that he then arranged them in such a way that he is now in a space capsule, orbiting the earth. But although such orbiting is "physically possible" in the sense in question, it is quite certain that, in our present sense of "could," the man we are talking about *could* not so have arranged things this morning that *he* is now thus orbiting the earth.

The other thing we might mean, when we say of a state of affairs that is "physically possible," is this: that no *other* states of affairs have obtained such that it is a law of nature that if such states of affairs obtain then the state of affairs in question does not obtain. Or, more exactly, if we say that it is physically possible, in this sense, for a state of affairs A to obtain at a certain time *t*, we mean that there have been no earlier states of affairs such that it is a law of nature that, if those earlier states of affairs obtain, then A does not obtain at *t*. In short, if A is physically possible, in this sense, then there is no sufficient causal condition for not-A. And so if it was physically possible for our agent to do otherwise, in the present sense of "physically possible," then there was no sufficient causal condition of his *not* doing otherwise.

Is our "could" thus one of simple indeterminism? In saying "You could have arranged things so that you would be in Boston now," are we saying merely: "Your *not* being in Boston now has no sufficient causal condition"? It would seem not. For it may well be that, although this morning the man could have arranged things so that he would be in Boston now, he has been in Chelmsford for the past 15 minutes. And this will mean that for the past 15 minutes, if not for considerably longer, there has been a set of conditions constituting a sufficient causal condition for his not being in Boston now.

Could we modify this indeterministic answer by saying: "Even though for the past 15 minutes there has been a sufficient causal condition for your not being in Boston now, there *was* a time (say, 10 o'clock this morning) when there was *no* sufficient causal condition for your not being in Boston now"? This, too, seems wrong. Suppose that between 9 and 11 o'clock this morning a certain *other* man had it within *his* power, in this present indeterministic sense, to render our agent incapable of moving from the place where he then happened to be and that our agent was incapable of depriving him of this power; and suppose further that at 11 o'clock the other man exercised this power but without there being any sufficient causal condition for his so doing. These suppositions would be consistent with saying to our agent, "At 10 o'clock this morning there was no sufficient causal condition for your not being Boston now." But they are not consistent with saying "At 10 o'clock this morning you could have arranged things so that you would be in Boston now."

We should remind ourselves, finally, that these indeterministic answers are frequently criticized in still another way. Thus there may be cases of indeterminism that are not cases of ability to do otherwise. Suppose that an atomic particle is so situated that there is a place such that there has been no sufficient causal condition for the particle *not* now being in that place. This fact alone would hardly imply that the particle *could* have made it happen that it is now in a place other than where it is in fact.

III

I shall now describe the type of answer that I shall propose to our question. Then I shall attempt to set it forth more precisely. I shall assume that the agent himself is a causal factor. In other words, at least one of the events that is involved in any act is caused, not by any other event or set of events, but by the agent, by the man. Causation is thus a relation that holds, not only between states or events, but also between agents, as causes, and states or events, as effects. I shall also assume that the concept of an act is essentially teleological: action involves *endeavor* or *purpose*, one thing occurring *in order that* some other thing may occur. Purpose or endeavor is "intentional" in the philosophical sense of this term; from the fact that one thing occurs in order that some other thing may occur, it does not follow that the other thing does in fact occur.

In attempting to explicate the concept expressed by the words "He could have done otherwise," I shall make use of the intentional concept of *undertaking*, or *endeavoring*. The technical expression "He undertakes (or endeavors) to make it happen that ——" will be used to mean, simply, that there is something that the agent makes happen with an end to making it happen that ——. The blank may be filled by any propositional expression, e.g., "He goes to Boston." [6]

The "could" I shall attempt to define will be indeterministic in this respect: our definitions will imply, in effect, that if our agent had it within his power at 10 o'clock this morning to arrange things so that he would be in Boston now, then there were certain things such that at 10 o'clock this morning there was no sufficient causal condition for his not then *undertaking* those things. (But presumably in the case of the undetermined subatomic particle, the absence of the equipment necessary for undertaking or endeavoring constitutes a sufficient causal condition for *its* not undertaking anything, and our definitions, therefore, will not apply to it.)

In addition to being thus indeterministic, our "could" will also be constitutionally iffy. For the definitions will imply that *if* our agent had undertaken some of the things just referred to, and *if* further conditions, which I shall try to specify, had obtained, then he *would* be in Boston now.

---

[6] I have discussed undertaking, or endeavoring, in greater detail in "Freedom and Action," in Keith Lehrer, ed., *Freedom and Determinism* (New York: Random House, 1966), esp. pp. 30–44. [See pp. 284–292 above. Ed.] The following is a simplified statement of what I take to be the logic of this notion. We take as undefined, "He makes it happen that —— in the endeavor to make it happen that . . . ," where the blanks may be filled by propositional expressions. We assume with respect to any instance of this locution, i.e., any sentence formed by filling its blanks: (1) it implies "There is a p and a q such that he makes it happen that p in the endeavor to make it happen that q"; (2) it implies the corresponding instance of "——"; and (3) it implies the corresponding instance of "He makes it happen that, he makes it happen that —— in the endeavor to make it happen that . . . ," in the endeavor to make it happen that . . . ." If we abbreviate "He makes p happen in the endeavor to make q happen" as "M(p,q)," we may summarize the third point by saying that "M(p,q)" implies "M[M(p,q),q]." We define the expression introduced above, viz., "He undertakes to make it happen that ——" as "There is a p such that he makes p happen in the endeavor to make it happen that ——." Instances of the latter expression will not ordinarily imply the corresponding instances of "——"; for undertakings are intentional and may not be successful. But, because of (3), "He undertakes" will imply "He makes it happen that he undertakes" (though not "he undertakes to undertake"). "He makes it happen that ——" would be defined as "There is a p such that he makes it happen that —— in the endeavor to make it happen that p"; and "He intentionally makes it happen that ——" would be "He makes it happen that —— in the endeavor to make it happen that ——."

But what we say must be consistent with the possibility that, for the past fifteen minutes, there has been a sufficient causal condition for the fact that our agent has not been in Boston now. To ensure this consistency I shall attempt to make a technical distinction between what we may describe as being "directly" in our agent's power and what we may describe as being "indirectly" in his power. Thus he may have had it *directly* within his power at 10 o'clock this morning to take the first step in a journey toward Boston, but he may have had it only *indirectly* in his power then to arrange things so that he would be in Boston now. And perhaps, although he then had it directly within his power to take the first step, he had it only indirectly in his power to take the second, and only indirectly in his power to take any of the others. But he may have been so situated that, if he *had* taken the first step, then he *would* have had it directly within his power to take the second, and if he had then taken the second, then he would have had it directly within his power to take the third, and so on, until he stepped into Boston. One could say that the first step "directly enabled" him to take the second (since taking the first put taking the second directly within his power) and that each step, had he continued the journey, would have directly enabled him to take the next.

I shall formulate three preliminary definitions: first, a definition of what it is for our agent to be free to undertake a certain action; secondly, a definition of "directly within his power"; and thirdly, a definition of "indirectly within his power." Then we will be able to say that an act is in the agent's power, in the sense that we have been concerned with, just in case it is either directly or indirectly within his power.

IV

Our first definition, then, will be this:

(D1) At *t* he is *free to undertake* to make it happen that ——, provided only: there is no sufficient causal condition at *t*, or prior to *t*, either for his undertaking at *t* to make it happen that ——, or for his not undertaking at *t* to make it happen that ——.

In other words, if the agent is free to undertake a certain act, then there is no sufficient causal condition for his undertaking it and there is no sufficient causal condition for his *not* undertaking it.[7]

The sense of "sufficient causal condition" that is here intended may be suggested by the following. If C is a *sufficient causal condition* for E, then C is a set of events no member of which begins after E begins and which is such that it is a law of nature, but not a law of logic, that if C were to occur then E would occur. (Ordinarily, when we say that one event "causes" another, we do not mean that the one event is a sufficient causal condition, in the present sense, for the other. We mean only that the one event is a "partial cause" of the other. An event that is a *partial cause* of an event E would be any proper subset of a "minimal" sufficient causal condition for E; and a "minimal" sufficient causal condition for

---

[7] "There is no sufficient causal condition for his not undertaking to make it happen that ——" would be spelled out in the technical locution we have introduced, as: "There is no sufficient causal condition for it not being the case that there is a p such that he makes it happen that p in the endeavor to make it happen that ——."

E would be a sufficient causal condition for E and would have no proper subset that is also a sufficient causal condition for E.)

Our second definition concerns the technical concept, "directly within his power":

(D2) It is *directly within his power* at *t* to make it happen that ——, provided only: there is a p such that (i) at *t* he is free to undertake to make it happen that p, and (ii) if he were to undertake at *t* to make it happen that p, he would make it happen that ——.

It may be that our agent is free, in this sense, to undertake to get himself to the piano. It may also be that if he were now to undertake to get himself to the piano, then he would cause himself to be three feet closer to Boston. Our definition would allow us to say, therefore, that getting three feet closer to Boston is now directly within his power. But if he does not know that there is such a place as Boston, then he will not know that getting three feet closer to Boston is now directly within his power. Or if he knows that there is such a place but does not know where it is, then he may know that getting three feet closer to Boston is directly within his power (for he knows, say, that going three feet in any direction is directly within his power) but he may not know what it is that he needs to undertake to get himself three feet closer to Boston. It is quite possible, therefore, that although there are various things such that his undertaking any one of them would get him three feet closer to Boston, his undertaking to get three feet closer to Boston is not among them.

It may be noted, in passing, that the point just made is essential to marking off the sense of "could" and "can" that is implied by "ought." Consider a man in the position of Jimmy Valentine, for whom it is imperative to open the safe in the shortest time possible: he has it directly within his power to turn the dials to any one of the 10,000 possible combinations within 10 seconds (there being 100 positions for the left dial and 100 for the right), but he has no idea at all of what the proper combination is. Our definition would allow us to say that it is directly within his power to turn the dials to the proper combination within 10 seconds; for if he undertook to set the dials to L-84 and R-32, then he would have the proper combination. But it would be unjust to say to him: "You could have done it within 10 seconds; therefore you ought to have."

Unless our agent is very close indeed to Boston, it is not likely that getting to Boston is directly within his power in the sense just defined. But there is a clear sense in which it may be *indirectly* within his power. For, as we have noted, if he takes the first step, which is directly within his power, then he will put taking the second step directly within his power, and if he takes the second, then taking the third will become directly within his power, and so on until the trip is completed. We need, therefore, a definition of "indirectly within his power."

Our definition, in effect, should tell us this. If there is a certain state of affairs such that it is indirectly within our agent's power to make that state of affairs happen, then there is a possible series of successive acts, each of which is such that, either he *is* free to undertake it, or he *would* be free to undertake it if he undertakes all its predecessors in the series; and if he does undertake all of those acts then he will make happen the state of affairs in question. I suggest, therefore, the following definition:

(D3) It is *indirectly within his power* at *t* to make it happen at *t'* that ——, provided only: there is a p such that it is directly within his power at *t* to make it happen that p; there is a series of states of affairs, the first of which is his undertaking at *t* to make it happen that p, and each of the others of which is a state of affairs such that it would be directly within his power to make that state of affairs happen if he were to make its predecessors in the series happen; and if he were to make those states of affairs happen, then he would make it happen at *t'* that ——.[8]

If these definitions are adequate, then we may say, of any given agent at any time, that his making a certain thing happen is *within his power* at that time if, only if, his making that thing happen is either directly within his power or indirectly within his power at that time. (Strictly speaking, "directly" is here redundant, since our definition implies that what is directly within the agent's power is also indirectly within his power.)

We may also say that the agent's undertakings are among the things that he makes happen.[9] Thus Suarez had said: "If we understand the term 'effect' so that it includes not only the thing produced but also everything that flows from the power of the agent, then we may say that the action itself is in a certain sense the effect of the agent." [10] And we may also say that these undertakings are among the things that are within his power to make happen. But we need not say that, if an agent undertakes to make a certain thing happen, he thereby *undertakes to undertake* to make that thing happen (". . . to say, I can will if I will, I take to be an absurd speech." [11]).

And so what do we mean when we say, "This morning you could have arranged things in such a way that you would be in Boston now, but you didn't"? We mean that, although the agent did not make it happen this morning that he so arranged things, nevertheless it was then within his power to make it happen. The "could," as definition (3) makes clear, is constitutionally iffy, and the proposed explication is consistent with saying that for some time now there has been a sufficient causal condition for the agent's not being in Boston now. But the "could" is also indeterministic. For we are saying that this morning the agent was free to undertake such arrangements. And this means, according to definition (1),

---

[8] An alternative procedure would be this: First, define "directly enabling" (e.g., "his making p happen would directly enable him to make q happen provided only: if he makes p happen, then his making q happen will be directly within his power") and then use this concept to formulate a definition of "indirectly within his power" patterned after Frege's definition of the ancestral. Thus we might say: "It is indirectly within his power at *t* to make it happen at *t'* that ——, provided only: (a) there is a state of affairs p such that his making p happen is directly within his power at *t*; and (b) its happening at *t'* that —— is a member of every class of states of affairs C such that (i) p is a member of C and (ii) whatever any member of C directly enables him to make happen is also a member of C."

[9] This follows from the third assumption referred to in footnote 6 above.

[10] F. Suarez, *Disputationes Metaphysicae,* Disp. XVIII, Sec. 10, para. 6.

[11] Thomas Hobbes, in *The Questions concerning Liberty, Necessity, and Chance;* the quotation may be found on page 42 of the excerpt reprinted in Sidney Morgenbesser and James Walsh, *Free Will* (Englewood Cliffs, N.J.: Prentice-Hall, Inc., 1962).

that there was no sufficient causal condition for his undertaking them and no sufficient causal condition for his not undertaking them.

The things that our agent *can* make happen, therefore, will be those things which are within his power to make happen. And so to say of him, "He could have done otherwise," is to say that there was a time at which his doing otherwise was within his power.

THE EVENT APPROACH

THE LOGIC OF CHANGE AND ACTION

Georg Henrik von Wright

THE LOGIC OF CHANGE

. . .

There is a main type of event which can be regarded as an *ordered pair* of two states of affairs. The ordering relation is a relation between two occasions which are successive in time. We shall not here discuss the nature of this relation in further detail. Simplifying, we shall speak of the two occasions as the earlier and the later occasion. The event "itself" is the *change* or transition from the state of affairs which obtains on the earlier occasion, to the state which obtains on the later occasion. We shall call the first the *initial*-state, and the second the *end*-state.

The event, for example, which we call the opening of a window, consists in a change or transition from a state of affairs when this window is closed, to a state when it is open. We can also speak of the event as a *transformation* of the first state to the second. Alternatively, we can speak of it as a transformation of a world in which the initial state obtains, or which contains the initial state, into a world in which the end-state obtains, or which contains the end-state. Such transformations will also be called *state-transformations*.

Sometimes an event is a transition, not from one state to another state, but from a state to a process (which begins) or from a process (which ceases) to a state. Sometimes an event is a transition from one process to another process. Some-

From *Norm and Action: A Logical Enquiry* by Georg Henrik von Wright (New York: Humanities Press Inc., 1963), pp. 27–69. Reprinted by permission of Humanities Press Inc. and Routledge & Kegan Paul Ltd.

times, finally, it is a transition from one "state" of a process to another "state" of the same process—*e.g.*, from quicker to slower or from louder to weaker.

Events of these more complicated types we shall, in general, not be considering in this inquiry. "Event" will, unless otherwise expressly stated, always mean the transition from a state of affairs on a certain occasion to a state of affairs (not necessarily a different one) on the next occasion. If the occasion is specified the event is an individual event; if the occasion is unspecified the event is generic.

7. We introduce a symbol of the general form T, where the blanks to the left and to the right of the letter T are filled by p-expressions. The symbol is a schematic representation of sentences which describe (generic) events. The event described by pTq is a transformation of or transition from a certain initial state to an end-state, *viz.* from the (generic) state of affairs described by p to the (generic) state of affairs described by q. Or, as we could also put it: pTq describes the transformation of or transition from a p-world to a q-world. The states of affairs will also be called "features" of the worlds.

We shall call expressions of the type T *atomic* T-expressions. We can form molecular compounds of them. By a *T-expression* we shall understand an atomic T-expression or a molecular compound of atomic T-expressions.

T-expressions may be handled in accordance with the rules of the p-calculus (propositional logic). As will be seen, there also exist special rules for the handling of T-expressions. The rules for handling T-expressions, we shall say, define the *T-calculus*.

Let p mean that a certain window is open. $\sim p$ then means that this same window is closed (= not open). $\sim pTp$ again means that the window is being opened, strictly speaking: that a world in which this window is closed changes or is transformed into a world in which this window is open. Similarly, $pT \sim p$ means that the window is being closed (is closing). We could also say that $\sim pTp$ describes the event called "the opening of the window" and that $pT \sim p$ describes the event named "the closing of the window."

Consider the meaning of pTp. The letter to the left and that to the right of T describe the same generic state of affairs. The occasions on which this generic state is thought to obtain are successive in time. Hence pTp expresses that the state of affairs described by p obtains on both occasions, irrespective of how the world may have otherwise changed from the one occasion to the other. In other words: pTp means that the world remains *unchanged* in the feature described by p on both occasions. It is a useful generalization to call this too an "event" or a "transformation," although it strictly speaking is a "not-event" or a "not-transformation."

In a similar manner, $\sim pT \sim p$ means that the world remains unchanged in the generic feature described by $\sim p$ on two successive occasions.

Again let p mean that a certain window is open. pTp then means that this window remains open and $\sim pT \sim p$ that it remains closed on two successive occasions.

We shall call the events or state-transformations, described by pTp, $pT \sim p$, $\sim pTp$, and $\sim pT \sim p$, the four *elementary (state-) transformations* which are possible with regard to a given (generic) state of affairs or feature of the world. The four transformations, be it observed, are *mutually exclusive;* no two of them can happen on the same pair of successive occasions. The four transformations, moreover, are *jointly exhaustive*. On a given occasion the world either has the feature described by p or it lacks it; if it has this feature it will on the next occasion either have retained or lost it; if again it lacks this feature it will on the next occasion either have acquired it or still lack it.

By an *elementary T*-expression we understand an atomic T-expression in which the letter to the left of T is either an atomic p-expression or an atomic p-expression preceded by the negation-sign, and the letter to the right of T is this same atomic p-expression either with or without the negation-sign before itself.

8. We shall in this section briefly describe how every state-transformation—strictly speaking: proposition to the effect that a certain change or event takes place—may be regarded as a truth-function of elementary state-transformations.

Consider the meaning of pTq. A p-world changes to a q-world. p and q, let us imagine, describe logically independent features of the two worlds. The p-world either has or lacks the feature described by q. It is, in other words, either a p & q-world or a p & $\sim q$-world. Similarly, the q-world is either a p & q-world or a $\sim p$ & q-world. The event or transformation described by pTq is thus obviously the same as the one described by $(p \& q \text{ v } p \& \sim q) T (p \& q \text{ v } \sim p \& q)$.

Assume that the p-world is a p & q-world and that the q-world is a p & q-world too. Then the transition from the initial state to the end-state involves no change at all of the world in the two features described by p and q respectively. The schematic description of this transformation is $(p \& q) T (p \& q)$, and the transformation thus described is obviously the same as the *conjunction* of the two elementary transformations described by pTp and qTq.

Assume that the p-world is a p & q-world and that the q-world is a $\sim p$ & q-world. Then the transition from the initial state to the end-state involves a change from "positive" to "privative" in the feature described by p. The transformation described by $(p \& q) T (\sim p \& q)$ is obviously the same as the conjunction of the elementary transformations described by $pT \sim p$ and qTq.

Assume that the p-world is a p & $\sim q$-world and the q-world a p & q-world. The world now changes from being a $\sim q$-world to being a q-world, but remains unchanged as p-world. The transformation described by $(p \& \sim q) T (p \& q)$ is the conjunction of the elementary transformations described by pTp and $\sim qTq$.

Assume, finally, that the p-world is a p & $\sim q$-world and the q-world a $\sim p$ & q-world. The world now changes from p-world to $\sim p$-world and from $\sim q$-world to q-world. The transformation described by $(p \& \sim q) T (\sim p \& q)$ is the conjunction of the elementary transformations described by $pT \sim p$ and $\sim qTq$.

Thus the atomic T-expression pTq is identical in meaning with the following disjunction-sentence of conjunction-sentences of elementary T-expressions:
$(pTp) \& (qTq) \text{v} (pT \sim p) \& (qTq) \text{v} (pTp) \& (\sim qTq) \text{v} (pT \sim p) \& (\sim qTq)$.

From the example which we have been discussing it should be plain that every atomic T-expression can become transformed into a molecular complex (disjunction-sentence of conjunction-sentences) of elementary T-expressions. Thus every atomic T-expression expresses a truth-function of elementary state-transformations. Since truth-functionship is transitive, it follows that every molecular complex too of atomic T-expressions expresses a truth-function of elementary state-transformations.

Consider an arbitrary T-expression. We replace its (not-elementary) atomic constituents by disjunction-sentences of conjunction-sentences of elementary T-

expressions. The original T-expression has thus become transformed into a molecular complex of elementary T-expressions. These last will be called the *T-constituents* of the original T-expression.

It follows from what has been said that every T-expression expresses a truth-function of (the propositions expressed by) its T-constituents. Which truth-function it expresses can be investigated and decided in a truth-table. This truth-table differs from an "ordinary" truth-table of propositional logic only in the feature that certain combinations of truth-values are excluded from it. The excluded combinations are those, and only those, which would conflict with the principle that, of the four elementary T-expressions which answer to a given atomic p-expression, *no two* must be assigned the value "true," and *not all* may be assigned the value "false."

If a T-expression expresses the tautology of its T-constituents we shall call (the proposition expressed by) it a *T-tautology*. An example of a T-tautology is (pTp) $v(pT \sim p)v(\sim pTp)v(\sim pT \sim p)$.

The negation of a T-tautology is a *T-contradiction*. An example of a T-contradiction is (pTp) & $(pT \sim p)$. It follows that $\sim (pTp)$ v $\sim (pT \sim p)$ is a T-tautology.

We consider, finally, some special formulae.

The first is $(p$ v $\sim p)Tp$. Its normal form is $(pTp)v(\sim pTp)$. The formula, in other words, expresses a true proposition if, and only if, on the later of two successive occasions the world has the feature described by p, independently of whether it had this feature or lacked it on the earlier of the two occasions.

The second is $(p$ v $\sim p)$ T $(p$ v $\sim p)$. It is a T-tautology. Its normal form is (pTp) $v(pT \sim p)v(\sim pTp)v(\sim pT \sim p)$.

A special rule must be given for dealing with T-expressions in which contradictory p-expressions occur. This is necessary because of the fact that a contradictory formula has no perfect disjunctive normal form. Or, as one could also put it: its normal form "vanishes," is a 0-termed disjunction. The rule which we need is simply this: An atomic T-expression, in which the p-expression to the left or right of T expresses the contradiction of the propositions expressed by its atomic p-constituents, expresses a T-contradiction. The intuitive meaning of this is obvious: since a contradictory state of affairs cannot obtain, it cannot change or remain unchanged either. Nor can it come into existence as a result of change.

9. Consider an arbitrary T-expression. We replace the (not-elementary) atomic T-expressions of which it is a molecular complex by disjunction-sentences of conjunction-sentences of elementary T-expressions. Thereupon we transform the molecular complex thus obtained into its (perfect) disjunctive normal form. (See above Section 3.) This is a disjunction-sentence of conjunction-sentences of elementary T-expressions and/or their negation-sentences.

It may happen that some (or all) of the conjunction-sentences contain two (or more) elementary T-expressions of different type but of the same variable (atomic p-expression). For example: (pTp) & $(\sim pT \sim p)$. Since the four elementary types of state-transformations are mutually exclusive, such conjunction-sentences are contradictory. We omit them from the normal form.

Consider next the negation-sentence of some elementary T-expression, *e.g.*, the formula $\sim (pTp)$. Since the four elementary types of state-transformations are jointly exhaustive, the negation of the formula for one of the types will be tautologously equivalent to the disjunction of the unnegated formulae for the three other types. Thus, *e.g.*, the formula $\sim(pTp)$ is tautologously equivalent to the disjunction-formula $pT \sim p \vee \sim pTp \vee \sim pT \sim p$.

Because of the joint exhaustiveness of the four elementary types of state-transformations, we can replace each negated elementary T-expression by a three-termed disjunction-sentence of (unnegated) elementary T-expressions. We make these replacements throughout in the above perfect disjunctive normal form of the molecular complex—having omitted from the normal form the contradictory conjunctions, if any, which occur in it. Thereupon we distribute the conjunction-sentences which contain disjunction-sentences as their members into disjunction-sentences of conjunction-sentences of elementary T-expressions. The formula thus obtained we call the *positive normal form* of the original arbitrary T-expression. It is a disjunction-sentence of conjunction-sentences of elementary T-expressions. No negated T-expressions occur in it.

10. *p*-expressions, we have said (Section 5), may be regarded as (schematic) descriptions of (generic) states of affairs. T-expressions again are schematic descriptions of generic changes. Thus, in a general sense, *p*-expressions could be called "state-descriptions" and T-expressions "change-descriptions." Following an established terminology, however, we here make a restricted use of the term *state-description* to mean a conjunction-sentence of n atomic *p*-expressions and/or their negation-sentences (cf. Section 3). By analogy, we shall make a restricted use of the term *change-description* to mean a conjunction-sentence of some n elementary T-expressions of n different atomic variables (*p*-expressions). Thus, for example, (pTp) & $(qT \sim q)$ is a change-description.

n atomic *p*-expressions (variables p, q, etc.) determine 2^n different possible state-descriptions. To each state-description of n atomic *p*-expressions there correspond 2^n possible change-descriptions. n atomic *p*-expressions therefore determine in all $2^n \times 2^n$ or 2^{2n} different possible change-descriptions. Thus, for example, to the state-description p & $\sim q$ there correspond the four change-descriptions (pTp) & $(\sim qT \sim q)$ and (pTp) & $(\sim qTq)$ and $(pT \sim p)$ & $(\sim qT \sim q)$ and $(pT \sim p)$ & $(\sim qTq)$.

Given n atomic *p*-expressions, we can list in a table the 2^n state-descriptions and the 2^{2n} change-descriptions which answer to the atomic variables. This is a list for the case of two atomic variables, p and q. [See table on next page. Ed.]

The positive normal-form of a T-expression which contains n variables for states of affairs is a disjunction-sentence of (none or) one or two . . . or 2^{2n} conjunction-sentences of n elementary T-expressions. If the disjunction has no terms the T-expression expresses a T-contradiction. If it has 2^{2n} terms the T-expression expresses a T-tautology.

ACT AND ABILITY

1. The concept of a human act is of basic importance to the questions which are discussed in this book. It is not one of the aims of deontic logic to clarify this concept. The notion of an act is more like a tool, which this logic has to use for other purposes of clarification. Considering, however, the complex and obscure nature of this notion, we must try to throw light on some of its aspects before we can be reasonably sure that our use of it as a tool in deontic logic stands on a firm basis.

I find it surprising that the concept of a human act has, *as such*, been relatively little discussed in philosophic literature. The same is true of the related notions of

	State-descriptions	Change-descriptions	
	p & q	(pTp) & (qTq) (pTp) & $(qT\sim q)$ $(pT\sim p)$ & (qTq) $(pT\sim p)$ & $(qT\sim q)$	
	p & $\sim q$	(pTp) & $(\sim qT\sim q)$ (pTp) & $(\sim qTq)$ $(pT\sim p)$ & $(\sim qT\sim q)$ $(pT\sim p)$ & $(\sim qTq)$	
	$\sim p$ & q	$(\sim pT\sim p)$ & (qTq) $(\sim pT\sim p)$ & $(qT\sim q)$ $(\sim pTp)$ & (qTq) $(\sim pTp)$ & $(qT\sim q)$	
	$\sim p$ & $\sim q$	$(\sim pT\sim p)$ & $(\sim qT\sim q)$ $(\sim pT\sim p)$ & $(\sim qTq)$ $(\sim pTp)$ & $(\sim qT\sim q)$ $(\sim pTp)$ & $(\sim qTq)$	

activity and behavior. Traditional philosophic discussion, bearing on these concepts, has concentrated on the problem of the so-called freedom of the will. In this discussion it is all too often taken for granted that it is clear what action *is*. In fact, much of what has been said about the problem of freedom can be shown to be void of interest, because based on some logically defective notion of acting.

In our discussion of acts we renounce every pretension of being systematic, and shall try to confine ourselves to a necessary minimum of conceptual distinctions and observations. The freedom of the will we shall not discuss at all. But of the related topic of the *ability to act* (do), we shall have to say something.

2. The notion of a human act is related to the notion of an event, *i.e.* a change in the world. What is the nature of this relationship?

It would not be right, I think, to call acts a kind or species of events. An act *is* not a change in the world. But many acts may quite appropriately be described as the bringing about or *effecting* ("at will") of a change. To act is, in a sense, to *interfere* with "the course of nature."

An event, we have said, is a transition from one state of affairs to another, or from a state to a process, or from a process to a state; or it is a transformation of processes. The Logic of Change, which we sketched in the preceding chapter, is primarily a logic of events of the first type. Events of the second and third type are also called the beginning (commencing, starting) and the end (ceasing, stopping) of processes.

The events which are effected through action can be of any of the several types just mentioned. The acts of opening a window or of killing a person effect changes in states of affairs. Starting to run or stopping to talk may be acts which effect a change from a state to a process and from a process to a state respectively. But when a walking man starts to run, his action effects a transformation of processes.

The Logic of Action, which we are going to outline in the next chapter, will primarily be a logic of acts which effect changes among states of affairs. Other types of action will not be explicitly dealt with in our formal theory.

The examples of acts which we have here mentioned are examples of what I shall call *generic acts* or *act-categories*. There is an, in principle, unlimited number of cases of window-opening or of starting to run.

The several cases of generic acts I shall call *individual acts* or *act-individuals*. It is noteworthy that the word "act" is used ambiguously in ordinary language to mean sometimes a generic and sometimes an individual act. It is, *e.g.*, correct to call murder an act; this is an act-category. It is also correct to call the murder of Caesar an act; this is an act-individual.

To the generic act of opening a window there answers the generic change of a window becoming open. To the individual act, which was the murder of Caesar, there answers the individual event of Caesar's death.

The logical difference between acts and events is a difference between "activity" and "passivity." An act requires an agent. An individual event is the taking place or happening of some generic event on a specified *occasion*. An individual act again is the doing of a generic act on a specified occasion by a specified *agent*.

3. When we say that an individual event happens on a certain occasion we may regard this occasion for the happening of the event as constituted by two successive occasions for the obtaining of certain states of affairs. Similarly, when we say that an individual act is done on a certain occasion we may regard this occasion for the doing of the act as constituted by the two successive occasions for the corresponding individual event.

Not every occasion (or pair of successive occasions) is an occasion on which just any individual event may happen or act be done. Thus, for example, only on an occasion when a certain window is closed *can* this window open or become opened. Generally speaking, only on an occasion on which the generic state of affairs described by p obtains, *can* the generic change described by $pT \sim p$ or that described by pTp take place or become effected ("at will").

We shall say that an occasion constitutes an *opportunity* for the happening of a certain generic event or for the doing of an act of a certain category, when the occasion has some generic feature which makes the happening of this event or the doing of this act (logically) possible on that occasion. For example: Only on an occasion when the window is closed, is there an opportunity for opening it.

Any opportunity for the doing of an act of a certain category is also an opportunity for the happening of the corresponding generic event, *i.e.* for the event effected through the act. The converse entailment, however, does not hold. Not every opportunity for the happening of a certain generic event is also an opportunity for the doing of a corresponding act. The occasion for the happening of the event has to satisfy additional conditions in order to constitute an opportunity for the doing of the corresponding act, *i.e.* the act of bringing about this event. Which these additional conditions are will be discussed later (Section 7).

4. The notion of an agent is essential to the distinction between acts and events. We shall here make only a few brief comments on this notion.

We may distinguish between *empirical* (natural) and *super-empirical* (supernatural) agents. An agent is empirical, I shall say, if the agent's existence is a contingent or empirical fact. Super-empirical agents have necessary existence. The difference between the two categories of agent can also be expressed by saying that an empirical agent is a "perishable," a super-empirical agent an "eternal" being.

The ideas of necessary existence and of super-empirical agents cannot be discussed within the limits of this work.

Agents who perform human action are empirical. But not all agents of human acts are human individuals.

We can distinguish between *personal* and *impersonal* agents. An impersonal agent is, for example, any so-called legal or juristic person (such as a corporation), a law court, a legislative assembly, or the state.

The action of impersonal agents is certainly "human action" in some sense of the word. The question may be raised whether acts which we impute to juristic persons and other impersonal agents of human acts are "logical constructions," *i.e.* could be defined (conceptually explicated) in terms of acts of some personal agents. This question, however, we shall not discuss.

Of what I here call personal agents we can further distinguish two kinds, *viz.* *individual* and *collective* agents.

When an act is performed by one man we shall say that it is performed by him *individually*.

Sometimes the performance of an act requires the joint acting of several men. The table may be too heavy to be removed from the room by one person alone, but two or more persons may do it by their joint efforts. We then say that the act of removing the table is performed by two or more men *collectively*.

That an act is performed by several agents collectively may also be described by saying that the *agent* who performs this act is a collectivity of men or a collective agent.

A collective agent must not be confused with an impersonal agent such as, say, a corporation or the state or some other juristic person. But the acts of a juristic person *may* entail the collective acting of some men.

Whenever several men perform an action collectively ("by joint efforts"), each man does something individually. The question may be raised whether acts attributed to collective agents could not be regarded as "logical constructions" of acts of some individual agents. This is another problem which will not be discussed here.

5. To every act (of the kind which we are here considering) there corresponds a change or an event in the world. The terms "change" and "event" must then be understood in the broad, generalized sense, which covers both changes (events) and not-changes (not-events). This correspondence between act and change is an *intrinsic* or logical tie. The act is, as it were, "defined" as the act of effecting such and such a change. For example: the act of opening a certain window is, logically, the act of changing or transforming a world in which this window is closed to a world in which it is open.

By the *result* of an act we can understand either the change corresponding to this act or, alternatively, the end-state of this change. Thus, by the result of the act of opening a certain window we can understand either the fact that the window is opening (changes from closed to open) or the fact that it is open.

On either way of understanding the notion of a result of action the tie between the act and its result is intrinsic. The act cannot be truly described as being an act of the category in question unless it effects a change or ends in a state of affairs of the kind in question, which we call its result. An act cannot be truly called an act of opening the window unless it ends (results) in the window's being open —at least for a short time. *Trying* to open the window need not, of course, result in this.

When the world changes in a certain respect it may happen that it also, by virtue of so-called causal or natural necessity, becomes transformed in a certain other respect. We then say that the second transformation is a *consequence* of the first. If the first transformation is effected through action, is the result of an act, then the second is a consequence of action, is a consequence of this act.

For example: a consequence of the act of opening a window may be that the temperature in a certain room sinks (is subsequently lower than it was before).

Whether a certain transformation will cause a certain other transformation to take place or not will usually depend upon the presence or absence of a number of other features of the world *beside* the states associated with the two transformations themselves. This is true also of human action. Whether the temperature in a room will sink or not as a consequence of opening a window will depend, among other things, upon the antecedent difference in outdoor and indoor temperature. Sometimes the temperature will not sink but rise.

Unlike the relation between an act and its result, the relation between an act and its consequences is *extrinsic* (causal).

Someone may wish to object to our terms "result" and "consequence" (of action) on the ground that what is here called a consequence is quite commonly in ordinary language spoken of as the result of an act, and vice versa. Thus, for example, we say that as a result of the window's being opened he caught a cold. The catching of the cold, however, was a consequence, to use our terminology, of the act whose result was that the window became open.

I am, of course, not anxious to correct the ordinary use of "result" and "consequences." What matters are not the terms, but the conceptual distinction between such changes and states as have an intrinsic and such as have an extrinsic relation to a given act. This distinction is important to note, and it is somewhat unfortunate that no clear terminological indication of it in ordinary parlance should exist.

Perhaps this "defect" of ordinary language is connected with the fact that the distinction between the result and the consequences of an act, although logically sharp, is at the same time in an important sense relative. What I mean by this can be explained as follows:

Consider again the act whose result we said was that a certain window is open (at a certain time and place). Could one not truthfully answer the question of what the person who opened the window *did*, by saying that he let cool air into the room (thus lowering the temperature)? Is not the cooling of the room the result, rather than the consequence? A consequence may be that someone in the room began to shiver and went out or subsequently caught a cold.

The answer is that we can certainly speak of an act of cooling the room, but that this is a *different* act from that of opening the window. The act of cooling the room requires *logically* that the temperature should go down, and *may* require *causally* that the window should be opened. The act of opening the window again requires *logically* that the window is opened, and *may* lead *causally* to the fact that the indoor temperature sinks.

Thus, one and the same change or state of affairs can be both the result and a consequence of an action. What makes it the one or the other depends upon the agent's *intention* in acting, and upon other circumstances which we shall not discuss in this work.

The act of opening a window and that of cooling a room are *logically distinct,* because of the nature of their results. But there is a sense in which the two acts may be said to "look" exactly alike. The sense in which they look alike is that the *activity* involved in performing the two acts may be identical, *viz.* certain muscular contractions and movements of the agent's limbs.

6. We shall distinguish between *act* and *activity*. To close a window or to kill a person is to perform an act. To smoke or to run or to read is to be engaged in activity.

The distinction is obviously important, but philosophers have so far done very little to clarify it. Here I shall make only a few scattered observations on the topic.

As acts are related to *events,* so are activities related to *processes.* Events happen, processes go on. Acts effect the happening of events, activities keep processes going.

Activity is not internally related to changes and to states of affairs in the same manner in which acts are related to their results. Activity, however, may be externally or causally related to changes and states which are consequences of performing this activity. Running need not leave any "imprint" on the world, but smoking may leave smoke. As a consequence of drinking a person may get drunk. Getting drunk is an event, and drunkenness a state.

The question may be raised whether activity is logically prior to acts, or vice versa.

In some sense activity seems to be prior. Action may be said to presuppose or require activity. The bodily movements which are a prerequisite of most human acts may be regarded as activity in which the agent has to engage in order to perform those acts. The changes and states which we call *results* of action may be viewed as *consequences* of such prerequisite activities.

Yet in another way action seems prior. Human activity has a beginning and an end. The beginning and the ending of activity have, sometimes at least, the character of acts. To *run* is an activity, but to *start* running or to *stop* running are acts of a kind. These acts, however, differ characteristically from acts which effect changes in states of affairs. The first of them implies a change or transition from a state to a process, the second again from a process to a state.

Beside the distinction between act and activity, we have to note a distinction between *acting* and *doing*. To do something is to perform an act. To be doing something is to be engaged in some activity. That which we have called the result of an act is that which any agent who (successfully) performs this act on a certain occasion *has done* on that occasion. When an act fails of its intended result the agent *has tried* to do something which, in fact, he failed to accomplish (do). Trying is thus a "logically incomplete" mode of acting. It is not immediately clear whether trying should be counted as falling in the category of act or in that of activity (cf. below, Section 10).

7. We have previously introduced the notion of an *elementary change*. The four types of elementary change, we said, are the four types of change and not-change which are possible with regard to a given (atomic) state of affairs and a pair of successive occasions. As schematic descriptions of the four types of change we introduced pTp, $pT \sim p$, $\sim pTp$, and $\sim pT \sim p$.

We now introduce the notion of an *elementary act*. By an elementary act we shall understand an act the *result* (Section 5) of which is an elementary change. The correspondence between elementary act and elementary change is one to one.

We shall use the symbol d for acting. The schematic descriptions of the four types of elementary act shall be $d(pTp)$, $d(pT \sim p)$, $d(\sim pTp)$, and $d(\sim pT \sim p)$. It should be observed that $d(pTp)$, etc., are schematic representations of *sentences* which describe acts, just as pTp, etc., are schematic representations of sentences which describe changes, and p, etc., are schematic representations of sentences which describe (generic) states of affairs.

We shall now consider the nature of the four types of elementary act in turn. For purposes of illustration, let p represent the sentence "The door is open."

Take first $d(\sim pTp)$. It describes the act of changing or transforming a $\sim p$-world to a p-world. In terms of our illustration: it describes the act of opening the door. We could say that $d(\sim pTp)$ represents the sentence "the door is being opened." A way of reading the schema $d(\sim pTp)$ would be "it is being done that p." For purposes of convenience, however, we shall read it, though this is somewhat inaccurate, "p is done" and call the act which the schema describes, "the doing of p." (A more accurate, but clumsier, name would be "the doing so that p.")

It is easy to see that the act described by $d(\sim pTp)$ *can* (logically) be done only provided two conditions are satisfied. The first condition is that the state described by $\sim p$ prevails on the first of the two successive occasions which jointly constitute an occasion for doing the act. Only when the door *is* closed *can* it become opened. One cannot open an open door. The second condition is that the change described by $\sim pTp$ does not happen, as we say, "of itself," *i.e. independently of the action of an agent,* from the first to the second of the two occasions. If a door is so constructed that a spring or other mechanism pulls it open as soon as it has become closed, then there is no such *act* as the act of opening this door. (But there may be an act of closing it and of keeping it closed. See below.)

Consider next $d(pT \sim p)$. It describes the act of changing a p-world to a $\sim p$-world. If we call the act described by the schema $d(\sim pTp)$, "the doing of p," we could call the act described by the schema $d(pT \sim p)$, "the destroying of p." If we apply the schema to our example it describes the act of closing the door.

The conditions for the doing of the act described by $d(pT \sim p)$ are as follows: The state described by p should prevail on the first of two successive occasions, *and* not "of itself" change to its opposite from this occasion to the next. For example: A door can become closed as a result of action, only provided it is open and does not close "of itself." Here the words "of itself" mean that the change is due to some "natural" cause, such as, *e.g.*, the operation of a spring, and is independent of the action of an agent.

Which act does $d(pTp)$ describe? pTp means that the world does not change in the feature described by p on two successive occasions. Can this be a result of action? It certainly can. The world might change in a certain feature, unless there is some agent to prevent it from changing. This is the sort of action that $d(pTp)$ describes. We might call it "the preserving of p." This act can be done, provided that the state described by p initially obtains, and would change into its contradictory state unless the change were prevented through action. For example: It could happen that a door which is open will close, e.g., under the influence of a spring-mechanism, unless somebody keeps it open.

$d(\sim pT \sim p)$, finally, describes the act of keeping the world unchanged in the feature described by $\sim p$. We could call this act "the suppression of p." This act can be done provided that the state described by $\sim p$ obtains, but would change into the state described by p unless prevented through action. For example: It could happen that a door which is closed will open, unless someone keeps it closed.

If by the result of an act we understand, not a change, but the end-state of a change, then the correspondence between act and result is not a one-to-one correspondence. The same state may be the result of more than one act. Thus, the state described by p can be the result both of the elementary act described by $d(pTp)$ and of the elementary act described by $d(\sim pTp)$. The fact that a certain window is open can be a result either of an act of opening it or of an act of keeping it open.

Each one of the four types of elementary act can be performed only provided a certain state of affairs obtains. The types of act described by $d(\sim pTp)$ and $d(pT \sim p)$, moreover, can be done only provided the change, which is their result, *does not* take place "of itself," i.e. independently of action. The types of act described by $d(pTp)$ and $d(\sim pT \sim p)$ again can be done only provided that the changes described by $pT \sim p$ and $\sim pTp$ respectively would take place unless prevented by action. But this is the same as to say that the changes (not-changes) described by pTp and $\sim pT \sim p$, i.e. the changes which are the results of the respective acts, *do not* take place "of themselves," i.e. independently of action.

The question may be raised what we shall say of the case when some *other* agent besides the agent in question effects the change, which must not happen "of itself," if we are to say truly that the agent in question has *done* it. Shall we say, then, that neither agent does the act? Or shall we say that both do it? If a person shoots at another at the very moment when the latter dies of a stroke the first person cannot be rightly said to have killed the second. The second died, but was not killed. The first did not commit murder, although he may have attempted to do so. Suppose, however, that two persons at the same time shoot at a third, and that each shot individually would have killed him. Obviously, we must say that the third man was killed, i.e. that his death was a result of action. But by whom was he killed? If the assumption is that each shot individually would have killed him it is not correct to say that the two murderers killed him "jointly" or "by joint efforts," and that therefore the agent, technically speaking, was a collective agent. The right thing to say is, in my opinion, that he was killed by each one of the two murderers, i.e. that his death was the result of an act of the one murderer *and* of an act of the other murderer. *Both* did it, not "jointly," but "individually."

We must thus think of the changes, the not-happening of which are conditions for the performance (performability) of an act, that they are changes *in nature,* *i.e.* such changes as happen independently of the interference of agents. This explains the meaning of the phrase "of itself," which we have been using when speaking of those changes.

8. Besides acts we have also to study their "correlatives," *forbearances.* What is it to forbear (to do) something?

Forbearing is not the same as not-doing *simpliciter.* That one forbears to produce through action the change described by $\sim pTp$, or the state of affairs described by p, cannot be described by $\sim d(\sim pTp)$. If, for example, a certain window is closed on a certain occasion one *does not* close it on that occasion—but neither does one *forbear* closing it then. Furthermore, things which are beyond human capacity to do (*e.g.* to change the weather), one does not do—but neither does one forbear doing them.

It is also clear that forbearing cannot be defined as the doing of not-changes. $d(\sim pT \sim p)$ does not mean that an agent forbears to produce the state of affairs described by p. It means that he ("actively") prevents this state from coming into existence—*e.g.* keeps open a door which otherwise would close.

It seems that forbearing cannot be defined in terms of action and change (and truth-functional notions) alone. But we can define it in terms of action, change, and ability. We propose the following definition:

An agent, on a given occasion, forbears the doing of a certain thing if, and only if, he *can do* this thing, but *does* in fact *not do* it.

The notion of forbearing, thus defined, is the logically *weakest* member of a series of progressively stronger notions of forbearing. On our definition, forbearing to do something which one can do does not presuppose *awareness* of the opportunity. In a stronger sense of "forbear," an agent forbears only such action as he knows he can perform on the occasion in question. In a still stronger sense, an agent forbears only such action as he knows he can perform but *decides* (chooses, prefers) to leave undone on the occasion in question. If, in addition, he feels an inclination or temptation to do the action, which he chooses not to do, then he is in a still stronger sense forbearing it. Of this strongest sense of "forbear" we also use such words as "abstain" or "forsake."

We shall introduce a special symbol f for forbearing.

$f(\sim pTp)$ shall mean that one forbears to change through action a $\sim p$-world to a p-world. We shall call this kind of action *forbearing to do.* The forbearance described by $f(\sim pTp)$ is possible only in a $\sim p$-world which does not, on the occasion in question, "of itself" change into a p-world. For example: To forbear to close a door is possible only provided this door is open *and* does not close "of itself."

$f(pT \sim p)$ means that one *forbears to destroy* (annihilate, undo) the state described by p. This forbearance is possible only in a p-world, which does not, on the occasion in question, "of itself" change into a $\sim p$-world.

$f(pTp)$ means that one *forbears to preserve* the state of affairs described by p. This is possible only in a p-world which will, on the occasion in question, change into a $\sim p$-world, unless the change is prevented through action.

$f(\sim pT \sim p)$, finally, means that one *forbears to suppress* the state of affairs described by p. This is possible only in a $\sim p$-world, which will, on the occasion in question, change into a p-world unless the change is prevented through action.

The modes of conduct which we have just been discussing we shall call the four types of *elementary forbearances*. It should be clear in which sense we can talk of "corresponding" elementary acts and forbearances. To the elementary act described by $d(pTp)$ corresponds the elementary forbearance described by $f(pTp)$, and so forth.

Forbearing, just as much as acting, has results and consequences.

Primarily, the results of forbearing are that certain changes do *not* take place. Thus, the forbearance described by $f(\sim pTp)$ results in that the change described by $\sim pTp$ does not occur. And similarly for the other elementary types of forbearance.

There is a *prima facie* objection to this way of arguing, which has to be answered. The result of my forbearing to open a certain window, say, is that I do not open it. But what if somebody else opens it? Cannot, in spite of my forbearance, the change from "window closed" to "window open" take place as the result of some *other* agent's interference with the state of the world? The answer seems to me to be this:

At the very moment when another agent opens a window, which I have up to this moment forborne to open, the *opportunity* for (continued) forbearing gets lost. What I may forbear to do, when the window is being opened by another person, is to keep the window closed or to prevent the other person from opening it. But I *can* no longer forbear to open the window. Thus, my forbearance to do this will necessarily be "reflected" in the fact that the window remains closed.

Using our generalized notion of change, which includes not-changes, we can also say that the results of forbearing are that certain changes *take* place. There is a certain convenience in this mode of expression.

Thus, instead of saying that the forbearance described by $f(\sim pTp)$ results in the fact that the change described by $\sim pTp$ does not take place, we can say that it results in the fact that the change described by $\sim pT \sim p$ takes place. For, if the state of affairs described by $\sim p$ obtains on a certain occasion and if the world does not change in this feature, then—by the laws of the Logic of Change—the world remains unchanged in this feature.

By similar argument we can say that the forbearances described by $f(pT \sim p)$, $f(pTp)$, and $f(\sim pT \sim p)$ respectively result in the changes described by pTp, $pT \sim p$ and, $\sim pTp$ respectively.

Instead of calling certain changes the results of forbearance, we can also call certain states of affairs the results of forbearance. These states are the *end*-states of the resulting changes. Unlike the correspondence between forbearances and changes as their results, the correspondence between forbearances and states is not one-to-one, but one-to-two. Thus, *e.g.*, the state of affairs described by p can be the result either of a forbearance to prevent it from coming into being or of a forbearance to destroy it. It can also, as will be remembered, be the result either of an act of doing or of an act of preserving it. Finally, this state can exist, without being the result of either an act or a forbearance.

It should now be clear what has to be understood by the *consequences* of forbearances—and also clear that forbearance can have consequences. The consequences of a certain forbearance are the consequences of the state or change which is the result of this forbearance. Thus, *e.g.*, if the state described by p is the result of a forbearance to prevent it from coming into being, then everything which is a consequence of the change described by $\sim pTp$ is a consequence of this forbearance. There is no difference "in principle" between the consequences of acts and of forbearances. (This is a logical observation of some importance to a certain type of ethical theory.)

We can exhibit the correspondences between the elementary acts, forbearances, and changes, together with the conditions of acting and forbearing and the results of acts and forbearances, in a table.

Condition of action	Act or forbearance	Result of action
$pT\sim p$ p is but vanishes, unless preserved	$d(pTp)$ p is preserved	pTp p remains
Same	$f(pTp)$ one lets p vanish	$pT\sim p$ p vanishes
pTp p is and remains, unless destroyed	$d(pT\sim p)$ p is destroyed	$pT\sim p$ p vanishes
Same	$f(pT\sim p)$ one lets p remain	pTp p remains
$\sim pT\sim p$ p is not and does not happen, unless produced	$d(\sim pTp)$ p is produced	$\sim pTp$ p happens
Same	$f(\sim pTp)$ one lets p remain absent	$\sim pT\sim p$ p remains absent
$\sim pTp$ p is not but happens, unless suppressed	$d(\sim pT\sim p)$ p is suppressed	$\sim pT\sim p$ p remains absent
Same	$f(\sim pT\sim p)$ one lets p happen	$\sim pTp$ p happens

In ordinary language, it seems, the words "act" and "action" are used pretty much as synonyms. The philosopher is free to give to the two words different meanings for the purpose of marking some conceptual distinction which he thinks important. Here I shall employ the term "action" as a common name for acts and forbearances. Acts and forbearances, we could say, are two *modes of action*.[1]

---

[1] Sir David Ross, too, makes a distinction between act and action. The distinction for which he uses the two terms is quite different from the distinction for which they are used here. See *The Right and the Good* (1930), p. 7.

9. From the discussion of *acts* (and forbearances) we now move to a discussion of *abilities* or the notion of "can do."

We have distinguished between generic and individual acts (Section 2), between the result and the consequences of an act (Section 5), and between act and activity (Section 6). These distinctions are relevant to the present discussion.

When do we say of an agent that he *can do* a certain thing—for example, can open a window, or can get up from his bed, or can tell a lie? This is a very complicated question. What is said about it here will be confined to a necessary minimum for our theory of norms.

To be able to do some act, we shall say, is to *know how* to do it. Sometimes we can also say that it is to master a certain technique. The mere fact that by some haphazard movements of my hands and fingers I succeed in opening a door with a complicated lock-mechanism does not entitle me to say that I *can* open a door with this type of lock. But if normally, *i.e.* on most occasions, when I set myself to the task I succeed in opening the door without much trial and error, then I may be said to be able to do this sort of thing. I then *know how* to do it. I also master a certain technique.

Ability to do a certain act must be distinguished from ability to perform a certain activity, such as to walk, to run, or to speak. Of the ability to perform a certain activity we do not normally use the phrase "know how." A child who has learnt to walk or to speak is not ordinarily said to know how to walk or to speak. But ability to perform an activity can sometimes quite naturally be characterized as mastership of a technique; for example, when a child has learnt to handle knife and fork in eating.

The "can do" which we are here discussing is the "can do" of acts, and not the "can do" of activities.

One can make a distinction between *ability* and *skill,* and relate it to a distinction between knowing how and having the mastership of a technique. The man who is able to do a certain thing knows how to do it. Only if the activity which is involved in doing the thing is of a complicated kind does this ability amount to mastership of a technique. When it does this we call such ability a skill.

We can also make a distinction between *ability* and *capacity.* Capacity often has the character of "second order" ability. It is within a man's capacity to do a certain thing, we may say, when he *can* acquire the ability or skill needed for doing this thing, although he does not yet possess it.

On the view of ability which we are here adopting, a criterion for judging truly that a man can do a certain act is that normally, on most occasions for doing it, he should succeed. But is this not like saying that he *can do* something only if, on most occasions, he *can do* this? Are we not moving in a circle here?

I do not think that we have a circle here but a noteworthy shift in the meaning of certain words. That I "can do" something has a different meaning when it refers to an act-individual and when it refers to an act-category. That on some occasion a certain state of affairs, say that a door is open, comes (came) into being as a *consequence* of some *activity* on my part, say some movements of my hands and fingers, is a necessary and sufficient condition for saying that I can (could) do this thing or produce this state *on that occasion.* The sole criterion of the "can do" is here the success of certain efforts. Of this "can do" no "know how" and no reasonable assurance of success before the attempt is required. These are requirements of that "can do" which refers to act-categories and which alone amounts to ability. It is, moreover, only when these requirements are satisfied that consequences of activity assume the character of *results* of *action*.

I shall call the "can do" which refers to individual acts the *can do of success*, and that which refers to generic acts the *can do of ability*. The first "can do" is always relative to an occasion for acting. The second is *independent* of occasions for acting. By this I mean that it makes no sense to say that we can do—in this sense of "can do"—the thing on one occasion, but not on another—unless that other occasion belongs to a stage in our life-history which is either before we have learnt to do this thing or after we have forgotten how to do it.

Before we have acquired the ability, success and failure on the individual occasion for acting is the only sense in which we can or cannot do a certain thing. When the ability (or skill) has become acquired, however, we can also do things which we *sometimes* fail to accomplish in spite of efforts. We may fail because of some unforeseen obstacle, or because another agent interferes and prevents us from completing the act. When this happens we describe what we *did* on the occasion by saying that we *tried to do* something, but failed.

Yet, as already observed, we cannot be said to have the ability, unless *on most occasions,* when we set ourselves to do the act, we succeed in doing it. In this way success can be said to be the measure and criterion of ability, and yet the meaning of the "can do" of ability be different from the meaning of the "can do" of success.

10. It would be a mistake to think that whenever an agent has successfully accomplished an act he has also tried to accomplish it. A similar remark can be made of activity. Normally, when I shut a door or walk or read I cannot be said to *try,* successfully, to shut the door or to move my legs or to read out the words. To construe every act as a result or consequence of trying to act would be a distortion.

Although doing does not entail trying to do, it would seem that ability to do entails capacity for trying to do. If I *can do,* I also *can try.*

It would also be a mistake to think that, although one cannot *do* any given thing, one can at least *try to do* it. One cannot, for example, jump to the moon. But can one not *try* to jump to the moon? It is not clear what sort of behavior we should describe as "trying to jump to the moon." Not until we have at least some idea of how to do a thing, can we try to do that thing. To "have an idea" of how to do a thing again presupposes that we are not convinced that it is humanly impossible to do that thing. Since we *are* convinced that it is humanly impossible to jump to the moon, in the ordinary sense of "jump," we can rightly say that we are unable even to try to perform this feat. To say "I try, although I know that I shall fail" is to state a contradiction in terms.

There are also many things which I know are humanly possible and which I may learn or otherwise acquire the ability to do, but which at present I cannot even try to do, because of my ignorance.

The question may be raised: Is trying act or activity? In the course of trying to do something, one may perform various acts. But, basically, trying seems to me to belong to the category of activity. Trying to do something may, as we say, "result" in the act's being successfully performed. But performing the act is not tied to trying to perform it in the same way as the resulting change is tied to the doing of the act. One is inclined to call the successful performance a consequence rather than a result, in our sense of the terms. It is *contingent* whether trying leads to result, but it is *necessary* that acting result in change.

When an agent *tries* to do something which he *can* do, but *fails* to accomplish the act, has he then forborne to do the thing in question? We are free to answer Yes or No, depending upon how we wish to mould the notion of forbearing. *Here* we shall understand "forbear" in such a way that unsuccessful trying to do something which it is within the agent's *ability* to accomplish, counts as forbearing. "Forbearing to do," in other words, will not be understood so as to entail "forbearing to try."

On this ruling, doing and forbearing are two *jointly exhaustive* modes of action. If an agent can do a certain thing, then, on any given occasion when there is an opportunity for him to do this thing, he will either do it or forbear doing it.

We could, however, also mould the notions in a way which would make unsuccessful trying a "middle" between doing and forbearing. That which is *here* called "forbearing" could then be called "failing to do" or "leaving undone." Perhaps it would be more in accordance with ordinary usage to call the two jointly exhaustive and mutually exclusive modes of action "doing" and "failing to do" rather than "doing" and "forbearing." But usage seems to be vacillating. The important thing is not whether we should choose this or that terminology, but that it should be clear how the terminology actually chosen is to be understood.

11. The notion of forbearing we have thus defined (see Section 8) that ability to do and ability to forbear doing the same thing are *reciprocal abilities*.

It may appear more plausible to say that what an agent can do he can also forbear doing than to say that what an agent can forbear doing he can also do. It is inviting to think that it is somehow "easier" to forbear than to do, and that there are many more things which we can forbear than things we can do.

The appearance of asymmetry between the abilities is partly, I think, due to confusions and to neglect to observe certain conceptual distinctions.

First, the idea may be guilty of a confusion between *not-acting* and *forbearing*. On an occasion which is not an *opportunity* (see Section 3) for doing a certain act, an agent necessarily does not do this act. Of course, we could so define "forbear" that an agent is said to forbear those acts also which he has not even an opportunity of doing. But this would be an odd use. We should then have to say such things as that an agent who is in a room where the window is open "forbears" to *open* the window in that room.

Secondly, the impression that there are more things one can forbear than things one can do may be due to a confusion between *doing* and *trying to do*. Consider a man on the bank of a river, which is, as a matter of fact, too wide for him to cross swimming. He *cannot* cross it, but if he can swim and is not certain whether he will reach the other shore he may *try* to cross it. If he can try he can also forbear trying. He forbears trying by not plunging into the water and setting out for the other shore. This is exactly the same "negative behavior," by which our man would manifest his forbearance to swim across the river, could he perform this feat. But this does not mean that forbearing to swim across the river and forbearing to try to swim across the river are one and the same thing. They are different just because they are forbearances relative to different modes of action.

In a sense, therefore, forbearing is precisely as "difficult" as doing. But in another sense, forbearing can quite rightly be said to be, normally, *easier* than doing. That an agent can or is able to do a certain thing shall mean, we have said (Section 9), that he knows how to do this, has learnt it, sometimes that he has acquired mastership of a technique. However, in order to be able to forbear, an agent need not, normally, learn anything in addition to learning to *do* the thing in question. We could express this insight in several ways. "Can do," we might say, is *prior* to "can forbear," although the two "cans" are reciprocal. There is no special "know how" of forbearing.

Consider again the eight elementary acts and forbearances which answer to a given state of affairs.

An agent's abilities with regard to corresponding acts and forbearances, we have found, are reciprocal. That which an agent can effect as a result of his action he can also forbear to effect as a result of his action, and conversely.

An agent's abilities with regard to acts and/or forbearances of different types, but relative to the same state of affairs, are *not* reciprocal. They are, on the contrary, *logically independent* of one another. The fact that an agent can, through his action, destroy a state of affairs which exists and does not vanish "of itself" is no guarantee that he can produce this same state of affairs, if it does not exist and does not come into being independently of his action. There are plenty of examples of this. To take a drastic but convincing one: Men can kill each other, but they cannot raise the dead. Generally speaking: that a man can or cannot do the act described by $d(\sim pTp)$ is logically independent of the proposition that he can or cannot do the act described by $d(pT \sim p)$.

The same seems to be true, "in principle," of the pairs of acts described by $d(\sim pTp)$ and $d(pTp)$ and by $d(pT \sim p)$ and $d(\sim pT \sim p)$ respectively. That I can suppress something which happens unless it is suppressed does not entail that I can destroy it if it exists. Nor does the converse entailment hold. And that I can prevent from vanishing something which exists, does not entail that I can produce it if it does not exist, or vice versa.

12. There are two types of act which are of great importance to deontic logic and which relate to one agent's ability to interfere with the ability of another agent to perform a certain act. These are the types of act which we call *hindering* or *preventing* and *compelling* or *forcing*.

These two types of act are obviously interdefinable. Therefore we can here limit the discussion to one of them. To compel an agent to do something is the same as to prevent him from forbearing this thing. And to hinder an agent from doing something is the same as to force him to forbear it.

To hinder an agent from doing something is to act in such a manner that it becomes impossible for that agent to do that thing. To hinder or prevent is to "make impossible." The result of the act of hindering an agent from doing a certain thing on a certain occasion is to change the world in such a way that the agent cannot do that thing on that occasion. But this result, be it observed, can be effected only on condition that the agent *can* do this thing. One cannot prevent people from doing that which they, in any case, cannot do. An act of preventing thus results in the fact that an agent, in some sense, cannot do that which he, in some sense, can do.

This may look like a paradox, though it certainly is not one. But it is an interesting illustration of the two senses of "can do," which we distinguished and discussed in Section 9. The sense in which one must be able to do something in order to become prevented from doing this thing is that sense of "can do" which refers to act-categories. The sense, again, in which one is not able to do that which one has become prevented from doing is the sense of "can do" which refers to act-individuals. Preventing from doing does not annihilate ability to perform the generic act. Preventing, on the contrary, presupposes this ability, and destroys the successful exercise of it only on an individual occasion.

This, of course, is not to say that abilities could not become annihilated or destroyed as a result or consequence of action. By injuring a person I may temporarily or even permanently make him unable to perform a certain generic act, which before he could do. This, however, is not what we ordinarily call "preventing." We call it "disabling."

THE LOGIC OF ACTION

1. By an *elementary d-expression* we shall understand an expression which is formed of the letter d followed by an elementary T-expression (within brackets). The letter f followed by an elementary T-expression will be said to form an *elementary f-expression*.

By an *atomic d*-expression we shall understand an expression which is formed of the letter d followed by a (atomic or molecular) T-expression. The letter f followed by a T-expression will be said to form an *atomic f*-expression.

By *df-expressions*, finally, we shall understand atomic d- and atomic f-expressions and molecular complexes of atomic d- and/or f-expressions.

Examples: $d(qT \sim q)$ is an elementary d-expression. $f((p \And \sim q) T(r \vee s) \vee \sim pTp)$ is an atomic f-expression. $d(pTp) \And f(\sim qTq)$ is a df-expression.

Elementary d-expressions describe elementary acts, and elementary f-expressions, elementary forbearances. Generally speaking, a df-expression describes a certain (mode of) action which is performed by *one and the same* unspecified agent on *one and the same* unspecified occasion.

The logic of df-expressions or the df-calculus is a fragment of a (general) Logic of Action.

2. We shall in this section briefly discuss the logical relations between the eight elementary acts and forbearances, which answer to one given state of affairs.

Firstly, we note that corresponding elementary acts and forbearances are *mutually exclusive*. One and the same agent cannot both do and forbear the same thing on the same occasion. But one and the same agent can do something on some occasion and forbear doing the (generically) same thing on a different occasion.

Secondly, we note that any two of the four types of elementary act (relative to a given state of affairs) are mutually exclusive. Consider, for example, the acts described by $d(pTp)$ and by $d(\sim pTp)$. They cannot be both done by the same agent on the same occasion. This is a consequence of the fact that no occasion constitutes an opportunity for doing both acts. This again is so, because a given state and its contradictory state cannot both obtain on the same occasion. Or consider the acts described by $d(pTp)$ and by $d(pT \sim p)$. They, too, cannot both be done by the same agent on the same occasion. For a given state of affairs either changes or remains unchanged. If, independently of action, it would remain unchanged the agent may destroy it, but cannot preserve it. That is: there is then an opportunity for destroying it, but not for preserving it. If again, independently of action, the world would change in the feature under consideration the agent may preserve, but cannot destroy, this feature.

Thirdly, we note that any two of the four types of elementary forbearances are mutually exclusive. Since no state and its contradictory state can both obtain on the same occasion, no agent can, for example, both forbear to preserve and forbear to suppress a given state on a given occasion. And since a state which obtains either changes or remains unchanged independently of action, no agent can, for example, both forbear to preserve and forbear to destroy it on one and the same occasion.

From the above observations we may conclude that all the eight elementary acts and forbearances which answer to one given state of affairs are mutually exclusive.

The question may be raised: Are the eight elementary acts and forbearances *jointly exhaustive?* Let, for example, the state of affairs described by p be that a certain window is closed. Is it necessarily true, given an agent and an occasion, that this agent will on that occasion either close the window or leave it open, open the window or leave it closed, keep the window closed or let it (become) open, or keep the window open or let it close?

I think we must, when answering this question, take into account considerations of human *ability*. Assume that the state of affairs is one which the agent can neither produce nor suppress, if it does not exist, nor destroy or preserve, if it exists. Then he can, of course, not be said truly to produce or suppress or destroy or preserve it. But neither can he be rightly said to *forbear* to produce or suppress or destroy or preserve it. For forbearing, as we understand it here, *makes sense* only when the act *can* be done.

There are many states towards whose production or suppression or destruction or preservation human beings can do nothing. Most states of the weather are of this kind, and states in remote parts of the universe. And there are states with which some agents cannot interfere in any way whatsoever, but with which other, more "powerful," agents can interfere in some, if not in every, way. A child may have learnt to open a window, but not to close it.

The correct answer to the above question concerning the jointly exhaustive character of the eight elementary acts and forbearances, answering to a given state of affairs, therefore is as follows:

Only on condition that the agent *can* produce *and* suppress *and* destroy *and* preserve a given state of affairs, is it the case that he necessarily will, on any given occasion, either produce *or* forbear producing, suppress *or* forbear suppressing, destroy *or* forbear destroying, *or* preserve *or* forbear preserving this state of affairs.

In the subsequent discussion it will be assumed that this requirement as regards ability is satisfied and that consequently the eight types of elementary acts and forbearances may be treated as not only mutually exclusive but also jointly exhaustive.

3. Every *df*-expression expresses a truth-function of elementary *d*- and/or *f*-expressions. This is so because of the fact that the operators d and f have certain

distributive properties. These properties are "axiomatic" to the df-calculus: that is, they cannot be proved in the calculus. Their intuitive plausibility, however, can be made obvious from examples.

Consider an atomic d-expression. Let the T-expression in it be in the positive normal form. It is then, normally, a disjunction of conjunctions of elementary T-expressions. The conjunctions describe mutually exclusive ways in which the world changes and/or remains unchanged. Obviously the proposition that some of these ways are effected through the action of some unspecified agent on some unspecified occasion is equivalent to the proposition that the first of these ways is effected through the action of that agent on that occasion or . . . or the last of these ways is effected through the action of that agent on that occasion.

For example: $d(\sim pTp \vee pT \sim p)$ says that some agent on some occasion either produces the state described by p or destroys it. The same thing is also expressed by $d(\sim pTp) \vee d(pT \sim p)$.

Thanks to the disjunctive distributivity of the d-operator, every atomic d-expression may become replaced by a disjunction of atomic d-expressions, in which the d-operator stands in front of a change-description.

Now consider for example the meaning of $d((pT \sim p)$ & $(qT \sim q))$. An agent, on some occasion, through his action makes both of two states vanish. Does this not mean that he makes the one and makes the other state vanish, *i.e.* does the above expression not mean the same as $d(pT \sim p)$ & $d(qT \sim q)$?

I shall answer in the affirmative and accept the identity of the expressions. I also think this answer accords best with ordinary usage. Be it observed, however, that ordinary usage is not perfectly unambiguous in cases of this type. To say that somebody through his action has become "responsible" for two changes in the world *could* be taken to mean that he effected one of the two changes, whereas the other took place independently of his action. But to say that he effected or produced the two changes would not seem quite accurate, unless he actually produced the one and also produced the other. We must not, however, be pedantic about actual usage. But we must make the intended meaning of our symbolic expressions quite clear. Therefore we rule that the d-operator is conjunctively distributive in front of change-descriptions.

Consider an atomic f-expression. Is the f-operator too disjunctively distributive in front of a disjunction which describes some mutually exclusive alternative changes in the world? What does it mean to say that an agent forbears this *or* that? Since the changes (the "this" and the "that") are mutually exclusive, the occasion in question cannot afford an opportunity for forbearing to produce more than one of the changes. The agent therefore, on the occasion in question, either forbears to produce the first or . . . or forbears to produce the last of the mutually exclusive alternative changes in the world.

It is essential to this argument that the changes are *mutually exclusive*. To forbear this *or* that, when both things *can* be done on the same occasion, would, I think, ordinarily be understood to mean that the agent forbears both things, *i.e.* does neither the one nor the other.

Thus the f-operator too is disjunctively distributive in front of a T-expression in the perfect normal form. For example: $f((\sim pTp) \vee (pT \sim p))$ means the same as $f(\sim pTp) \vee f(pT \sim p)$.

Remains the case when the f-operator stands in front of a change-description. For example: $f((pT \sim p) \& (qT \sim q))$. What does the agent do, who, on some occasion, forbears to destroy two existing states? The question can be answered in more than one way. If, however, we stick to the view that forbearing is not-doing on an occasion for doing *and* accept the above interpretation of $d((pT \sim p) \& (qT \sim q))$, then we must answer the question as follows: To forbear to destroy two existing states is to forbear the destruction of at least one of them. $f((pT \sim p) \& (qT \sim q))$ thus equals $f(pT \sim p) \vee f(qT \sim q)$. Generally speaking: the f-operator is *disjunctively* distributive in front of change-descriptions.

These four rules for the distributivity of the d- and f-operators secure that every atomic d- or f-expression expresses a truth-function of elementary d- or f-expressions. Since truth-functionship is transitive, it follows *a fortiori* that every df-expression expresses a truth-function of elementary d- and/or f-expressions.

The elementary d- and/or f-expressions, of which a given df-expression expresses a truth-function, will be called the *df-constituents* of the df-expression. Which truth-function of its df-constituents a given df-expression expresses can be investigated and decided in a truth-table. The distribution of truth-values over the df-constituents in the table is subject to the limitations imposed by the mutually exclusive and jointly exhaustive nature of the eight types of elementary acts and forbearances (relative to the same state of affairs).

If a df-expression expresses the tautology of its df-constituents we shall call it a *df-tautology*. If it expresses their contradiction we call it a *df-contradiction*.

$d(pTp) \& f(pTp)$ is an example of a df-contradiction. Hence $\sim d(pTp) \vee \sim f(pTp)$ is a df-tautology.

Assume that the T-expression in an atomic d- or f-expression is a T-contradiction. Then the positive normal form of the T-expression is a 0-termed disjunction. We cannot use the distributivity of the d- and f-operators for transforming the atomic d- or f-expression into a molecular complex of elementary d- and/or f-expressions. A special rule has to be introduced for the case. The rule is simple: the atomic d- or f-expression in question is a df-contradiction. The intuitive meaning of this rule is obvious: If it is logically impossible that a certain change should happen, then it is also logically impossible to effect or leave uneffected this change through one's action.

4. On the assumption, which we are here making, that the eight types of elementary acts and forbearances are jointly exhaustive of "logical space," every df-expression has what I propose to call a *positive normal form*. It is a disjunction-sentence of conjunction-sentences of elementary d- and/or f-expressions. It is called "positive," because it does not contain negation-sentences of elementary d- and/or f-expressions.

The positive normal form of a given df-expression is found as follows: The df-expression is first transformed into a molecular complex of elementary d- and/or f-expressions, according to the procedure described in Section 3. The new df-expression thus obtained is thereupon transformed into its perfect disjunctive normal form. This is a disjunction-sentence of conjunction-sentences of elementary d- and/or f-expressions and/or negation-sentences of elementary expressions. We replace each negation-sentence of an elementary d- or f-expression by a 7-termed disjunction-sentence of elementary expressions. The new df-expression thus obtained is transformed into its perfect disjunctive normal form. From the normal form we omit those conjunction-sentences, if there are any, which contain two or more different elementary d- or f-expressions of the same variable (p, q, etc.). What remains after these omissions is the perfect normal form of the original df-expression.

We give a simple example to illustrate this procedure:

Let the df-expression be $d(pTp) \vee d(qTq)$. Its perfect disjunctive normal form is $d(pTp)$ & $d(qTq) \vee d(pTp)$ & $\sim d(qTq) \vee \sim d(pTp)$ & $d(qTq)$. We replace $\sim d(pTp)$ by the 7-termed disjunction-sentence $d(pT \sim p) \vee d(\sim pTp) \vee d(\sim pT \sim p) \vee f(pTp) \vee f(pT \sim p) \vee f(\sim pTp) \vee f(\sim pT \sim p)$, and $\sim d(qTq)$ by the 7-termed disjunction-sentence $d(qT \sim q) \vee d(\sim qTq) \vee d(\sim qT \sim q) \vee f(qTq) \vee f(qT \sim q) \vee f(\sim qTq) \vee f(\sim qT \sim q)$. After distribution we get the 15-termed disjunction-sentence of 2-termed conjunction-sentences $d(pTp)$ & $d(qTq) \vee d(pTp)$ & $d(qT \sim q) \vee d(pTp)$ & $d(\sim qTq) \vee d(pTp)$ & $d(\sim qT \sim q) \vee d(pTp)$ & $f(qTq) \vee d(pTp)$ & $f(qT \sim q) \vee d(pTp)$ & $f(\sim qTq) \vee d(pTp)$ & $f(\sim qT \sim q) \vee d(pT \sim p)$ & $d(qTq) \vee d(\sim pTp)$ & $d(qTq) \vee d(\sim pT \sim p)$ & $d(qTq) \vee f(pTp)$ & $d(qTq) \vee f(pT \sim p)$ & $d(qTq) \vee f(\sim pTp)$ & $d(qTq) \vee f(\sim pT \sim p)$ & $d(qTq)$. This is the positive normal form of the original df-expression. It is a complete enumeration of the 15 mutually exclusive generic modes of action, which are covered by the description $d(pTp) \vee d(qTq)$.

5. We have previously introduced the notions of a state-description and a change-description. By analogy, we now introduce the notion of an *act-description*. An act-description is a conjunction-sentence of some n elementary d- and/or f-expressions of n different atomic variables. Thus, for example, $d(pTp)$ & $f(qT \sim q)$ is an act-description.

As we know, n atomic variables determine 2^n different possible state-descriptions and 2^{2n} different possible change-descriptions. An act-description is obtained from a given change-description through the insertion of the letter d or the letter f in front of each of the n T-expressions in the change-description. The insertion can take place in 2^n different ways. Consequently, the total number of act-descriptions which are determined by n atomic variables is $2^n \times 2^{2n}$ or 2^{3n}.

(pTp) & $(qT \sim q)$ is a change-description. To it answer four act-descriptions, viz. $d(pTp)$ & $d(qT \sim q)$ and $d(pTp)$ & $f(qT \sim q)$ and $f(pTp)$ & $d(qT \sim q)$ and $f(pTp)$ & $f(qT \sim q)$.

Given n atomic variables, we can list in a table the 2^n state-descriptions, the 2^{2n} change-descriptions, and the 2^{3n} act-descriptions, which these variables determine. On the next page there is a fragment of such a list for the case of two variables, p and q.

The positive normal form of a df-expression which contains n variables for states of affairs is a disjunction-sentence of (none or) one or two or . . . or 2^{3n} conjunction-sentences of n elementary d- and/or f-expressions. If the disjunction-sentence has no members the df-expression expresses a df-contradiction. If it has 2^{3n} members the df-expression expresses a df-tautology.

It is often convenient to regard the positive normal form of a df-expression as consisting of "bits" or segments answering to the various conditions (change-descriptions), which constitute opportunities for doing the act in question. Thus, for example, the 15-termed disjunction-sentence, which is the positive normal form

State-descriptions	Change-descriptions	Act-descriptions
	(pTp) & (qTq)	$d(pTp)$ & $d(qTq)$ $d(pTp)$ & $f(qTq)$ $f(pTp)$ & $d(qTq)$ $f(pTp)$ & $f(qTq)$
p & q	(pTp) & $(qT{\sim}q)$	
	$(pT{\sim}p)$ & (qTq)	
	$(pT{\sim}p)$ & $(qT{\sim}q)$	
	$({\sim}pT{\sim}p)$ & $({\sim}qT{\sim}q)$	
	$({\sim}pT{\sim}p)$ & $({\sim}qTq)$	
4. ${\sim}p$ & ${\sim}q$	$({\sim}pTp)$ & $({\sim}qT{\sim}q)$	
	16. $({\sim}pTp)$ & $({\sim}qTq)$	$d({\sim}pTp)$ & $d({\sim}qTq)$ $d({\sim}pTp)$ & $f({\sim}qTq)$ $f({\sim}pTp)$ & $d({\sim}qTq)$ 64. $f({\sim}pTp)$ & $f({\sim}qTq)$

of the expression $d(pTp) \vee d(qTq)$ (Section 4), may become divided into the following seven "bits":

$d(pT {\sim}p)$ & $d(qTq) \vee f(pT {\sim}p)$ & $d(qTq)$ answering to (pTp) & $(qT {\sim}q)$; $d(pTp)$ & $d(qT {\sim}q) \vee d(pTp)$ & $f(qT {\sim}q)$ answering to $(pT {\sim}p)$ & (qTq); $d(pTp)$ & $d(qTq) \vee d(pTp)$ & $f(qTq) \vee f(pTp)$ & $d(qTq)$ answering to $(pT {\sim}p)$ & $(qT {\sim}q)$; $d(pTp)$ & $d({\sim}qTq) \vee d(pTp)$ & $f({\sim}qTq)$ answering to $(pT {\sim}p)$ & $({\sim}qT {\sim}q)$; $d(pTp)$ & $d({\sim}qT {\sim}q) \vee d(pTp)$ & $f({\sim}qT {\sim}q)$ answering to $(pT {\sim}p)$ & $({\sim}qTq)$; $d({\sim}pTp)$ & $d(qTq) \vee f({\sim}pTp)$ & $d(qTq)$ answering to $({\sim}pT {\sim}p)$ & $(qT {\sim}q)$; and $d({\sim}pT {\sim}p)$ & $d(qTq) \vee f({\sim}pT {\sim}p)$ & $d(qTq)$ answering to $({\sim}pTp)$ & $(qT {\sim}q)$.

6. We shall distinguish between the *external* and the *internal* negation of a *df*-expression.

External negation is negation in the "ordinary" sense. Its symbol is $\sim$. If the positive normal form of a given *df*-expression has m members (conjunction-sentences), then the positive normal form of the external negation of this *df*-expression has 2^{3n}-m members, n being the number of atomic variables of the expression. Thus, for example, the positive normal form of $\sim(d(pTp) \vee d(qTq))$ is a disjunction-sentence of 49, *i.e.* of 64—15, conjunction-sentences of two elementary *df*-expressions. It is readily seen that this normal form has 16 "bits," of which the shortest is $f(pTp)$ & $f(qTq)$. The other segments are either 2-termed or 4-termed disjunction-sentences (of conjunction-sentences of two elementary *df*-expressions).

The internal negation of a given *df*-expression is obtained as follows: The expression is transformed into its positive normal form, and the normal form is divided up into segments. We form the disjunction-sentence of all those conjunction-sentences (of elementary df-expressions of the same atomic variables) which do *not* occur in the segments but answer to the same conditions for acting (change-descriptions) as the conjunction-sentences in the segments. The expression thus formed is the (positive normal form of the) internal negation of the given df-expression.

For example: The internal negation of $d(pTp) \vee d(qTq)$ is the 13-termed disjunction-sentence $d(pT \sim p) \& f(qTq) \vee f(pT \sim p) \& f(qTq) \vee f(pTp) \& d(qT \sim q)$ $\vee f(pTp) \& f(qT \sim q) \vee f(pTp) \& f(qTq) \vee f(pTp) \& d(\sim qTq) \vee f(pTp) \& f(\sim qTq)$ $\vee f(pTp) \& d(\sim qT \sim q) \vee f(pTp) \& f(\sim qT \sim q) \vee d(\sim pTp) \& f(qTq) \vee f(\sim pTp)$ $\& f(qTq) \vee d(\sim pT \sim p) \& f(qTq) \vee f(\sim pT \sim p) \& f(qTq)$.

The internal negation of $d(pTp) \& d(qTq)$ is the 3-termed disjunction-sentence $d(pTp) \& f(qTq) \vee f(pTp) \& d(qTq) \vee f(pTp) \& f(qTq)$. Its external negation is (in the normal form) a 63-termed disjunction-sentence.

The internal negation of $d(pTp)$ is $f(pTp)$. Generally speaking: *the internal negation of doing is forbearing.*

The external negation of $d(pTp)$ is, in the normal form, the 7-termed disjunction-sentence $d(pT \sim p) \vee d(\sim pTp) \vee d(\sim pT \sim p) \vee f(pTp) \vee f(pT \sim p) \vee f(\sim pTp)$ $\vee f(\sim pT \sim p)$.

The external negation says that the action described by the expression in question is *not* done (by the agent in question on the occasion in question). The internal negation says that, under the same conditions of action, the "opposite" of the action described by the expression in question *is* done (by the agent in question on the occasion in question).

An action and its external negation are incompatible (modes of action). This means: they cannot both be performed by the same agent on the same occasion. An action and its internal negation are also incompatible.

We can distinguish between external and internal incompatibility of actions (and of expressions for action). Two actions will be called externally incompatible when the proposition that the one has been performed (by some agent on some occasion) entails the proposition that the external negation of the other has been performed (by the same agent on the same occasion). Two actions will be called internally incompatible when the proposition that the one has been performed entails the proposition that the internal negation of the other has been performed.

For example: The actions described by $d(pTp) \& d(qTq)$ and by $d(pT \sim p)$ $\& d(qT \sim q)$ are *externally* incompatible. The actions described by $d(pTp) \&$ $d(qTq)$ and $d(pTp) \& f(qTq)$ are *internally* incompatible. Also: the actions described by $d(pTp)$ and $f(pT \sim p)$ are externally, the actions described by $d(pTp)$ and $f(pTp)$ internally incompatible.

It is readily seen that internal incompatibility entails external incompatibility, but not vice versa.

The notions of external and internal incompatibility can be generalized so as to become applicable to any number n of actions (and of descriptions of actions).

n actions are externally incompatible when they cannot be all performed by the same agent on the same occasion. n actions are internally incompatible when they are externally incompatible *and* the conditions under which each of them can be performed are the same.

Speaking of descriptions of action, we can say that n df-expressions are externally incompatible when their conjunction is a *df*-contradiction. They are internally incompatible when they are externally incompatible *and* answer to the same change-descriptions.

Three or more actions can be (externally or internally) incompatible, even though no two of them are incompatible. An example would be the three actions described by $d(pTp)$ & $d(qTq)$ v $d(pTp)$ & $f(qTq)$ and $d(pTp)$ & $f(qTq)$ v $f(pTp)$ & $d(qTq)$ and $d(pTp)$ & $d(qTq)$ v $f(pTp)$ & $d(qTq)$. Their incompatibility, moreover, is internal, since the condition under which each of them can be performed is the same, *viz.* $(pT \sim p)$ & $(qT \sim q)$.

7. We shall also distinguish between the external and the internal *consequences* of (the proposition expressed by) a given *df*-expression.

A *df*-expression entails (in the Logic of Action) another *df*-expression if, and only if, the implication-sentence whose antecedent is the first and whose consequent is the second *df*-expression is a *df*-tautology. When a *df*-expression entails another the second is called an external consequence of the first.

For example: $d(pTp)$ & $d(qTq)$ entails $d(pTp)$ & $d(qTq)$ v $d(pT \sim p)$ & $d(qT \sim q)$. "If a person on some occasion continues both of two states, then, trivially, he either continues them both or destroys them both." This entailment is valid already by virtue of the laws of the Logic of Propositions.

A *df*-expression is an internal consequence of another *df*-expression if, and only if, the first is a (external) consequence of the second *and* the two expressions answer to the same change-description (conditions of action).

For example: $d(pTp)$ & $d(qTq)$ v $f(pTp)$ & $f(qTq)$ is an internal consequence of $d(pTp)$ & $d(qTq)$. "If an agent on some occasion continues both of two states, then, trivially, he either continues both or lets both vanish."

8. Two or more *df*-expressions which contain exactly the same variables for states of affairs will be called *uniform* with regard to the variables. Expressions which are not uniform can be made uniform by a vacuous introduction of new variables into them.

If, *e.g.*, the variable p does not occur in a given *df*-expression, we can introduce it into the expression by forming the conjunction-sentence of the given *df*-expression and, *e.g.*, the *df*-expression $d(pTp)$ v $\sim d(pTp)$. In a similar manner, the variable p can be introduced into a given T-expression by conjoining the expression with (pTp) v $\sim(pTp)$, and into a given p-expression by conjoining it with p v $\sim p$.

Consider the T-expression pTp. If we want to introduce the variable q into it, we can form the conjunction-sentence (pTp) & $(qTq$ v $\sim(qTq))$ or the conjunction-sentence (pTp) & $(qTq$ v $qT \sim q$ v $\sim qTq$ v $\sim qT \sim q)$. But we can achieve the same by replacing p in the original expression by the conjunction-sentence p & $(q$ v $\sim q)$. The reader can easily satisfy himself that the two operations lead to the same result, *i.e.* that after the appropriate transformations we reach in the end the same T-expression. Because of this fact we say that T-expressions are *extensional* with regard to p-expressions. This means, generally speaking, that if for some p-expression which occurs in a T-expression we substitute a (in the p-calculus) tautologously equivalent p-expression the new T-expression which we get through the substitution is (in the T-calculus) tautologously equivalent to the original T-expression.

df-expressions, be it observed, are *not* extensional with regard to *p*-expressions, nor with regard to *T*-expressions. If for some *p*-expression which occurs in a *df*-expression we substitute a (in the *p*-calculus) tautologously equivalent *p*-expression the new *df*-expression is not necessarily (in the *df*-calculus) tautologously equivalent to the first. And similarly, if for some *T*-expression which occurs in a *df*-expression we substitute a (in the *T*-calculus) tautologously equivalent *T*-expression. In the said respect *df*-expressions may be said to be *intensional* and the *df*-calculus may be called an intensional calculus.

Consider some elementary *d*-expression, *e.g.*, $d(pTp)$. As known from the Logic of Propositions, p is tautologously equivalent to $p \& q \vee p \& \sim q$. Consider now the atomic *d*-expression $d((p \& q \vee p \& \sim q) \; T \; (p \& q \vee p \& \sim q))$. According to the laws of the Logic of Change, $(p \& q \vee p \& \sim q) \; T \; (p \& q \vee p \& \sim q)$ is tautologously equivalent to $pTp \& (qTq \vee qT \sim q \vee \sim qTq \vee \sim qT \sim q)$. Consider next the atomic *d*-expression $d(pTp \& (qTq \vee qT \sim q \vee \sim qTq \vee \sim qT \sim q))$. According to the Logic of Action, this is tautologously equivalent to the molecular *d*-expression $d(pTp) \& d(qTq \vee qT \sim q \vee \sim qTq \vee \sim qT \sim q)$, which in its turn is equivalent to $d(pTp) \& (d(qTq) \vee d(qT \sim q) \vee d(\sim qTq) \vee d(\sim qT \sim q))$.

Let us compare the first and the last of our above *d*-expressions. Do the two mean the same? The first says that a certain agent on a certain occasion through his action preserves a certain state of affairs, *e.g.*, keeps a certain door open. The second says that a certain agent on a certain occasion does this same thing and also another thing in addition to it. This additional thing is that he, through his action, either preserves or destroys or produces or suppresses a certain state of affairs, *e.g.*, the state of affairs that a car is parked in the front of his house. It is plain that, even if it were (which it need not be) possible for the agent to do the first thing *and* one of the mutually exclusive four other things on one and the same occasion it is not necessary that he should do any of the four other things on an occasion when he does the first. Hence, the meaning of $d(pTp)$ is *not* the same as the meaning of $d(pTp) \& (d(qTq) \vee d(qT \sim q) \vee d(\sim qTq) \vee d(\sim qT \sim q))$.

That the two meanings must be different is not at all difficult to understand. The disjunction of changes described by $qTq \vee qT \sim q \vee \sim qTq \vee \sim qT \sim q$ is a tautology, something which necessarily *happens* on any occasion. But neither the disjunctive act, described by $d(qTq \vee qT \sim q \vee \sim qTq \vee \sim qT \sim q)$, nor the equivalent disjunction of acts described by $d(qTq) \vee d(qT \sim q) \vee d(\sim qTq) \vee d(\sim qT \sim q)$ is a tautology, *i.e.* something which will necessarily be *done* on every occasion. If, for example, an agent forbears to do one of the four acts, then he does not do any of them. And if, for some reason or other, he *cannot* do any of them, then he neither does nor forbears any of them on a given occasion.

Though it is easy to see that the two expressions have different meanings, it may yet appear as something of a paradox that there should be this difference— considering how the two expressions are related to each other "formally." We reached the last from the first through a series of substitutions of tautologously equivalent expressions and of a series of transformations of expressions into tautologously equivalent forms. We have no reason to deny or to doubt any of these equivalences. What we have to do, then, is to reject some of the substitutions (as not leading from one expression to another, which is tautologously equivalent to the first). The substitution which we reject is the first. The *act* described by $d(pTp)$

is not the same as the act described by $d((p \& q \vee p \& \sim q) \ T \ (p \& q \vee p \& \sim q))$ — although the *change* described by $(p \& q \vee p \& \sim q) \ T \ (p \& q \vee p \& \sim q)$ is the same as the change described by pTp and the *state* described by $p \& q \vee p \& \sim q$ is the same as the state described by p.

When *df*-expressions are uniform with regard to the variables and in the positive normal form it can instantly be seen from the "look" of the expressions whether they are compatible or not. They are compatible if, and only if, the normal forms have at least one disjunct in common.

When *df*-expressions are uniform with regard to the variables and in the positive normal form it can also instantly be seen from the "look" of the expressions whether the one entails (or is a consequence of) the other. The one entails the other if, and only if, the normal form of the first is a part of the normal form of the other.

BIBLIOGRAPHY

I. *Historical Background.* Aristotle is the starting point for an investigation into the nature of human action. See his *Ethica Nicomachea*, especially Book III, Chapters 1–5 and *Ethica Eudemia*, especially Book II; also his *De Anima*, especially Book III. The standard English translation is *The Works of Aristotle*, under the editorship of W. D. Ross (Oxford: The Clarendon Press). Among the medievals, there is an extremely interesting essay by .Anselm, written about 1090, in F. S. Schmitt, "Ein neues unvollendetes Werk des Hl. Anselm von Canterbury," *Beiträge zur Geschichte der Philosophie und Theologie des Mittelalters 33* (1936), pp. 23–45. (There is an unpublished English translation from the Latin by Ernst van Haagen under the title "Power and Impotence, Possibility and Impossibility, Necessity and Freedom.") Aquinas, however, is the primary medieval writer on action theory: see his *Summa Theologica*, I–II, questions 6–10, 12–17, translated in the *Basic Writings of Saint Thomas Aquinas*, ed. Anton C. Pegis (New York: Random House, Inc., 1945), vol. II, 225–265, 272–316; *Summa de Veritate Catholicae Fidei Contra Gentiles*, Book II, Chapters 47 and 48, in *On the Truth of the Catholic Faith*, translated by J. F. Anderson (New York: Doubleday & Company, Inc., Image Books, 1956), pp. 142–146; and *Commentum in Libros Sententiarum*, II, Distinctio XXIV, quaestio 1, in *Opera Omnia*, Parmcee 1852–1873, tom. VI, pp. 592–597.

Among the moderns, see Hobbes' *Leviathan* (first published 1651), Part I, Section 6, and *Liberty and Necessity* (first published 1654), "My Opinion about Liberty and Necessity," reprinted from *The English Works of Thomas Hobbes*, ed. Sir William Molesworth (London: John Bohn, 1841) in *Hobbes Selections*, ed. Frederick J. E. Woodbridge (New York: Charles Scribner's Sons, 1958), pp. 185–211. See, too, John Locke, *An Essay Concerning Human Understanding*, Book II, Chapter xxi. A. C. Fraser's edition of Locke's *Essay* (originally published in 1894 and reprinted by Dover, New York, in 1959), is quite accessible but unfortunately unreliable; A. D. Woozley's text (New York: The World Publishing Company, Meridian Books, 1964) of the posthumous fifth (1706) edition is reliable but unfortunately abridged. The empiricist's view is best represented by David Hume in *A Treatise of Human Nature* (first published 1739), especially Book II, Part iii, Sections 1–4, and in his *Inquiry Concerning Human Understanding* (originally published 1748), Sections VII and VIII. An accessible edition of the *Treatise* is by L. A. Selby-Bigge (Oxford: The Clarendon Press), first published 1888 and reprinted 1960, and for the *Inquiry*, see Charles Hendel's edition (New York: The Bobbs-Merrill Co., Inc., Library of Liberal Arts, 1955). Also see Thomas Reid, *Essays on the Active Powers of Man* (first published 1768), especially Essays I–IV. The standard edition is *The Works of Thomas Reid*, edited by Sir William Hamilton (London, 8th ed., 1895; reprinted by Georg Olms, 1967). Ignore Hamilton's notes. Finally, see Jeremy Bentham, *The Principles of Morals and Legislation* (first published 1789), especially Chapters VII–XII. An accessible reprint of the revised 1823 edition is edited by Laurence Lafleur (New York: Hafner Publishing Company, Inc., 1965).

From the nineteenth century, see John Stuart Mill, *A System of Logic* (first published 1843), Book I, Chapter III, Sections 3–5 and Book III, Chapter V. Longmans, Green & Co. Ltd. have reprinted (London, 1961) the revised eighth edition, originally published 1872. Jurists, traditionally, have adopted the volitional theory; an influential part of this tradition is John Austin's *Lectures on Jurisprudence* (London: John Murray, 1863), Lectures XVIII and XIX. Much of William James' *The Principles of Psychology* (first published 1890, and reprinted by Dover, New York, 1950) is also relevant, especially Chapter XXVI.

II. *Selected Recent Work.* The contemporary dialogue on action theory began, more or less, with Gilbert Ryle's *The Concept of Mind* (1949). What follows is a selected and annotated list of books, anthologies, and journal articles which (on the whole) have appeared since Ryle's book. Only material directly relevant to action theory has been included: related material on the free will problem, scientific explanation, practical inference, and so on, does not appear on the list. The italicized Roman numerals immediately following an entry refer to the pertinent sections in this volume. Materials reprinted are not included. The following abbreviations for journals are used:

APQ   *American Philosophical Quarterly*
JP   *The Journal of Philosophy*
PAS   *Proceedings of the Aristotelian Society*
PPR   *Philosophy and Phenomenological Research*
PQ   *Philosophical Quarterly*
PR   *The Philosophical Review*

1. Abelson, R. "Because I Want To," *Mind*, LXXIV (1965), 540–553. *I*. On causes and reasons, especially relevant to the logical relatedness argument.
2. ———. "Doing, Causing and Causing to Do," *JP*, LXVI (1969), 178–192. *I*. Primarily a review of Richard Taylor's *Action and Purpose*.
3. Alker, H. "Will Power," *Analysis*, XXI (1960–1961), 78–81. *I*.
4. Alston, W. "Wants, Actions, and Causal Explanation" in *Intentionality, Minds and Perception*, ed. H. Castaneda. Detroit: Wayne State University Press, 1967, pp. 301–356. *I* and *III*. Includes comments by K. Lehrer and rejoinder by Alston.
5. Anderson, A. R. "The Formal Analysis of Normative Systems" in *The Logic of Decision and Action*, ed. N. Rescher. Pittsburgh: University of Pittsburgh Press, 1967, pp. 147–213. *III*.
6. Anscombe, G. E. M. *Intention*. Oxford: Basil Blackwell & Mott Ltd., 1957. *I* and *III*. Difficult to read, but philosophically and historically important. Cf. review by J. Jarvis in *JP*, LVI (1959), 31–41.
7. ———. "The Two Kinds of Error in Action," *JP*, LX (1963), 393–401. *I*.
8. Ardal, P. S. "Motives, Intentions and Responsibility," *PQ*, XV (1965), 146–154. *I*.
9. Aune, B. "Abilities, Modalities and Free Will," *PPR*, XXIII (1962–1963), 397–413. *II*. Defends the Moore-type thesis that "can"-statements can be "unpacked" only by "will if"-statements. Worth considering.
10. ———. "Can" in *The Encyclopedia of Philosophy*, vol. 2, ed. Paul Edwards. New York: The Macmillan Company and the Free Press, 1967, 18–20. *II*. A catalogue of the uses of "can."
11. ———. "Hypotheticals and Can, Another Look," *Analysis*, XXVII (1967), 191–195. *II*.

12. Austin, J. L. "A Plea for Excuses," *PAS*, LVII (1956–1957), 1–30. *I* and *II*. Hints of an action theory.

13. ——. "Three Ways of Spilling Ink," *PR*, LXXV (1966), 427–440. *I* and *III*.

14. Ayers, M. R. "Austin on 'Could' and 'Could Have,'" *PQ*, XVI (1966), 113–120. *II*. Cf. D. Gallop's reply "Ayers on 'Could' and 'Could Have,'" *PQ*, XVII (1967), 255–256.

15. Baier, K. "Could and Would," *Analysis*, XXIII (1961), Supplement, 20–29. *II*. Critique of Austin's "Ifs and Cans," O'Connor's "Choice and Possibility," and an attempt to defend Moore. An important article.

16. ——. *The Moral Point of View*, abridged edition. New York: Random House, Inc., 1965. *I*. Provides the background in moral theory for Baier's views about action and responsibility.

17. ——. "Action and Agent," *Monist*, XLIX (1965), 183–195. *I* and *III*. Essential background reading for Baier's "Responsibility and Action."

18. Barnes, W. H. F. "Action," *Mind*, L (1941), 243–257. *I*.

19. Beck, L. W. "Agent, Actor, Spectator and Critic," *Monist*, XLIX (1965), 167–182. *I*. Develops the Actor-Spectator metaphor for action theory. This metaphor has roots in Hegel's *Phenomenology of Mind*. Cf. J. Loewenberg's *Hegel's Phenomenology*. La Salle, Illinois: Open Court Publishing Company, 1965.

20. ——. "Conscious and Unconscious Motives," *Mind*, LXXV (1966), 155–179. *I* and *III*.

21. Bennett, D. "Action, Reason and Purpose," *JP*, LXII (1965), 85–96. *I* and *III*.

22. Bennett, J. "Whatever the Consequences," *Analysis*, XXVI (1966), 83–102. *I*. See comments by P. J. Fitzgerald, "Acting and Refraining," *Analysis*, XXVII (1967), 133–139, and Bennett's rejoinder "Acting and Refraining," *Analysis*, XXVIII (1967), 30–31. One of the few discussions on the important topic of *inaction*.

23. Binkley, R. W. "A Theory of Practical Reason," *PR*, LXXIV (1965), 423–448. *III*. A formal action language.

24. Black, M. "Making Something Happen" in *Determinism and Freedom*, ed. S. Hook. New York: Collier Books, 1961, pp. 31–45. *I* and *III*.

25. Brand, M. "Danto on Basic Actions," *Nous*, II (1968), 187–190. *III*.

26. ——. "A Note on von Wright's Logic of Action," *Philosophical Studies* forthcoming. *III*.

27. ——. "Choosing and Doing," *Ratio* forthcoming. *I*.

28. Brandt, R., and Kim, J. "Wants as Explanations of Actions," *JP*, LX (1963), 425–435. *I* and *III*. Reinforces the view that the concepts of physics and biology are not adequate to account for human action.

29. Braybrooke, D., Anderson, Alan R., Belnap, Nuel, Fleming, Noel, and Wallace, John. "Some Questions for Miss Anscombe About Intention," *Analysis*, XXII (1961–1962), 49–54. *I* and *III*.

30. Broadie, F. "Trying and Doing," *PAS*, LXVI (1965–1966), 27–40. *I*.

31. Brodbeck, M. "Meaning and Action," *Philosophy of Science*, XXX (1963), 309–324. *III*. Important.

32. Bronaugh, R. N. "The Logic of Ability Judgments," *PQ*, XVIII (1968), 122–130. *II*.

33. Brown, D. G. *Action*. Toronto: University of Toronto Press, 1968. *I* and *III*. Only slightly helpful.

34. Brown, R. "On Having One's Reasons," *Philosophy,* XXXVIII (1963), 264–271. *III.* On the relation between explanations in terms of goals and in terms of the agent's reasons for acting.

35. Browning, D. "Acts," *Review of Metaphysics,* XIV (1960), 3–17. *I.* Only slightly helpful.

36. Bunge, M. *Causality: The Place of the Causal Principle in Modern Science.* Cleveland: The World Publishing Company, Meridian Books, 1963. *I* and *III.* Knowledge of the nature of causation is a prerequisite for the study of human action.

37. "Can I Decide to Do Something Immediately Without Trying to Do It Immediately?" *Analysis,* XVI (1955–1956), 1–5. *I. Analysis* problem no. 7, proposed and judged by R. B. Braithwaite. Answers by Brian Ellis, "Candidus," and Nicholas Rescher.

38. Care, N. S., and Landesman, C. "Introduction" in *Readings in the Theory of Action,* eds. Care and Landesman. Bloomington: Indiana University Press, 1968, pp. xi–xxxv. *I* and *III.* Helpful in elucidating the meaning of "behavior" as it is used in recent discussions about action.

39. Castaneda, H. N. "The Logic of Change, Action, and Norms," *JP,* LXII (1965), 333–344. *III.* An excellent critical and positive discussion of Von Wright's *Norm and Action.* Cf. the defense by D. Sidorsky, "A Note on Three Criticisms of von Wright," *JP,* LXII (1965), 739–742.

40. Chisholm, R. M. "What Is It to Act Upon a Proposition?" *Analysis,* XXII (1961–1962), 1–6. *I.* Cf. comments by R. A. George, "Acting Upon a Proposition," *Analysis,* XXIII (1962–1963), 116–118, and P. Kashop, "Can a Man Act Upon a Proposition Which He Believes to Be False?" *Analysis,* XXII (1961–1962), 31–36.

41. ———. "The Descriptive Element in the Concept of 'Action,'" *JP,* LXI (1964), 613–624. *I* and *III.* An early version of the material reprinted from *Freedom and Determinism,* ed. Lehrer.

42. ———. *Human Freedom and the Self.* Kansas: The Lindley Lecture of the University of Kansas, 1964. *III.*

43. Chopra, Y. N. "The Consequences of Human Actions," *PAS,* LXV (1964–1965), 147–166. *I.* On the act-consequence distinction.

44. Cody, A. B. "Can a Single Action Have Many Different Descriptions?" *Inquiry,* X (1967), 164–180. *III.* Cf. R. E. Dowling's "Can an Action Have Many Descriptions?" *Inquiry,* X (1967), 447–448, and Cody's rejoinder "Reply to Mr. Dowling," 449–452.

45. Danto, A. C. "What We Can Do," *JP,* LX (1963), 435–445. *III.* Concerned mostly with the thesis that some actions are not basic.

46. ———. "Freedom and Forbearance" in *Freedom and Determinism,* ed. K. Lehrer. New York: Random House, Inc., 1966, pp. 45–63. *I* and *III.* Concerned with the problem of *inaction.*

47. D'Arcy, E. *Human Acts.* Oxford: The Clarendon Press, 1963. *I.* Contains an important discussion on the act-consequence distinction. Cf. review by D. Sachs, "A Few Morals About Acts," *PR,* LXXV (1966), 91–98.

48. Daveney, T. F. "Wanting," *PQ,* XI (1961), 135–144. *I.* Defends the view that wants are *not* causes.

49. ———. "Intention and Causes," *Analysis,* XXVII (1966), 23–28. *I.*

50. Davidson, D. "The Logical Form of Action Sentences" in *The Logic of Decision*

and Action, ed. N. Rescher. Pittsburgh: University of Pittsburgh Press, 1966, pp. 81–95. III. Cf. the comments of E. J. Lemmon, H. N. Castaneda, and R. M. Chisholm, and Davidson's rejoinders, pp. 96–120. An extremely important paper.

51. Dore, C. "On the Meaning of 'Could Have,'" Analysis, XXIII (1962–1963), 41–43. II. Cf. D. S. Scarrow's comments in "On an Analysis of 'Could Have,'" Analysis, XXIII (1962–1963), 118–120, and Dore's rejoinder "More on the Meaning of 'Could Have,'" Analysis, XXIV (1963–1964), 41–43.

52. ———. "On Being Able to Do Otherwise," PQ, XVI (1966), 137–145. II.

53. Dray, W. "Choosing and Doing," Dialogue, I (1962–1963), 129–152. II. On "cans" and "ifs."

54. Ducasse, C. J. Nature, Mind, and Death. La Salle, Illinois: Open Court Publishing Company, 1949, Part II. I and III. An important contribution to the analysis of causation.

55. Edwards, R. B. "Agency Without a Substantive Self," Monist, XLIX (1965), 273–289. III.

56. Ehman, R. R. "Causality and Agency," Ratio, IX (1967), 140–154. I and III. Defends the view that causal explanation is inapplicable to the relation of an agent to his action.

57. Evans, J. L. "Choice," PQ, V (1955), 303–315. I. The impetus for other work on choosing. Defends the view that choosing is an action.

58. Ewing, A. C. "May Can-Statements Be Analyzed Deterministically," PAS, LXIV (1963–1964), 157–176. II.

59. Falk, D. "Action-guiding Reasons," JP, LX (1963), 702–718. I. Cf. comments by K. Baier, "Reasons for Doing Something," JP, LXI (1964), 198–203.

60. Feinberg, J. "Action and Responsibility" in Philosophy in America, ed. M. Black. Ithaca: Cornell University Press, 1965, pp. 134–160. I. Important.

61. ———. "Causing Voluntary Actions" in Metaphysics and Explanation, eds. W. H. Capitan and D. D. Merrill. Pittsburgh: University of Pittsburgh Press, 1964, pp. 29–47. I and III. The 1964 Oberlin Philosophy Colloquium. Cf. comments by K. S. Donnellan and K. Lehrer, and rejoinders by Feinberg, pp. 48–61.

62. Fisk, M. "Causation and Action," Review of Metaphysics, XVIX (1965), 235–247. III. Relevant to Chisholm's notion of agent causation.

63. Fleming, B. N. "On Intention," PR, LXXIII (1964), 301–320. I.

64. Flew, A. "Motives and the Unconscious" in Minnesota Studies in the Philosophy of Science, vol. 1, eds. H. Feigl and M. Scriven. Minneapolis: University of Minnesota Press, 1956, 155–173. I and III.

65. Franks, O. C. "Choice," PAS, XXXIV (1933–1934), 269–294. I.

66. Gauthier, D. P. Practical Reasoning. Oxford: Oxford University Press, 1963. I and III. Chapter III is particularly relevant.

67. Gean, W. D. "Reasons and Causes," Review of Metaphysics, XIX (1965), 667–688. I and III. Defends the view that reason-explanations are a type of causal explanation.

68. Glasgow, W. D. "On Choosing," Analysis, XVII (1956), 135–139. I. Defends the view that choosing is the same as deciding.

69. ———. "The Concept of Choosing," Analysis, XX (1959–1960), 63–67. I.

70. Goldberg, B. "Can a Desire Be a Cause?" Analysis, XXV (1965), 70–72. I. On the logical relatedness of reasons and actions.

71. Gordon, L. M. "The Range of Application of 'Voluntary,' 'Not Voluntary' and 'Involuntary,'" *Analysis,* XXVI (1965–1966), 149–152. *I.*

72. Gustafsen, D. F. "Voluntary and Involuntary," *PPR,* XXIV (1962–1963), 493–501. *I.*

73. ———. "Momentary Intentions," *Mind,* LXXVII (1968), 1–13. *I* and *III.*

74. Hamlyn, D. W. "Behavior," *Philosophy,* XXVIII (1953), 132–145. *I.*

75. Hamlyn, D. W., and Smart, J. J. C. "Causality and Human Behavior" (Symposium), *PAS* Supplement, XXXVIII (1964), 125–142. *I* and *III.*

76. Hampshire, S. *Thought and Action.* London: Chatto & Windus Ltd., 1959. *I* and *III.* Cf. T. Long's "Hampshire on Animals and Intentions," *Mind,* LXXIII (1963), 414–416; also cf. J. J. Walsh's "Remarks on *Thought and Action,*" *JP,* LX (1963), 57–65, and Hampshire's "Reply to Walsh on *Thought and Action,*" *JP,* LX (1963), 410–424. An important contribution.

77. ———. *Freedom of the Individual.* London: Chatto & Windus Ltd., 1965. *II.* Chapter 1 is relevant to McCall's paper "Ability as a Species of Possibility."

78. Hampshire, S., and Hart, H. L. A. "Decision, Intention, and Certainty," *Mind,* LXVII (1958), 1–12. *I* and *III.* Cf. K. Stern's "Mr. Hampshire and Prof. Hart on Intention: A Note," *Mind,* LXVIII (1959), 98–99.

79. Hart, H. L. A. "The Ascription of Responsibility and Rights," *PAS,* XLIX (1948–1949), 171–194. Reprinted in *Logic and Language,* ed. A. Flew, Oxford: Basil Blackwell & Mott Ltd., 1951, and by New York: Doubleday & Company, Inc., Anchor Books, 1965, pp. 151–174. *I.* Essential reading.

80. ———. *Punishment and Responsibility.* Oxford: Oxford University Press, 1968. *I.* A collection of recently published papers. Most relevant are "Acts of Will and Responsibility" (Chapter 4), "Legal Responsibility and Excuses" (Chapter 2), and "Postscript: Responsibility and Retribution" (Chapter 9).

81. Hart, H. L. A., and Honoré, A. M. *Causation in the Law.* Oxford: The Clarendon Press, 1959. *I* and *III.* An important contribution to the literature on causation, including a helpful discussion of the notion of *the* cause. Reviewed by P. H. Nowell-Smith in *Mind,* LXX (1961), 553–561, and by P. Foot, "Hart and Honoré: Causation in the Law," *PR,* LXXII (1963), 505–515.

82. Henschen-Dahlquist, Ann-Mari. "Remarks to Austin's Criticism of Moore's Analysis of 'Can,'" *Theoria,* XXIX (1963), 305–315. *II.* Relevant to Lehrer's "Ifs, Cans, and Causes."

83. Hicks, G. D. "The Nature of Willing," *PAS,* XIII (1912–1913), 27–65. *I.* Interesting.

84. Honoré, A. M. "Can and Can't," *Mind,* LXXIII (1964), 463–479. *II.* Relevant to the distinction drawn in the Introduction to section II between the ability "can," which pertains to general actions, and the within-one's-power "can," which pertains to individual actions.

85. Imlay, R. A. "Do I Ever Directly Raise My Arm?" *Philosophy,* XLII (1967), 119–127. *I* and *III.* Cf. G. N. A. Vesey's comments in "Do I Ever Directly Raise My Arm?" *Philosophy,* XLII (1967), 148–149, in which he defends the view that he took in "Volition."

86. Jeffrey, R. C. "Ethics and the Logic of Decision," *JP,* LXII (1965), 528–539. *I.* Uses probability theory to shed light on the nature of deliberation.

87. Jenkins, J. S. "Motives and Intention," *PQ,* XV (1965), 155–164. *I.* Critical dis-

cussion of the analyses of "intending" and "being motivated" proposed by Passmore and Heath in "Intention," and by Kenny in *Action, Emotion and Will.*

88. Kaufman, A. S. "Moral Responsibiilty and the Use of 'Could Have,'" *PQ,* XII (1962), 120–128. *II.* Consists mainly of comments on Austin's "Ifs and Cans."

89. ———. "Practical Decision," *Mind,* LXXV (1966), 25–44. *I* and *III.* An analysis of "decision."

90. Kenny, A. *Action, Emotion and Will.* London: Routledge & Kegan Paul Ltd., 1963. *I, II,* and *III.* An important book.

91. ———. "Intention and Purpose," *JP,* LXIII (1966), 642–651. *III.*

92. King, H. R. "Professor Ryle and *The Concept of Mind,*" *JP,* XLVIII (1951), 280–296. *I.*

93. Kotarbinski, T. "The Concept of Action," *JP,* LVII (1960), 215–222. *I.*

94. Ladd, J. "Free Will and Voluntary Action," *PPR,* XII (1951), 392–405. *I.* Relevant to the distinction between voluntary and involuntary action.

95. ———. "The Ethical Dimensions of the Concept of Action," *JP,* LXII (1965), 633–645. *I.* Cf. comments by K. Baier, "Acting and Producing," *JP,* LXII (1965), 645–648, and J. B. Schneewind, "Responsibility and Liability," *JP,* LXII (1965), 649–650.

96. Lehrer, K. "Decisions and Causes," *PR,* LXXII (1963), 224–227. *I.*

97. ———. "'Could' and Determinism," *Analysis,* XXIV (1963–1964), 159–160. *II.* Cf. K. Baier's "Could and Would."

98. ———. "An Empirical Disproof of Determinism" in *Freedom and Determinism,* ed. Lehrer. New York: Random House, Inc., 1966, pp. 175–202. *II.* See especially pp. 189 ff. for a proof that the "if" in "I can if I choose" is not conditional. Also see J. Cornman and Lehrer, *Philosophical Problems and Arguments.* New York: The Macmillan Company, 1968, Chapter 3, in which Lehrer defends his claim that determinism can be refuted empirically.

99. ———. "Cans Without Ifs," *Analysis,* XXVIII (1968), 29–32. *II.*

100. Leonard, H. "Authorship and Purpose," *Philosophy of Science,* XXVI (1959), 272–294. *III.* Part I is relevant to Chisholm's action language in "Freedom and Action."

101. Lewis, C. I. *An Analysis of Knowledge and Valuation.* La Salle, Illinois: Open Court Publishing Company, 1950, pp. 5–9, 365–373. *I.*

102. Locke, D. "Ifs and Cans Revisited," *Philosophy,* XXXVII (1962), 245–256. *II.*

103. Louch, A. R. *Explanation and Human Action.* Berkeley and Los Angeles: University of California Press, 1966. *I* and *III.*

104. McAdam, J. I. "Choosing Flippently or Non-rational Choice," *Analysis,* XXV (1964–1965), 132–136. *I.* On the analysis of "choosing."

105. McCormich, S., and Thalberg, I. "Trying," *Dialogue,* VI (1967), 29–46. *I.*

106. McCracken, D. J., Peters, R. S., and Urmson, J. O. "Motives and Causes" (Symposium), *PAS Supplement,* XXVI (1952), 139–194. *I* and *III.*

107. MacIntyre, A. C. "The Antecedents of Action" in *British Analytical Philosophy,* ed. Williams and Montefiore. London: Routledge & Kegan Paul Ltd., 1966, pp. 205–225. *I.* On the volitional theory.

108. MacIntyre, A. C., and Nowell-Smith, P. H. "Purpose and Intelligent Action" (Symposium), *PAS Supplement,* XXXIV (1960), 79–112. *III.*

109. McLaughlin, R. N. "Human Action," *Australasian Journal of Philosophy,* XLV (1967), 141–158. *I* and *III.*

110. MacMurray, J., Ewing, A. C., and Franks, O. S. "What Is Action?" (Symposium), *PAS Supplement*, XVII (1938), 69–120. *I.*

111. Madell, G. "Action and Causal Explanation," *Mind*, LXXVI (1967), 34–48. *III.* Defends the view that causal explanation is applicable to human action.

112. Malcolm, N. "The Conceivability of Mechanism," *PR*, LXXVI (1968), 45–72. *III.*

113. Mannison, D. S. "My Motive and Its Reason," *Mind*, LXXIII (1964), 423–429. *III.* In part, criticism of Peter's *The Concept of Motivation;* cf. Peter's rejoinder "More About Motives," *Mind*, LXXVI (1967), 92–97.

114. Margolis, J. "Actions and Ways of Failing," *Inquiry*, III (1960), 89–101. *I.* Also relevant to the analysis of "trying."

115. ——. "Motives, Causes and Action," *Methodos*, XVI (1964), 83–89. *I.*

116. Mayo, B. "Commitments and Reasons," *Mind*, LXIV (1955), 342–360. *I.* On the relation between having a reason and being committed.

117. Meiland, J. W. "Motives and Ends," *PQ*, XIII (1963), 64–71. *I.* Defends a dispositional analysis of "motives."

118. ——. "Are There Unintentional Actions?" *PR*, LXXII (1963), 377–381. *I* and *III.* Defends the thesis that all actions are intentional.

119. Melden, A. I. "Willing," *PR*, LXIX (1960), 475–484. *I.* An early version of Chapter 5 of *Free Action.*

120. ——. "Reasons for Action and Matters of Fact," *Proceedings and Addresses of the American Philosophical Association*, XXXV (1962), 45–60. *I* and *III.*

121. ——. "Philosophy and the Understanding of Human Fact" in *Epistemology*, ed. A. Stroll. New York: Harper & Row, Inc., 1967, pp. 229–249. *I* and *III.* The text of a public lecture.

122. Mischel, T. "Psychology and Explanations of Human Behavior," *PPR*, XXIII (1962–1963), 578–594. *III.* Defends the view that motive-explanation is fundamentally different from the kind of explanation offered by the sciences, including psychology.

123. Mish'Alani, J. K. "Can Right Acts Be Voluntary," *Analysis*, XX (1959–1960), 67–72. *I.* On Ryle's analysis of "voluntary."

124. Montague, R. "Choosing Chisels and Deciding to Get Up," *Mind*, LXXVI (1967), 428–429. *I.* Argues that Daveney in "Choosing" has not shown that decision and choice can proceed without prior deliberation.

125. Morris, H., ed. *Freedom and Responsibility.* Stanford: Stanford University Press, 1961. *I, II,* and *III.* Relevant material by legal theorists.

126. Myers, G. E. "Motives and Wants," *Mind*, LXXIII (1964), 173–185. *I* and *III.* Critique of behavioristic analyses of "motive."

127. Nowell-Smith, P. H. "Choosing, Deciding and Doing," *Analysis*, XVIII (1958), 63–69. *I.* Defends the view that in choosing to perform actions, choosing is deciding, but in choosing an object, it is acting.

128. ——. "Ifs and Cans," *Theoria*, XXVI (1960), 85–101. *II.* Rejoinder to Austin's criticisms in "Ifs and Cans." An important article.

129. O'Connor, D. J. "Possibility and Choice," *PAS Supplement*, XXXIV (1960), 1–24. *I* and *II.* Cf. K. Baier's "Could and Would."

130. Ofstad, H. "Libertarianism and the Belief in Transempirical Entities, E. J. Russell on Causation and Agency" in *Philosophical Essays Dedicated to Gunnar Aspelin.* Lund, Sweden: C. W. K. Gleerup, 1963. *III.* Relevant to Chisholm's notion of agent causation.

131. ——. "Recent Work on the Free Will Problem," *APQ*, IV (1967), 179–207. *I*, *II*, and *III*. Gives a perspective to the connections between action theory and the free will problem.

132. Oldenquist, A. "Choosing, Deciding, and Doing" in *The Encyclopedia of Philosophy*, vol. 2, ed. Paul Edwards. New York: The Macmillan Company and the Free Press, 1967, 96–104. *I* and *III*. A superior introduction to some of the problems about human action.

133. Osborn, J. M. "Austin's Non-conditional Ifs," *JP*, LXII (1965), 711–715. *II*.

134. O'Shaughnessy, B. "The Limits of the Will," *PR*, LXV (1956), 443–490. *I*. Relevant to the volitional theory.

135. ——. "Observation and the Will," *JP*, LIX (1963), 367–392. *I*.

136. Parsons, T. *Towards a General Theory of Action*. Cambridge: Harvard University Press, 1951. *I* and *III*. A sociologist's view of action theory. See also *The Social Theories of Talcott Parsons*, ed. M. Black. Englewood Cliffs, New Jersey: Prentice-Hall, Inc., 1961, "Some Questions About Parson's Theories" by Black, pp. 268–288, and Parson's reply "The Point of View of the Author," especially pp. 323 ff.

137. Passmore, J. A., and Heath, P. L. "Intentions" (Symposium), *PAS Supplement*, XXIX (1955), 131–146. *I* and *III*.

138. Pears, D. F., ed. *Freedom and the Will*. London: Macmillan & Co. Ltd., 1963. *I* and *II*.

139. ——. "Are Reasons for Actions Causes?" in *Epistemology*, ed. A. Stroll. New York: Harper & Row, Inc., 1967, pp. 204–228. *I*. Carefully written.

140. Peters, R. S. *The Concept of Motivation*. London: Routledge & Kegan Paul Ltd., 1958. *I* and *III*. Cf. J. J. Jenkin's "Dr. Peter's Motives," *Mind*, LXXV (1966), 248–254.

141. Peters, R. S., and Tojfel, H. "Hobbes and Hull—Metaphysicians of Behavior," *British Journal for the Philosophy of Science*, VIII (1957), 30–44. *I*.

142. Pitcher, G. "Hart on Action and Responsibility," *PR*, LXIX (1960), 226–235. *I*. In attacking Hart's "The Ascription of Responsibility and Rights," Pitcher defends the view that a person is not responsible for his acts, but rather for their consequences.

143. Potts, T. C., and Taylor, C. C. W. "States, Activities and Performances" (Symposium), *PAS Supplement*, XXXIX (1965), 65–84. *I* and *III*. Cf. Chapter 8 of Kenny's *Action, Emotion and Will*.

144. Prior, A. N., and Raphael, D. D. "The Consequences of Action" (Symposium), *PAS Supplement*, XXX (1956), 91–119. *I*.

145. Raab, F. V. "Free Will and the Ambiguity of 'Could,'" *PR*, LXIV (1955), 60–77. *II*.

146. ——. "The Relevance of Morals to Our Denials of Responsibility" in *Morality and the Language of Conduct*, eds. H. Castaneda and G. Nakhnikian. Detroit: Wayne State University Press, 1963, pp. 351–363. *I*.

147. Radcliff, P. "Beliefs, Attitudes and Actions," *Dialogue*, IV (1965–1966), 456–464. *I*. On the connection between belief and action and the intelligibility of "deciding to believe."

148. Rankin, K. W. "Causal Modalities and Alternative Action," *PQ*, VII (1957), 289–304. *II*.

149. ——. "Doer and Doing," *Mind*, LXIX (1960), 361–371. *I* and *III*.

150. Rankin, N. L. "The Unmoved Agent and the Ground of Responsibility," *JP*, LXIV (1967), 403–408. *I* and *III*.

151. Rawls, J. "Two Concepts of Rules," *PR*, LXIV (1955), 3–32. Reprinted (for example) in *Ethics*, eds. J. J. Thomson and G. Dworkin. New York: Harper & Row, Inc., 1968, pp. 104–135. *I*. Relevant to the Melden-Wittgenstein attempt to analyze action as rule-following behavior.

152. Rayfield, D. "Action," *Nous*, II (1968), 131–145. *I* and *III*. An attempt to state the necessary and sufficient conditions for the performance of an action.

153. Rescher, N., ed. *The Logic of Decision and Action*. Pittsburgh: University of Pittsburgh Press, 1967. *I*, *II*, and *III*.

154. ——. "Values and the Explanation of Behavior," *PQ*, XVII (1967), 130–136. *III*.

155. Ritchie, A. M. "Agent and Act in Theory of Mind," *PAS*, LII (1951–1952), 1–22. *I*.

156. Rorty, A. O. "Wants and Justifications," *JP*, LXIII (1966), 765–772. *I*. On the logical relatedness between reasons and actions. Cf. Abelson's "Because I Want To."

157. *Royal Institute of Philosophy, The Human Agent: Royal Institute of Philosophy Lectures*, vol. 1, 1966–1967. London: Macmillan & Co. Ltd., 1968. *I*, *II*, and *III*. See especially essays by Aurel Kolnai, "Agency and Freedom," Alan R. White, "On Being Obliged to Act," D. Pears, "Desires as Causes of Actions," and C. H. Whitely, "Mental Causes."

158. Russell, B. *The Analysis of Mind*. London: George Allen & Unwin Ltd., 1921. *I*. See especially Chapters 2 and 3, which concern the nature of habitual action and introspection.

159. Ryle, G. "Knowing How and Knowing That," *PAS*, XLVI (1945–1946), 1–16. *I* and *II*.

160. Sartre, Jean-Paul. *Being and Nothingness*, trans. Hazel E. Barnes. New York: Philosophical Library, Inc., 1956, Part Four. *I*.

161. Schuetz, A. "Choosing Among Projects of Action," *PPR*, XII (1951–1952), 161–184. *I*.

162. Sellars, W. "Imperatives, Intentions and the Logic of 'Ought'" in *Morality and the Language of Conduct*, eds. Castaneda and Nakhnikian. Detroit: Wayne State University Press, 1965, pp. 159–218. *I* and *III*.

163. ——. "Thought and Action" in *Freedom and Determinism*, ed. K. Lehrer. New York: Random House, Inc., 1966, pp. 105–139. *III*. An *important* systemic attempt to understand the nature of action.

164. ——. *Form and Content in Ethical Theory*, The Lindley Lecture of the University of Kansas (Kansas, 1967). *III*.

165. ——. *Science and Metaphysics*. London: Routledge & Kegan Paul Ltd., 1967, Chapter 7. *III*.

166. Shwayder, D. *The Stratification of Behavior*. London: Routledge & Kegan Paul Ltd. 1965. *I* and *III*.

167. Silber, J. R. "Human Action and the Language of Volitions," *PAS*, LXIV (1964), 199–220. *I*.

168. Skinner, B. F. *Science and Human Behavior*. New York: The Macmillan Company, 1953. *I*. A psychologist's viewpoint.

169. Sparshott, F. E. "The Concept of Purpose," *Ethics*, LXXII (1961–1962), 157–170. *III*.

170. Stoljar, S. "Ascriptive and Prescriptive Responsibility," *Mind,* LXVIII (1969), 350–360. *I*. Cf. Hart's "The Ascription of Responsibility and Rights."

171. Stroup, T. "Austin on 'Ifs,'" *Mind,* LXXVII (1968), 104–108. *II*.

172. Sutherland, N. S. "Motives as Explanations," *Mind,* LXVIII (1959), 145–149. *I* and *III*.

173. Taylor, C. *The Explanation of Behavior.* London: Routledge & Kegan Paul Ltd., 1964. *III*. An attempt to show that an account of human behavior must include teleological and purposive concepts. An important work. Cf. D. H. Mellor's "Two Fallacies in Charles Taylor's Explanation of Behavior," *Mind,* LXXVII (1968), 124–126, and J. Peyton's unpublished thesis, University of Pittsburgh, 1968, which is a careful critical review of Taylor's book. Also cf. the critical review by N. Malcolm, "Explaining Behavior," *PR,* LXXVI (1967), 97–104.

174. Taylor, R. *Metaphysics.* Englewood Cliffs, New Jersey: Prentice-Hall, Inc., 1963, Chapters 4 and 5. *II*.

175. ——. *Action and Purpose.* Englewood Cliffs, New Jersey: Prentice-Hall, Inc., 1966. *I, II,* and *III*. An important book.

176. Thalberg, I. "Abilities and Ifs," *Analysis,* XXII (1961–1962), 121–126. *II*.

177. ——. "Do We Cause Our Own Actions?" *Analysis,* XXVII (1967), 196–201. *III*.

178. Thomas, George B. "Abilities and Physiology," *JP,* LXI (1964), 321–328. *II*. A careful critical study of Kaufman's "Ability."

179. ——. "He Could Not Have Chosen Otherwise," *Southern Journal of Philosophy,* V (1967), 269–274. *II*.

180. Tolman, E. C. *Purposive Behavior in Animals and Men.* Berkeley and Los Angeles: University of California Press, 1949. *I* and *III*. An eminent psychologist's viewpoint.

181. ——. *Behavior and Psychological Man.* Berkeley and Los Angeles: University of California Press, 1966. *I* and *III*.

182. Vesey, G. N. A. "Volition," *Philosophy,* XXXVI (1961), 352–365. *I* and *III*. Important.

183. Von Wright, G. H. "The Logic of Action—A Sketch" in *The Logic of Decision and Action,* ed. N. Rescher. Pittsburgh: University of Pittsburgh Press, 1966, pp. 121–136. *III*. Cf. comments by R. M. Chisholm and J. Robison and Von Wright's rejoinders, pp. 137–146. The next step after *Norm and Action.* Essential reading.

184. Walker, K. F. "Motive and Behavior," *Australasian Journal of Philosophy,* XX (1942), 16–29. *I*. Demonstrates the need for Ryle's *Concept of Mind.*

185. "What Sort of 'If' Is the 'If' in 'I Can *If* I Choose'?" *Analysis,* XII (1951–1952), 125–132. *Analysis* problem no. 1. Proposed and judged by J. L. Austin. Answers by "Cuckoo," Brian Ellis, Douglas Gasking, and G. M. Matthews, pp. 125–132. *II*.

186. White, A. R. *Explaining Human Behavior: Inaugural Lecture Delivered in the University of Hull, January 1962.* Hull University Press, 1962. *III*.

187. ——. "On What Could Have Happened," *PR,* LXXVII (1968), 73–89. *II*. On analyzing "could have" in terms of possibility.

188. ——. "Introduction" in *The Philosophy of Action.* Oxford: Oxford University Press, 1968, pp. 1–18. *I, II,* and *III*.

189. Whiteley, C. H. "'Can,'" *Analysis,* XXIII (1962), 91–93. *II*.

190. Williams, B. A. O. "Personal Identity and Individuation," *PAS,* LVI (1956–1957), 229–252. *III*. Contains an interesting discussion on individuating action descriptions.

191. Winch, P. *The Idea of a Social Science*. London: Routledge & Kegan Paul Ltd., 1963. *I* and *III*. Cf. A. R. Louch's "On Misunderstanding Mr. Winch," *Inquiry*, VIII (1965), 212–216, and M. Martin's "Winch on Philosophy, Social Science and Explanation," *Philosophical Forum*, XXIII (1965–1966), 29–41.

192. ———. "Wittgenstein's Treatment of the Will," *Ratio*, X (1968), 38–53. *I*. Exegesis of Wittgenstein's view of the will.

193. Wittgenstein, L. *Philosophical Investigations*, trans. G. E. M. Anscombe. Oxford: Basil Blackwell & Mott Ltd., 1953. *I, II,* and *III*. See especially paragraphs 611–660 and Part II, Section viii. The frame of reference from which Melden, Kenny, and others work.

194. Yolton, J. W. "Ascriptions, Descriptions and Action Sentences," *Ethics*, LXVII (1956–1957), 307–310. *I*.

195. ———. "Act and Circumstance," *JP*, LIX (1962), 337–350. *I*.

196. ———. "Agent Causality," *APQ*, III (1966), 14–26. *I* and *III*. Also relevant to the issue of the logical relatedness between reasons and actions.